Learning
Excel 7
for Windows® 95

Vento / Blanc

TO OUR FAMILIES   Alan, Pamela and Jaime

Jim, Chris, Dirk, Jim, Mindy and Anthony

Acknowledgments

We wish to express our gratitude to **Karl Schwartz** and **Joanne Schwartz**, authors of the *DDC Excel 7.0 Quick Reference Guide*, for their dedication to this project.

Editors:

Stephanie Finucane

Yonkers, NY

Harriet Goldstein

Rio Rancho, NM

Desktop Publishing:

Joanne Schwartz and Karl Schwartz

Staten Island, NY

Copyright 1996 by DDC Publishing

Published by DDC Publishing

First DDC printing

CAT. NUMBER: Z-11

10 9 8 7 6 5 4 3 2

Printed in the United States of America

INTRODUCTION

ABOUT THIS BOOK

LEARNING EXCEL 7.0 is to be used with Excel 7.0 for Windows® 95 on an IBM PC or compatible computer.

Each lesson in this book explains Excel concepts, provides exercises with step by step instructions to apply those concepts, and illustrates the necessary keystrokes or mouse actions to complete the applications. The concepts taught in each exercise are illustrated with annotated screen captures, outputs, and toolbars. Lesson summary exercises are provided to challenge and reinforce the concepts learned.

The last chapter in the book provides exercises containing many Excel features that can be completed as culminating activities.

Become familiar with the information that is available in the Appendices, Index and Alphabetical List of Procedures. These references can provide answers to frequently asked questions.

After completing the 100 exercises in this book, the user will be able to use Excel 7.0 software with ease.

SUPPLEMENTARY MATERIALS

The following materials are available to enhance your use of this text:

Data disk

The data disk contains each exercise necessary to begin the application. The instructions to open the file with the disk icon 🖫 refer to the files on the data disk. The disk enables the user to begin the exercise immediately and eliminates the need to create the worksheet. The text may be used without this disk, using the instructions provided for creating files, by opening the files with the keyboard icon ⌨.

Solutions disk

The solution file for each exercise are included on the solutions disk. Formulas and formats may be checked using this disk.

Teacher's Manual

The manual provides assistance for teachers and trainers. The contents of the manual are listed on the next page.

Transparencies of solutions

Each exercise solution is provided on a transparency that can be used for training, checking formats and reviewing previously created files.

Tests for Excel 7

For each lesson in the text, a set of short answer and computer tests have been developed. The tests are provided in Test A and Test B format so that each test has two versions.

Transparencies for Training

Transparencies of the dialog boxes, screens and toolbars are provided for training. Each illustration is labeled with clear, easy-to-read callouts to be used to introduce or review vocabulary and procedures.

FEATURES OF THIS TEXT

- Lesson Objectives
- Exercise Objectives
- Excel concepts and vocabulary
- Alphabetical List of Procedures
- Directory of Files, which lists files alphabetically with the exercises in which they are used
- Log of Exercises, which lists filenames and data filenames in exercise order
- Annotated screen illustrations
- Exercises to apply each Excel worksheet concept
- End-of-Chapter exercises to review and test your knowledge of lesson concepts
- Procedures necessary to complete each exercise application
- Notes and hints to assist the user at difficult junctures
- Glossary (Appendix A)
- Functions (Appendix B)
- Toolbars (Appendix C)
- Error Messages (Appendix D)
- Visual Basic (Appendix E)
- Worksheet Planning Grid (Appendix F)
- Index

continued...

INTRODUCTION

HOW TO USE THIS BOOK

Each exercise contains four parts:

- **Notes** — explain the Excel 7 concept being introduced. Concepts are illustrated with annotated toolbars, screen captures and/or sample outputs. The parts of the dialog boxes or window can be compared to your computer screen. After reading the Notes section introducing the Excel concept, you should complete the exercise using the procedures provided.

- **Exercise Directions** — tell you how to complete the exercise.

  The book is written to be used with or without the optional DDC Data disk. If the book is used without the DDC Data disk, files that are created and saved will be reused in later exercises. These files will be indicated with a keyboard ⌨ icon.

  The disk 🖫 icon indicates that the file noted is available on the optional DDC Data disk. For example, in "Open ⌨ SALARY; or 🖫 06SALARY," the keyboard icon is used to indicate a file that you have previously created and the disk icon indicates the name of the required file on the optional Data disk. Each data file on the DDC data disk has a descriptive name and an exercise number.

  The DDC Data disk will save keyboarding time and can be used for short courses, one-day seminars, or for students who have missed earlier lessons.

- **Exercise Application** — applies the concept that was introduced. Problems or applications are selected to include only those features that have already been learned and to highlight new concepts and exercise objectives.

- **Keystroke/Mouse Procedures** — outline the keystroke or mouse actions required to complete the exercise.

  Keystroke procedures include mouse actions, keystrokes and shortcut keystrokes, if applicable. The keystrokes are provided, as a reference, in the exercise where the feature is first discussed and utilized. If you need to refer to them again, you may look in the index, use Excel's Answer Wizard or the Alphabetical List of Procedures on pages vii-xi.

FILE MANAGEMENT

- As files are created, you will be instructed to save the file using the name provided in the exercise. It is advisable to save the files on a new, formatted disk. When the files are recalled in later exercises, you will add to the file and change or enhance the data. When you save the file after these changes, the original data is overwritten. If you wish to save each exercise as a separate file, you can use the exercise name and number.

THE TEACHER'S MANUAL

While this text can be used as a self-paced learning book, a comprehensive instructor's guide is available for training purposes. The Teacher's Manual contains

- Lesson objectives
- Exercise objectives
- Related vocabulary
- Points to emphasize
- Teaching suggestions
- Formulas
- Data/Solutions file names
- Solutions

TABLE OF CONTENTS

continued...

TABLE OF CONTENTS

LESSON SIX - WORKING WITH WORKBOOKS, WORKSHEETS AND TEMPLATES

- **Insert and Delete Columns and Rows**
- **Move (Cut/Paste)**
- **Edit Undo**
- **Copy and Paste Special**
- **Copy (Drag and Drop)**
- **Transpose Data**
- **AutoCorrect**
- **Freeze Titles**
- **Create New Workbook**
- **Select Workbook**
- **Split Worksheet**
- **Copy and Paste Special (Extract and Combine Data)**
- **Scroll Tips**
- **Workbook Sheets**
- **Print Workbook**
- **Print Worksheet on Specified Number of Pages**
- **Named Ranges**
- **Replace**
- **Templates**
- **Spreadsheet Solutions**
- **Arrange Workbooks**
- **Link Workbooks**
- **3-D Formulas**
- **Duplicate Workbook Window**

LESSON SEVEN - ADVANCED FEATURES AND FUNCTIONS

- **Insert IF Functions**
- **Print Compressed Worksheet**
- **Auditing**
- **Enter a Date as Numerical Data**
- **Format Numerical Dates**
- **AutoFormat**
- **Color Buttons**
- **Insert Lookup Functions**
- **Copy/Paste Special**
- **Protect a Sheet**
- **Lock Cells in a Worksheet**
- **Hide Data**
- **Non-Consecutive References in a Function**

TABLE OF CONTENTS

TABLE OF CONTENTS

ALPHABETICAL LIST OF PROCEDURES

continued…

ALPHABETICAL LIST OF PROCEDURES

continued..

ALPHABETICAL LIST OF PROCEDURES

continued…

ALPHABETICAL LIST OF PROCEDURES

continued...

ALPHABETICAL LIST OF PROCEDURES

DIRECTORY OF FILES

DIRECTORY OF FILES

LOG OF EXERCISES

LESSON 1

GETTING STARTED

Exercises 1-3

- Start Microsoft Excel

- The Microsoft Excel 7.0 Window

- The Workbook Window

- The Mouse and Keyboard

- The Excel 7 Keyboard Template

- Menus, Toolbars and Commands

- Exit Excel

- Select Menu Items

- Options in a Dialog Box

- Set View Preferences

- The View Menu

- The Zoom Control Box

- Change Window Displays

- Get Help

- Answer Wizard

EXERCISE

■ Start Microsoft Excel ■ The Microsoft Excel 7.0 Window
■ The Workbook Window ■ The Mouse and Keyboard ■ Exit Excel
■ The Excel 7 Keyboard Template ■ Menus, Toolbars and Commands

1

NOTES:

Start Microsoft Excel

- Microsoft® Excel® 7.0 is a spreadsheet tool that may be started in Windows® 95 as follows:

  - Click Start on the Windows 95 Taskbar, highlight Programs, and highlight and select Microsoft Excel

- If you own Excel as part of the Microsoft® Office '95® suite, the program may be started using the method noted above or as follows:

  - Click Start, highlight and select New Office Document, select Blank Workbook from the Windows 95 Taskbar

  - Click Start a New Document and select Blank Workbook, from the Shortcut bar

The Microsoft Excel 7.0 Window

- The Microsoft® Excel® 7.0 window that displays when the program is first started appears below:

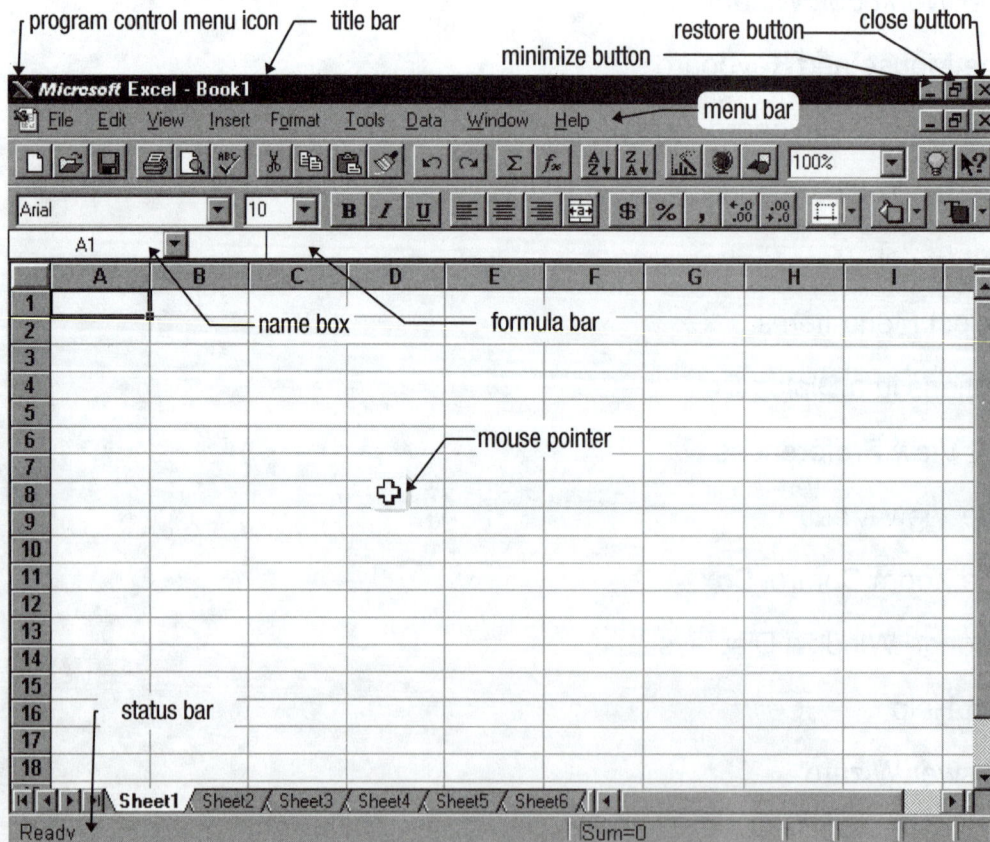

THE EXCEL APPLICATION WINDOW

Note the following Excel window parts:

- The **application window title bar**, located at the top of the application window, displays the program name (Microsoft Excel), and may also display the filename of an open workbook window if the window is maximized. You can drag the title bar to move the Excel window, or double–click it to maximize or minimize the window.

- The **program control menu icon**, located to the left of the application window title bar, can be clicked to access a drop-down menu with commands to control the Excel window.

- The application window minimize, restore and close buttons, are located on the right side of the application window title bar. Clicking the **minimize** ▬ **button** shrinks the Excel window to a button on the Windows 95 Taskbar. Clicking the **restore** 🗗 **button** reduces the Excel screen to a window on your desktop. When Excel is a window on the desktop, the **maximize** ▢ **button** appears so it can be brought back to a full screen. The **close** ✕ **button** exits or closes the program.

- The **menu bar**, located below the Excel title bar, displays menu names from which drop-down menus may be accessed.

- The **toolbars**, located below the menu bar, contain buttons that can be used to select commands quickly without opening a menu or dialog box. Pointing to and resting the pointer on a toolbar button displays the tool name, while an explanation of the button's function is displayed on the Status Bar. This is called the ToolTips function.

- The **name box**, located below the toolbars and to the left of the window, displays the active cell reference, i.e. the location of your cursor.

- The **formula bar**, located next to the name box, provides a space for typing or editing cell data.

- The **mouse pointer** moves as you move the mouse. Its shape changes to signal different functions. Use the mouse pointer to select cells, menu items, toolbar buttons or worksheets.

- The **status bar**, located at the bottom of the Excel window, displays information about the current mode, selected command, or option. At the right of the Status Bar is the AutoCalculate box. The results of automatically calculating selected cells using a variety of formulas are displayed here.

The Workbook Window

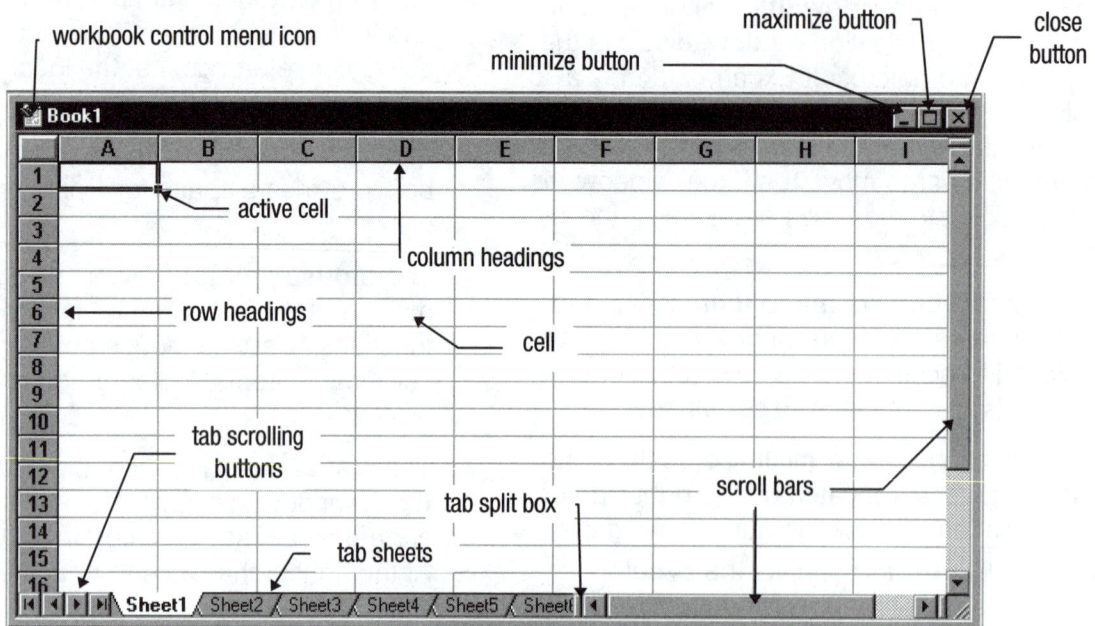

EXCEL WORKBOOK WINDOW

Note the following workbook window parts:

■ A **workbook** (Book1) displaying the active **worksheet** (Sheet1) is the document window that opens when you start Excel 7. By default, workbooks contain sixteen worksheets (Sheet1 – Sheet16). You can have up to 255 sheets in a workbook to enter your data and formulas or to create charts and macros. Several workbooks may be open at one time.

■ The **workbook window title bar**, located at the top of a workbook window, displays the workbook filename. You can drag the title bar to move the window or double–click it to maximize the window size. A maximized workbook window does not have a title bar. Its filename appears on the application window title bar.

■ The **workbook control menu icon** is at the left of the document window title bar. If the workbook window is maximized, its control menu icon is located on the left side of the Excel window menu bar. Clicking the document window control menu box opens a drop-down menu with commands that control the workbook window.

■ The workbook window minimize, maximize, and close buttons are located on the right side of the document window title bar. Clicking the **minimize button** ⬜ shrinks the workbook window to an icon. Clicking the **maximize button** ⬜ enlarges the workbook to its largest size. Once the window has been maximized, the maximize button changes to the **restore button** 🗗 and these buttons are located on the right side of the Excel window menu bar. Clicking the restore button returns the workbook window to the previous size.

The **close button** ❌ will close the workbook window.

■ **Row** and **column headings** are the areas at the left and top of the worksheet. Rows are numbered and columns are lettered. A worksheet can have up to 16,384 rows and 256 columns.

- The intersection of rows and columns forms a grid of cells. A **cell** is a single location on a worksheet in which data is stored. A cell reference refers to a column letter and row number. For example, A1 is the cell reference of the cell where row 1 intersects column A. The **active cell** contains a dark outline, cell A1 in the illustration on the previous page. When a cell is active, you can type data into it.

- When you enter data or double–click a cell, Excel displays the **insertion point**, a flashing line that indicates the cell is ready to receive data or be edited.

- When you click the **select all button**, located at the intersection of the row and column headings in upper-left hand corner of worksheet, all the cells in the worksheet become selected.

- The **tab scrolling buttons**, located at the bottom left of the workbook window, provide a way for you to scroll to hidden sheet tabs.

- The **sheet tabs** are located next to the tab scrolling buttons, at the bottom of the workbook window. Clicking a sheet tab displays that sheet in the workbook window. The active sheet tab is shown in bold, Sheet1 in the illustration on the previous page.

- The **tab split box** is located between the sheet tabs and the horizontal scroll bar at the bottom of the workbook window. This box can be dragged to the right to display more sheet tabs or to the left to show more of the horizontal scroll bar. The mouse pointer will change to a ←| |→ to denote that the split box may be dragged to the left or right.

- The **scroll bars**, located at the right and bottom borders of the workbook window, are used to display areas of the workbook that are not in view. You can click a scroll arrow to move one row or column at a time, click a scroll bar to move one screen at a time, or drag a scroll box to move quickly to a desired sheet area.

The Mouse and Keyboard

■ You can use the mouse or the keyboard to choose commands and perform tasks.

Using the Mouse

• When the mouse is moved on the tabletop, a corresponding movement of the mouse pointer occurs on the screen. The mouse pointer changes shape depending upon the object it is pointing to and actions it can perform. The mouse pointer will not move if the mouse is lifted up and placed back on the tabletop.

• The mouse terminology and the corresponding actions described below will be used throughout the book:

Point to	Move the mouse (on the tabletop) so the pointer touches a specific item.
Click	Point to item and quickly press and release the left mouse button.
Right–click	Point to item and quickly press and release the right mouse button.
Double–click	Point to item and press the left mouse button twice in rapid succession.
Drag	Point to item and press and hold down the left mouse button while moving the mouse. When the item is in the desired position, release the mouse button to place the item.
Right–drag	Point to item and press and hold down the right mouse button while moving the mouse. When the item is in the desired position, release the mouse button to place the item.

Using the Keyboard

In addition to the alphanumeric keys found on most typewriters, computers contain additional keys:

• **Function keys** (F1 through F10 or F12, depending on your keyboard) perform special functions and are located across the top of an enhanced keyboard (which has 12 function keys) or on the side (which has ten function keys).

• **Modifier keys** (Shift, Alt, Ctrl) are used in conjunction with other keys to select certain commands or perform actions. To use a modifier key with another key, you must hold down the modifier key while tapping the other key.

• **Numeric keys**, found on keyboards with a number pad, allow you to enter numbers quickly. When Num Lock is ON, the number keys on the pad are operational, as is the decimal point. When Num Lock is OFF, the cursor control keys (Home, PgUp, End, PgDn) are active. The numbers on the top row of the keyboard are always active.

• **Escape key** (Esc) is used to cancel some actions, commands, menus, or an entry.

• **Enter keys** (there are two on most keyboards) are used to complete an entry of data into a cell.

• **Directional arrow keys** are used to move the active cell when in the Ready mode or the insertion point when in the Edit mode.

The Excel 7 Keyboard Template

■ To assist you in remembering special key combinations, you may use the keyboard template of frequently used commands illustrated below. The key combinations will be presented in the keystroke procedures as the topics are discussed in this text.

Calculate active worksheet	Shift + F9	Enter current date	Ctrl + ;	Repeat	F4
Calculate open workbooks	F9	Enter current time	Ctrl + Shift + :	Replace	Ctrl + H
Change reference type	F4	Find	Ctrl + F	Select column	Ctrl + Space
Copy selection	Ctrl + C	Format cells/object	Ctrl + 1	Select entire worksheet	Ctrl + A
Cut selection	Ctrl + X	Go to	F5	Select row	Shift + Space
Display values/formulas	Ctrl + `	Paste	Ctrl + V	Spell check	F7
Edit cell	F2	Paste named reference	F3	Undo	Ctrl + Z

Menus, Toolbars and Commands

■ In Excel, commands are used to change or enter data and are applied to selected cells or objects. The menu bar, shortcut menus, and toolbar buttons may be used to select commands.

The menu bar may be used with the keyboard or the mouse.

To access menu bar commands:

• Use the mouse to point to a menu on the menu bar and click once, or

• Press Alt + *underlined letter* in the menu name.

Note the drop-down menu that appears when the Tools menu is accessed:

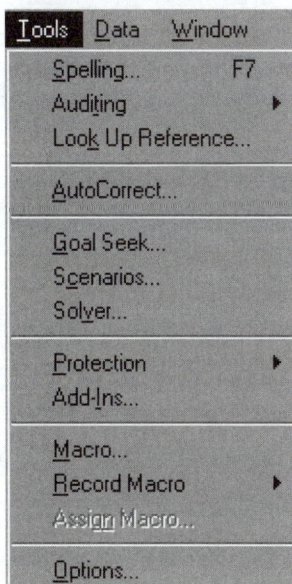

Tools Data Window

Spelling...   F7
Auditing   ►
Look Up Reference...

AutoCorrect...

Goal Seek...
Scenarios...
Solver...

Protection   ►
Add-Ins...

Macro...
Record Macro   ►
Assign Macro...

Options...

To select a command from the drop-down menu:

• Use the mouse to point to the command on the drop-down menu and click once, or

• Press the underlined letter in the command name, or

• Use the up or down arrow key to highlight the command, then press Enter.

Shortcut menus are only available by using the mouse.

To access shortcut menu commands:

• Use the mouse to point to the object you want the command to act on and right–click once.
  NOTE: Not all objects display a menu when right–clicked.

Note the pop-up menu that appears when a cell in a worksheet is right–clicked:

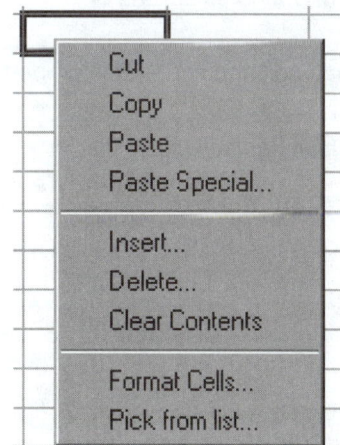

Cut
Copy
Paste
Paste Special...

Insert...
Delete...
Clear Contents

Format Cells...
Pick from list...

Menus, Toolbars and Commands (continued)

To select a command from the pop-up (shortcut) menu:

- Use the mouse to point to the command on the pop-up menu and click once, or

- Use the up or down arrow key to highlight the command, then press Enter.

  The toolbars provide icons that represent commands which are activated using the mouse.

To select a command from a toolbar:

- Use the mouse to point to a button and click once.

Exit Excel

- The quickest way to exit Excel with the mouse is to use the Close button in the top right corner of the screen on the Excel title bar.

EXERCISE DIRECTIONS:

1. Roll the mouse up, down, left and right on the tabletop (or the mousepad).

2. Click **File**.

   ✓ *Note the drop-down menu selections.*

3. Click off the menu once to close the **F**ile menu.

4. Click **Edit**.

   ✓ *Note the drop-down menu selections.*

5. Click once off the menu to close the Edit menu.

6. Select the **V**iew menu.

   ✓ *Note the drop-down menu selections.*

7. Close the **V**iew menu.

8. Select the **I**nsert menu.

   ✓ *Note the drop-down menu selections.*

9. Close the **I**nsert menu.

10. Select each remaining menu.

    ✓ *Note the drop-down menu selections of each menu.*

11. Point to any worksheet cell and right–click to open a shortcut menu.

    ✓ *Note the pop-up menu selections.*

12. Click once off the pop-up menu to close it.

13. Point to and rest the pointer on a toolbar button to display its name. Do this procedure for all buttons on the toolbars.

    ✓ *Note the purpose of the tool is shown on the status bar and the ToolTip displays the name of the button.*

14. Use keystrokes to select a column by pressing Ctrl+Space Bar. The column where the cursor was will be selected. Click on any other cell to deselect the column.

15. Use keystrokes to select a row by pressing Shift+Space Bar. The row where the cursor was will be selected. Click on any other cell to deselect the row.

16. Use keystrokes to select the entire worksheet by pressing Ctrl+A. The entire worksheet will be selected. Click on any cell to deselect the worksheet.

17. Exit Excel by clicking the close button.

NOTE: Mouse action procedures are indicated on the left; keyboard procedures are indicated on the right. You may use either the mouse or the keystrokes, or a combination of both.

START EXCEL

1. Click Start on Taskbar......... `Ctrl` + `Esc`
2. Select Programs............................ `P`
3. Select Microsoft Excel.................. `↓`

SELECT A MENU BAR ITEM

1. Click desired menu name .. `Alt` +*letter*
2. Click desired menu item ....*letter*

SELECT A SHORTCUT MENU ITEM

1. Right–click desired object.
2. Click desired menu item.

CLOSE A MENU

- Click anywhere off the menu.

OR

Press **Escape**.............................. `Esc`

VIEW TOOLBAR BUTTON DESCRIPTIONS

- Point to and rest pointer on desired toolbar button.

  NOTE: The tool name is displayed next to the button and its purpose is shown on the Status Bar.

EXIT WITHOUT SAVING

- Press **Alt** + **F4**...................... `Alt` + `F4`

OR

1. Click **File** menu .... `Alt` + `F`
2. Click **Exit**.................................... `X`

   NOTE: If a message box appears prompting you to save changes to the open workbook, click the No button.

OR

- Click **Close** button .... `X`

EXERCISE

■ Select Menu Items ■ Options in a Dialog Box
■ Set View Preferences ■ The View Menu ■ The Zoom Control Box

2

NOTES:

Select Menu Items

■ In Exercise 1, you selected menus from the menu bar. Once a menu is selected, it opens a **drop-down menu** that lists items from which you can choose. The menus Excel displays will vary. For example, if no workbook is open, Excel displays only the **File** and **Help** menus. The items on a drop-down menu will depend on the object that is selected.

Note the drop-down menus that appear when the **View** and **Tools** menus are selected:

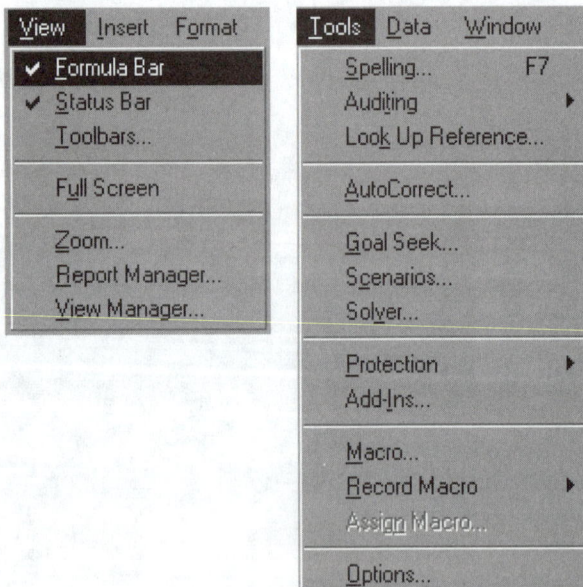

View Insert Format
✔ Formula Bar
✔ Status Bar
Toolbars...
Full Screen
Zoom...
Report Manager...
View Manager...

Tools Data Window	
Spelling...	F7
Auditing	▶
Look Up Reference...	
AutoCorrect...	
Goal Seek...	
Scenarios...	
Solver...	
Protection	▶
Add-Ins...	
Macro...	
Record Macro	▶
Assign Macro...	
Options...	

■ Note on the Tools menu some menu options are dimmed, while others appear black. **Dimmed options** are not available for selection at this time while **black options** are.

■ A **check mark** next to a drop-down menu item means the option is currently selected.

■ A menu item followed by an **arrow** (▶) opens a **submenu** with additional choices.

■ A menu item followed by an **ellipsis** (...) indicates that a **dialog box** (which requires you to provide additional information to complete a task) will be forthcoming.

Options in a Dialog Box

- A **dialog box** contains different ways to ask you for information:

  - The **title bar** identifies the title of the dialog box.

  - The **text box** is a location where you type information.

  - **Command buttons** carry out actions described on the button. When command names have an ellipsis following them, they will access another dialog box.

  - The **drop-down list** is marked with a down arrow. Clicking the drop-down list arrow accesses a short list of options. Make a choice from the options provided.

  - An **increment box** provides a space for typing a value. An up or down arrow (usually to the right of the box) gives you a way to select a value with the mouse.

  - A **named tab** is used to display options related to the tab's name in the same dialog box.

- **Option buttons** are small circular buttons marking options appearing as a set. You may choose only one option from the set. A selected option button contains a dark circle.

- A **check box** is the small square box where options may be selected or deselected. An "X" in the box indicates the option is selected. If several check boxes are offered, you may select more than one.

- A **list box** displays a list of items from which selections can be made. A list box may have a scroll bar that can be used to show hidden items in the list.

- A **scroll bar** is a horizontal or vertical bar providing scroll arrows and a scroll box that can be used to show hidden items in a list.

Note the labeled parts in the dialog boxes below:

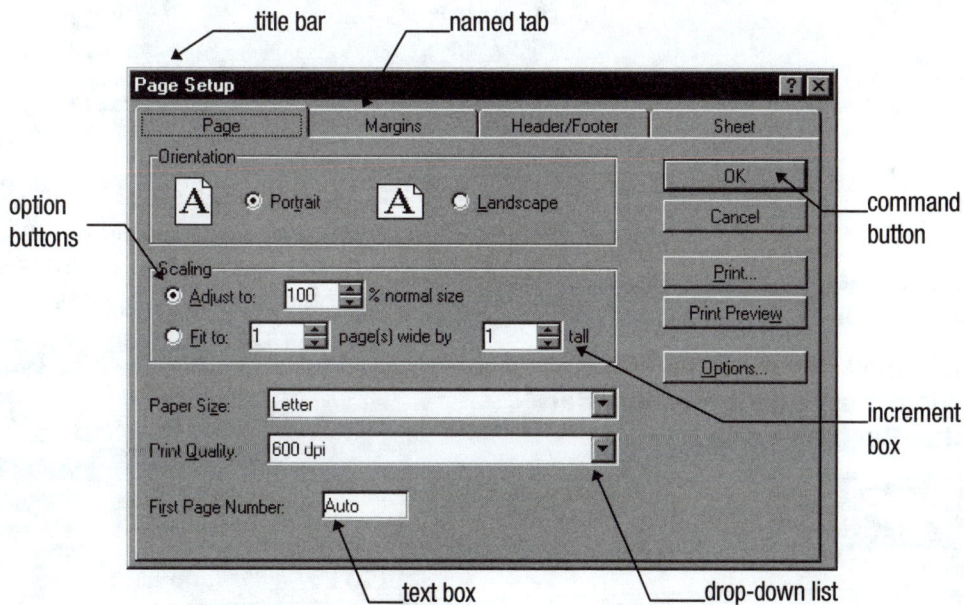

Set View Preferences

■ The default view settings for windows are indicated in the View tab in the Options dialog box indicated below. To customize view preferences, select **Options** from the **Tools** menu and then select the View tab in the Options dialog box.

To change the settings, you may deselect or select any combination of features in the View tab. The items are selected or deselected by clicking the check boxes or option buttons. When selected, check boxes contain a "✓" and option buttons contain a dark dot.

Note the illustration of the View tab in the Options dialog box and the default view settings:

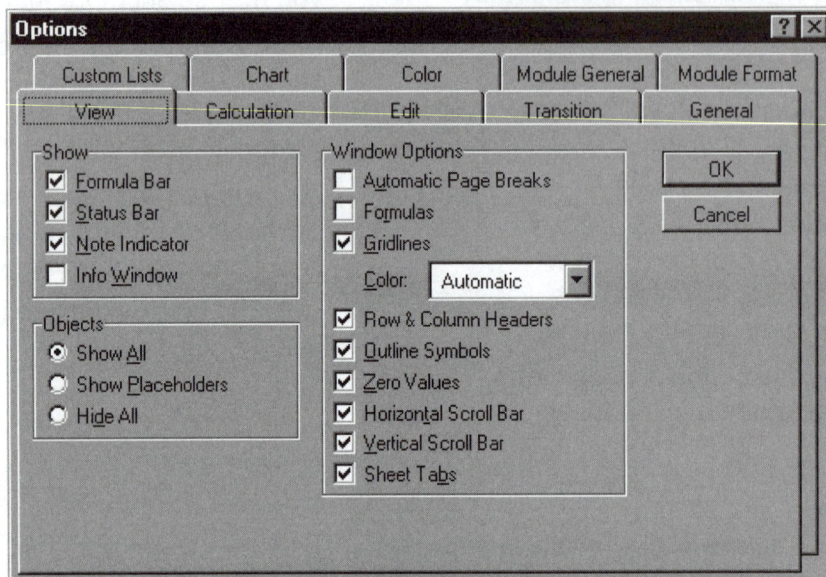

The View Menu

■ A quick way to view or hide the Formula or Status Bars is to select or deselect these items from the **View** menu.

Note the check marks on the **View** menu below which indicates that the **Formula Bar** and the **Status Bar** are selected:

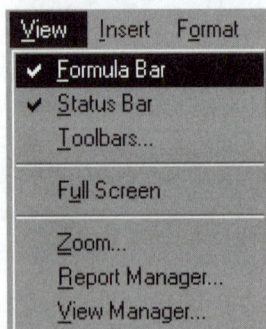

■ The **View** menu also contains a **Zoom** option that allows you to set the magnification of cells in a worksheet. When **Zoom** is selected, the following dialog box appears:

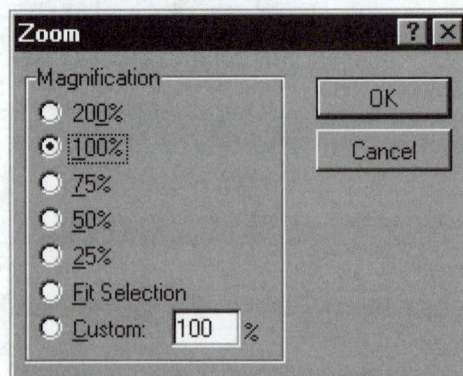

By clicking an option button, you can display the cells at **25%**, **50%**, **75%**, **100%** or **200%** of the normal display. The **Custom** option sets the zoom percentage anywhere from 10% – 400%. The **Fit Selection** option sizes a selected range to the current window size.

The Zoom Control Box

- The **Zoom Control box** `100%` located on the Standard toolbar, lets you easily set the magnification of cells in a worksheet without opening a menu or a dialog box.

EXERCISE DIRECTIONS:

1. Select **Tools** from the menu bar.
2. Select **Options**.
3. Select the View tab in the Options dialog box.
4. Deselect the **Formula Bar** check box.
5. Select **OK**.
   ✓ *Note the change.*
6. Repeat steps 1–2.
7. Select the **Formula Bar** check box.
8. Select **OK**.
   ✓ *Note the change.*
9. Repeat steps 1–2.
10. Make the following changes:

    Deselect the **Status Bar**.

    Deselect **Vertical Scroll Bar** and **Horizontal Scroll Bar**.

    Click the **Gridlines, Color** drop-down arrow, then click the red color box in the palette.
11. Select **OK**.
    ✓ *Note the changes.*
12. Restore View options to the default settings by reversing all actions listed above.
13. Select **View** from the menu bar.
14. Select **Zoom**.
15. Select the **50%** magnification option.
16. Select **OK**.
    ✓ *Note the changes.*
17. Repeat steps 13–16 several times choosing a different magnification each time.
18. Select **Zoom** from the **View** menu.
19. Select **Custom** and type 300 in the text box.

20. Select **OK**.
    ✓ *Note the changes.*
21. Click in the Zoom Control box on the Standard toolbar, type 60 and press Enter.
    ✓ *Note the change.*
22. Open the Zoom Control box and select **200%**.
    ✓ *Note the change.*
23. Select **Zoom** from the **View** menu.
24. Select **100%** magnification to return to the default zoom setting.
25. Select **OK**.
26. Select **Page Setup** from the **File** menu.
27. Click the Margins tab.
    ✓ *Note the margin options displayed in the dialog box.*
28. Press the Escape key to close the dialog box.
29. Select **Page Setup** from the **File** menu.
30. Practice selecting options in a dialog box:

    - Select the Page tab.
      ✓ *Note the dialog box selections.*

    - Click the **Landscape** option button to select it.

    - Click the **Paper Size** drop-down arrow.
      ✓ *Note the choices, but do not select one.*

    - Click the Margins tab.

    - Click the up arrow in the **Top** increment box until a 2 appears.

    - Double–click in the **Left** increment box and type 2.5.

    - Press Tab and type 2.5 in the **Right** increment box.
      ✓ *Note effects of changes in the sample Preview.*

    - Exit Page Setup (Click Cancel or press Escape.).
31. Select **Exit** from the **File** menu to exit Excel.

SET VIEW PREFERENCES

1. Click **Tools** menu .... `Alt`+`T`
2. Click **Options...** .... `O`
3. Click **View** tab .... `Ctrl`+`Tab`

To set general view options:

Select or deselect desired **Show** options:

- **Formula Bar** .... `Alt`+`F`
- **Status Bar** .... `Alt`+`S`
- **Note Indicator** .... `Alt`+`N`
- **Info Window** .... `Alt`+`W`

To set view of window options:

Select or deselect desired **Window Options:**

- **Automatic Page Breaks** .... `Alt`+`U`
- **Formulas** .... `Alt`+`R`
- **Gridlines** .... `Alt`+`G`
- **Gridline Color** .... `Alt`+`C`
- **Row & Column Headers** .... `Alt`+`E`
- **Outline Symbols** .... `Alt`+`O`
- **Zero Values** .... `Alt`+`Z`
- **Horizontal Scroll Bar** .. `Alt`+`T`
- **Vertical Scroll Bar** ...... `Alt`+`V`
- **Sheet Tabs** .... `Alt`+`B`

4. Click `OK` .... `↵`

EXIT EXCEL USING THE MENU

1. Click **File** menu.................... `Alt`+`F`
2. Click **Exit** .... `X`

ZOOM USING THE ZOOM CONTROL BOX

To specify a custom zoom:

1. Click in `100%` on Standard Toolbar, where 100% is the current setting.
2. Type zoom percentage (10–400) .... *number*
3. Press **Enter** .... `↵`

To select a zoom:

1. Click drop-down arrow in `100%` on Standard Toolbar, where 100% is the current setting.
2. Select desired zoom percentage.

ZOOM USING THE MENU

1. Click **View** menu .... `Alt`+`V`
2. Click **Zoom** .... `Z`
3. Select desired **Magnification** option:

- **200%**............................. `0`
- **100%**............................. `1`
- **75%**............................... `7`
- **50%**............................... `5`
- **25%**............................... `2`

OR

a. Select ◯ **Custom**................. `C`
b. Type zoom percentage (10–400) .... *number*
4. Click `OK` .... `↵`

NEXT EXERCISE

EXERCISE

■ **Change Window Displays** ■ **Get Help** ■ **Answer Wizard**

3

NOTES:

Change Window Displays

■ The **minimize** ⬚, **maximize** ⬚ and **close** ⬚ **buttons** on the top line with the application name (Microsoft Excel) may be used to shrink, enlarge and close the program window on the desktop.

Once the application window has been maximized, the maximize button is replaced with a **restore button** ⬚. Use the restore button to return the Excel window to its previous size.

■ The minimize and maximize buttons on the title bar of the workbook window may be used to shrink, enlarge and close the workbook window within the Excel window.

Once the workbook window has been maximized, the title bar disappears and the maximize button is replaced with a restore button to the right of the menu bar. Use the restore button to return the workbook window to its previous size.

Get Help

■ Help may be accessed by clicking **Help** on the menu bar, or by pressing F1.

NOTE: If you are in a Help window, F1 will close the window and open the How to Use Help screen.

■ You may also get help on a particular screen item by pressing Shift+F1 or clicking the Help button ⬚, then pointing to any screen icon or location. A help screen appears explaining the item in question.

Note the **Help** menu options below:

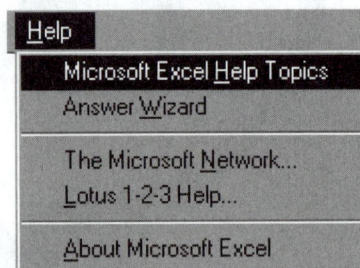

Help
Microsoft Excel Help Topics
Answer Wizard
The Microsoft Network...
Lotus 1-2-3 Help...
About Microsoft Excel

Microsoft Excel Help Topics and **Answer Wizard** bring you to the Microsoft Excel Help Topics dialog box explained and illustrated below.

Lotus 1-2-3 provides information about Excel 7 equivalents to Lotus 1-2-3 commands.

About Microsoft Excel provides system status information.

The Answer Wizard

- After accessing Help, the Help Topics dialog box displays with four tabs. The Answer Wizard tab displays by default, but it may be selected by highlighting Answer Wizard from the Help menu.

  - Answer Wizard searches for answers to your question about a particular topic. In the Step 1 text box, enter your question and click the Search button. A series of topics in answer to your question displays in the Step 2 list box as illustrated below. Double-click any topic in the Step 2 area or select the topic and click Display to view the help screen.

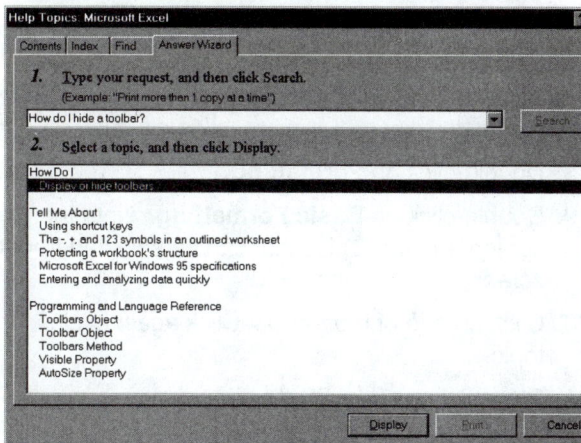

Contents

- The contents tab displays a page listing help contents for Excel. Double-clicking on a topic presents a list of subtopics and/or display screens. Note the Excel contents page and an example of a help display screen illustrated below.

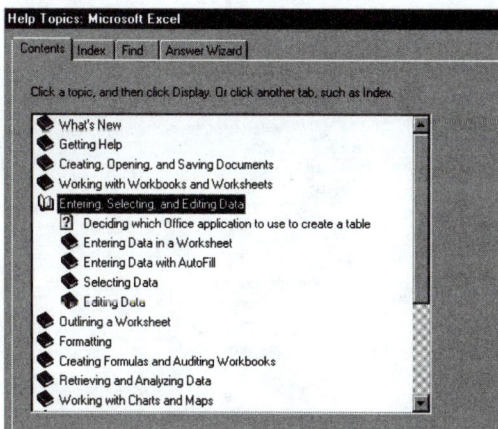

Index

- The Index tab allows you to enter the first few letters of your topic which brings you to the index entry. Double-click the entry or select the entry and click Display. The help screen related to your topic is then displayed.

Find

- The Find tab accesses the Help database feature. It allows you to search the Help database for the occurrence of any word or phrase in a Help topic. The Index and Find features are similar; however, Find offers more options for finding a topic.

TipWizard

- The TipWizard® is represented by a light bulb icon on the Standard Toolbar. When you click the icon, the TipWizard toolbar appears with a useful tip. To hide the toolbar, click the icon again.

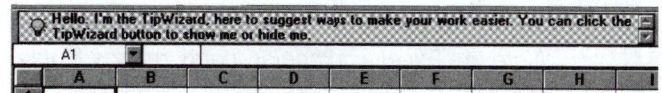

Exit Help

- To exit Help: Double–click the Help window control menu box.

  NOTE: *It may be necessary to click Cancel or Close, or press Escape to close a dialog box before exiting Help.*

EXERCISE DIRECTIONS:

1. Select **Help** from the menu bar. Note the selections. Deselect **Help**.

2. Click the **TipWizard** icon [💡]. Note the message. Click the icon again to hide the toolbar.

3. Press F1 to access Help.

4. Click the **Answer Wizard** tab if it is not active.

5. Type the following question: How do I minimize the window?

6. Click **Search**.

7. Double-click on Minimize a Workbook Window to an Icon.

8. Read and then close the Help screen.

9. Click the minimize button on the title bar (which contains the software name).

   ✓ *Note the Microsoft Excel icon on the Taskbar.*

10. Double–click the Microsoft Excel icon to return to the program.

11. Click the restore button on the menu bar.

    ✓ *Note the Excel workbook window returns to its previous size.*

12. If the window is not maximized, click the maximize button on the workbook window title bar.

13. Click the minimize button on the workbook window title bar.

    ✓ *Note the workbook icon in the Excel window.*

14. Double–click the icon to return the workbook to a window.

15. Select **Microsoft Excel Help Topics** from the **Help** menu.

16. Select the **Contents** tab if it is not active.

17. Do the following:

    Double-click **Working with Workbooks and Worksheets** from the list.

    Double-click the **Workbooks and Worksheets** help topic.

    Read the topic and click on the vocabulary word *worksheets* to see the definition.

    Read the definition for active sheet.

    Click on the **Options** menu and note the <u>P</u>rint topic option.

    Click on **Help <u>T</u>opics** to return to the Help Contents menu.

18. Double-click on **Formatting**.

19. Double-click on **Basic Formatting**. Note the Help screen and the topics that can be selected from the screen.

20. Click on one of the topics. Click again to close the topic.

21. Close the screen.

22. Exit Excel.

USE HELP DIALOG BOX

1. a.   Click **Help** menu........... `Alt` + `H`

    b.   Click **Answer Wizard** .... `W`

    OR

    Press **F1** .... `F1`

2. Click tab:

    ### Answer Wizard
    a.   Type question in Step 1 text box.

    b.   Click **Search** .... `S`

    c.   Double-click topic in Step 2 box.

    OR

    a.   Select topic.

    b.   Click **Display** .... `D`

    ### Contents
    a.   Double-click a book or topic.

    b.   Double-click a submenu item or a display item.

    ### Index
    a.   Type first letters of topic word in Step 1 text box.

    b.   Double-click topic in Step 2 box.

    OR

    a.   Select topic.

    b.   Click **Display** .... `D`

Find
a.   Type and enter search word or phrase in Step 1 text box.

b.   Select matching words in Step 2, if presented.

c.   Double-click topic in Step 3 box.

OR

a.   Select topic

b.   Click **Display** .... `D`

EXIT HELP OR HELP SCREENS

NOTE: It may be necessary to click Cancel or Close, or press Escape to close a dialog box before exiting Help.

•   Click **Cancel** button............. `Cancel`

    OR

    Press **Escape** .... `Esc`

    OR

    Click **close** button .... `X`

    OR

    Double-click Help Screen Control icon

MAXIMIZE A WINDOW

•   Click **maximize** button .... `□`

    NOTE: After a window is maximized, the maximize button is replaced with the restore button.

OR

1. Click Workbook Control icon

2. Click **Maximize** .... `X`

RESTORE A MAXIMIZED WINDOW

•   Click **restore** button .... `🗗`

    NOTE: After a window is restored, the restore button is replaced with the maximize button.

OR

1. Click Workbook Control icon.

2. Click **Restore** .... `R`

MINIMIZE A WINDOW

•   Click desired window **minimize** button .... `_`

    NOTE: To minimize the window, use Steps 1 and 2 below.

OR

1. Click Workbook Control icon.

2. Click **Minimize** .... `N`

NEXT LESSON

LESSON 2

EXPLORE WORKSHEET

Exercises 4-5

■ Explore the Worksheet Using the Mouse
  and Keyboard

EXERCISE

Explore the Worksheet Using the Mouse and Keyboard

4

NOTES:

- The **active cell** is the cell that is ready to receive data or a command.

- When you change the active cell, the **name box** located on the left side of the formula bar shows the new **cell reference**.

- The cell reference identifies the location of the active cell in the worksheet by the column and row headings.

- You can change the active cell in a worksheet using the mouse or keyboard.

- The workbook window displays a limited portion of the worksheet. It is possible to view other portions of the worksheet by **scrolling** to the desired location.

- You can scroll to different areas in a worksheet using the mouse or keyboard. Scrolling does not change the active cell.

- There are 256 columns and 16,384 rows in a worksheet.

Note the illustrations of the outer edges of a worksheet:

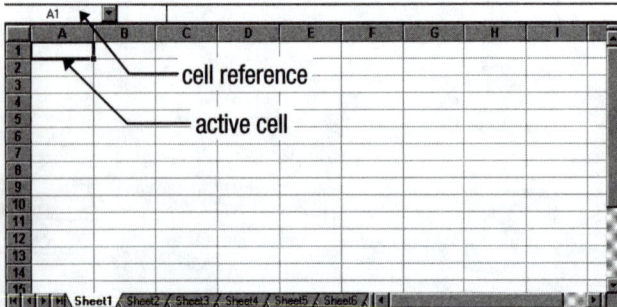

TOP LEFT OF WORKSHEET

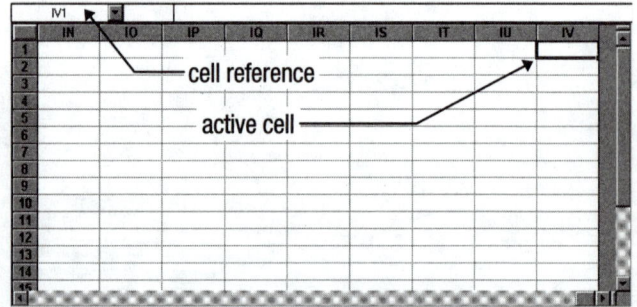

TOP RIGHT OF WORKSHEET

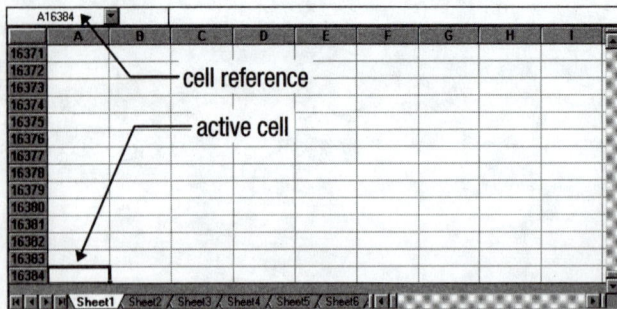

BOTTOM LEFT OF WORKSHEET

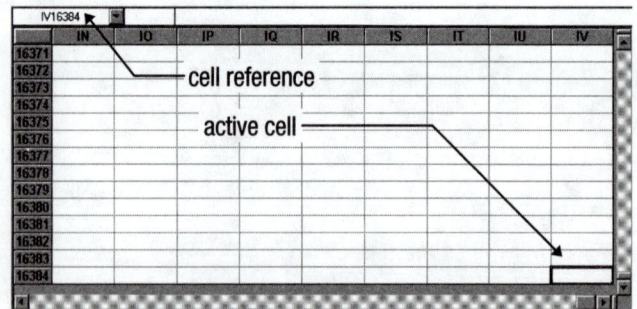

BOTTOM RIGHT OF WORKSHEET

You can scroll through the worksheet by clicking on the scroll arrows or by moving the scroll box. When the scroll box is clicked,

Excel displays the destination row or column. This is called a ScrollTip.

EXERCISE DIRECTIONS:

1. Click cell E5 to make it active.

   ✓ *Note the cell reference in the name box.*

2. Press the left arrow key until cell C5 is selected.

   ✓ *Note the cell reference in the name box.*

3. Select cell C9.

   ✓ *Note the cell reference in the name box.*

4. Use the arrow keys to select the following cells:

   - A6
   - B14
   - G2
   - H20
   - R19
   - AA45
   - J33
   - A1

5. Click the down scroll arrow on the vertical scroll bar.

   ✓ *Note the worksheet moves down by one row.*

6. Click the right scroll arrow on the horizontal scroll bar.

   ✓ *Note the worksheet moves right by one column.*

7. Click the scroll bar below the scroll box on the vertical scroll bar.

   ✓ *Note the row ScrollTip and that the worksheet moves down by one screen.*

8. Click the scroll bar to the right of the scroll box on the horizontal scroll bar.

   ✓ *Note the column ScrollTip and that the worksheet moves right by one screen.*

9. Drag the horizontal scroll box all the way to the right on the scroll bar.

   ✓ *Note how the view of the worksheet has changed.*

10. Drag the vertical scroll box all the way down on the scroll bar.

    ✓ *Note how the view of the worksheet has changed.*

11. Use the scroll bars or keystrokes to move in the following ways or to the parts of the worksheet listed below:

    - Down one screen
    - Up one screen
    - Right one screen
    - Left one screen
    - Lower left of worksheet
    - Top right of worksheet
    - Bottom right of worksheet

12. Exit Excel.

CHANGE ACTIVE CELL USING THE KEYBOARD

One cell right .... →

One cell left .... ←

One cell down .... ↓

One cell up .... ↑

One screen up .... Page Up

One screen down .... Page Down

One screen right .... Alt + Page Down

One screen left .... Alt + Page Up

First cell in current row .... Home

Last cell in current row .... Ctrl + →

First cell in worksheet .... Ctrl + Home

Last occupied cell in
worksheet .... Ctrl + End

CHANGE ACTIVE CELL USING THE MOUSE

- Click desired cell.
  - *NOTE: If desired cell is not in view, use the scroll bars to move area of worksheet containing cell into view. Then click the cell.*

SCROLL USING THE MOUSE

✓ *The **vertical scroll bar** is located on the right side of the workbook window. The **horizontal scroll bar** (illustrated below) is located on the bottom of the workbook window. Excel shows the destination row or column (ScrollTips) when you drag a scroll box.*

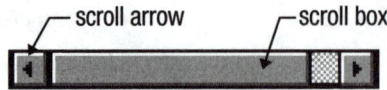

scroll arrow ─────   ─── scroll box

SCROLL BAR

To scroll one column left or right:

- Click left or right scroll arrow.

To scroll one row up or down:

- Click up or down scroll arrow.

To scroll one screen up or down:

- Click vertical scroll bar above or below the scroll box.

To scroll one screen right or left:

- Click horizontal scroll bar to right or left of the scroll box.

To scroll to the beginning columns:

- Drag horizontal scroll box to the extreme left of the scroll bar.

To scroll to the beginning rows:

- Drag vertical scroll box to the top of the scroll bar.

To scroll quickly to an area in worksheet:

- Drag scroll box to desired position on the scroll bar.
  - *NOTE: The limits of the scrolling area will depend on the location of data in the worksheet.*

To scroll quickly to the last row where data was entered:

- Press **Ctrl** and drag vertical scroll box to the bottom of the scroll bar.

SCROLL USING THE KEYBOARD

One screen up .... Page Up

One screen down .... Page Down

One screen right .... Alt + Page Down

One screen left .... Alt + Page Up

NEXT EXERCISE

EXERCISE

Explore the Worksheet Using the Mouse and Keyboard

5

NOTES:

- You can also change the active cell in a worksheet by selecting the **Go To** command on the **Edit** menu or by pressing F5.

  Note the **Go To** dialog box that appears when **Go To** is selected or F5 is pressed:

- You can also change the active cell in a worksheet by typing or selecting a reference in the **name box** [   ].

  Note the location of the name box with an active reference displayed.

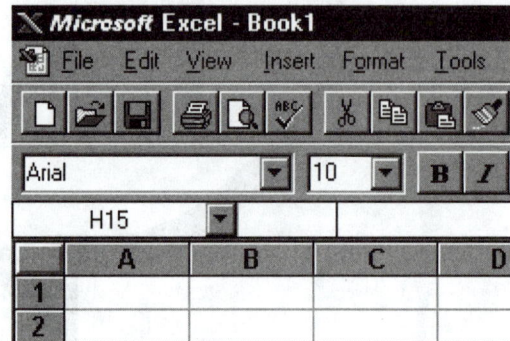

EXERCISE DIRECTIONS:

1. Select **Edit** on the menu bar.

2. Select **Go To**.

3. Type A10 in the **Reference** text box.

4. Click **OK**.

   ✓ *Note the active cell is A10.*

5. Using the **Go To** command, change the active cell to the following:

   - AB105
   - A8150
   - K965
   - BG200
   - C28
   - A1 (Home)

   ✓ *Note the **Go To** list box displays the last four references you chose to go to.*

6. Click in the name box on the left side of the formula bar.

   ✓ *Note A1 becomes highlighted.*

7. Type C6 and press Enter.

   ✓ *Note C6 is now the active cell.*

8. Using the name box, change the active cell to the following:

   - P365
   - GH67
   - IV56
   - Q80
   - Lower left of worksheet (A16384)
   - Top right of worksheet (IV1)
   - Bottom right of worksheet (IV1684)
   - Top of worksheet (A1)

9. Press F5 and go to the following cells:

   - BC15
   - GZ495
   - DA15000

10. Close Excel.

CHANGE ACTIVE CELL USING GO TO

1. Press **F5** F5

   OR

   a. Click **Edit** menu .... Alt + E

   b. Click **Go To** .... G

2. Type cell reference .... *cell reference* in **Reference** text box.

   NOTE: *The **Go To** list box displays the last four references you chose to go to.*

3. Click OK .... ↵

CHANGE ACTIVE CELL USING THE NAME BOX

1. Click in name box ▢ on left side of formula bar.

2. Type cell reference .... *cell reference*

3. Press **Enter** .... ↵

LESSON 3

WORKSHEET BASICS

Exercises 6-10

- Enter Labels and Values

- Make Simple Corrections

- Save a Workbook

- Close a Workbook

- Exit Excel

- Numeric Labels and Values

- Align Labels

EXCEL

EXERCISE

■ **Enter Labels** ■ **Make Simple Corrections**
■ **Save a Workbook** ■ **Close a Workbook** ■ **Exit Excel**

6

NOTES:

Enter Labels

- The **status** of a cell is determined by the first character entered.

- When an alphabetical character or a symbol (` ~ ! # % ^ & * ( ) _ \ | [ ] { } ; : ' " < > , ?) is entered as the first character in a cell, the cell contains a **label**.

- By default, each cell is approximately nine (9) characters wide; however, it is possible to view an entered label that is longer than the cell width if the cell to the right is blank.

- A label is entered in the cell after you do one of the following:

  • Press the Enter key, or

  • Press an arrow key, or

  • Click another cell, or

  • Click the Enter box ☑ on the formula bar.

- The contents in a label will automatically align to the left of the cell, making it a left–justified entry.

Make Simple Corrections

- Before data is entered, the Backspace key may be used to correct an error. To delete the entire entry, press the Escape key or click the Cancel box ☒ on the formula bar. Note the illustration of the formula bar below. After text is entered, a correction may be typed directly over the existing text. This is referred to as the **strikeover** method of correction.

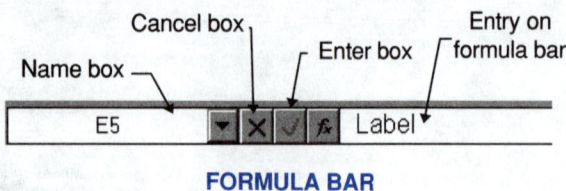

FORMULA BAR

Save a Workbook

- Each workbook is saved on a data disk or hard drive for future recall, and must be given a name for identification. A saved workbook is called a **file.**

- Previously, a **filename** could not exceed eight (8) characters. However, with Windows® 95, you may use descriptive filenames up to 255 characters long. Since the name has to be remembered and typed for recall, it is still advisable to limit the length of the names. When you save a file, Excel automatically adds a period and a **filename extension** (usually .XLS) to the end of the filename. Because Excel identifies file types by their extension, you should not type the filename extension.

  NOTE: Filenames may be typed in either uppercase or lowercase characters.

- A workbook must be saved before closing it or all current or updated entries will be lost. If you attempt to close a workbook or exit Excel before saving, you will be asked if you want to save the changes.

  NOTE: If you make a mistake and want to begin again, you may choose to close the workbook without saving it.

- A file may be saved by using the **File, Save As** commands or by clicking the Save icon 💾 on the Standard Toolbar. The Save dialog box that appears allows you to name the path, folder and file.

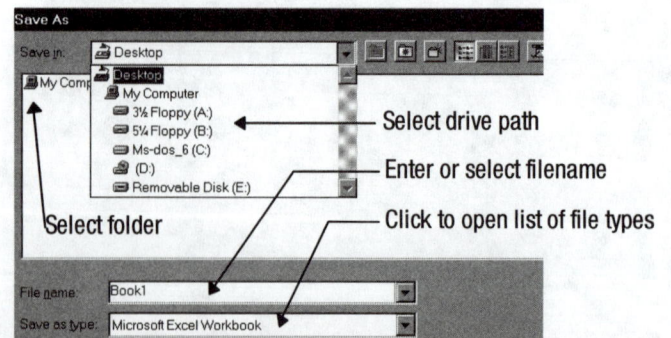

In this exercise, you will begin to create a worksheet for the Family Pharmacy by entering labels. Numeric data will be entered in a later exercise.

EXERCISE DIRECTIONS:

1. Go to cell B2.

2. Type your name and look at the formula bar.

   ✓ *Note the Cancel and Enter boxes to the left of the formula bar.*

   NOTE: *If the formula bar is not visible, see SET VIEW PREFERENCES, page 14, and follow steps to select the **Formula Bar** option.*

3. Cancel the entry by pressing the Escape key, or by clicking the Cancel box ☒.

4. Create the worksheet below.

5. Enter the labels in the exact cell locations shown in the illustration.

6. Correct errors using the Backspace or strikeover method.

7. Save the workbook; name it **DAILY**.

8. Close the workbook.

	A	B	C	D	E	F	G	H
1				FAMILY PHARMACY				
2				DAILY SALES REPORT				
3	DATE:							
4								
5	CODE	DEPARTMENT		SALES	TAX	TOTAL	% OF TOTAL	
6								
7	A	BEAUTY AIDS						
8	B	CANDY						
9	C	CARDS						
10	D	MEDICINE (OTC)						
11	E	TOILETRIES						
12	F	VITAMINS						
13	G	PRESCRIPTIONS						
14								
15								
16								
17								
18								
19								
20								

ENTER A LABEL

NOTE: Labels are right–aligned and cannot be calculated.

1. Click cell.................................... ⬍
    to receive label.

2. Type label text........................ *label text*

3. Press **Enter** .... ⏎

    OR

    Click **Enter** box.............................. ✓
    on the formula bar.

    OR

    Press any **arrow key**................... ⬍
    to enter label and move to next cell.

SAVE A NEW WORKBOOK

1. Click **F**ile menu .... Alt + F

2. Click **Save As**............................... A

    ### To select a drive:

    a.   Click **Save in** .... Alt + I

    b.   Click desired drive letter........ ↓

    ### To select a folder:

    •   Click on desired folder
        in list............................ Tab , ↓

3. Double–click in **File name:** .. Alt + N

4. Type filename .... *filename*

5. Click **Save** .... Alt + S

CLOSE A WORKBOOK

•   Click **close** button........................ ✕

OR

1. Click **F**ile menu.................... Alt + F

2. Click **Close** C

    If **Save Changes in Workbook**
    message appears:

    •   Click [Yes] .... Y
        to save changes to the workbook.

        *NOTE: If you have not previously saved the workbook, the **Save As** dialog box appears. (See SAVE A NEW WORKBOOK, left.)*

    OR

    Click [No] .... N
    to close without saving the changes.

EXIT EXCEL

•   Click **close** button......................... ✕

OR

•   Press **Alt + F4** .... Alt + F4

OR

1. Click **F**ile menu.................... Alt + F

2. Click **Exit** X

    If **Save Changes in Workbook**
    message appears:

    •   Click [Yes] .... Y
        to save changes to the workbook.

        *NOTE: If you have not previously saved the workbook, the **Save As** dialog box appears. (See **SAVE A NEW WORKBOOK**, left.)*

    OR

    Click [No] .... N
    to close without saving the changes.

NEXT EXERCISE

EXERCISE

7

■ **Enter Labels** ■ **Numeric Labels and Values** ■ **Save a Workbook**
■ **Close a Workbook** ■ **Make Simple Corrections**

NOTES:

Numeric Labels and Values

■ When a number or a symbol (+ - . = $) is entered as the first character in a cell, the cell contains a **value**.

■ A value is entered after you do one of the following:

- Press the Enter key, or

- Press an arrow key, or

- Click another cell, or

- Click the Enter box on the formula bar.

■ If a value is longer than the cell, Excel displays the number in scientific notation or number signs (######) appear in the cell. In this case, the column width must be reset. Setting column width will be covered in **Exercise 21**, page 70.

■ A **numeric label** is a number that will not be used in calculation. Examples of numeric labels are social security numbers or identification numbers. To indicate that such numbers are to be treated as *labels* and not *values*, it is necessary to begin the entry with a **label prefix**, an apostrophe ('). Therefore, a card number 12567 would be entered as '12567 and would appear left-aligned as a label without the apostrophe or label prefix.

■ The label prefix is not displayed on the worksheet, but is shown on the formula bar.

Label Alignment

■ A value automatically aligns to the right of the cell, making it a right–justified entry.

■ Since labels are left–justified and values are right–justified in a cell, column titles (which are labels) will not appear centered over numeric data.

Note the illustration of how entered data is aligned in cells:

TEXT	◄─────	left-justified label
123	◄─────	right-justified value
123	◄─────	left-justified numeric label

In this exercise, you will create a payroll for employees of the Burlington National Bank. GROSS PAY refers to total salary earned before taxes; NET PAY refers to salary received after taxes are deducted; F.I.C.A. (Federal Insurance Contributions Act) is a designation for social security tax; and F.W.T. refers to Federal Withholding Tax.

EXERCISE DIRECTIONS:

1. Create the worksheet below.

2. Enter the labels and values in the exact cell locations shown in the illustration.

   NOTE: The time card numbers (in the CARD NUMBER column) are to be entered as NUMERIC LABELS, not as values.

3. Correct any errors.

4. Save the workbook; name it **SALARY**.

5. Close the workbook.

	A	B	C	D	E	F	G	H
1		BURLINGTON NATIONAL BANK						
2			PAYROLL					
3								
4	CARD	EMP.	HOURLY	HOURS	GROSS			NET
5	NUMBER	NAME	RATE	WORKED	PAY	F.I.C.A.	F.W.T.	PAY
6								
7	12567	CARTER	5.55	15				
8	12750	FINCKEL	7.23	32				
9	12816	JAMISON	6.18	16				
10	12925	MILLS	4.66	28				
11	12345	POTTER	6.57	12				
12	12716	SAMUELS	8.65	21				

ENTER A NUMERIC LABEL

NOTE: Numbers, entered as numeric labels, are left–aligned and cannot be calculated.

1. Click cell........................... 🔀 to receive numeric label.

2. Press ' (label prefix) .... ▮

3. Type number.............................number

4. Press **Enter** .... ⏎

ENTER A VALUE

NOTE: Numbers, entered as values, are right–aligned and can be calculated.

1. Click cell..................................... 🔀 to receive value.

2. Type number ....number

   NOTE: Begin entry with a number from zero to nine, or a decimal point. Precede a negative number with a minus sign (-) or enclose it in within parentheses ().

3. Press **Enter** .... ⏎

   NOTE: If Excel displays number signs (######) or the number in scientific notation, the column is not wide enough to display the value. Excel stores the value in the cell, but cannot display it. To see the entry, double–click the right border of the column heading. If the value has more than eight decimal places, Excel automatically rounds it to eight places.

EXERCISE

■ Enter Labels and Values ■ Align Labels ■ Save a Workbook
■ Close a Workbook ■ Make Simple Corrections

8

NOTES:

- Note the label and value entries in the worksheet on the right. The label text is left–aligned while the values are right–aligned in the cell. Column title labels above numeric data may be centered or right–aligned to improve the appearance of the worksheet.

- You can align a label by using the **alignment buttons** on the Formatting toolbar.

- Labels may also be aligned by selecting the cells containing the label(s) to align and choosing an alignment through the menu system.

TEXT	◄	left-justified label	
TEXT	◄	centered label	
TEXT	◄	right-justified label	
123	◄	right-justified value	
123	◄	left-justified numeric label	

Note the illustration of the alignment buttons on the Formatting toolbar below:

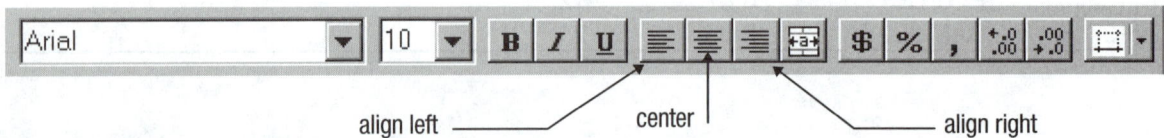

align left ——— center | ——— align right

In this exercise you will create an invoice. An invoice is a bill sent to a buyer by a seller. UNIT PRICE refers to the price of an item quoted by the way the item is packaged for sale. For example, the unit price for pencils may be quoted by the dozen.

EXERCISE DIRECTIONS:

1. Create the worksheet on the right.

2. Enter the labels and values in the exact cell locations shown in the illustration. Right–align the labels UNIT PRICE and TOTAL PRICE.

   NOTE: Stock numbers, the address, and the terms are to be entered as NUMERIC LABELS, not as values.

3. Correct any errors.

4. Save the workbook; name it **BILL**.

5. Close the workbook.

	A	B	C	D	E	F	G	H
1				INVOICE				
2								
3				PAPER PALACE OFFICE SUPPLIES				
4								
5	SOLD TO:	Imani Taylor						
6		65 First Street						
7		Beverly Hills, CA 90210						
8								
9	TERMS:	30 days						
10								
11	QUANTITY	UNIT	DESCRIPTION			STOCK	UNIT	TOTAL
12						NUMBER	PRICE	PRICE
13								
14	5	DOZ	PENCILS #2			2BJ442	2.47	
15	4	BOXES	FOLDERS - LEGAL SIZE			1FJ154	7.86	
16	2	BOXES	DISKS - 3.5"			6SD879	8.21	
17								

SELECT (HIGHLIGHT) A RANGE OF CELLS USING THE MOUSE

1. Point to interior of first cell to select.
   Pointer becomes a ✛.
2. Drag through adjacent cells until desired cells are highlighted.

SELECT (HIGHLIGHT) A RANGE OF CELLS USING THE KEYBOARD

1. Press **arrow keys**...................... [↑↓←→]
   until first cell to select is outlined.
2. Press **Shift + arrow
   keys**.................................. [Shift] + [↑↓←→]
   until adjacent cells to select are highlighted.

ALIGN LABELS USING THE TOOLBAR

1. Select cell(s) containing label(s).
   —FROM FORMATTING TOOLBAR—
2. Click **Align Left** button................. [≡]
   OR
   Click **Center** button..................... [≡]
   OR
   Click **Align Right** button .... [≡]

ALIGN LABELS USING THE MENU

Aligns data in labels horizontally or vertically in cells.

1. Select cell(s) containing label(s) to align.
2. a. Click **Format** menu ...... [Alt] + [O]
   b. Click **Cells**............................. [E]
   OR
   a. Right–click a selected cell.
   b. Click **Format Cells**.
3. Click **Alignment** tab........... [Ctrl] + [Tab]

To align data horizontally:

Select desired **Horizontal** option:
- **General**
  (default alignment) .... [Alt] + [G]
- **Left** .... [Alt] + [L]
- **Center**...................,,,,.... [Alt] + [C]
- **Right**............................. [Alt] + [R]
- **Fill**................................. [Alt] + [F]
  cell appears filled with its contents.
- **Justify** .... [Alt] + [J]
  aligns and wraps text evenly within its horizontal limits.
- **Center across
  selection**..................... [Alt] + [A]

To align data vertically:

Select desired **Vertical** option:
- **Top**............................... [Alt] + [T]
- **Center** .... [Alt] + [E]
- **Bottom**......................... [Alt] + [B]
- **Justify**.......................... [Alt] + [U]
  aligns and wraps text evenly within its vertical limits.
4. Click [OK] .... [↵]

EXERCISE
Summary

9

You want to keep track of the fees paid by the members of the Millstown Regional High School Drill Team. Data provided includes student names, school identification numbers, dates of birth (entered as left–aligned labels) and fees paid to date.

EXERCISE DIRECTIONS:

1. Include a two-line report title and appropriate column titles. Center all entries in the school identification numbers column. Right–align the column title for the fees column.

2. Using the data below, create the worksheet.

Allison, John	2314	03/14/80	55
Darkin, Bill	4376	12/02/81	25
Gallina, Lawrence	7543	02/28/80	15
Johnson, Sean	3265	05/12/81	55
Marks, Samuel	5376	08/30/81	30
Potter, George	2943	04/19/80	35
Ryan, Mike	4328	11/07/81	40
Timmons, Robert	3178	10/27/81	10

3. Save the workbook; name it **TEAM**.

EXERCISE

10

Mr. Wiggins, the owner of the Pringle Repair Shop, has asked you to prepare an inventory listing the items he stocks in his repair shop with the item numbers, unit cost and selling price of each item.

EXERCISE DIRECTIONS:

1. Using the data below, create the worksheet. Include an appropriate two-line worksheet title. Leave a blank column (column C) between ITEM and UNIT COST. Enter item numbers as numeric labels. Right–align column labels for UNIT COST and SELLING PRICE.

ITEM NUMBER	ITEM	UNIT COST	SELLING PRICE
142	carburetor	120	168
321	spark plugs	2	3
093	tires	55	77
393	brakes	60	84
659	alarm	125	195
572	mats	45	63
175	battery	45	70
421	radio	185	265
932	fan belt	15	28

2. Save the workbook; name it **PARTS**.

NEXT LESSON

LESSON 4

FILES, FORMULAS AND FORMATTING

Exercises 11-18

- Use Formulas

- File Functions (Open, Resave, Save As, Backup)

- Format Data

- Use Ranges

- Copy Data

- Print a Worksheet

- Copy a Formula (Absolute and Relative References)

- Format Fractions and Mixed Numbers

- Spelling

EXERCISE
Use Formulas

11

NOTES:

- A **formula** is an instruction to calculate a number.

- A formula is entered in the cell where the answer should appear. As you type the formula, it appears in the **cell** and in the **formula bar**. After a formula is entered, the answer is displayed in the cell, and the formula is displayed in the formula bar.

- **Cell references** and **mathematical operators** are used to develop formulas. The cell reference can be typed or inserted into a formula. An equal sign (=) must precede a formula. For example, the formula =C3+C5+C7 results in the addition of the values in these cell locations. Therefore, any change to a value made in these cell locations causes the answer to change automatically.

  NOTE: If you are using the number pad and enter the formula (+C3+C5+C7) using a plus sign as the first character, Excel will substitute the equal sign.

- The standard mathematical operators used in formulas are:

  + Addition   - Subtraction

  * Multiplication   / Division

  ^ Exponentiation

- It is important to consider the **order of mathematical operations** when preparing formulas. Operations enclosed in parentheses have the highest priority and are executed first; exponential calculations are executed second. Multiplication and division operations have the next priority and are completed before any addition and subtraction operations.

- All operations are executed from left to right in the order of appearance. For example, in the formula =A1*(B1+C1), B1+C1 will be calculated before the multiplication is performed. If the parentheses were omitted, A1*B1 would be calculated first and C1 would be added to that answer. This would result in a different outcome.

- Multiplication and division formulas may result in answers with multiple decimal places. These numbers can be rounded off using a formatting feature. (See Format Data, Exercise 13, page 48.)

- When using a **percentage** as a numeric factor in a formula, you can enter it with a decimal or with the percent symbol. For example, you may enter either .45 or 45% to include 45 percent in a formula.

EXERCISE DIRECTIONS:

1. Create the worksheet below.

2. Enter the labels and values in the exact cell locations shown in the illustration.

3. Enter the formulas, as shown in the indicated cells.

4. Enter the appropriate formulas to complete the problem.

5. Save the workbook; name it **PRICE**.

6. Close the workbook.

	A	B	C	D	E	F	G	H
1			LIST	DIS-	SALE	SALES	TOTAL	
2	PRODUCT		PRICE	COUNT	PRICE	TAX	PRICE	
3								
4	RED GOWN		745	185	=C4-D4	=E4*.08	=E4+F4	
5	BLUE JACKET		985	265				
6	BROWN SLACKS		395	98				
7								
8								
9								
10								
11								
12								
13								
14								
15								
16								
17								
18								
19								
20								

ENTER A FORMULA USING MATHEMATICAL OPERATORS

1. Click cell............................... [↑↓ ←→]
   to receive formula.

2. Press **Equal** .... [=]

3. Type formula............................*formula*
   using cell references and
   mathematical operators.

   Example: =A1*(B2+B10)/2

NOTE: You can select cells instead of
   typing references to tell Excel
   which cells you wish the
   formula to reference.

To insert cell references by selecting cells:

a. Click formula where cell
    reference will be inserted.

    NOTE: If necessary, type
       preceding operator
       or parenthesis.

b. Select cell(s) you want the
    formula to reference.
    Reference appears in formula.

c. Type desired operator or
    parenthesis.

d. Repeat steps a–c as needed.

4. Press **Enter** .... [↵]

EXERCISE

■ Use Formulas ■ File Functions (Open, Resave, Save As, Backup)

12

NOTES:

Open Files

■ Workbooks that have been saved and closed must be opened using the same drive designation and filename used during the saving process. The Open dialog box contains a drop-down list with the drives or folders and a box containing a list of the files in that directory. In addition to opening a previously saved file, you may preview, search for a file and list details on a file from the Open dialog box.

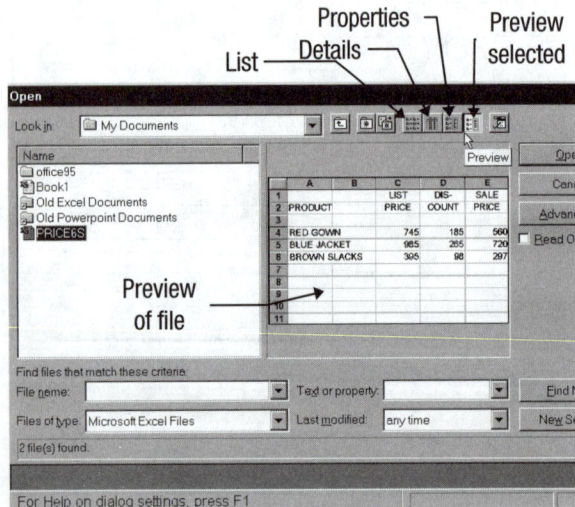

OPEN DIALOG BOX

■ When the **File** menu is accessed, a list of the last four files used is provided. One of these files may be opened by clicking the filename.

■ A newly opened workbook becomes the **active workbook** and hides any other open workbook. A previously opened workbook will *not* be closed automatically and can be made the active workbook.

Save Files

■ When resaving a workbook, the **Save** option on the File menu or the Save icon on the Standard Toolbar overwrites the previous version.

■ The **Save As** command allows for the changing of the filename as well as other save conditions. A new version of a previously saved workbook may be saved under a new name in order to keep both files.

■ It is also possible to backup all workbooks as they are being saved. This setting can be made using the Options button on the Save As dialog box, which brings you into the dialog box shown below. You can activate Always Create Backup which will create a copy of your file with a .BAK extension.

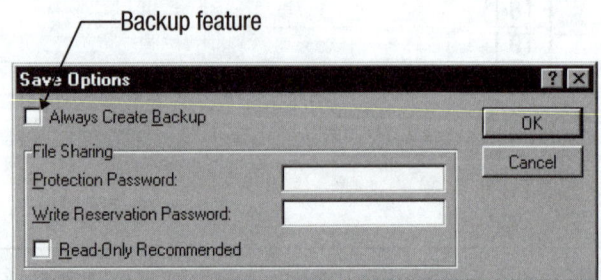

OPTIONS DIALOG BOX

In this exercise, you will complete the invoice for Paper Palace Office Supplies by finding the TOTAL PRICE for each item and the TOTAL DUE. The workbook will be saved again, backed up and saved using a new filename.

EXERCISE DIRECTIONS:

1. Open ⌨ **BILL** or 💾 **12BILL**.

2. Enter a formula to multiply QUANTITY by UNIT PRICE to find the TOTAL PRICE for each item.

3. Enter the label TOTAL DUE where indicated.

4. Enter a formula to add the TOTAL PRICE column to find TOTAL DUE.

5. Resave/overwrite the workbook file using the **Save** command or icon. Name the file **BILL.**

6. To create a backup file:

   - Select File, Save As, Options.
   - Select Always Create Backup.
   - Select OK.
   - Resave the file.

7. Save the workbook as **BILL2**.

8. Select File, Open to check for the new files.

   ✓ You should have BILL, BILL2, and Backup of BILL.

9. Close the workbook.

	A	B	C	D	E	F	G	H
1				INVOICE				
2								
3			PAPER PALACE OFFICE SUPPLIES					
4								
5	SOLD TO:	Imani Taylor						
6		65 First Street						
7		Beverly Hills, CA 90210						
8								
9	TERMS:	30 days						
10								
11	QUANTITY	UNIT	DESCRIPTION			STOCK	UNIT	TOTAL
12						NUMBER	PRICE	PRICE
13								
14	5	DOZ	PENCILS #2			2BJ442	2.47	
15	4	BOXES	FOLDERS - LEGAL SIZE			1FJ154	7.86	
16	2	BOXES	DISKS - 3.5"			6SD879	8.21	
17								
18			TOTAL DUE					
19								
20								

OPEN A WORKBOOK FILE

1. Click **Open** button......................... 📂
   on the Standard Toolbar.

   OR

   a. Click **File** menu .... `Alt`+`F`

   b. Click **Open**............................. `O`

To select a drive:

a. Click **Look in** .... `Alt`+`I`

b. Select desired drive ..... `↑↓`, `↵`

   Files in current directory of selected drive appear in File Name list box.

To select a folder in the drive:

• Double-click folder name
  in list box .... `↑↓`, `↵`

  Files in selected folder appear in File name list box.

To list files of a different type:

a. Click **Files of Type:** ...... `Alt`+`T`

b. Click file type .... `↑↓`, `↵`
   to list.
   Only files of specified type appear in File name list box.

✓ *Use this option to change the kinds of files displayed in the File name list box. For example, if you want to open a Lotus file into Excel, you would select the Lotus 1-2-3 Files item in the drop-down list.*

2. Click file to open in File Name list box.

   OR

   a. Select **File Name**
      list box .... `Alt`+`N`

   b. Type filename .... *filename*
      to open.

3. Click `Open` .... `Alt`+`O`

RESAVE/OVERWRITE A WORKBOOK FILE

• Click **Save File** button .... 💾
  on Standard Toolbar.

  OR

1. Click **File** menu............... `Alt`+`F`

2. Click **Save** .... `S`

SAVE AS

Saves and names the active workbook.

1. Click **File** menu.................... `Alt`+`F`

2. Click **Save As** .... `A`

To select a drive:

a. Click **Save in** .... `Alt`+`I`

b. Select desired drive .... `↑↓`, `↵`

To select a folder in the drive:

• Double-click folder name
  in list box .... `↑↓`, `↵`

3. Click **File name** .... `Alt`+`N`

4. Type filename ....*filename*

To set Excel to always create a backup of previous version when saving:

a. Click `Options` .... `Alt`+`O`

b. Select **Always Create**
   Backup...................... `Alt`+`B`

c. Click `OK` .... `↵`

5. Click `OK` .... `↵`

NEXT EXERCISE

EXERCISE

■ Open and Resave a Workbook File ■ Format Data ■ Use Ranges

13

NOTES:

Format Data

■ You can change the appearance of data to make it more attractive and readable by **formatting** it. Some available number formats are currency, percent, date, time and scientific notation.

■ The following formats may be used for formatting money values:

Number Displays number with or without decimal places and commas.

Currency Displays number with currency symbols: dollar signs, commas, and decimals.

NOTE: Other formats will be introduced in future exercises.

■ Formats may be set using the menu, with the **Format**, **Cells** commands, or using the format buttons on the toolbar. The Currency button **$** on the Formatting toolbar will format numbers for two decimal places and dollar signs.

Use Ranges

■ A **range** is a defined area of a worksheet. For example, if you select the cells F4, F5 and F6, this range of cells can be indicated as F4:F6. You can format data in a column or row by selecting the range of cells containing the data to format.

■ A **block of cells** may be defined as a range. For example, A1:G2 includes all the cells in columns A through G in rows one and two.

■ As noted in Exercise 7, label text is left–aligned while values are right–aligned in a cell. The alignment buttons on the Formatting toolbar, or the alignment settings through the menu system, may be used to align a column title in a single cell or all the column titles in a selected range.

■ Cell contents may be formatted or aligned before or after data is entered.

In this exercise, you will format money columns and column titles for the PRICE worksheet.

EXERCISE DIRECTIONS:

1. Open ⌨ **PRICE or** 💾 **13PRICE**.

2. Select the range C1:G2 shown in the illustration and center all column titles.

3. Select the range C4:G6 shown in the illustration and format data for two decimal places using the Number format.

4. Select the data in column G, G4:G6, and format for **Currency**.

5. Save the workbook file as **PRICE**.

6. Close the workbook.

	A	B	C	D	E	F	G	H
1			LIST	DIS-	SALE	SALES	TOTAL	range C1:G2
2	PRODUCT		PRICE	COUNT	PRICE	TAX	PRICE	
3								
4	RED GOWN		745	185	560	44.8	604.8	range C4:G6
5	BLUE JACKET		985	265	720	57.6	777.6	
6	BROWN SLACKS		395	98	297	23.76	320.76	
7								
8								
9								
10								
11								
12								
13								
14								
15								
16								
17								
18								
19								
20								

SELECT (HIGHLIGHT) A RANGE OF CELLS USING THE MOUSE

NOTE: *A range of cells is two or more cells. Cells in a selected range are highlighted and the active cell within the selection is white.*

To select a range of adjacent cells:

1. Point to interior of first cell to select. *Pointer becomes a* ✛.

2. Drag through adjacent cells until desired cells are highlighted.

To select entire row or column:

- Click row heading or column heading to select.

To select adjacent rows or columns:

1. Point to first row heading or column heading to select.

   Pointer becomes a ✛.

2. Drag through adjacent headings until desired rows or columns are highlighted.

SELECT (HIGHLIGHT) A RANGE OF CELLS USING THE KEYBOARD

NOTE: *A range of cells is two or more cells. Cells in a selected range are highlighted and the active cell within the selection is white.*

To select a range of adjacent cells:

1. Press **arrow keys** .... [↕↔]

   until first cell to select is highlighted.

2. Press **Shift + arrow keys** .... [Shift] + [↕↔]

To select entire row containing active cell:

- Press **Shift + Space** .... [Shift] + [Space]

To select entire column containing active cell:

- Press **Ctrl + Space** .... [Ctrl] + [Space]

To select adjacent rows:

1. Press **arrow keys** .... [↕↔]

   until a cell in first row to select is outlined.

2. Press and hold **Shift** .... [Shift]

   then press **Space** .... [Space]

   to highlight first row to select.

3. Still pressing **Shift**, press **up or down key** .... [↑↓]

   to highlight adjacent rows to select.

FORMAT NUMBERS USING THE MENU

1. Select cell(s) to format.

2. a. Click **Format** menu ...... [Alt] + [O]

   b. Click **Cells...** .... [E]

   OR

   a. Right–click a selected cell.

   b. Click **Format Cells**.

3. Click **Number** tab .... [Ctrl] + [Tab]

4. Click desired category .... [Alt] + [C], [↑↓]

   in **Category** list.

   Category list items include: All, Custom, Number, Accounting, Date, Time, Percentage, Fraction, Scientific, Text Currency.

5. Select option(s) for selected category .... [Tab], [↓]

6. Click [OK] .... [↵]

FORMAT NUMBERS USING THE TOOLBAR

Applies commonly used number formats.

- Select cell(s) to format.

—FROM FORMATTING TOOLBAR—

To apply currency style:

- Click **Currency Style**
  button .... $ \boxed{\$} $

To apply percent style:

- Click **Percent Style** button... $ \boxed{\%} $

To apply the comma style:

- Click **Comma Style** button ... $ \boxed{,} $

To increase or decrease decimal places:

- Click **Increase Decimal**
  button .... $ \boxed{\substack{+.0 \\ .00}} $

  OR

  Click **Decrease Decimal**
  button .... $ \boxed{\substack{.00 \\ +.0}} $

ALIGN (JUSTIFY) LABELS USING THE MENU

Aligns data horizontally or vertically in their cells.

1. Select cell(s) containing data to align.

2. a. Click **Format** menu ...... $ \boxed{Alt} + \boxed{O} $

   b. Click **Cells** .... $ \boxed{E} $

   OR

   a. Right–click a selected cell.

   b. Click **Format Cells**.

3. Click **Alignment** tab .... $ \boxed{Ctrl} + \boxed{Tab} $

To align data horizontally:

Select desired **Horizontal** option:

- **Left** .... $ \boxed{Alt} + \boxed{L} $
- **Center** .... $ \boxed{Alt} + \boxed{C} $
- **Right** .... $ \boxed{Alt} + \boxed{R} $
- **General** .... $ \boxed{Alt} + \boxed{G} $
- **Full** .... $ \boxed{Alt} + \boxed{F} $
- **Justify** .... $ \boxed{Alt} + \boxed{J} $

To align data vertically:

Select desired **Vertical** option:

- **Top** .... $ \boxed{Alt} + \boxed{T} $
- **Center** .... $ \boxed{Alt} + \boxed{E} $
- **Bottom** .... $ \boxed{Alt} + \boxed{B} $
- **Center across**
  selection .... $ \boxed{Alt} + \boxed{A} $

4. Click $ \boxed{\text{OK}} $ .... $ \boxed{\hookleftarrow} $

NOTE: *You may also use the alignment buttons on the Formatting toolbar to left-align, center, and right-align labels, see **ALIGN LABELS USING THE TOOLBAR**, page 37.*

NEXT EXERCISE

EXERCISE

■ Open and Resave a Workbook File ■ Use Formulas ■ Copy Data
■ Format Data ■ Print a Worksheet

14

NOTES:

Copy Data

- Using the Copy command from the Edit menu or the Copy icon on the Standard Toolbar, formulas may be **copied**:

  - Horizontally or vertically, or

  - To another cell or range of cells, or

  - To another worksheet or workbook.

- When a formula is copied to a new location, the cell references change relative to their new location.

Print a Worksheet

- The workbook, the selected worksheet(s), or the selected range of data may be **printed** using the Print command. When the Print command is accessed, Excel allows you to select various print options. One way you can preview the print output is by selecting the Preview button in the Print dialog box. You may print multiple copies of a report by entering the number in the Copies section of the dialog box *(see below)*.

Preview button ———

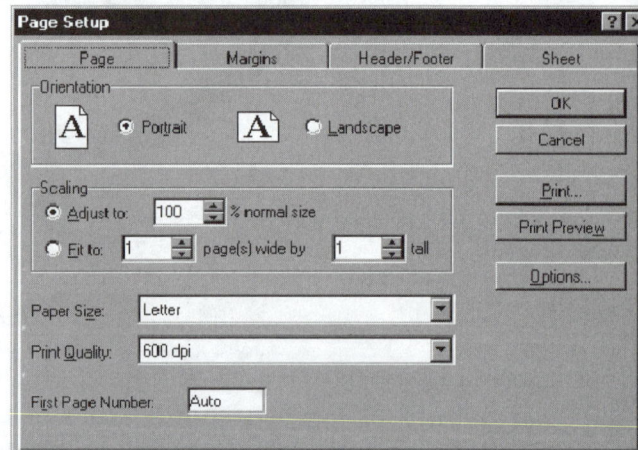

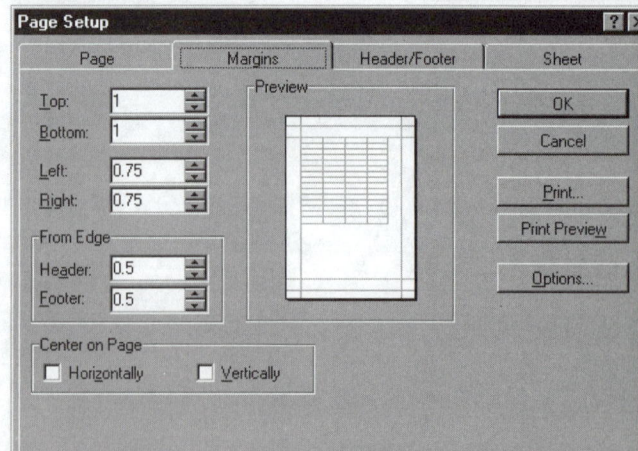

- To set print options, select Page Setup from the File menu and a dialog box with four tabs will appear. The page size settings can be accessed by selecting the Page tab. Excel uses the default page size (usually 8 1/2" x 11") of the installed printer. The margin page settings can be accessed by selecting the Margins tab. The top and bottom default page margins are set at 1", the right and left default page margins are set at 0.75".

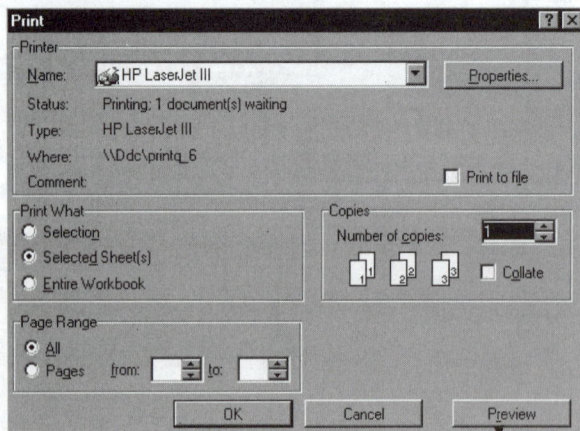

PAGE SETUP DIALOG BOX WITH THE PAGE AND MARGINS TABS SELECTED

In this exercise, you will prepare and print a payroll where Federal Withholding Tax is calculated using a fixed percentage.

NOTE: F.W.T. is actually determined using a table where the tax varies according to your salary and number of exemptions.

EXERCISE DIRECTIONS:

1. Open ⌨ **SALARY** or 💾 **14SALARY**.
2. Enter a formula to calculate GROSS PAY for the first employee using the hourly rate and hours worked.
3. Copy the GROSS PAY formula for each employee.
4. Enter a formula to compute F.I.C.A. at 7.65%.
5. Copy the F.I.C.A. formula for each employee.
6. Enter a formula to calculate F.W.T. at 20%.
7. Copy the F.W.T. formula for each employee.
8. Enter a formula to calculate NET PAY which is the amount received after taxes are deducted.
9. Copy the NET PAY formula for each employee.
10. Format columns E, F, G and H for two decimal places using the **Number** format option.
11. Center all column heading labels.
12. Save the workbook file as **SALARY**.
13. Print Preview the file.
14. Select Page Setup from the file menu and check all print settings.
15. Print two copies of the worksheet.
16. Close the workbook.

	A	B	C	D	E	F	G	H
1			BURLINGTON NATIONAL BANK					
2				PAYROLL				
3								
4	CARD	EMP.	HOURLY	HOURS	GROSS			NET
5	NUMBER	NAME	RATE	WORKED	PAY	F.I.C.A.	F.W.T.	PAY
6								
7	12567	CARTER	5.55	15				
8	12750	FINCKEL	7.23	32				
9	12816	JAMISON	6.18	16				
10	12925	MILLS	4.66	28				
11	12345	POTTER	6.57	12				
12	12716	SAMUELS	8.65	21				
13								

COPY USING THE MENU

Copies the data once and overwrites existing data in the destination cells.

1. Select cell(s) to copy.
2. Click **Edit** menu .... `Alt`+`E`
3. Click **Copy** .... `C`

   OR

   Click **Copy** button .... 🖹
   on Standard Toolbar.
   A flashing outline surrounds selection.

4. Select destination cell(s).
   NOTE: *Select an area to copy to, or select the upper left cell in the destination cell range. The destination can be in the same worksheet, another sheet or another workbook.*

5. Press **Enter** .... ⏎

PRINT A WORKSHEET

Prints worksheet data using the current page settings.

NOTE: *When printing a worksheet, Excel will only print the print area, if you defined one.*

- Click **Print** button .... 🖨
  on Standard Toolbar.

OR

1. Click **File** menu .... `Alt`+`F`
2. Click **Print** .... `P`
3. Select ◯ **Selected Sheet(s)** .... `Alt`+`D`
4. Click [OK] .... ⏎

EXERCISE

■ Copy a Formula (Absolute and Relative Reference)
■ Format Data (Bold, Italics and Underscore) ■ Print a Worksheet
■ Open and Resave a Workbook File

15

NOTES:

Copy Formulas (Absolute and Relative Reference)

■ When formulas are copied the cell references change relative to their new location. This is called **relative reference.** In some cases, a value in a formula must remain constant when copied to other locations. This is called an absolute reference.

■ To identify a cell as an absolute value, a dollar sign ($) must precede the column and row references for that cell. For example, in the formula =F7/$F$15, F15 is an absolute reference. The dollar sign ($) may be typed in the formula in the correct locations or F4 may be used to enter the absolute reference codes.

■ In this exercise, we must divide each department's sales by the total to find each department's percentage of total sales. Therefore the formula, =F7/$F$15, represents the sales for BEAUTY AIDS divided by the TOTAL SALES for the store. F15 is made an absolute reference so that when the formula is copied, the F15 or TOTAL SALES remains

constant in every formula. The department sales, F7, will change depending on the formula location since it is a relative reference in the formula.

■ If a formula with relative references is copied, a zero (0) appears if the formula is referring to empty cells.

Format Data

■ Formatting may be used to change decimal answers into a percentage format.

Styles such as **Bold**, *Italics* and Underscore may be applied to labels or values to enhance, highlight or organize your worksheet. The Formatting Toolbar contains buttons for each of these styles, which are used by selecting the data and clicking the appropriate toolbar button or buttons. Additional formatting enhancements will be discussed in Lesson 9. The Toolbar buttons are illustrated below:

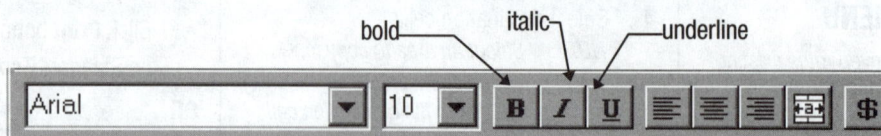

FORMATTING TOOLBAR

In this exercise, you will complete the Family Pharmacy daily sales report by calculating sales, tax and total sales. To analyze departmental sales, the owner requests an analysis showing what percent each department's sales is of the total sales. Labels and values will be bolded, italicized and underscored.

EXERCISE DIRECTIONS:

1. Open ⌨ **DAILY** or 💾 **15DAILY**.
2. Enter sales data, as shown in italics.
3. Enter a formula to calculate a 5% TAX on Beauty Aids.
4. Copy the TAX formula for each department *except* PRESCRIPTIONS.
5. Enter a formula to determine TOTAL for Beauty Aids.
6. Copy the TOTAL formula for each department including PRESCRIPTIONS.
7. Enter the label TOTAL SALES in cell B15.
8. Enter a formula in cell D15 to calculate TOTAL SALES.
9. Copy the TOTAL SALES formula to cells E15 and F15.
10. Enter the indicated formula using an absolute reference in the % OF TOTAL column.
11. Copy the % OF TOTAL formula for each department.

12. Copy the TOTAL SALES formula to find the total of the % OF TOTAL column.

    NOTE: The % OF TOTAL column should add up to 100% or 1 if not formatted for percents.

13. Using the **Number** formatting option, format the money columns (E and F) for two decimal places.
14. Using the **Percentage** formatting option, format the % OF TOTAL column for two decimal places.
15. Center SALES, TAX and TOTAL column headings.
16. Bold and underscore the two-line title of the worksheet.
17. Bold the Date line.
18. Bold, underscore and italicize the Totals line.
19. Save the workbook file as **DAILY**.
20. Print one copy of the worksheet.
21. Close the workbook.

	A	B	C	D	E	F	G	H
1				FAMILY PHARMACY				
2				DAILY SALES REPORT				
3	DATE:							
4								
5	CODE	DEPARTMENT		SALES	TAX	TOTAL	% OF TOTAL	
6								
7	A	BEAUTY AIDS		2238.02			=F7/$F$15	
8	B	CANDY		543.98				
9	C	CARDS		326.85				
10	D	MEDICINE (OTC)		1654.83				
11	E	TOILETRIES		196.37				
12	F	VITAMINS		413.29				
13	G	PRESCRIPTIONS		1245.65				
14								
15		TOTAL SALES						
16								
17								
18								

ENTER FORMULAS FOR ABSOLUTE CONDITIONS

1. Select cell to receive formula.

2. Press **Equal** .... ▣

3. Type formula .... *formula*
   using absolute references
   and mathematical operators.

   Example of a formula using absolute
   references: =$A$1*($B$2+$B$10)/2

   *NOTE: You can select cells instead of
   typing absolute references
   to tell Excel which cells you
   wish the formula to reference.*

To insert cell references by selecting cells:

a. Click formula where cell
   reference will be inserted.
   *NOTE: If necessary, type
   preceding operator
   or parenthesis.*

b. Select cell(s) you want formula
   to reference.
   Reference appears in formula.

c. Press **F4** .... ⌨F4

   until absolute reference appears.

d. Type desired operator or
   parenthesis.

e. Repeat steps a–d as needed.

4. Press **Enter** .... ⏎

FORMAT FOR BOLD, ITALICS AND UNDERSCORE

1. Select data to be formatted.

2. Click **Bold** button .... **B**

   OR

   Click **Italics** button .... *I*

   OR

   Click **Underscore** button .... U

NEXT EXERCISE

EXERCISE
■ Format Fractions and Mixed Numbers ■ Spelling
■ Copy a Formula

16

NOTES:

Fractions and Mixed Numbers

- Values can be formatted as fractions or mixed numbers automatically by entering them in a specific way, or values may be changed to fraction format using the Format, Cells commands.

- To enter a value as a **fraction**, which is part of a whole number, type a zero, a space and then type the fraction. For example: 0 1/3.

- To enter a value as a **mixed number**, which is a whole number with a fraction, type the whole number, a space, and then type the fraction. For example: 5 1/3.

- To format a value as a fraction after it has been entered, you must format the cell (**Format, Cells**) as a fraction number type.

- When you enter or format a value as a fraction, it appears as a decimal (which is also part of a whole number) in the formula bar.

Spelling

- Labels and text entries can be checked for spelling by using the Spelling feature. The Spelling icon on the Standard Toolbar or the **Spelling** item on the **Tools** menu, or pressing **F7** will access the feature. The words on the worksheet are checked and replacement words are suggested when misspelled words are found.

In this exercise, the Main Street Bakery wants to computerize their recipes so that they can adjust the amounts of ingredients depending on the desired yield. Fractions and mixed numbers will be used in the recipes.

EXERCISE DIRECTIONS:

1. Create the worksheet as illustrated. Bold titles and column headings.
2. Enter the values in the AMT column as shown in the illustration.
   NOTE: Enter fractions or mixed numbers as detailed above.
3. Format the whole numbers in the AMT column as fractions to align them with the mixed numbers.
4. Center all column headings except for INGREDIENTS as shown.
5. Center the yield and measure data as shown.
6. In cell A8, enter the formula to find the NEW AMT value for milk as shown in the illustration (AMT/YIELD*DESIRED YIELD).
   NOTE: In the formula, the YIELD and DESIRED YIELD references must be absolute since they remain constant (=B8/$B$4*$A$4).
7. Copy the formula to the remaining ingredients.
8. Format the NEW AMT values as fractions using the menu system.
9. Spell check the worksheet.
   NOTE: Ignore abbreviations, such as AMT and tbl. that will appear as misspellings. Along with any errors you might have made, you should find misspellings for cinnamon and whole-wheat.
10. Change the DESIRED YIELD value to 36 and note the changes.
11. Preview and print the worksheet.
12. Save the workbook; name it **MUFFIN**.

58

	A	B	C	D	E	F
1				MAIN STREET BAKERY		
2	DESIRED			BASIC MUFFIN RECIPE		
3	YIELD	YIELD				
4	24	12	Muffins	enter formula =B8/$B$4*$A$4		
5						
6	NEW					
7	AMT	AMT	MEAS.	INGREDIENTS		
8		3/4	cup	milk		
9		3	tbl.	vegatable oil		
10		1	large	egg		
11		1 1/4	cups	flour, all-purpose		
12		1/2	cup	flour, whole-wheat		
13		1/4	cup	oats, rolled		
14		1/2	cup	sugar, brown		
15		1/4	cup	sugar, white		
16		1/4	tsp.	salt		
17		2	tsp.	baking powder		
18		1/8	tsp.	cinamon		
19						
20				enter amounts as fractions and mixed numbers as shown		
21						
22						
23						

ENTER NUMBERS AS FRACTIONS

1. Select cell to receive number.
2. Press **Zero** .... [0]
3. Press **Space** .... [Space]
4. Type fraction .... *fraction*
   Example: 0 1/4
5. Press **Enter** .... [↵]

ENTER MIXED NUMBERS

1. Select cell to receive number.
2. Type whole number ...... *whole number*
3. Press **Space** .... [Space]
4. Type fraction .... *fraction*
   Example: 5 1/4
5. Press **Enter** .... [↵]

FORMAT NUMBERS FOR FRACTIONS

1. Select cell(s) to format.
2. a. Click **Format** menu ...... [Alt]+[O]
   b. Click **Cells** .... [E]
   OR
   a. Right–click a selected cell.

b. Click **Format Cells**.
3. Click **Number** tab .... [Ctrl]+[Tab]
4. Click fractions .... [Alt]+[C], [↗↓]
   in **C**ategory list.
5. Click **Type** and
   select option .... [Alt]+[T], [↓]
6. Click [OK] .... [↵]

SPELL CHECK

1. Select any cell.
   NOTE: When you select any cell, Excel spell checks all cells, headers, footers, embedded charts, text boxes, cell notes, and text in buttons on selected sheet.
   OR
   Select cells to spell check.
   OR
   Select sheets to spell check.
2. Click **Spelling** button .... [ABC✓]
   on Standard Toolbar.
   OR
   a. Click **Tools** menu .... [Alt]+[T]
   b. Click **Spelling** .... [S]

To replace word not found in dictionary with suggested word:

a. Type replacement word in **Change To:** [ ]
   OR
   Select word in **Suggestions** list box .... [Alt]+[N], [↗↓]
b. Click [Change] .... [Alt]+[C]
   to replace only current instance.
   OR
   Click [Change All] .... [Alt]+[L]
   to replace all instances.

To undo last change:

• Click [Undo Last] .... [Alt]+[U]

To skip word not found in dictionary:

- Click [Ignore] .... [Alt]+[I]
  to skip only current instance.

  OR

  Click [Ignore All] .... [Alt]+[G]
  to skip all instances.

To add word not found to dictionary:

- Click [Add] .... [Alt]+[A]

To ignore uppercase words:

- Select ☐ **Ignore UPPERCASE** .... [Alt]+[R]

To end spell checking:

- Click [Cancel] .... [Esc]

  OR

  Click [Close] .... [Esc]

3. Click [OK] .... [↵]

NEXT EXERCISE

EXERCISE
Summary
17

You are employed by the **PALMER TOY MANUFACTURING CO.**, and need to prepare a summary of the number of employees located in branches throughout the United States.

EXERCISE DIRECTIONS:

1. Create an appropriate two-line title for your worksheet.
2. Create a listing of each STATE and the number of EMPLOYEES at each location.

Arizona	1060
California	120
Montana	450
New Mexico	695
Oregon	543
South Dakota	267

3. At the bottom of the list, enter a label and find:
   - TOTAL EMPLOYEES
4. Create a new column heading and find for each state:
   - The PERCENT of the (total) firm's employees employed at each location.
     Hint: Use a formula with an absolute reference.
5. Find the Total of the Percent of Employees column.
6. Format values in the EMPLOYEES column for commas with no decimal places.
7. Format PERCENT OF EMPLOYEES column for two-place percents.
8. Right-align all column titles over numeric data.
9. Print one copy of the worksheet.
10. Save the workbook; name it **TOY**.

EXERCISE

Summary

18

You are asked to set up a worksheet to tally the February sales and compensation for agents in the Spring Car Rental Agency. Each salesperson receives a 4% commission on their car rental sales in addition to their monthly salary.

EXERCISE DIRECTIONS:

1. Create an appropriate two-line title for the worksheet.

2. Enter the following information for the sales staff (use columns A and B for AGENT data):

AGENT	SALES	TAX	TOTAL SALES	COMMIS-SION	MONTHLY SALARY	TOTAL
Deb Billings	9567.54				850.00	
Janine Diloren	14356.87				890.00	
Greg Milloy	15321.65				920.00	
Alan Nicks	16754.87				950.00	
Peter Simms	7536.76				820.00	
Kelly Timmer	6675.43				820.00	

3. For each AGENT, find:

   - TAX - sales tax rate is 8%

   - TOTAL SALES

   - COMMISSION - 4% on pre-tax sales

   - TOTAL - monthly salary plus commission

4. Format all money columns for two decimal places.

5. Skip one row and enter a Totals label below the worksheet. Find the totals for all money columns.

6. Right-align all column headings for money values.

7. Format title and total lines to bold.

8. Print one copy of the worksheet.

9. Save the workbook; name it **AGENT.**

LESSON 5
FUNCTIONS, FORMATS, FEATURES, AND PRINT OPTIONS

Exercises 19-29

- Use Formulas and Functions
- Function Wizard
- AutoCalculate
- Change Column Width
- Create a Series
- AutoComplete
- Comma Format
- Edit
- Print Options
- Print Preview
- Cell Notes
- AutoSum
- Bold Text
- Spell Check
- Page Breaks
- Solve What-If Problems (Data Tables, Goal Seek)
- PMT Function

EXCEL

EXERCISE

■ Use Functions ■ Function Wizard

19

NOTES:

Use Functions

■ A **function** is a built-in formula that performs a special calculation automatically. For example, the SUM function can be used with a range of cells to add all values in the range specified. To add the values in A4, A5 and A6, the function appears in the formula as follows: =SUM(A4:A6).

■ Functions appear in formulas in the following order: first the *function name* (in either uppercase or lowercase); followed by an *open parenthesis*; then the *number, cell, or range* of cells to be affected; followed by a *closed parenthesis*. You can type or insert functions into formulas. If you are typing a function and you wish to start the formula with a function, first type an equal sign (=).

■ A function may be used by itself, or it may be combined with other functions.

■ Excel provides functions that are used for statistical and financial analysis or for database operations. Some of the more commonly used functions are:

AVERAGE() Averages values in a range of cells.

COUNT() Counts all the non-blank cells in a range. Cells containing values as well as labels are counted.

MAX() Indicates the highest value in a range of cells.

MIN() Indicates the lowest value in a range of cells.

SUM() Adds all values in a range of cells.

■ The data the functions require you to supply are called **arguments**. For example, in =MAX(A1:A5), the range of cells is the argument.

Function Wizard

■ The **Function Wizard button** [fx], located on the Standard Toolbar or active formula bar, lets you insert functions into formulas by selecting the function from a list. It provides steps that prompt for required and optional arguments. When you use the **Function Wizard** to insert a function at the beginning of a formula, you do not type an equal sign since the Function Wizard enters one for you.

In this exercise, you will enter summary labels and find summary data using the AVERAGE, COUNT, MAX and MIN functions to complete the PRICE worksheet.

NOTE: Only the most commonly used functions are covered in this text. Appendix B (page 314), however, provides the methods to access information on the functions available in Excel.

EXERCISE DIRECTIONS:

1. Open ⌨ **PRICE** or 💾 **PRICE19**.
2. Enter new labels in column A, as indicated.
3. Enter the **SUM** function to total the LIST PRICE column and copy the formula to the remaining columns.
4. Enter the **AVERAGE** function to average the LIST PRICE column. Copy the formula to the remaining columns.
5. Use the Function Wizard and follow the steps to create a function formula for COUNT. Copy the formula to the remaining columns.
6. Enter the MAX and MIN function formulas to complete the worksheet. Copy formulas to the remaining columns.
7. Format summary data money amounts for two decimal places.
8. Save the workbook file as **PRICE**.
9. Close the workbook.

	A	B	C	D	E	F	G	H
1			LIST	DIS-	SALE	SALES	TOTAL	
2	PRODUCT		PRICE	COUNT	PRICE	TAX	PRICE	
3								
4	RED GOWN		745.00	185.00	560.00	44.80	604.80	
5	BLUE JACKET		985.00	265.00	720.00	57.60	777.60	
6	BROWN SLACKS		395.00	98.00	297.00	23.76	320.76	
7								
8	TOTALS						▶	
9	AVERAGE						▶	
10	COUNT						▶	
11	MAXIMUM						▶	
12	MINIMUM						▶	
13								

INSERT A FUNCTION USING FUNCTION WIZARD

1. Click cell....................................... [↔]
   to contain formula.

   OR

   a. Double–click cell containing
      formula..................................... [F2]

   b. Click formula....................... [↵]
      where function will be inserted.

2. Click **Function Wizard**
   button... [fx]
   on Standard Toolbar or formula bar.

   OR

   a. Click **Insert** menu .... [Alt]+[I]

   b. Click **Function** .... [F]

   —FUNCTION WIZARD – STEP 1 OF 2—

3. Select a
   category.................... [Alt]+[C], [↔]
   in **Function Category** list.

4. Select a function .... [Alt]+[N], [↕]
   in **Function Name** list.

5. Click [Next >] .... [↵]

   —FUNCTION WIZARD – STEP 2 OF 2—

6. Click desired argument box........... [Tab]

7. Type data .... data
   Depending on the function, enter
   the following kinds of data:

   • **numbers (constants)** — type
     numbers (integers, fractions,
     mixed numbers, negative
     numbers) as you would in a cell.

   • **references** — type or insert cell
     references.

   • **named references or formulas**
     — type or insert named
     references or formulas.

   • **functions** — type a function or
     click **Function Wizard** button
     [fx] (to left of argument box)
     to insert a function into an
     argument (nest functions).

The Function Wizard describes the
current argument, indicates if
the argument is required, and shows
you the result of the values
you have supplied.

8. Repeat steps 6 and 7, as needed.

9. Click [Finish] .... [↵]

10. Type or insert remaining parts of
    formula.

    OR

    Press **Enter** .... [↵]

EXERCISE

■ **Use Functions** ■ **AutoCalculate**

20

NOTES:

AutoCalculate

■ AutoCalculate is a new feature that automatically provides the Average, Count, Count Nums, Max, Min or Sum for a selected range. After selecting the range to be calculated, you can right-click the mouse on the AutoCalculate section of the Status Bar to get a pop-up list of automatic functions. There is an additional feature called Count Nums. The Count feature will count all entries in a range and the Count Nums will count only the numbers in a range.

■ After selecting the desired function, the answer will appear on the Status Bar as indicated in the illustration. This result is for your use and cannot be transferred to the worksheet.

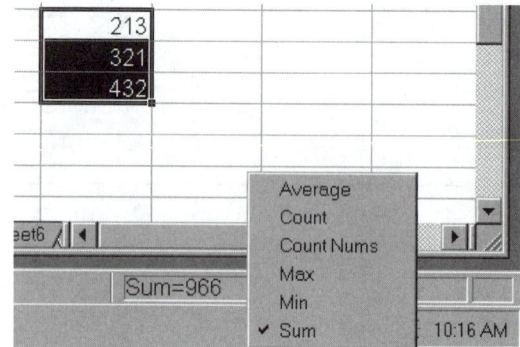

■ **Markup** is the difference between the selling price and cost of an item.

The **% markup** on cost is determined by dividing the markup by the unit cost.

In this exercise, you will use the AVERAGE, COUNT, MAX and MIN functions to analyze the Pringle Auto Repair Shop's inventory list. You will use AutoCalculate to preview the answers. In addition, you will find the MARKUP and % MARKUP on each item.

EXERCISE DIRECTIONS:

1. Open ⌨ **PARTS** or 💾 **20PARTS**.
2. Enter new labels, as indicated.
3. Center all column titles.
4. Find MARKUP.
5. Copy the formula to the remaining items.
6. Format all money columns for two decimal places.
7. Find % MARKUP on cost. *Hint: Markup/Cost*
8. Format % MARKUP column for two-place percent.
9. Copy the formula to the remaining items.
10. Enter the **AVERAGE** function to average the UNIT COST column. Copy the formula to the remaining columns.
11. Preview the answer to the HIGHEST VALUE answer by using AutoCalculate as follows:
    • Select the values in the UNIT COST column.

• Point to the AutoCalculate box on the Status Bar.
• Right-click right mouse to view the pop-up list of functions.
• Select MAX.
• View the answer on the Status Bar.

12. Enter the **MAX** function formula to complete the HIGHEST VALUE data. Copy formulas to the remaining columns.
13. Repeat the AutoCalculate process to review the answer for LOWEST VALUE or MIN data.
14. Enter the **MIN** function formula to complete the LOWEST VALUE data. Copy formulas to the remaining columns.
15. Format summary data, if necessary.
16. Save the workbook file as **PRICE**.
17. Close the workbook.

	A	B	C	D	E	F	G	H
1			INVENTORY LIST					
2			PRINGLE AUTO REPAIR SHOP					
3								
4	ITEM			UNIT	SELLING			
5	NUMBER	ITEM		COST	PRICE	*MARKUP*	*% MARKUP*	
6								
7	142	carburetor		120.00	168.00			
8	321	spark plugs		2.00	3.00			
9	093	tires		55.00	77.00			
10	393	brakes		60.00	84.00			
11	659	alarm		125.00	195.00			
12	572	mats		45.00	63.00			
13	175	battery		45.00	70.00			
14	421	radio		185.00	265.00	▼	▼	
15	932	fan belt		15.00	28.00			
16								
17	*AVERAGES*						►	
18	*HIGHEST VALUE*						►	
19	*LOWEST VALUE*						►	
20								
21								

AUTOCALCULATE VALUES IN A WORKSHEET

Displays a calculated value for selected cells in a worksheet.

1. Select cells to calculate....... Shift + ↓

2. Right-click on Status Bar AutoCalculate area.

3. Click .... *desired function*
    Average, Count, Count Nums, Max, Min, Sum
    Excel displays result, such as Sum+123, on the AutoCalculate area of the Status Bar.

EXERCISE

■ Use Functions ■ Change Column Width ■ Create a Series
■ AutoComplete ■ Comma Format ■ AutoCalculate

21

NOTES:

Change Column Width

- All worksheets in a workbook are set for a **standard column width** (default setting). This number represents the number of characters displayed in a cell using the standard font.

- It is sometimes desirable to change (widen or narrow) the column widths so text or values can fit or have a better appearance. Only the width of an entire column or a group of columns may be changed, not the width of a single cell. You can use the **Column, AutoFit Selection** command on the **Format** menu, or the mouse to set the column width to fit the longest entry.

- When you enter long *labels*, the text flows into the next column if the cell to the right is empty. If the next cell is not empty, text that exceeds the column width is covered by the data in the cell to the right.

- Unlike label text, *numeric data* that exceeds the column width does *not* flow into the next column. If the column is not wide enough to display a numeric value, Excel fills the cell with number signs (######) or displays the number in scientific notation to indicate a need to widen the column.

Create A Series

- You can use the **Fill ▸, Series** command on the **Edit** menu to quickly enter sequential values in a range of cells. You can enter sequential numbers, dates or times in any increment (e.g., 2, 4, 6, 8 or 5, 10, 15, 20 or January, February, March, April).

- Another way to fill a range with a series is to drag the **fill handle** of a selection containing the first or first and second series values of a range into which you want the series to be entered. Excel completes the series based on the value(s) in the selected cell(s).

AutoComplete

- A new feature, AutoComplete, allows you to enter labels automatically after making repetitive entries. For example, if labels in a list are repeated randomly, you may use the quick menu and the Pick from list item, to select the next label from a list.

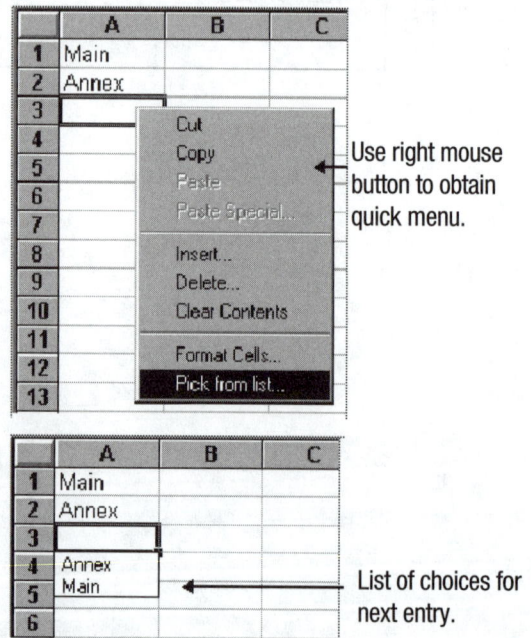

Use right mouse button to obtain quick menu.

List of choices for next entry.

- A more efficient method may also be used for repetitive entries. You will note that when you enter the first few letters of data, Excel will guess or "AutoComplete" the rest of the entry. You may press Enter to confirm the entry.

Comma Format

- To make large numbers more readable, **formatting** may be used to include commas. When formatting for commas, the number of decimal places to display may also be set.

In this exercise, you will create a worksheet for the Woodworks Furniture Company showing employees' quarterly SALES and COMMISSION earned. You will use the AutoComplete, AutoCalculate, comma format and function features. Each employee receives a 5% commission on sales.

EXERCISE DIRECTIONS:

1. Create the worksheet as shown, or open 🖫 **21WOOD**.

2. Set column widths as follows:

   Column A: 4   Column B: 18   Column C: 10

   Column E: 12   Column F: 12   Column G: 12

3. Practice using the F<u>i</u>ll, <u>S</u>eries option as follows:

   - Using the <u>E</u>dit menu enter employee numbers starting with 110 and stopping at 114.
   - Delete the employee numbers.

4. Enter 1 and 2 as employee numbers for the first two employees. Select the numbers and use the fill handle to extend the series.

5. Practice using the AutoComplete feature as follows:

   - Enter BUILDING as the column heading for column C.
   - Enter Main for Judy Abrams and Annex for Peter Chang.
   - Place mouse cursor in the next cell (C9) for Kelly Linsey.
   - Right-click to display a shortcut menu.
   - Select Pick from list.
   - Select Main for Kelly Linsey.
   - Use this procedure to enter Annex for Johnson and Main for Rivera.

6. Copy BASE SALARY to the remaining employees.

   ✓ *All employees have the same base salary.*

7. Enter a formula to find COMMISSION for the first employee. The commission rate is 5% of sales. Copy the formula to the remaining employees.

8. Enter a formula to find QUARTERLY SALARY for the first employee by adding BASE SALARY and COMMISSION for the quarter. Copy the formula to the remaining employees.

9. Use AutoCalculate to check the total of the Base Salary column.

10. Enter formulas to find TOTALS, AVERAGES, HIGHEST, and LOWEST values. Copy the formulas to each column.

11. Center column title labels.

12. Format numeric data to include commas and two decimal places.

13. Save the workbook; name it **WOOD**.

14. Print one copy.

15. Close the workbook.

	A	B	C	D	E	F	G
1		WOODWORKS FURNITURE COMPANY					
2		QUARTERLY SALES AND SALARY REPORT - JANUARY-MARCH					
3							
4	EMP.			BASE		5%	QUARTERLY
5	NO.	NAME	BUILDING	SALARY	SALES	COMMISSION	SALARY
6							
7		ABRAMS, JUDY		1,500.00	113,456.67		
8		CHANG, PETER			150,654.87		
9		LINSEY, KELLY			234,765.36		
10		JOHNSON, LETOYA			89,765.43	▼	▼
11		RIVERA, TONY			287,987.76		
12							
13		TOTALS					▶
14		AVERAGES					▶
15		HIGHEST					▶
16		LOWEST					▶

CHANGE COLUMN WIDTHS USING THE MENU

1. Select any cell(s) in column(s) to change.

2. Click **Format** menu .... `Alt`+`O`

3. Click **Column** .... `C`

4. Click **Width** .... `W`

5. Type number (0-255) .... *number* in **Column Width** text box.

   ✓ *Number represents number of characters that can be displayed in cell using the standard font.*

6. Click `OK` .... `↵`

CHANGE COLUMN WIDTHS USING THE MOUSE

Change One Column Width

1. Point to right border of column heading to size.
   Pointer becomes a ↔.

2. Drag ↔ left or right.
   Excel displays width on left side of formula bar.

Change Several Column Widths

1. Select columns to size.

2. Point to right border of any selected column heading.
   Pointer becomes a ↔.

3. Drag ↔ left or right.
   Excel displays width on left side of formula bar.

Use Right Mouse Button

1. Highlight column by clicking on label.

2. Right-click mouse.

3. Click **Column Width**

4. Type in width........................... *number*

5. Click `OK` .... `↵`

SET COLUMN WIDTH TO FIT LONGEST ENTRY

- Double-click right border of column heading.

OR

1. Select column to size .... `↕`, `Ctrl`+`Space`

2. Click **Format** menu .... `Alt`+`O`

3. Click **Column** .... `C`

4. Click **AutoFit Selection**................... `A`

SET STANDARD COLUMN WIDTH

Changes column widths that have not been previously adjusted in a worksheet.

1. Click **Format** menu .... `Alt`+`O`

2. Click **Column**.............................. `C`

3. Click **Standard Width** .... `S`

4. Type new number (0-255) .... *number* in **Standard Column Width** text box.

   ✓ *Number represents number of characters that can be displayed in cell using the standard font.*

5. Click `OK` .... `↵`

RESET COLUMNS TO STANDARD COLUMN WIDTH

1. Select column(s) to format.

2. Click **Format** menu .... `Alt`+`O`

3. Click **Column**.............................. `C`

4. Click **Standard Width** .... `S`

5. Click `OK` .... `↵`

CREATE A SERIES OF NUMBERS, DATES, OR TIMES USING THE MENU

1. Enter first series value in a cell to create a series from a **single value**.
   OR
   Enter first and second series values in consecutive cells to create a series from multiple values.

2. Select cell(s) containing series value(s) **and** cells to fill.

   ✓ *Select adjacent cells in rows or columns to fill.*

3. Click **Edit** menu .... `Alt`+`E`

4. Click **Fill**................................... `I`

5. Click **Series** .... `S`

To change proposed step value:

- Type step value................ *number* in **Step Value** text box.

To change proposed direction of series:

Select desired **Series in** option:

- **Rows**........................... `Alt`+`R`

- **Columns**...................... `Alt`+`C`

To change proposed series type:

Select desired **Type** option:

- **Linear**......................... `Alt`+`L`
  to increase/decrease each value in series by number in Step Value text box.

- **Growth**........................ `Alt`+`G`
  to multiply each value in series by number in Step Value text box.

- **Date**............................ `Alt`+`D`
  to set increment by days, weekdays, months, or years.

- **AutoFill**....................... `Alt`+`F`
  to fill cells based on values in selection.

   If Date was selected:

   Select desired **Date Unit** option:

   - **Day**...................... `Alt`+`A`

   - **Weekday**............... `Alt`+`W`

   - **Month** .... `Alt`+`M`

   - **Year** .... `Alt`+`Y`

To set stop value for series:

✓ *Type a stop value if you want series to end at a specific number.*

a. Click **Stop Value**:......... `Alt`+`O`

b. Type stop value............... *number*

6. Click `OK` .... `↵`

NEXT EXERCISE

EXERCISE

■ Use Functions ■ Edit ■ Print Preview ■ Cell Notes ■ AutoSum

22

NOTES:

Edit

■ Data may be changed either *before* or *after* it has been entered in a cell.

■ To clear a cell's content before it is entered:

- Backspace to clear, or
- Press the Escape key, or
- Click the Cancel box on the formula bar.

■ To clear a cell's content after data is entered:

- Replace the entire entry with new data.
- Edit part of an entry by **enabling cell editing**.
- Erase a single cell entry.
- Erase a range of cell entries.

Print Options

■ When the **Print** command is accessed, Excel allows you to set various print options. You can choose to print a range of cells, one page, or the entire workbook. You can also set print Properties or Preview your settings by using the buttons provided. The properties button accesses settings for Paper, Fonts, Graphics or Device Options. The Print dialog box can also be accessed by clicking on the Print icon on the Standard Toolbar.

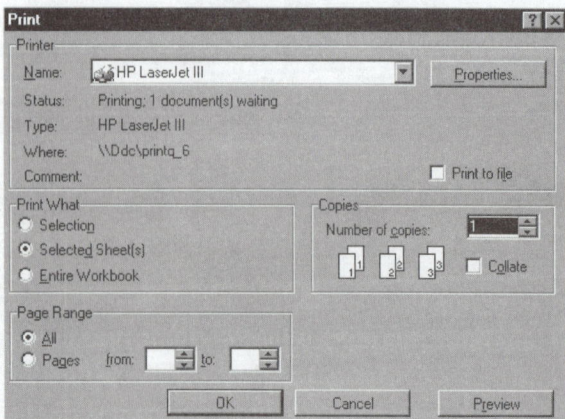

Print Preview

■ In both dialog boxes you can select the preview button to review, on screen, the output your settings will yield. The Print Preview dialog box can also be accessed by clicking on the Print Preview icon on the Standard Toolbar.

Cell Notes

■ It is possible to attach a text or audio note to a cell that displays or plays when the cursor is placed on the cell. This feature is useful to document formulas or assumptions built into the worksheet. A note is entered using the **Insert, Note** commands and will display when the mouse moves to the cell. A red dot appears in the corner of the cell to indicate the presence of a cell note. Note the illustration below of a cell note and the dot showing a cell note in the cell to the right of the selection.

F.I.C.A.	F.W.T.
6.37	16.65
Tax	46.27
calculated	19.78
at 7.65%	26.10

AutoSum

■ You can use the **AutoSum** feature to quickly enter the SUM function to total values in a worksheet. Clicking the AutoSum icon on the Standard Toolbar displays a suggestion (with a dotted line) for a range of cells to total. You can accept that range or change it by dragging through the cells you wish to total.

In this exercise, you will complete the payroll for the Burlington National Bank for the week ending May 15, 199–. You will then copy the entire worksheet to a new location and edit entries to create another payroll for the week ending May 22, 199–. You will enter cell notes and print the worksheet.

EXERCISE DIRECTIONS:

1. Open ⌨ **SALARY** or 💾 **22SALARY**.
2. Edit the first line of the title, as illustrated.
3. Erase the second line of the title. Replace it, as indicated.
4. Enter the new row labels, as indicated.
5. Find TOTALS for GROSS PAY, F.I.C.A., F.W.T. and NET PAY columns by using the AutoSum feature.
6. Find the AVERAGES for the same columnar data.
7. Format TOTALS and AVERAGES for two decimal places.
8. Enter cell notes as follows:

   In F7: Tax calculated at 7.65%

   In G7: Tax calculated at 20%
9. View the cell notes.

10. Copy the range of data shown to a new location on the worksheet.

   ✓ *When copying a range, it is only necessary to specify the first position in the destination range.*

– ON THE BOTTOM PAYROLL –

11. Edit the title to read:

   FOR THE WEEK ENDING MAY 22, 199-
12. Edit the HOURS WORKED as follows:

   CARTER, 20   FINCKEL, 31   JAMISON, 23

   MILLS, 22   POTTER, 15   SAMUELS, 25
13. Preview the printout of this file.
14. Print one copy of the MAY 22nd payroll.
15. Close and save the workbook, or *save as* **SALARY**.

	A	B	C	D	E	F	G	H
1			BURLINGTON NATIONAL BANK			*PAYROLL*		
2			~~PAYROLL~~		*FOR THE WEEK ENDING MAY 15, 19 -*			
3								
4	CARD	EMP.	HOURLY	HOURS	GROSS			NET
5	NUMBER	NAME	RATE	WORKED	PAY	F.I.C.A.	F.W.T.	PAY
6								
7	12567	CARTER	5.55	15	83.25	6.37	16.65	60.23
8	12750	FINCKEL	7.23	32	231.36	17.70	46.27	167.39
9	12816	JAMISON	6.18	16	98.88	7.56	19.78	71.54
10	12925	MILLS	4.66	28	130.48	9.98	26.10	94.40
11	12345	POTTER	6.57	12	78.84	6.03	15.77	57.04
12	12716	SAMUELS	8.65	21	181.65	13.90	36.33	131.42
13								
14	*TOTALS*							➤
15	*AVERAGES*							➤
16								
17	(copy)							
18	↓							
19								
20								

EDIT CELL CONTENTS AFTER DATA IS ENTERED (Enable Cell Editing)

1. Double-click cell to edit.
   OR
   a. Select cell to edit. .... ⬍
   b. Press **F2** F2
   An insertion point appears in the active cell and these buttons appear on the formula bar:

   ☒ **Cancel** button – cancels changes made in cell.

   ☑ **Enter** button – accepts changes made in cell.

2. Click desired data position........... ⬌
   in cell or in formula bar.

3. Type new data...............................*data*
   OR
   Press **Backspace**.............. Backspace
   to delete character to left of insertion point.
   OR
   Press **Delete**................................ Del
   to delete character to right of insertion point.

   ### To accept changes:
   • Press **Enter** .... ⏎
     OR
     Click **Enter** button .... ☒
     on the formula bar.

   ### To cancel changes:
   • Press **Escape** .... Esc
     OR
     Click **Cancel** button............... ☑
     on the formula bar.

EDIT CELL CONTENTS WHILE TYPING

To delete character to the left of insertion point:
• Press **Backspace**.............. Backspace

To cancel all characters:
• Press **Escape** .... Esc

ERASE CONTENTS OF CELL OR RANGE

1. Select cell or range containing contents to erase.
2. Press **Delete**............................... Del

CREATE TEXT CELL NOTES

1. Select cell to attach note to.
2. Click **Insert** menu............... Alt + I
3. Click **Note**..................................... O
4. Type note in ....**Text Note:** box
5. Click [OK] .... ⏎
   Excel marks each cell containing a note with a note marker (small square).

   Point to the cell containing the note to view it.

PRINT RANGE OF CELLS

Prints data in range using the current page settings.

✓ *When printing a range, this procedure will override a print area if you defined one.*

1. Select range of cells to print.
2. Click **File** menu.................... Alt + F
3. Click **Print**.................................... P
4. Click **Selection** .... N
5. Click [OK] .... ⏎

USE AUTOSUM

1. Select cell(s) to receive sum(s).
   NOTE: Select blank cell(s) below or to the right of cells containing values to total.

2. Click **AutoSum** button .... Σ
   on Standard Toolbar.
   OR

   Press **Alt + Equal**................ Alt + =
   Excel inserts =SUM() function in formula bar, and a flashing outline may surround cells to be totaled.

   ### To change proposed range to total:
   • Select cells to total.

3. If necessary, press **Enter**.............. ⏎

NEXT EXERCISE

EXERCISE

■ Use Functions ■ Change Column Width ■ Edit
■ Print Options (Page Setup, Scale)

23

NOTES:

Page Setup

- Excel 7 uses the default page size (usually 8 1/2"x11") of the installed printer. To change the page size, click the **Page Setup** option on the **File** menu, then select the Page tab.

- The Page Setup option is also used to control the print output for the selected page size. The Page Setup dialog box (*see below*) may be accessed directly from the File menu, or from the Print Preview screen.

- The Page Setup dialog box has several tabs. Each tab contains options that control the print output.

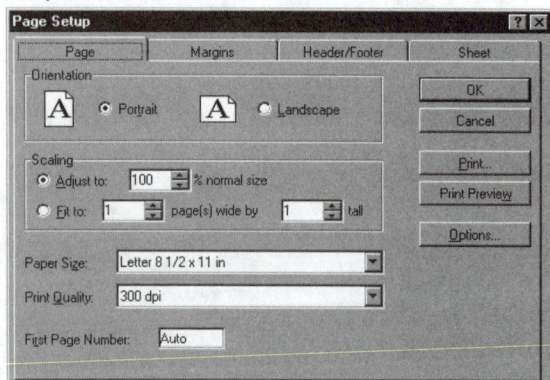

PAGE SETUP DIALOG BOX WITH PAGE TAB SELECTED

- Page Setup options include:

Page Tab

- **Orientation** The worksheet data may be printed in either **Portrait** (vertical) or **Landscape** (horizontal) paper orientation.

- **Scaling** The printed worksheet can be enlarged or reduced. The scaling options are: **Adjust to** % of normal size, or **Fit to** pages wide by pages tall. Both scaling options proportionally scale the worksheet.

  NOTE: Scaling is often needed when you want a printed worksheet to fit on a page. You can use the Print Preview option to check how it will fit before printing.

- **Paper Size** The paper size options include: letter, legal and other size options.

- **First Page Number** The starting page number for the pages on the current sheet.

Margins Tab

- **Margins** The page margins, the distance of the worksheet data to the **Top**, **Bottom**, **Left** or **Right** edge of the page, may be set in inches. The **Header** and **Footer** margins, the distance of the header and footer data from the top and bottom edges of the worksheet, can be set in inches.

- **Center on Page** The worksheet data can be **Horizontally** and/or **Vertically** centered within the page margins.

Header/Footer Tab

- **Header/Footer** A line of text may be included above or below the worksheet. This may be used to include a title, a date or a page number. *(See **Exercise 24**, page 82.)*

Sheet Tab

- **Print Area** Only define this area if you always want to print the same range of cells when printing a worksheet.

- **Print Titles** Descriptive information from designated **Rows** that will print on the top of each page and/or **Columns** that will print on the left of each page. *(See **Exercise 25**, page 88.)*

- **Print** Includes the following print options: **Gridlines**, **Notes**, **Draft Quality**, **Black and White**, **Row and Column Headings**.

- **Page Order** The setting that determines the printed page order: **Down, then Across** or **Across, then Down**.

In this exercise, you will open the quarterly sales worksheet for the Woodworks Furniture Company, expand the worksheet to include quarterly data, and print the worksheet using scaling options and gridlines.

EXERCISE DIRECTIONS:

1. Open ⌨ **WOOD or** 💾 **23WOOD.**

2. Edit the second line of the title. Replace MARCH with JUNE.

3. Replace QUARTERLY with JAN-MAR.

4. Select the column heading and data in the BUILDING column and erase all data.

5. Change column widths as follows:

   Column C: 3

   Columns H, I, J: 12

6. Copy column titles SALES, 5% COMMISSION and SALARY to columns H, I and J. Insert the label APR-JUN over SALARY in column J.

7. Center all new labels where necessary.

8. Enter new sales data in column H.

9. Copy the COMMISSION formula for the first employee in column F to column I.

10. Copy the COMMISSION formula down for each employee.

11. Enter a formula in column J to compute BASE SALARY + COMMISSION for the second quarter.

12. Copy the BASE SALARY + COMMISSION formula down for each employee.

13. Find TOTALS, AVERAGES, HIGHEST and LOWEST for the second quarter. (Copy formulas using one copy command.)

14. Format numeric data for commas and two decimal places.

15. Change the scale setting to fit worksheet on one page.

16. Change the sheet setting to print gridlines.

17. Check your scale setting, using Print Preview.

18. Print one copy.

19. Close and save the workbook; or save as **WOOD**.

	A	B	C	D	E	F	G	H	I	J
1				WOODWORKS FURNITURE COMPANY				←12→	←12→	←12→
2		QUARTERLY SALES AND SALARY REPORT - JANUARY-MARCH					JUNE			
3							JAN - MAR			
4	EMP.			BASE		5%	QUARTERLY			APR - JUN
5	NO.	NAME	BUILDING	SALARY	SALES	COMMISSION	SALARY			
6										
7	1	ABRAMS, JUDY	Main	1,500.00	113,456.67	5,672.83	7,172.83	114342.90		
8	2	CHANG, PETER	Annex	1,500.00	150,654.87	7,532.74	9,032.74	143276.70		
9	3	LINSEY, KELLY	Main	1,500.00	234,765.36	11,738.27	13,238.27	187956.80		
10	4	JOHNSON, LETOYA	Annex	1,500.00	89,765.43	4,488.27	5,988.27	9398469		
11	5	RIVERA, TONY	Main	1,500.00	287,987.76	14,399.39	15,800.30	254768.60		
12										
13		TOTALS		7,500.00	876,630.09	43,831.50	51,331.50			
14		AVERAGES		1,500.00	175,326.02	8,766.30	10,266.30			
15		HIGHEST		1,500.00	287,987.76	14,399.39	15,899.39			
16		LOWEST		1,500.00	89,765.43	4,488.27	5,988.27			
17			→3←							
18										

SET PRINT OPTIONS FOR WORKSHEET

Sets a print area and shows or hides gridlines on printed sheet.

1. Click **File** menu .... Alt + F
2. Click **Page Setup**... .... U
3. Click **Sheet**.......................... Ctrl + Tab

To set a print area:

✓ *Use this option to print a specific area of a worksheet each time you print.*

a. Click in **Print Area**: ...... Alt + A

b. Select range of cells in worksheet to print.

OR

Type cell reference(s) ..*references* of area to print.

NOTE: To remove a print area, delete the reference.

To show or hide gridlines:

• Select or deselect **Gridlines** .... Alt + G

4. Click [OK] .... ↵

CHANGE SCALE OF PRINTED DATA

1. Click **File** menu................... Alt + F
2. Click **Page Setup** .... U

3. Select **Page** .... Ctrl + Tab

To reduce or enlarge data on printed sheet:

a. Click **Adjust to:**........... Alt + A

b. Type percentage (10-400)......................... *number*

✓ *You can also click the increment box arrows to select a percentage.*

4. Click [OK] .... ↵

NEXT EXERCISE

EXERCISE

■ Use Functions ■ Change Column Widths ■ Edit ■ Bold Text
■ Print Options (Headers/Footers) ■ Page Breaks

24

NOTES:

Page Breaks

■ Before printing, you may set page breaks and add headers and footers to a worksheet that requires more than one page. When the **Page Break** option is set, Excel stops printing on the current page and starts printing on the top of a new page.

■ Excel inserts **automatic page breaks** based on the current paper size, scaling, and margin settings. Automatic page breaks appear as dashed lines on the worksheet. To view automatic page breaks, the **Automatic Page Breaks** check box must be selected on the View tab in the Options dialog box. You can override the automatic page breaks by inserting **manual page breaks** in your worksheet. Manual page breaks appear as bold dashed lines.

Headers and Footers

■ **Headers** and **footers** are used when you want to repeat the same information at the top (header) or bottom (footer) of every page.

■ With Excel, you can select from built-in headers and footers, or you can customize them. These print enhancements can be set in the Page Setup dialog box from the Header/Footer tab.

■ Headers/footers are limited to a single line of text and may be formatted. Header/footer text may be separated into segments, as shown in the illustration.

■ When you create a custom header, text entered in the left-most section will be left-justified. Text entered in the middle section will be centered, and text entered in the right-most section will be right-justified.

■ You may insert **codes** to print the current date, current time, page number, and/or workbook filename as part of the header/footer text by clicking a code button representing the desired item.

✓ *Note the illustration on the next page.*

Bold Text

■ To emphasize headings or labels, you may want to bold the text. This can be accomplished by selecting the cell and then clicking the Bold icon **B** on the Formatting Toolbar.

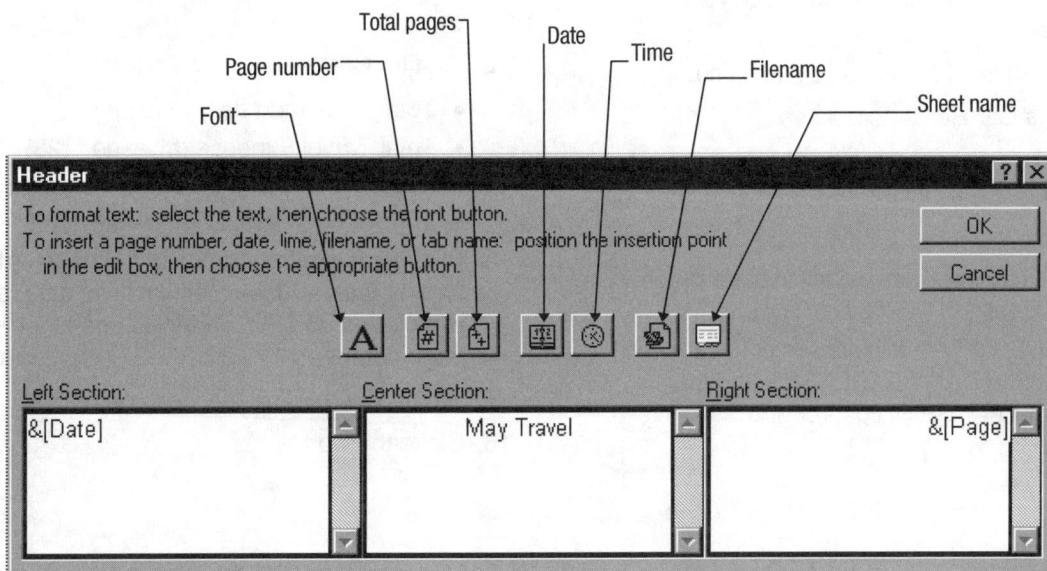

Font┐ Page number┐ Total pages┐ Date┐ Time┐ Filename┐ Sheet name┐

Header

To format text: select the text, then choose the font button.
To insert a page number, date, time, filename, or tab name: position the insertion point
  in the edit box, then choose the appropriate button.

OK
Cancel

Left Section: Center Section: Right Section:
&[Date]   May Travel   &[Page]

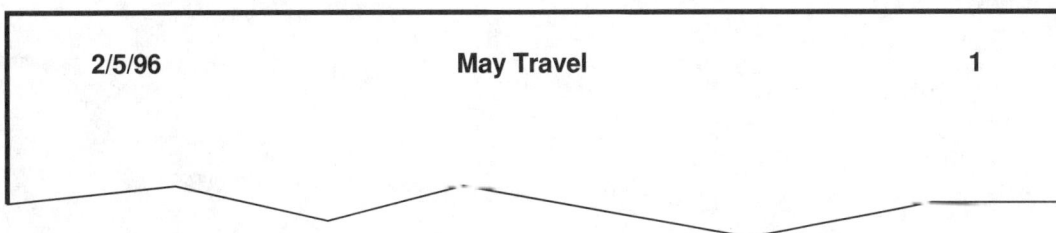

2/5/96   **May Travel**   1

In this exercise, you will create a travel expense report for one of the salespeople at the Quick-Print Publishing Company. The May travel report will include two trips, each printed on a separate page with a header. The reports will be spell checked.

EXERCISE DIRECTIONS:

1. Create the **top** worksheet shown on the next page, including bold styles, or open 🖫 **24TRIPS.**

   ✓ *Enter the days of the month as numeric labels.*

2. Set column widths as follows:

   Column A: 15

   Column B: 3

3. Use the Spell Check feature to check your worksheet.

4. In the Total Travel Expenses column find:

   Total of the Car Rental Expenses

5. Copy the formula to each expense item as illustrated.

6. Find:

   - TOTALS for each day (which include the rows in the TRANSPORTATION section).
   - Total of Total Travel Expenses column (which includes the DAILY EXPENSES and the TRANSPORTATION costs).

7. Format all money columns for two decimal places.

8. Center all column titles.

9. Copy the entire top worksheet to cell A34.

10. Create a page break at cell A33.

11. Edit the DATES, PURPOSE, and DAILY EXPENSES to display the data for the next trip, as indicated. Include the TRANSPORTATION expenses.

12. Find for Car(miles):

    - Total Miles (add daily mileage)
    - Total Travel Expense (mileage * .28)

13. Edit the formula for the Total of Total Travel Expenses to include the Driving Expenses.

14. Print the file to fit columns to the page with a custom header that includes a left-justified date, a centered title that reads MAY TRAVEL, and a right-justified page number.

15. Save the workbook file; name it **TRIPS.**

16. Close the workbook.

	A	B	C	D	E	F	G	H
1	←—15—→		QUICK-PRINT PUBLISHING COMPANY					
2			TRAVEL EXPENSE REPORT					
3		→3←						
4	NAME:		John McCarthy					
5								
6	DATES:		5/3-5/6/9-		PURPOSE:		School Visits - Chicago	
7								
8								
9					*enter as numeric labels*		Total	Total
10							Miles	Travel
11			May 3	May 4	May 5	May 6	@ $.28	Expenses
12	TRANSPORTATION							
13	Car (miles)		168	55	43	175		
14								
15	Car Rental							
16	Plane							
17	Train							
18								
19	DAILY EXPENSES							
20	Hotal		125.65	125.65	125.65	125.65		
21	Breakfast		0.00	5.59	15.95	7.55		
22	Lunch		15.60	12.95	45.95	43.55		
23	dinner		39.35	95.86	135.85	0.00		
24	Tolls		0.00	1.50	2.00	0.00		
25	Parking		0.00	15.00	12.00	7.00		
26	Tips		6.00	18.00	22.00	11.00		
27	Phone		3.25	7.53	8.52	4.76		
28	Misc.		0.00	12.00	15.00	3.00		
29								
30	TOTALS							
31								
32						*enter page break*		
33		*copy*						
34			QUICK-PRINT PUBLISHING COMPANY					
35			TRAVEL EXPENSE REPORT					
36								
37	NAME:		John McCarthy					
38								
39	DATES:		5/14-5/16/9-		PURPOSE:		School Visits - Los Angeles	
40								
41								
42							Total	Total
43							Miles	Travel
44			May 14	May 15	May 16		@ $.28	Expenses
45	TRANSPORTATION							
46	Car (miles)							
47								
48	Car Rental		65.00	65.00	65.00			
49	Plane		375.89					
50	Train							
51								
52	DAILY EXPENSES							
53	Hotal		135.65	135.65	135.65			
54	Breakfast		0.00	6.68	5.76			
55	Lunch		35.55	13.64	43.32			
56	dinner		88.75	145.76	0.00			
57	Tolls		3.50	4.50	4.00			
58	Parking		18.50	22.15	16.75			
59	Tips		10.00	25.00	15.00			
60	Phone		8.95	9.95	6.25			
61	Misc.		0.00	16.50	0.00			
62								
63	TOTALS							

INSERT MANUAL PAGE BREAKS

✓ *After you insert a manual page break, Excel adjusts the automatic page breaks that follow it. To display automatic page breaks see **SHOW AUTOMATIC PAGE BREAKS**, right.*

Insert a Horizontal Page Break:

1. Select row where new page will start.
2. Click **Insert** menu.................. `Alt`+`I`
3. Click **Page Break**...................... `B`

Insert a Vertical Page Break:

1. Select column where new page will start.
2. Click **Insert** menu.................. `Alt`+`I`
3. Click **Page Break**...................... `B`

Insert a Horizontal and Vertical Page Break:

1. Click cell..................................... `↔` where new pages will start.
2. Click **Insert** menu.................. `Alt`+`I`
3. Click **Page Break**...................... `B`

REMOVE MANUAL PAGE BREAKS

✓ *After you remove a manual page break, Excel adjusts the automatic page breaks that follow it. To display automatic page breaks see **SHOW AUTOMATIC PAGE BREAKS**, right.*

Remove a Horizontal Page Break:

1. Select a cell immediately below page break.
2. Click **Insert** menu.................. `Alt`+`I`
3. Click **Remove Page Break** .... `B`

Remove a Vertical Page Break:

1. Select a cell immediately to the right of page break.
2. Click **Insert** menu.................. `Alt`+`I`
3. Click **Remove Page Break** .... `B`

Remove All Manual Page Breaks:

1. Click blank button at top left corner of worksheet grid.
2. Click **Insert** menu.................. `Alt`+`I`
3. Click **Remove Page Break** .... `B`

SHOW AUTOMATIC PAGE BREAKS

1. Click **Tools** menu .... `Alt`+`T`
2. Click **Options**......................... `O`
3. Select **View** tab .... `Ctrl`+`Tab`
4. Click **Automatic Page Breaks**...................... `Alt`+`U`
5. Click `OK` .... `↵`

BOLD TEXT

1. Select any cell.
2. Click Bold button........................ **B**
   OR
   Press **Ctrl + B** .... `Ctrl`+`B`

SET HEADER AND FOOTER OPTIONS

Adds text or special codes to top or bottom of each page.

1. Click **File** menu.................... `Alt`+`F`
2. Click **Page Setup** .... `U`
3. Select **Header/Footer** tab ... `Ctrl`+`Tab`

To select a built-in header:

a. Click **Header**............... `Alt`+`A` drop-down list.
b. Select desired header type .. `↔`

To select a built-in footer

a. Click **Footer** .... `Alt`+`F` drop-down list.
b. Select desired footer type .... `↔`

To customize selected header or footer:

a. Click `Custom Header...` .... `Alt`+`C`
   OR
   Click `Custom Footer...` .... `Alt`+`U`
b. Click in section to change:
   - **Left**................... `Alt`+`L`
   - **Center** .... `Alt`+`C`
   - **Right** .... `Alt`+`R`
c. Type or edit text.....................*text* to appear in header or footer section.

To change font of header or footer text:

i. Select text to format.
ii. Click Font button **A** .... `Tab`+`↵`
   ✓ *Press **Tab** until **Font** button is highlighted.*
iii. Select desired font options.
iv. Click `OK` .... `↵`

To insert a header or footer code:

i. Place insertion point where code will appear.
ii. Click desired .... `Tab`+`↵` code button from the following choices:
   ✓ *Press **Tab** until desired code button is highlighted.*

   `#` **Page Number** Inserts page number code.

   `↟` **Total Pages** Inserts total pages code.

   `📅` **Date** Inserts current date code.

   `🕙` **Time** Inserts current time code.

   `🗐` **Filename** Inserts filename code.

   `🗒` **Sheet Name** Inserts active sheet name code.

d. Repeat steps b and c for each custom header or footer to change.
e. Click `OK` .... `↵`
4. Click `OK` .... `↵`

NEXT EXERCISE

EXERCISE

■ Use Functions ■ Change Column Width ■ Create a Series
■ Print Options (Scale, Print Titles) ■ Print Preview

25

NOTES:

Print Titles

■ As a print option, you may print **column and row titles.** Titles may be useful when:

- printing a range that is too wide or too long to fit on one page requiring titles on the second page to clarify the data.

- printing a part of a columnar series of data that does not have column or row titles adjacent to the number values.

■ The columns or rows titles you select:

- will repeat only on the pages that follow the page containing the title data when an extra wide or extra long worksheet is set up as the print range.

- should not be included in the print range when printing part of a columnar series of data.

Note the illustration below. It shows the first and second pages of a worksheet that was too wide for one page, (using 100% sizing). Since column titles were set for column A, both pages show the labels contained in column A.

PAGE 1 OF 2

	A	B	C	D	E	F	G
1			COMPARATIVE INCOME STATEMENT				
2			GREEN THUMB LANDSCAPE SERVICE				
3							
4							
5			JANUARY	FEBRUARY	MARCH	APRIL	MAY
6							
7	INCOME:						
8	Service Fees		5342.87	5543.65	6165.87	8343.84	9862.89
9	Consultations		1564.98	1654.76	1689.76	1893.65	1498.62
10	Total Income						
11							
12	EXPENSES:						
13	Advertising		55	65	150	150	165
14	Salaries		754.65	754.65	1255.55	1255.55	1255.55
15	Supplies		154.76	245.65	589.53	769.54	965.62
16	Truck Maint.		95	125.54	243.98	185.87	543.51
17	Other		143.43	43.54	231.65	326.43	654.65
18	Total Expenses						
19							
20	NET INCOME						

column titles on page 1

PAGE 2 OF 2

	A	H	I	J
5		JUNE	TOTALS	AVERAGES
6				
7	INCOME:			
8	Service Fees	10359.5		
9	Consultations	1287.49		
10	Total Income			
11				
12	EXPENSES:			
13	Advertising	165		
14	Salaries	1255.55		
15	Supplies	1276.54		
16	Truck Maint.	324.65		
17	Other	798.43		
18	Total Expenses			
19				
20	NET INCOME			

column titles on page 2

In this exercise, you will create a comparative income statement for the Green Thumb Landscape Service. You will use repeating column titles for labels in the first column to print the worksheet and part of the worksheet.

EXERCISE DIRECTIONS:

1. Create the worksheet as illustrated, or open 💾 25IS.

2. Enter the months by dragging the fill handle to create the series.

3. Set column widths as follows:

   Column A: 15

   Column B: 3

   Column C-J: 12

4. Find for each month:
   - Total Income
   - Total Expenses
   - NET INCOME

5. Find for each item in the income statement:
   - TOTALS
   - AVERAGE

6. Format all money columns for two decimal places.

7. Center all column titles.

8. Set column A as a repeating print title.

9. Create a header that includes the page number and total pages centered on the page.

10. Set the print range for the entire worksheet and be sure that scaling is set to 100% of normal size. Preview both pages of the worksheet.

    NOTE: Page one will show column A with JANUARY through MAY data. Page two will show column A with JUNE through AVERAGES data.

11. Print one copy of the two-page report.

12. Print one copy of the April-June data with column titles:
    - Highlight the April-June columns. Enter commands to print the selection.
    - Preview the print selection. (The column border was set previously.)

    NOTE: The April-June data will be shown with the column titles in column A.

    - Print the selection.

13. Change columns C-J back to the standard width.

14. Save the workbook file; name it IS.

15. Close the workbook.

	A	B	C	D	E	F	G	H	I	J
1	← 15 →		COMPARATIVE INCOME STATEMENT							
2			GREEN THUMB LANDSCAPE SERVICE							
3										
4										
5			JANUARY	FEBRUARY	MARCH	APRIL	MAY	JUNE	TOTALS	AVERAGES
6		→ 3 ←								
7	INCOME:									
8	Service Fees		5342.87	5543.65	6165.87	8343.84	9862.89	10359.45		
9	Consultations		1564.98	1654.76	1689.76	1893.65	1498.62	1287.49	↓	↓
10	Total Income								↓	↓
11										
12	EXPENSES:									
13	Advertising		55	65	150	150	165	165		
14	Salaries		754.65	754.65	1255.55	1255.55	1255.55	1255.55		
15	Supplies		154.76	245.65	589.53	769.54	965.62	1276.54		
16	Truck Maint.		95	125.54	243.98	185.87	543.51	324.65		
17	Other		143.43	43.54	231.65	326.43	654.65	798.43	↓	↓
18	Total Expenses								↓	↓
19										
20	NET INCOME								↓	↓
21										

SET REPEATING PRINT TITLES FOR WORKSHEET

Sets titles to print on current and subsequent pages.

1. Click **File** menu .... `Alt`+`F`

2. Click **Page Setup**... .... `U`

3. Select **Sheet** .... `Ctrl`+`Tab`

To set columns as repeating print titles:

a. Click **Columns**
    to Repeat at Left: .... `Alt`+`C`

b. Select columns in worksheet.

OR

Type column
reference .... *column reference*

*EXAMPLE: The cell reference $A:$A
indicates column A.*

✓   *Columns must be adjacent. To
    remove print titles, delete the
    reference.*

To set rows as repeating print titles:

a. Click **Rows**
    to Repeat at Top:........ `Alt`+`R`

b. Select rows in worksheet.

OR

Type row reference........ *row reference*

*EXAMPLE: The cell reference $1:$4
indicates rows 1 through 4.*

✓   *Rows must be adjacent. To remove
    print titles, delete the reference.*

4. Click `OK` .... `↵`
    to return to the worksheet.

OR

Click `Print...` .... `Alt`+`P`
to print worksheet using
current settings.

NEXT EXERCISE

EXERCISE

Solve What-If Problems (Data Tables, Goal Seek)

26

NOTES:

- A **What-if worksheet** is used to answer a question based on one or more factors that might influence the outcome. This exercise contains two methods of solving this type of problem: **data tables** and **Goal Seek**.

Data Table

- You can create a **data table** (what-if table) to evaluate a series of possible answers for values you supply in the first row and left-most column of the table. These values are called **substitution values**.

  For example, if a company wished to reduce its entire expense budget but was not certain of the effects of each cut, it might test a series of reductions on each of the expense values to allow the manager to decide which reduction was best for the company.

  When you use the data table command, Excel uses one **formula** in the upper-left corner of the table to calculate the substitution values. Data tables that require two sets of

substitution values (a row and a column) are called **two-input data tables.** Note illustration A.

- The format of a two-input data table must meet the following criteria:

  - The **column and row input values** that the formula will refer to must be outside the table.

  - The **formula** must be in the top-left cell of the table range and must refer to the column and row input values.

  - The **substitution values** for the table must be arranged in the first row and column of the table as shown in illustration A.

- To create the table values, you will select the **data table range** (which includes the formula), then indicate the row and column input cells (the cells that contain the column and row input values) from the Table dialog box.

ILLUSTRATION A

Goal Seek

■ The **Goal Seek** command on the **Tools** menu is another method of answering a what-if question. It will adjust a value in a cell (the changing cell) until a cell containing a formula (the set cell) reaches the value you specify. Illustration B shows the three items to identify for this problem and illustrates the steps in the procedure.

- **Set cell** Reference of the cell containing the formula to solve.

- **To value** Desired outcome or goal for the formula.

- **By changing cell** The cell that contains a value the Goal Seek command can change to achieve the desired result.

				changing cell (G6)
2.00%	3.00%	4.00%	5.00%	
53887.26	53337.39	52787.52	52237.65	
9648.10	9549.65	9451.20	9352.75	
2524.48	2498.72	2472.96	2447.20	
15188.04	15033.06	14878.08	14723.10	
5300.82	5246.73	5192.64	5138.55	
4310.04	4266.06	4222.08	4178.10	
6215.16	6151.74	6088.32	6024.90	
97073.90	96083.35	95092.80	94102.25	
				set cell (G15)

Goal Seek

Set cell:	$G$15
To value:	95500
By changing cell:	$G$6

OK   Cancel   Help

references to:
set cell
to value (goal), and
changing cell

ILLUSTRATION B

In this exercise, the Jumping Jack Gymnasium would like to reduce its budgeted expenses to $95,500. You are to create a data table that will show the effects of 2%, 3%, 4% and 5% budget cuts and to answer the same question using the Goal Seek method.

EXERCISE DIRECTIONS:

1. Create the worksheet below, as shown, or open 💾 **26CUT**.

   Be sure to enter the percentage values as percentages (i.e., 2% or .02).

2. Using the column and row input values located outside the table, enter a formula in the top left cell of the table that references these values.

   NOTE: The answer 53887.26 appears in the cell C6 containing the formula =C17-(C17*C18). The formula must reference the input values in cells C17 and C18. The input values will not affect the computed values in the table when it's generated.

3. Do the following:

   • Format entire table and cells that will contain totals for two decimal places.

   • Format percentage values as percentages with two decimal places.

4. Follow the procedure to create a two-input data table on page 95.

5. Copy Total formula below each column of values to complete the worksheet.

6. Save the workbook file; name it **CUT**.

7. Print one copy.

   ❷ Based on the data in the table, which estimated budget cut would result in expenses not exceeding $95,500?

8. Use Goal Seek to determine the *exact* percentage cut that would result in a total expense budget of $95,500.

   • Click Tools, Goal Seek.

   • Set cell: $G$15 (click on G15)

   • To value: 95500

   • By changing cell: $G$6 (click on G6)

   NOTE: The percent in the G6 location will change to the exact % cut necessary to achieve a $95,500 total expense figure.

   ❷ Based on the Goal Seek procedure, what is the exact percentage cut that will result in expenses of $95,500?

9. Close the workbook file *without* saving the Goal Seek results.

	A	B	C	D	E	F	G	H	I	J
1				JUMPING JACK GYM						
2				EXPENSE REDUCTION ANALYSIS						
3			Formula in D6					row substitution		
4			=C17-(C17*C18)	PRESENT		PERCENTAGE CUT		values		
5	EXPENSES		refers to input	BUDGET						
6			cells below.	53887.26		2%	3%	4%	5%	
7	Salaries			54987.00						
8	Insurance			9845.00						
9	Utilities			2576.00				data table		
10	Advertising			15498.00				range: D6:H13		
11	Office expenses		column	5409.00						
12	Maintenance		substitution	4398.00						
13	Other		values	6342.00						
14										
15	Total			99055.00						
16										
17		column input cell:	54987							
18		row input cell:	2%							
19										
20										
21										

TWO-INPUT DATA TABLES (What-If Tables)

Data tables generate values that change from one or two values in a formula. For example, a two-input table displays results of changing two values in a formula.

The **row input cell** is used to indicate an initial input value that the formula will reference.

The **column input cell** is used to indicate an initial input value that the formula will also reference.

NOTE: Because Excel uses a table function to generate answers for each pair of substitution values, you cannot edit or delete any single value in the answer set. You can, however, delete **all the answers** in the generated data table.

Although instructions listed below are for a two-input data table, you could also create a one-input data table that would find answers for a single row or column of substitution values.

CREATE A TWO-INPUT DATA TABLE

1. Enter initial value.....................*number* in row input cell.

2. Enter initial value.....................*number* in column input cell.

3. Enter series of substitution values ....*numbers* in a column.

4. Enter series of substitution values...................................*numbers* in a row.
   NOTE: The first value in row and column will contain a single formula.

5. Click upper-left cell ....[⬍] in table.

6. Type formula ....*formula*
   NOTE: Formula must refer to row and column input cells.

7. Select all cells in data table range.
   NOTE: Select cells containing formula, substitution values and cells where results will be displayed.

8. Click **Data** menu ....[Alt]+[D]

9. Click **Table**...................................[T]

10. Click row input cell in worksheet.

    OR

    Type reference ....*reference* of input cell in **Row Input Cell** text box.

11. Click **Column Input Cell:**
    [_____] ....[Alt]+[C]

12. Click cell in worksheet containing column input data.

    OR

    Type reference ....*reference* of column input cell.

13. Click [OK] ....[↵]

FIND A SPECIFIC SOLUTION TO A FORMULA (Goal Seek)

1. Enter formula and dependent values in cells.

2. Click **Tools** menu ....[Alt]+[T]

3. Click **Goal Seek** ....[G]

4. Click cell in worksheet containing formula.

    OR

    Type reference ....*reference* to cell containing formula in **Set cell** text box.

5. Click **To value:**
   [_____] ....[Alt]+[V]

6. Type desired formula result value............................. *number*

7. Click **By changing cell:**
   [_____] ....[Alt]+[C]

8. Select cell in worksheet containing value to change.

    OR

    Type reference ....*reference* to cell containing value to change.

9. Click [OK] ....[↵]
   Excel displays status of goal seeking.

EXERCISE

■ Solve What-If Problems (Data Tables) ■ PMT Function

27

NOTES:

Data Tables

■ The data table created in a what-if problem may be used to evaluate different situations based on certain variables, and enables you to find the best solution. For example, if you wanted to purchase a home and can only afford to spend $1,000 per month on your mortgage payment, you might want to determine the maximum mortgage amount you can afford to borrow and the number of years for which you should apply. A data table should be created showing the mortgage payments for various loan amounts and loan payment periods. Then you can determine what you can afford.

PMT Function

■ The **PMT** (payment) **function** can be applied to calculate a loan payment amount using principal, interest rate and number of payment periods. This might be used to determine your monthly mortgage payment when borrowing money over 30 years at a specified rate of interest. The PMT function uses the following format and contains three parts, which are defined on the right.

The arguments for the PMT function are:

=PMT	(*rate,nper,pv*)
rate	Interest rate per period (for example, interest/12).
nper	Number of payment periods (for example, term*12).
pv	Present value - total amount that a series of future payments is worth now (for example, the principal).

NOTE: *The rate and the number of payment periods (nper) must be expressed in the same manner. For example, if you are calculating a monthly payment at a 9% rate of interest for 25 years, and the interest is expressed as an annual rate, you must enter .09/12 as the monthly rate; and if the term is expressed in years, you must enter 25*12 to get the number of monthly payment periods (nper).*

In this exercise, you will create a mortgage payment table to determine payment amounts at 9% for various principal amounts and for various numbers of years.

EXERCISE DIRECTIONS:

1. Create the worksheet on the right, or open 🖫 **27TABLE**.

2. Find, in B4, the monthly mortgage payment for $100,000 at 9% for 15 years using the input cell data for principal and term.

   HINT: =PMT(*rate,nper,pv*)

   =PMT(.09/12,B16*12,-B15)

   function   *row input cell (term)*   *column input cell (principal)*

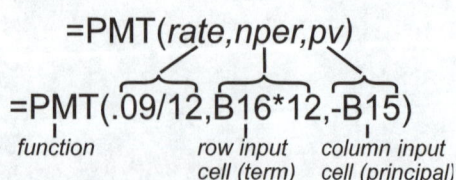

NOTE: *If you type a minus sign before the principal, Excel finds a positive number as the monthly mortgage payment; otherwise, the result will be a negative number.*

3. Format answer for two decimal places.

4. Create a two variable data table by completing the Table dialog box.

5. Save the file; name it **TABLE**.

6. Print one copy.

    ❷ Based on the data in the table, what would be the highest principal you can borrow, with a payment of approximately $1000 a month?

7. Use Goal Seek to determine the *exact* mortgage amount you can afford assuming a $1000 monthly payment, with a 9% interest rate and a 30-year term.

    • Place cursor on the mortgage payment in the 30-year column closest but less than $1000. (965.55)

    • Click Tools, Goal Seek.

    • Set cell: $F$9

    • To value: 1000

    • By changing cell: Click on Mortgage amount. $B$9

    ✓ *The mortgage in the B9 location will change to the exact loan available with a $1000 payment at 9% interest.*

    ❷ Based on the Goal Seek procedure, what is the exact mortgage loan available for a $1000 mortgage payment on a 30-year, 9% mortgage?

8. Close the file *without* saving.

	A	B	C	D	E	F	G
1		MORTGAGE PAYMENT TABLE AT 9%					
2							
3			TERM IN YEARS				
4			15	20	25	30	
5	PRINCIPAL	100000					
6		105000					
7		110000					
8		115000					
9		120000					
10		125000					
11		130000					
12		135000					
13							
14	Input cells						
15	column:	100000					
16	row:	15					
17							
18							

formula location

data table: B4:F12

USE THE PMT FUNCTION

Applies the PMT function to find the monthly payment for a principal for a specific number of years.

1. Click cell.............................. [⬦] where answer should appear.

2. Press **Equal** .... [=]

3. Type *PMT*.................... [P][M][T]

4. Press **(** (open parenthesis)............. [(]

5. Type rate /12.............. rate [/][1][2]

NOTE: *The **rate** is a percentage. You can type the percentage or type the cell reference containing the percentage.*

6. Press , (comma) .... [,]

7. Type term *12 .... term [*][1][2]

NOTE: *The **term** is the number of years. You can type the number or type the cell reference containing the number.*

8. Press , (comma) .... [,]

9. Type principal .... principal

NOTE: *The **principal** is the amount of the loan. You can type the amount or type the cell reference containing the amount. If you want the answer expressed as a positive number, type a minus sign before the principal.*

10. Press **)** (close parenthesis) .... [)]

EXAMPLES: *=PMT(.06/12,20*12,-100000)*

*=PMT(A1/12,A2*12,-A3)*

11. Press **Enter** .... [↵]

EXERCISE

Summary

28

You have been asked to develop a weekly worksheet showing bowling statistics for the Bloomington Kingpins.

On Friday, June 8, the Kingpins bowled three games. Their names and game scores were as follows: BENDER: 124, 112, 131; JEFFERS: 100, 150, 134; BHATT: 157, 135, 141; PEREZ: 148, 187, 163; ROSEN: 115, 109, 132.

Assign a player number to each player starting with 1000 and increase the numbers by 5.

EXERCISE DIRECTIONS:

1. Create a worksheet file that includes the score achieved in each game by each of the five players on the team using the layout provided. Arrange the names of players vertically in column A.

2. Using functions and ranges, find for each player:

   - TOTAL PINS
   - NUMBER OF GAMES
   - AVERAGE
   - HIGH GAME
   - LOW GAME

3. At the bottom of the worksheet, enter the labels listed below:

   - BEST PLAYER AVERAGE
   - TEAM AVERAGE
   - TEAM HIGH GAME
   - TEAM LOW GAME

4. Using functions and ranges that include all the players, find the values for each of the summary labels.

5. Copy the entire June 8 worksheet down to a new location.

6. Edit the date and scores to create a worksheet for June 15 using the data shown below:

   BENDER: 132, 121, 119

   JEFFERS: 115, 143, 135

   BHATT: 155, 137, 143

   PEREZ: 158, 183, 170

   ROSEN: 120, 119, 135

7. Insert a page break between the two worksheets.

8. Include a centered header which reads:

   BOWLING STATISTICS–JUNE

9. Right–align a page number in the header.

10. Center all column headings.

11. Format all numeric columns for no decimal places.

12. Print one copy of the two-page report scaled to 90%.

13. Save the file; name it **GAME**.

	A	B	C	D	E	F	G	H	I	J
1			THE BLOOMINGTON KINGPINS							
2			SUMMARY OF GAMES - FRIDAY,JUNE 8TH							
3										
4						TOTAL	NUMBER		HIGH	LOW
5	NAME	NUMBER	GAME 1	GAME 2	GAME 3	PINS	GAMES	AVERAGE	GAME	GAME
6										

EXERCISE

Summary

29

Your teacher, Ms. Ann McConnel, has asked you to help her set up a worksheet to organize her grades. She plans to administer three major examinations this term for her Business Marketing 101 class.

EXERCISE DIRECTIONS:

1. Create a worksheet file that summarizes student exam grades. *Use a format similar to the illustration below.* Provide each student with a consecutive ID number. Begin with the number 200 for Aaronson.

   The students and their exam grades for Test 1, 2 and 3 are:

   ✓ *A few of the students were absent for some of the exams. Leave the cell blank for absent grades. Line spacing was created to make it easier to copy data. Therefore, do not leave blank rows between data.*

   Aaronson: 78, 96, 80

   Barnett: 71, 89, 80

   Costello: 67, 79, 80

   Dionesios: 88, absent, 80

   Ellenberg: 90, 70, 73

   Falstaff: 76, 90, 90

   Garcia: 84, 91, 76

   Hamway: 87, 68, 80

   Ianelli: 98, absent, 70

   Jae Woo: absent, 80, 70

   Kelly: 75, 90, 93

2. Find for each student:
   - NUMBER OF TESTS TAKEN
   - TEST AVERAGE

3. Change column widths to fit the widest entries.

4. Enter these labels below the worksheet and find for each test:
   - NO. OF PAPERS
   - CLASS AVERAGE
   - HIGHEST GRADE
   - LOWEST GRADE

5. Format all averages to one decimal place.

6. Center all column titles.

7. Print one copy that is 75% of the actual worksheet size. (Your teacher wants to insert the printout into a notebook.)

8. Edit the names to include a first initial for each student as follows:

   Aaronson, M.

   Barnett, F.

   Costello, A.

   Dionesios, A.

   Ellenberg, S.

   Falstaff, L.

   Garcia, H.

   Hamway, R.

   Ianelli, J.

   Jae Woo, K.

   Kelly, G.

9. Save the file; name it **TEST**.

BUSINESS MARKETING 101				MS. ANN MC CONNELL		
EXAM GRADES						
					NO. OF	
					TESTS	TEST
ID #	STUDENT	TEST 1	TEST 2	TEST 3	TAKEN	AVERAGE

NEXT LESSON

LESSON 6

WORKING WITH WORKBOOKS, WORKSHEETS AND TEMPLATES

Exercises 30-42

- Insert and Delete Columns and Rows
- Move (Cut/Paste)
- Edit Undo
- Copy and Paste Special
- Copy (Drag and Drop)
- Transpose Data
- AutoCorrect
- Freeze Titles
- Create New Workbook
- Select Workbook
- Split Worksheet
- Copy and Paste Special (Extract and Combine Data)
- Scroll Tips
- Workbook Sheets
- Print Workbook
- Print Worksheet on Specified Number of Pages
- Named Ranges
- Replace
- Templates
- Spreadsheet Solutions
- Arrange Workbooks
- Link Workbooks
- 3-D Formulas
- Duplicate Workbook Window

EXERCISE

30

■ Insert and Delete Columns and Rows ■ Move (Cut/Paste)
■ Drag and Drop ■ Undo a Command

NOTES:

Insert and Delete Columns and Rows

- It is recommended that you save the workbook before you insert, delete, move, or copy data so you can retrieve the original worksheet in the event of an error.

- Columns and/or rows may be inserted or deleted to change the structure of a worksheet.

- When a column or row is **inserted**, a blank area is created. Existing columns or rows shift to allow for the newly created space.

- When a column or row is **deleted**, all data in that column or row is eliminated. Existing columns or rows shift to fill in the space left by the deletion.

Move (Cut/Paste)

- When **moving** data, the data is removed (cut) from one location and reinserted (pasted) into another location. You may choose to overwrite existing data or insert the data and shift existing data.

Drag and Drop

- Moving data can be accomplished using a combination of cutting and pasting to the paste location or selecting the range and dragging it to the paste location (known as **drag and drop**).

- If data is dragged and dropped it is pasted to the new location and cut from the previous location. If data is dragged to a cell where data exists, you will be asked if you wish to overwrite existing data. If you want to insert dragged data between cells or rows without deleting the existing data, you can press Control + Shift and drag the insertion outline onto the row or column insertion point on the gridline. This is essentially a copy, paste procedure.

- Inserting, deleting, moving, or copying data can affect formulas. Be sure formulas are correct after an insert, delete, move, or copy operation.

- The format of the data will be moved or copied along with the data.

Edit Undo

- As with the Word program, any edit activity can be reversed using **Edit, Undo**. For example, if you drag and drop data and find it did not move correctly, you would use this feature. As shown in the illustration, the Undo feature specifically names the last edit to be undone. The Undo/Repeat buttons ↶ ↷ on the Standard Toolbar have the same functions and both methods may be used to undo a series of edits.

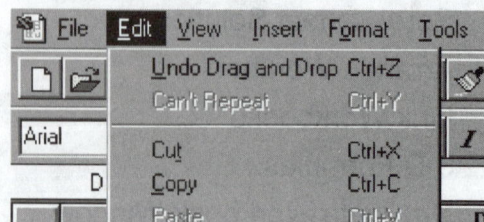

EXERCISE DIRECTIONS:

1. Open ⌨ **SALARY** or 💾 **30SALARY**.

2. Make the following changes on the top payroll as shown in the illustration on the following page:

   - Insert a new column A.
   - Move the data in the EMP. NAME column to column A. (Try using drag and drop.) Use Edit Undo if the move is not correct.) Adjust column width.
   - Edit EMP. NAME to EMPLOYEE NAME in both payrolls. Adjust column width.
   - Set column width for column C, which is now empty, to 11 and enter the label S.S. NO. as the column title.
   - Enter social security numbers as follows:

CARTER	069-65-4532
FINCKEL	123-75-7623
JAMISON	107-53-6754
MILLS	103-87-5698
POTTER	127-78-0045
SAMUELS	043-67-7600

   - Copy the social security number column title and data from the May 15 to the May 22 payroll.
   - Copy the entire May 22 payroll, including the title, to a new location below the existing worksheet.

3. Make the following changes on the bottom payroll:

   - Edit the title to read:
     FOR THE WEEK ENDING MAY 29, 199-

   - Delete the row containing data for FINCKEL.
   - Insert a row where necessary to maintain alphabetical order for a new employee named NELSON.
   - Enter the following information for NELSON:

Card Number:	12967
S.S. No.:	146-93-0069
Hourly Rate:	6.25

   - Edit the HOURS WORKED as follows:

CARTER	22
JAMISON	33
MILLS	21
NELSON	16
POTTER	18
SAMUELS	28

   - Copy payroll formulas to complete NELSON's data.

4. Format where necessary.

5. Print one copy of all three payrolls to fit on a page.

6. Close and save the workbook file, or *save as* **SALARY**.

	A	B	C	D	E	F	G	H
1	insert new column A		BURLINGTON NATIONAL BANK PAYROLL					
2			FOR THE WEEK ENDING MAY 15, 19-					
3	move							
4	CARD	EMP.	HOURLY	HOURS	GROSS			NET
5	NUMBER	NAME	RATE	WORKED	PAY	F.I.C.A.	F.W.T.	PAY
6								
7	12567	CARTER	5.55	15	83.25	6.37	16.65	60.23
8	12750	FINCKEL	7.23	32	231.36	17.70	46.27	167.39
9	12816	JAMISON	6.18	16	98.88	7.56	19.78	71.54
10	12925	MILLS	4.66	28	130.48	9.98	26.10	94.40
11	12345	POTTER	6.57	12	78.84	6.03	15.77	57.04
12	12716	SAMUELS	8.65	21	181.65	13.90	36.33	131.42
13								
14	TOTALS				804.46	61.54	160.89	582.03
15	AVERAGES				134.08	10.26	26.82	97.00
16								
17			FOR THE WEEK ENDING MAY 22, 19-					
18								
19	CARD	EMP.	HOURLY	HOURS	GROSS			NET
20	NUMBER	NAME	RATE	WORKED	PAY	F.I.C.A.	F.W.T.	PAY
21								
22	12567	CARTER	5.55	20	111.00	8.49	22.20	80.31
23	12750	FINCKEL	7.23	31	224.13	17.15	44.83	162.16
24	12816	JAMISON	6.18	23	142.14	10.87	28.43	102.84
25	12925	MILLS	4.66	22	102.52	7.84	20.50	74.17
26	12345	POTTER	6.57	15	98.55	7.54	19.71	71.30
27	12716	SAMUELS	8.65	25	216.25	16.54	43.25	156.46
28								
29	TOTALS				894.59	68.44	178.92	647.24
30	AVERAGES				149.10	11.41	29.82	107.87
31								
32		copy						
33								
34								

INSERT COLUMNS/ROWS

Inserts blank columns or rows and shifts existing columns or rows to make room for the insertion.

1. Select as many adjacent columns or rows as you want to add to worksheet.

   ✓ *Be sure to select the entire column or row. New columns will be placed to the left of the highlighted columns. New rows will be placed above the highlighted rows.*

2. Click **Insert** menu .... `Alt`+`I`

3. Click **Columns** .... `C`

   OR

   Click **Rows** .... `R`

INSERT COLUMNS/ROWS USING THE MOUSE

Inserts blank columns or rows and shifts existing columns or rows to make room for the insertion.

1. Select as many columns/rows as you want inserted.

2. Right-click any part of selection. *A quick menu appears.*

3. Click **Insert**

DELETE COLUMNS/ROWS

Deletes columns or rows and the data they contain. Existing columns or rows shift to fill in the space left by the deletion.

1. Select column(s) or row(s) to delete.

   ✓ *Be sure to select the entire column or row. When deleting more than one row or column, select adjacent columns or rows.*

2. Click **Edit** menu .... `Alt`+`E`

3. Click **Delete** .... `D`

MOVE (CUT/PASTE) USING THE MENU

Moves data in a cell or a range of cells to another area.

1. Select cell or range to move.

2. Click **Edit** menu .... `Alt`+`E`

3. Click **Cut** .... `T`

4. Select cell or range to receive data.

   ✓ *You only have to specify the top left cell. The destination range can be in another workbook or worksheet.*

To move and overwrite existing data in destination cells:

- Press **Enter** .... `↵`

To move and insert between existing cells:

a. Click **Insert** menu .... `Alt`+`I`

b. Click **Cut Cells** .... `E`

c. If prompted, select **Insert Paste** option:

   - **Shift Cells Right** .... `R`
   - **Shift Cells Down** .... `D`

MOVE (DRAG AND DROP)

Moves data in a cell or range of cells to another area.

1. Select cell or range to cut.

2. Move mouse pointer to edge of range. *Pointer becomes a* ⬉.

To move and overwrite existing data in destination cells:

a. Drag border outline to new location.

b. Click `OK` .... `↵`

To move and insert between existing cells:

a. Press **Shift** and drag .. `Shift`+*drag* insertion outline onto row or column gridline.

   ✓ *If you drag the insertion outline onto a column gridline, cells are shifted right; if dragged onto a row gridline, cells are shifted down.*

b. Release mouse button, then the key.

COPY (DRAG AND DROP)

Copies data in a cell or range of cells to another area.

1. Select cell or range to copy.

2. Move mouse pointer to edge of range. *Pointer becomes a* ⬉.

To copy and overwrite existing data in destination cells:

a. Press **Ctrl** and drag ..... `Ctrl`+*drag* border outline to new location.

b. Release the key, then mouse button.

c. Click `OK` .... `↵`

To copy and insert between existing cells:

a. Press **Ctrl + Shift** and drag insertion outline .... `Ctrl`+`Shift`+*drag* onto row or column gridline.

   ✓ *If you drag the insertion outline onto a column gridline, cells are shifted right; if dragged onto a row gridline, cells are shifted down.*

b. Release mouse button, then the key.

UNDO A COMMAND

NOTE: To successfully undo a command, undo before another command is selected. Not all commands can be undone.

- Click **Undo** button .... ↺ on Standard Toolbar.

   OR

   Press **Ctrl+Z** .... `Ctrl`+`Z`

   OR

a. Click **Edit** menu .... `Alt`+`E`

b. Click **Undo** .... `U`

EXERCISE

■ Copy and Paste Special ■ Transpose Data ■ AutoCorrect
■ Insert and Delete Columns and Rows ■ Move (Cut/Paste)

31

NOTES:

Copy and Paste Special

■ **Paste Special** is a feature that gives you added controls on the pasting process when data is copied. As shown in the illustration on the right, with the Paste Special command you can:

- Specify which characteristics of the selection should be copied. (Paste Options)
- Specify how data should be combined when the paste area contains data. (Operation Options)
- Skip blanks
- Transpose data
- Create a Pasted Link

Transpose Data

■ **Transpose data** to copy and rearrange data so data in rows can be copied to columns and vice versa.

✓ *Note the example below. The labels in column B, when transposed, are copied to row 3.*

	A	B	C	D	E	F	G
1							
2							
3		JAN					
4		FEB					
5		MAR	→	JAN	FEB	MAR	
6							

■ When transposing formulas, select the **Paste Values** option in the Paste Special dialog box. This selection ensures that only the values are copied to the new location, not the formulas. If you do not select the Paste Values option, the formulas will produce unwanted results.

AutoCorrect

■ The AutoCorrect feature automatically changes text as you type if you, *in advance*, specify the word that is often typed incorrectly. This feature also automatically corrects capitalization at the beginning of days of the week and changes the case of incorrectly capitalized letters in the first two positions in a word. Note the illustration of the AutoCorrect dialog box (right) with a new entry being placed into the AutoCorrect replace list.

PASTE SPECIAL DIALOG BOX

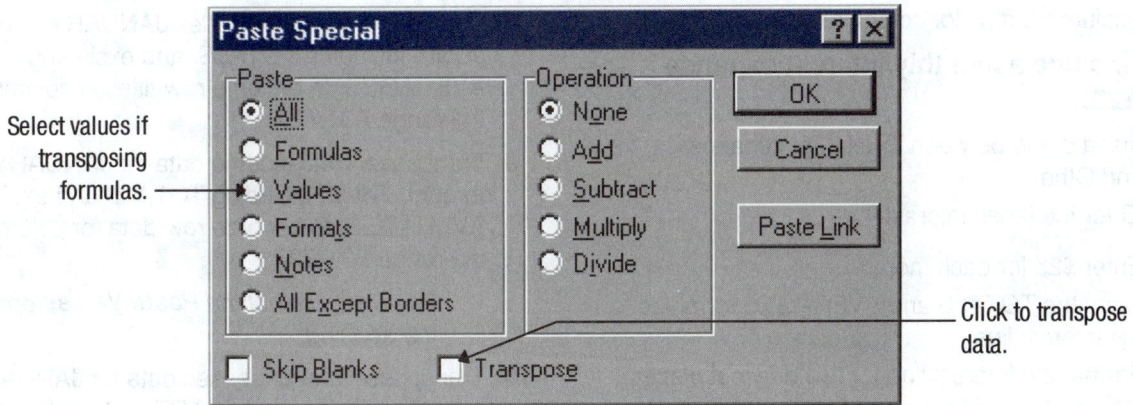

Paste Special ? X

Paste
- ● A**l**l
- ○ **F**ormulas
- ○ **V**alues ← Select values if transposing formulas.
- ○ For**ma**ts
- ○ **N**otes
- ○ All E**x**cept Borders

Operation
- ● **N**one
- ○ A**d**d
- ○ **S**ubtract
- ○ M**u**ltiply
- ○ D**i**vide

OK

Cancel

Paste **L**ink

☐ Skip **B**lanks   ☐ Transpos**e** ← Click to transpose data.

AUTOCORRECT DIALOG BOX

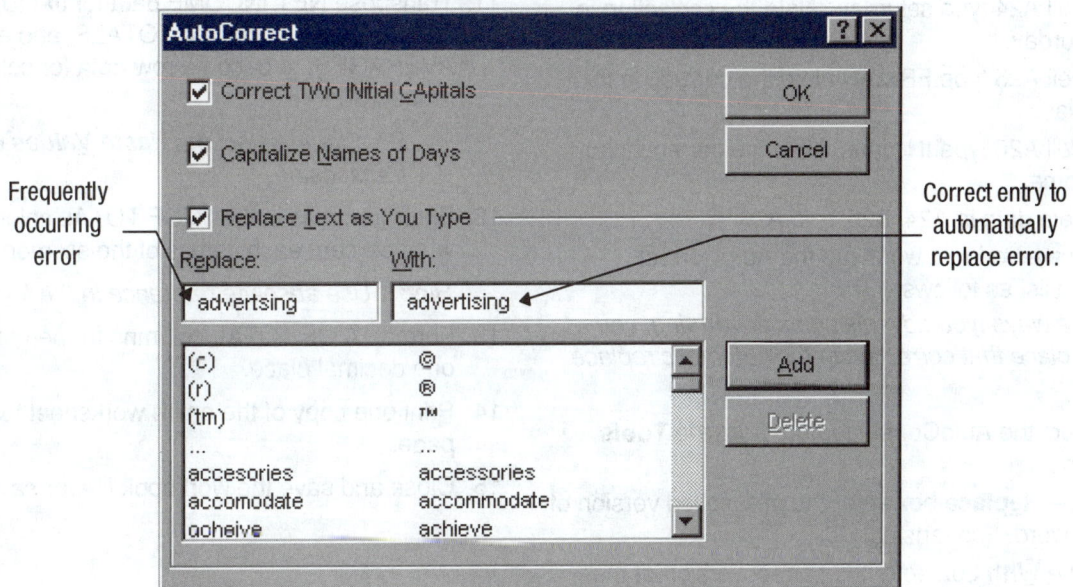

AutoCorrect ? X

☑ Correct TWo INitial CApitals

☑ Capitalize **N**ames of Days

☑ Replace **T**ext as You Type

Frequently occurring error →

Correct entry to automatically replace error. →

Replace: With:

advertsing   advertising

(c)	©
(r)	®
(tm)	™
...	...
accesories	accessories
accomodate	accommodate
aoheive	achieve

OK

Cancel

Add

Delete

In this exercise, you will insert a new expense item in the worksheet of the Green Thumb Landscape Service and practice using the AutoCorrect feature. In addition, you will use transposed data from the income statement to prepare an income statement analysis.

EXERCISE DIRECTIONS:

1. Open ⌨ **IS** or 💾 **31IS**.

2. Delete column B.

3. Set column widths for columns B through H to 10.

   To include a monthly interest expense of $25:

   - Insert a row between Truck Maintenance and Other.
   - Enter the label: Interest.
   - Enter $25 for each month.
   - Copy the TOTALS and AVERAGES formulas to the interest line.
   - Format the interest line for two decimal places.

4. Enter new title and column labels below the existing worksheet, as illustrated.

5. Center column labels.

6. Practice using the AutoCorrect feature by doing the following:
   - In cell A24 type saturday. Note the correction to Saturday.
   - In cell A25 type FRiday. Note the correction to Friday.
   - In cell A26 type INcome. Note the correction to Income.
   - Delete data in A24, A25, and A26.

7. Practice entering a word into the AutoCorrect replace list as follows:
   If you always type advertising as advertsing, you could place that correction in the automatic replace box.
   - Select the AutoCorrect feature from the **Tools** menu.
   - In the **Replace** box enter the misspelled version of the word. (advertsing)
   - In the **With** box enter the correct version of the word. (advertising)

   - In A13 type Advertising using the incorrect version.
   - Note the correction to Advertising.

8. Transpose the column titles JANUARY through JUNE, including TOTALS, and excluding AVERAGES, to become row titles in column A in the range A31:A37.

9. Transpose Total Income data for JANUARY through JUNE, including TOTALS and excluding AVERAGES, to become row data for column B in the range B31:B37.

   ✓ *Be sure to select the **Paste Values** option when transposing.*

10. Transpose Total Expenses data for JANUARY through JUNE, including TOTALS, and excluding AVERAGES, to become row data for column D in the range D31:D37.

    ✓ *Be sure to select the **Paste Values** option when transposing.*

11. Transpose NET INCOME data for JANUARY through JUNE, including TOTALS, and excluding AVERAGES, to become row data for column F in the range F30:F36.

    ✓ *Be sure to select the **Paste Values** option when transposing.*

12. Enter formulas in the % OF TOTAL columns to find what percent each item is of the six month total.

    Hint: Use absolute reference in the formula.

13. Format % OF TOTAL columns for percentage with one decimal place.

14. Print one copy of the entire worksheet to fit on a page.

15. Close and save the workbook file, or *save as* **IS**.

	A	B	C	D	E	F	G	H	I	J	K
1			COMPARATIVE INCOME STATEMENT								
2			GREEN THUMB LANDSCAPE SERVICE								
3											
4											
5			JANUARY	FEBRUARY	MARCH	APRIL	MAY	JUNE	TOTALS	AVERAGES	
6											
7	INCOME:										
8	Service Fees		5342.87	5543.65	6165.87	8343.84	9862.89	10359.45	45618.57	7603.10	
9	Consultations		1564.98	1654.76	1689.76	1893.65	1498.62	1287.49	9589.26	1598.21	
10	Total Income		6907.85	7198.41	7855.63	10237.49	11361.51	11646.94	55207.83	9201.31	
11											
12	EXPENSES:										
13	Advertising		55.00	65.00	150.00	150.00	165.00	165.00	750.00	125.00	
14	Salaries		754.65	754.65	1255.55	1255.55	1255.55	1255.55	6531.50	1088.58	
15	Supplies		154.76	245.65	589.53	769.54	965.62	1276.54	4001.64	666.94	
16	Truck Maint		95.00	125.54	243.98	185.87	543.51	324.65	1518.55	253.09	
17	Interest		25.00	25.00	25.00	25.00	25.00	25.00	150.00	25.00	
18	Other		143.43	43.54	231.65	326.43	654.65	798.43	2198.13	366.36	
19	Total Expenses		1227.84	1259.38	2495.71	2712.39	3609.33	3845.17	15149.82	2524.97	
20											
21	NET INCOME		5680.01	5939.03	5359.92	7525.10	7752.18	7801.77	40058.01	6676.34	
22											
23											
24											
25			INCOME STATEMENT ANALYSIS								
26			GREEN THUMB LANDSCAPING SERVICE								
27											
28	MONTH		TOTAL	% OF	TOTAL	% OF	NET	% OF			
29			INCOME	TOTAL	EXPENSES	TOTAL	INCOME	TOTAL			
30											
31											
32											
33											
34											
35											
36											
37											

Callouts: **delete column B**, **insert row**, **transpose**

SET AN AUTOCORRECT REPLACEMENT

1. Click **Tools** menu .... Alt + T
2. Click **AutoCorrect** .... A
3. Click **Replace** .... E
4. Type abbreviation or commonly misspelled word.
5. Click **With** .... W
6. Type replacement text.
7. Click **Add** .... A
8. Click OK .... ↵

TRANSPOSE DATA

Copies and transposes data from horizontal to vertical arrangement and vice versa.

1. Select range to transpose.
2. a. Click **Edit** menu .... Alt + E
   b. Click **Copy** C
   OR
   a. Right-click a cell in selection to open shortcut menu.
   b. Click **Copy** C
3. Click upper-left cell .... ⬍
   to receive transposed data.
4. a. Click **Edit** .... Alt + E
   b. Click **Paste Special** .... S
   OR
   a. Right-click destination cell to open shortcut menu.
   b. Click **Paste Special** .... S
5. Click **Transpose** .... E
   check box.

To paste transposed data as values, not formulas:

- Click **Values** V
6. Click OK .... ↵
7. Press **Escape** .... Esc
   to end copying.

EXERCISE

■ Insert and Delete Columns and Rows ■ Freeze Titles
■ Create New Workbook ■ Select Workbook
■ Copy and Paste Special (Extract Data) ■ Scroll Tips

32

NOTES:

- Excel provides two methods for working with large worksheets: freezing titles to keep titles in view and splitting the window into two panes or four panes.

Freeze Titles

- To keep headings or titles in view at the left or top edge of the worksheet when scrolling, it is necessary to hold, or **freeze**, them in place.

- To view different parts of a large worksheet at one time, the worksheet may be **split** horizontally or vertically so data may be viewed through each of the windows at the same time.

  When you split a window *vertically* the panes scroll together when you scroll up or down, but they scroll independently when you scroll left and right.

  When you split a window *horizontally* the panes scroll together when you scroll left or right, but they scroll independently when you scroll up and down.

- When you freeze a split worksheet, the top and/or left pane locks when you scroll through the worksheet.

Scroll Tips

- You may move through a large worksheet by moving the scroll box on the horizontal or vertical scroll bars. When you move the scroll box, Excel displays the row or column numbers near the scroll box as you move through the worksheet. Note the illustration below:

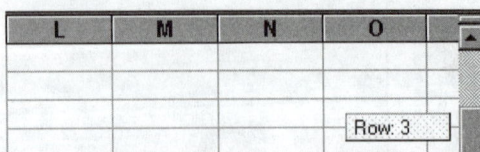

Copy and Paste Special

- Use the **Copy** and **Paste Special** commands to copy part of a worksheet into another workbook.

- Paste options in the Paste Special dialog box include:

All	Replaces paste area cells with all formulas, formats, and notes contained in copied cells.
Formulas	Copies data that exists in formula bar of copied cells (the formulas).
	✓ *Relative cell references in formulas will adjust.*
Values	Copies data as it appears in copied cells (results of formulas).
Formats	Copies only the formats of cells.
Notes	Copies cell notes.

- In the Paste Special dialog box, the **Formulas** and **Values** paste options affect the paste result. Select **Formulas** to extract values, labels and formulas *exactly as they exist.* Select **Values** to extract labels, values, *and the results of the formulas.* You should select **Values** if the range to be extracted contains formulas with references to cells that do not contain the values to be calculated.

Create New Workbook

- New workbooks can be created to store new or extracted data. You can access a new workbook by selecting the New Workbook icon ▢ on the Standard Toolbar or by selecting File, New.

Select Workbook

- When working with more than one workbook at a time, you can use the **Window** menu to select the desired file from the list of open files.

In this exercise, you will divide the data into quarterly information. To do this, you must insert and delete columns. However, because inserting or deleting columns from the top portion of the worksheet will affect the bottom portion, you will extract the bottom portion of the worksheet, save it to another file, and delete it from the original. The top portion of the worksheet will then be expanded and edited.

EXERCISE DIRECTIONS:

1. Open ⌨ **IS** or 💾 **32IS**.

2. Use the Copy and Paste Special commands to extract the Income Statement Analysis portion of the worksheet to a new workbook; name the new workbook file **ANA**.

   ✓ Select the **Values** option in the Paste Special dialog box to ensure that the results of the formulas are copied, and not the formulas themselves.

3. Switch to the IS workbook. Delete the Income Statement Analysis portion from the **IS** worksheet.

4. Insert a column between MARCH and APRIL and enter the column titles:

   1ST QTR.
   TOTALS

5. Format the new column for two decimal places.

6. Insert a column between JUNE and TOTALS and enter the column titles:

   2ND QTR.
   TOTALS

7. Format the new column for two decimal places.

8. Edit column title TOTALS to read:

   COMBINED
   TOTALS

9. Delete the AVERAGES column.

10. Find 1ST QTR. TOTALS.

    HINT: =January+February+March

11. Copy the formula to the remaining items.

12. Copy the formulas for 1ST QTR. TOTALS to the column for 2ND QTR. TOTALS.

13. Edit the formula in the COMBINED TOTALS column to add 1ST QTR. TOTALS and 2ND QTR. TOTALS.

14. Freeze titles in column A.

15. Practice using the scroll bar and scroll tips by moving the horizontal scroll box to bring the worksheet into position to enter data in column K.

16. Enter third quarter data indicated below beginning in the next available column of your worksheet.

	A	K	L	M
1				
2				
3				
4				
5		JULY	AUGUST	SEPT.
6				
7	INCOME:			
8	Service Fees	11986.45	11050.65	10573.87
9	Consultations	1343.27	1186.87	965.78
10	Total Income			
11				
12	EXPENSES:			
13	Advertising	165.00	165.00	150.00
14	Salaries	1255.55	1255.55	1255.00
15	Supplies	1887.98	1667.09	1654.98
16	Truck Maint.	486.98	245.90	327.65
17	Interest	25.00	25.00	25.00
18	Other	674.79	543.87	476.98
19	Total Expenses			
20				
21	NET INCOME			
22				

17. Copy and edit formulas, where necessary, to complete the worksheet.

18. Find 3RD QTR. TOTALS.

19. Copy the formula to the remaining items.

20. Center column title labels.

21. Format numeric data for two decimal places.

22. Save the file, or *save as* **IS**.

23. Print one copy of IS to fit on a page.

24. Switch to **ANA** workbook.

25. Format and align data as needed.

26. Resave **ANA**, then print one copy.

27. Close both workbook files.

	A	B	C	D	E	F	G	H	I
1		COMPARATIVE INCOME STATEMENT							
2		GREEN THUMB LANDSCAPE SERVICE							
3									
4									
5		JANUARY	FEBRUARY	MARCH	APRIL	MAY	JUNE	TOTALS	AVERAGES
6									
7	INCOME:								
8	Service Fees	5342.87	5543.65	6165.87	8343.84	9862.89	10359.45	45618.57	7603.10
9	Consultations	1564.98	1654.76	1689.76	1893.65	1498.62	1287.49	9589.26	1598.21
10	Total Income	6907.85	7198.41	7855.63	10237.49	11361.51	11646.94	55207.83	9201.31
11									
12	EXPENSES:								
13	Advertising	55.00	65.00	150.00	150.00	165.00	165.00	750.00	125.00
14	Salaries	754.65	754.65	1255.55	1255.55	1255.55	1255.55	6531.50	1088.58
15	Supplies	154.76	245.65	589.53	769.54	965.62	1276.54	4001.64	666.94
16	Truck Maint.	95.00	125.54	243.98	185.87	543.51	324.65	1518.55	253.09
17	Interest	25.00	25.00	25.00	25.00	25.00	25.00	150.00	25.00
18	Other	143.43	43.54	231.65	326.43	654.65	798.43	2198.13	366.36
19	Total Expenses	1227.84	1259.38	2495.71	2712.39	3609.33	3845.17	15149.82	2524.97
20									
21	NET INCOME	5680.01	5939.03	5359.92	7525.10	7752.18	7801.77	40058.01	6676.34
22									
23									
24		INCOME STATEMENT ANALYSIS							
25		GREEN THUMB LANDSCAPING SERVICE							
26									
27	MONTH	TOTAL	% OF	TOTAL	% OF	NET	% OF		
28		INCOME	TOTAL	EXPENSES	TOTAL	INCOME	TOTAL		
29									
30	JANUARY	6907.85	12.5%	1227.84	8.1%	5680.01	14.2%		
31	FEBRUARY	7198.41	13.0%	1259.38	8.3%	5939.03	14.8%		
32	MARCH	7855.63	14.2%	2495.71	16.5%	5359.92	13.4%		
33	APRIL	10237.49	18.5%	2712.39	17.9%	7525.10	18.8%		
34	MAY	11361.51	20.6%	3609.33	23.8%	7752.18	19.4%		
35	JUNE	11646.94	21.1%	3845.17	25.4%	7801.77	19.5%		
36	TOTALS	55207.83		15149.82		40058.01			
37									

Callouts: insert column 1ST QTR. TOTALS; insert column 2ND QTR. TOTALS; delete column; extract to new workbook and save new workbook as ANA

COPY AND PASTE SPECIAL (Extract Data)

Copies a portion of the current worksheet to a new workbook.

1. Copy range to extract to the clipboard:
   a. Select range of worksheet to extract.
   b. Click **Edit** menu .... Alt + E
   c. Click **Copy** C

2. Open a new workbook:
   a. Click **File** menu .... Alt + F
   b. Click **New** .... N

– FROM NEW WORKBOOK –

3. Use Paste Special command:
   a. Click **Edit** menu .... Alt + E
   b. Click **Paste Special** .... S
   c. Click **Values** V
   to copy data as it appears in cells (results of formulas).

   OR

   Click **Formulas** .... F
   to copy data as it exists in formula bar (formulas).
   ✔ Only relative cell references in formulas will adjust.
   d. Click [OK] .... ↵

4. Save and name the new workbook.
   a. Click **File** menu .... Alt + F
   b. Click **Save As** .... A
   c. Type new filename..........*filename*
   ✔ The filename you type replaces default name of the workbook.
   d. Click [OK] .... ↵

CREATE NEW WORKBOOK

Opens a new workbook based on the default template.

- Click **New Workbook** button ...... [icon] on Standard Toolbar.

OR

1. Click **File** menu .... [Alt] + [F]
2. Click **New** .... [N]

SELECT WORKBOOK

✓ *When more than one workbook is open, the workbook you want may be hidden or reduced to an icon. In order to use the workbook, you need to select the workbook window or open the workbook icon.*

To select a workbook window:

- Click anywhere on workbook window.

OR

1. Click **Window** menu .... [Alt] + [W]
2. Select name of workbook .... [↑↓], [↵] near bottom of the menu.

To open a workbook icon:

- Double-click workbook icon.

OR

1. Click **Window** menu .... [Alt] + [W]
2. Select name of workbook .... [↑↓], [↵] near bottom of the menu.

SPLIT WORKSHEET INTO PANES USING SPLIT BOXES

Provides simultaneous scrolling of up to four panes. You can freeze panes (see right) to prevent top, left, or both panes from scrolling.

✓ *If the scroll bars are not displayed in panes, see SET VIEW PREFERENCES, page 194.*

1. Point to horizontal split box ▭ or vertical split box [] on scroll bar.

   Pointer becomes a ⇳ or ⇻.

2. Drag ⇳ or ⇻ along scroll bar until split bar is in desired position.

SPLIT WORKSHEET INTO PANES USING THE MENU

Provides simultaneous scrolling of up to four panes. You can freeze panes (see right) to prevent top, left, or both panes from scrolling.

1. Select row below which horizontal split will occur.

   OR

   Select column to right of which vertical split will occur.

   OR

   Select cell below and to the right of which horizontal and vertical split will occur.

2. Click **Window** menu .... [Alt] + [W]
3. Click **Split** .... [S]

REMOVE SPLIT BARS

- Double-click any part of split bar.

OR

1. Click **Window** menu .... [Alt] + [W]
2. Click **Remove Split** .... [S]

ADJUST WORKSHEET PANES

1. Point to horizontal split box ▭ or vertical split box [] on scroll bar.

   Pointer becomes a ⇳ or ⇻.

2. Drag ⇳ or ⇻ along scroll bar until split bar is in desired position.

MOVE BETWEEN WORKSHEET PANES

- Click desired pane.

OR

   Press **F6** .... [F6] until active cell is in desired pane.

FREEZE PANES ON A SPLIT WORKSHEET

Locks top and/or left pane when scrolling.

1. Click **Window** menu .... [Alt] + [W]
2. Click **Freeze Panes** .... [F]

UNFREEZE PANES

1. Click **Window** menu .... [Alt] + [W]
2. Click **Unfreeze Panes** .... [F]

FREEZE TITLES

Locks display of title row and/or title column on the screen. This procedure is for a worksheet that has not been split into panes.

1. Select row below horizontal titles to freeze.

   OR

   Select column to right of vertical titles to freeze.

   OR

   Select cell below and to the right of horizontal and vertical titles to freeze.

2. Click **Window** menu .... [Alt] + [W]
3. Click **Freeze Panes** .... [F]

UNFREEZE TITLES

1. Click **Window** menu .... [Alt] + [W]
2. Click **Unfreeze Panes** .... [F]

SCROLL TIPS

1. Click on horizontal or vertical scroll bar.
2. Move bar as desired.
3. Note row or column Scroll Tip.

SET WINDOW OPTIONS

1. Click **Tools** menu .... [Alt] + [T]
2. Click **Options** .... [O]
3. From the View tab, select desired option.
4. Click [OK] .... [↵]

EXERCISE

■ Insert and Delete Columns and Rows ■ Workbook Sheets
■ Print Workbook ■ Print Worksheet on Specified Number of Pages

33

NOTES:

Workbook Sheets

- By default, each new workbook contains sixteen worksheets labeled Sheet1 through Sheet16. **Sheet tabs** show the names of the sheets *(see illustration below)*.

- You can select multiple sheets (grouping) to work on several sheets simultaneously. In a group selection **selected sheet tabs** are white, and the **active sheet tab** is bold.

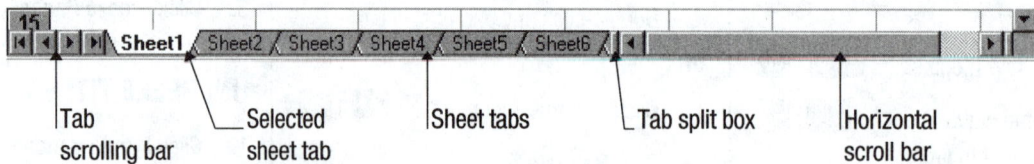

- Excel lets you work with sheets in many ways. For example, you can delete, insert, rename, move, copy, and hide sheets. These features let you arrange your workbook to fit your work objectives.

- Excel provides a **tab split box** between the sheet tabs and the horizontal scroll bar. You can drag this split box left or right to show more or fewer sheet tabs.

- You can use the **tab scrolling buttons** to scroll a hidden sheet tab into view. If no sheet tabs are visible, you can tell Excel to show them by selecting **Sheet Tabs** from the Options dialog box.

Print Workbook

- You can tell Excel on how many pages you want a worksheet to print. Then, Excel will automatically scale the worksheet to fit on the specified number of pages.

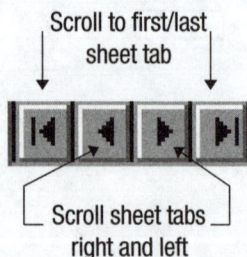

TAB SCROLLING BUTTONS

In this exercise, you will create a payroll template for future use. To do this you will delete unnecessary sheet tabs, insert and rename sheet tabs, and work with grouped sheets to quickly edit data on more than one worksheet at a time.

EXERCISE DIRECTIONS:

1. Open ⌨ **SALARY** or 💾 **33SALARY**.

2. Resave the workbook file as **SALNEW**.

3. Click sheet tab named Sheet2 to select it.

   ✓ Note that Sheet2 is empty.

4. Select Sheet1.

5. Use tab scrolling buttons to scroll to last sheet.

6. Use tab split box to increase, then decrease, the amount of visible sheet tabs.

7. Select Sheet16 and delete it.

8. Select Sheet2 through Sheet15.

   ✓ Note selected sheet tabs are white and [Group] appears on the title bar.

9. Delete the grouped worksheets.

   ✓ Note only Sheet1 remains.

10. Rename Sheet1 to May.

11. Insert a new worksheet; name it June.

12. Move the June sheet to the right of May.

13. Insert a new worksheet; name it July.

14. Move the July sheet to the right of June.

15. Select the May sheet and edit the titles in each week's payroll to read:

    FOR THE WEEK ENDING

    ✓ Delete the dates.

16. To make payrolls uniform on the May sheet:

    - Finckel has left our employment; delete the Finckel rows in the top two payrolls.
    - Copy the Nelson information from the last payroll to the first two payrolls in the correct order.

17. Select all the data in the May sheet and copy it to the clipboard.

    HINT: You can click the Select All button to select the entire worksheet.

18. Group the June and July sheets.

19. Select the June sheet and select cell A1.

20. Use the Paste command to copy the May worksheet data to the active cell in the grouped sheets (June and July).

21. Click cell A1 to deselect the range.

22. Select the May sheet.

23. Click cell A1 to deselect the range.

24. Select all the sheets in the workbook (May through July).

    —WHILE ALL SHEETS ARE GROUPED—

25. Clear the data in the cells containing the hours worked for each employee in each payroll week. (Do not delete the column.)

26. Mills has left our employment; delete the Mills row in each payroll week.

27. Deselect grouped sheets and check that each sheet contains identical data.

28. Set each worksheet to fit on one page when printed.

    ✓ You cannot set print page options for a group.

29. Print the entire workbook.

30. Close and save the workbook file.

	A	B	C	D	E	F	G	H	I
1				BURLINGTON NATIONAL BANK PAYROLL					
2				FOR THE WEEK ENDING MAY 15, 19—					
3									
4	EMPLOYEE	CARD		HOURLY	HOURS	GROSS			NET
5	NAME	NUMBER	S. S. NO.	RATE	WORKED	PAY	F.I.C.A.	F.W.T.	PAY
6									
7	CARTER	12567	069-65-4532	5.55	15	83.25	6.37	16.65	60.23
8	FINCKEL	12750	123-75-7623	7.23	32	231.36	17.70	46.27	167.39
9	JAMISON	12816	107-53-6754	6.18	16	98.88	7.56	19.78	71.54
10	MILLS	12925	103-87-5698	4.66	28	130.48	9.98	26.10	94.40
11	POTTER	12345	127-78-0045	6.57	12	78.84	6.03	15.77	57.04
12	SAMUELS	12716	043-67-7600	8.65	21	181.65	13.90	36.33	131.42
13									
14		TOTALS				804.46	61.54	160.89	582.03
15		AVERAGES				134.08	10.26	26.82	97.00
16									
17				FOR THE WEEK ENDING MAY 22, 19—					
18									
19	EMPLOYEE	CARD		HOURLY	HOURS	GROSS			NET
20	NAME	NUMBER	S. S. NO.	RATE	WORKED	PAY	F.I.C.A.	F.W.T.	PAY
21									
22	CARTER	12567	069-65-4532	5.55	20	111.00	8.49	22.20	80.31
23	FINCKEL	12750	123-75-7623	7.23	31	224.13	17.15	44.83	162.16
24	JAMISON	12816	107-53-6754	6.18	23	142.14	10.87	28.43	102.84
25	MILLS	12925	103-87-5698	4.66	22	102.52	7.84	20.50	74.17
26	POTTER	12345	127-78-0045	6.57	15	98.55	7.54	19.71	71.30
27	SAMUELS	12716	043-67-7600	8.65	25	216.25	16.54	43.25	156.46
28									
29		TOTALS				894.59	68.44	178.92	647.24
30		AVERAGES				149.10	11.41	29.82	107.87
31									
32									
33				FOR THE WEEK ENDING MAY 29, 19—					
34									
35	EMPLOYEE	CARD		HOURLY	HOURS	GROSS			NET
36	NAME	NUMBER	S. S. NO.	RATE	WORKED	PAY	F.I.C.A.	F.W.T.	PAY
37									
38	CARTER	12567	069-65-4532	5.55	22	122.10	9.34	24.42	88.34
39	JAMISON	12816	107-53-6754	6.18	33	203.94	15.60	40.79	147.55
40	MILLS	12925	103-87-5698	4.66	21	97.86	7.49	19.57	70.80
41	NELSON	12967	146-93-0069	6.25	16	100.00	7.65	20.00	72.35
42	POTTER	12345	127-78-0045	6.57	18	118.26	9.05	23.65	85.56
43	SAMUELS	12716	043-67-7600	8.65	28	242.20	18.53	48.44	175.23
44									
45		TOTALS				884.36	67.65	176.87	639.83
46		AVERAGES				147.39	11.28	29.48	106.64
47									

Annotations: **copy A1:I46 to June and July sheets** — **delete rows** (rows 8–10) — **delete rows** (rows 23–26) — **delete row** (row 40)

USE TAB SPLIT BOX

Lets you show more or fewer tabs.

1. Point to tab split box.
   Pointer becomes a ◄‖►.
2. Drag split box left or right.

SELECT SHEETS

Select One Sheet:

1. If necessary, click tab..... |◄ ◄ ► ►| scrolling buttons to scroll a hidden sheet tab into view.
2. Click desired sheet tab .... ＼Sheet #／

Select All Sheets:

1. Right-click any sheet tab .... ＼Sheet #／
2. Click **Select All Sheets** ....

Select (Group) Consecutive Sheets

IMPORTANT: When you group sheets, entries and formatting applied to one sheet are duplicated on all sheets in the group.

1. If necessary, click tab ..... |◄ ◄ ► ►| scrolling buttons to scroll hidden sheet tabs into view.
2. Click first sheet .... ＼Sheet #／ tab to select.
3. If necessary, click tab ..... |◄ ◄ ► ►| scrolling buttons to scroll hidden sheet tabs into view.
4. Press **Shift** and click .... ＼Sheet #／ last sheet tab to select.

[Group] appears in title bar.

Select (Group) Non-Consecutive Sheets

IMPORTANT: When you group sheets, entries and formatting applied to one sheet are duplicated on all sheets in the group.

1. If necessary, click .... |◄ ◄ ► ►| tab scrolling buttons to scroll hidden sheet tabs into view.
2. Click .... ＼Sheet #／ first sheet tab to select.
3. If necessary, click .... |◄ ◄ ► ►| tab scrolling buttons to scroll hidden sheet tabs into view.
4. Press **Ctrl** and click........ ＼Sheet #／ each sheet tab to select.

[Group] appears in title bar.

DESELECT GROUPED SHEETS

- Click any sheet tab that
  is not in the group .... ⎸ Sheet # ⎟

OR

1. Right-click .... ⎸ Sheet # ⎟
   any sheet tab in group.

2. Click **Ungroup Sheets** .... 🔳, ⏎

DELETE SHEETS

Delete One Sheet:

1. Right-click sheet tab
   to delete .... ⎸ Sheet # ⎟

2. Click **Delete** .... 🔳, ⏎

3. Click ⎸ OK ⎟ .... ⏎

Delete Multiple Sheets:

1. Select sheet tabs to delete.

2. Right-click any selected
   sheet tab .... ⎸ Sheet # ⎟

3. Click **Delete** .... 🔳, ⏎

4. Click ⎸ OK ⎟ .... ⏎

RENAME A SHEET

1. Double-click sheet tab
   to rename .... ⎸ Sheet # ⎟

   OR

   a. Right-click sheet tab
      to rename .... ⎸ Sheet # ⎟

   b. Select **Rename** .... 🔳, ⏎

2. Type new name .... *name*

3. Click ⎸ OK ⎟ .... ⏎

INSERT SHEETS

Insert One Worksheet:

1. Right-click sheet tab .... ⎸ Sheet # ⎟
   before which new sheet will be
   inserted.

2. Click **Insert** ... . 🔳, ⏎

3. Select **Worksheet** .... 🔳
   on General page.

4. Click ⎸ OK ⎟ .... ⏎

   *Excel inserts sheet and makes the new
   sheet active.*

Insert Multiple Worksheets:

1. Highlight as many sheets as you wish
   to insert.

2. Right-click sheet tab .... ⎸ Sheet # ⎟
   before which new sheets will be
   inserted.

3. Click **Insert** .... 🔳, ⏎

4. Select **Worksheet** .... 🔳
   on General page.

5. Click ⎸ OK ⎟ .... ⏎

   *Excel inserts sheets and
   makes the first new sheet active.*

MOVE SHEETS WITHIN A WORKBOOK

Move One Sheet:

1. If necessary, click .... 🔳🔳🔳🔳
   tab scrolling buttons to scroll a hidden
   sheet tab into view.

2. Drag sheet tab to desired sheet tab
   position.
   *Pointer becomes a ▯, and black
   triangle indicates point of insertion.*

Move Multiple Sheets:

1. If necessary, click tab ...... 🔳🔳🔳🔳
   scrolling buttons to scroll a hidden
   sheet tab into view.

2. Select sheets to move.

3. Drag selected sheet tabs to desired
   sheet tab position.
   *Pointer becomes a ▯, and black
   triangle indicates point of insertion.*

PRINT WORKBOOK

*Prints worksheet data using the current page
settings.*

1. Click **File** menu .... Alt + F

2. Click **Print** .... P

3. Click **Entire Workbook** .... Alt + E

4. Click ⎸ OK ⎟ .... ⏎

SET WORKSHEET TO PRINT ON SPECIFIED NUMBER OF PAGES

*Determines how much to scale printed data to
fit on a specified number of pages.*

✓ *Excel ignores manual page breaks when
  this setting is selected.*

1. Click **File** menu .... Alt + F

2. Click **Page Setup** ... . U

3. Select **Page** tab .... Ctrl + Tab

4. Select **Fit to:** .... Alt + F

To change settings for number of pages:

a. Type number of pages ..... *number*
   in **page(s) wide**.

b. Select **by tall** .... Tab

c. Type number of pages ..... *number*

5. Click ⎸ OK ⎟ .... ⏎

EXERCISE

■ **Insert and Delete Rows** ■ **Freeze Titles** ■ **Named Ranges**

34

NOTES:

Named Ranges

- Excel allows you to assign a **name** to a cell or range of cells rather than use the cell reference for identification.

- Naming ranges makes formulas easy to read and understand and makes printing and combining ranges easier to accomplish. For example, when you define a print area, you can type the name of a range (such as EMPS), rather than typing the cell reference (such as A1:D17). You should keep range names short and descriptive. Since spaces are not allowed, use an underscore to simulate a space character. Do not use range names that could be interpreted as a number or a cell reference.

- To name a range, use the **Insert**, **Name**, **Define** commands. You can name and select the range in the dialog box that appears.

- In your worksheet, you can insert a list of the existing named ranges and their locations by selecting the **Paste List** button in the Paste Name dialog box. Range names may contain up to 255 characters and may consist of letters, numbers, underscores (_), backslashes (\), periods (.), and question marks (?).

- A list of the named ranges you created and their corresponding cell references may be inserted into the worksheet, by selecting the **Paste List** button in the Paste Name dialog box.

- The name box [▼] provides a way to view a list of named ranges you have created and is an easy way to name or select a range.

- It is possible to modify a named range by changing the range or the name.

In this exercise, you will include third-quarter sales commission data and name ranges in the report for printing and for later use in combining files.

EXERCISE DIRECTIONS:

1. Open ▦ **WOOD** or 🖫 **34WOOD**.

2. Edit the title to read:

   QUARTERLY SALES AND SALARY REPORT – JANUARY– SEPTEMBER

3. Insert a row to include a new employee hired on July 1. Employee Number, 6; Name, THOMPSON, JIM; Base Salary, $1500.

   ✓ *Format base salary to be consistent with other formatting.*

4. Freeze columns A-D for vertical titles.

5. Change column widths to 12 for columns K, L, and M.

6. Enter the following data in columns K, L, and M:

	K	L	M
1			
2			
3			
4		5%	JULY-SEPT
5	SALES	COMMISSION	SALARY
6			
7	112469.32		
8	152643.36		
9	215050.16		
10	98463.14		
11	246315.19		
12	76451.13		
13			
14			
15			

7. Format all data to be consistent with other formatting.

8. Copy the COMMISSION formulas to the new column.

9. Find JULY-SEPT SALARY using the BASE SALARY + COMMISSION.

10. Copy the formula to the remaining employees.

11. Copy the formulas for TOTALS, AVERAGES, HIGHEST, and LOWEST to the new columns.

12. Clear the freeze.

13. Edit the formulas for TOTALS, AVERAGES, HIGHEST, and LOWEST in the BASE SALARY column to include the new employee data.

14. Copy the edited formulas to all columns.

15. Create the following named ranges:

    EMPS   A1:D17

    JAN_MAR   G1:G17

    APR_JUNE   J1:J17

    JUL_SEPT   M1:M17

16. Print one copy of the range EMPS.

17. In range beginning at cell B19, insert list of named ranges.

18. Close and save the workbook file, or *save as* **WOOD**.

	A	B	C	D	E	F	G	H	I	J	K	L	M
1		WOODWORKS FURNITURE COMPANY											
2		QUARTERLY SALES AND SALARY REPORT - JANUARY-SEPTEMBER											
3											◄—12◄	—12◄	—12
4	EMP.			BASE		5%	JAN-MAR		5%	APR-JUN		5%	JULY-SEPT
5	NO.	NAME		SALARY	SALES	COMMISSION	SALARY	SALES	COMMISSION	SALARY	SALES	COMMISSION	SALARY
6													
7	1	ABRAMS, JUDY		1,500.00	113,456.67	5,672.83	7,172.83	114,342.90	5,717.15	7,217.15			
8	2	CHANG, PETER		1,500.00	150,654.87	7,532.74	9,032.74	143,276.70	7,163.84	8,663.84			
9	3	LINSEY, KELLY		1,500.00	234,765.36	11,738.27	13,238.27	187,956.76	9,397.84	10,897.84			
10	4	JOHNSON, LETOYA		1,500.00	89,765.43	4,488.27	5,988.27	93,984.69	4,699.23	6,199.23			
11	5	RIVERA, TONY		1,500.00	287,987.76	14,399.39	15,899.39	254,768.60	12,738.43	14,238.43			
12										▼			
13		TOTALS		7,500.00	876,630.09	43,831.50	51,331.50	794,329.65	39,716.48	47,216.48	(insert row)		
14		AVERAGES		1,500.00	175,326.02	8,766.30	10,266.30	158,865.93	7,943.30	9,443.30			
15		HIGHEST		1,500.00	287,987.76	14,399.39	15,899.39	254,768.60	12,738.43	14,238.43			
16		LOWEST		1,500.00	89,765.43	4,488.27	5,988.27	93,984.69	4,699.23	6,199.23			
17													

NAME/MODIFY A RANGE USING THE MENU

1. Click **Insert** menu.................[Alt]+[I]

2. Click **Name** ....[N]

3. Click **Define**... ....[D]

   *Active cell reference appears in **Refers to** text box.*

To name a range:

a. Type name for range ....*name* in **Names in Workbook** text box.

b. Click [Add] ....[Alt]+[A]

c. Drag through existing reference ....[Alt]+[R] in **Refers to** text box.

d. Select cells in worksheet to name.

   OR

   Type range reference ....*reference* to name.

To delete a name:

a. Click name ....[Tab], [↑↓] to delete in list box.

b. Click [Delete] ....[Alt]+[D]

To change a name:

a. Click name ....[Tab], [↑↓] to change in list box.

b. Double-click in **Names in Workbook**...................[Alt]+[W]

c. Type new name...................*name* for range.

d. Click [Add] ....[Alt]+[A]

e. Click old name............[Tab], [↑↓] to delete in list box.

f. Click [Delete] ....[Alt]+[D]

To change reference a name refers to:

a. Click name.................[Tab], [↑↓] to edit in list box.

b. Drag through existing reference ....[Alt]+[R] in **Refers to** text box.

c. Select cells in worksheet to reference.

   OR

   Type new reference ......*reference*

4. Click [OK] ....[↵]

NAME A RANGE USING THE NAME BOX

1. Select range to name.

2. Click in name box on left side of formula bar.

3. Type name of range.................... *name* to create.

4. Press **Enter**..................................[↵]

SELECT A NAMED RANGE

Select a Named Range Using the Name Box:

1. Click drop-down arrow in name box on left side of formula bar.

2. Click desired named range.

Select a Named Range Using Go To:

1. Press **F5** ....[F5]

2. Type name............................... *name* to select in **Reference** text box.

3. Click [OK] ....[↵]

INSERT LIST OF NAMED RANGES

Inserts a list of named ranges and their corresponding references in current worksheet.

1. Select upper-left cell in range to receive list.

2. Click **Insert** menu................[Alt]+[I]

3. Click **Name**....................................[N]

4. Click **Paste** ....[P]

5. Click [Paste List] ....[Alt]+[L]

   ✔ *Excel includes sheet names in references.*

6. Press any arrow key ....[↑↓]

SET PRINT AREA FOR A NAMED RANGE

✔ *Use this option only when you want to print a specific area of a worksheet each time you print.*

1. Follow steps to **SET PRINT OPTIONS FOR WORKSHEET**, page 80.

2. When you set the print area, type named range *name* in **Print Area** text box.

3. Follow steps to **PRINT A WORKSHEET** PAGE 53.

PRINT A NAMED RANGE

1. Follow steps to **SELECT A NAMED RANGE**, left.

2. Follow steps to **PRINT RANGE OF CELLS**, page 76.

NEXT EXERCISE

EXERCISE
35

■ **Freeze Titles** ■ **Name Ranges** ■ **Create New Workbook**
■ **Select Workbook** ■ **Copy and Paste Special (Combine Data)**
■ **Print Workbook**

NOTES:

Copy and Paste Special

- When data is copied it is placed on the **clipboard**, a storage area, until it is pasted or replaced by another block of copied data.

- The **Paste Special** command gives you added controls on how data is pasted when copied. With the Paste Special command you can:
  - Indicate which attributes of the selection will be copied.
  - Indicate how to combine data when the paste area contains data.
  - Tell Excel to skip blanks.
  - Tell Excel to transpose data in the paste area.

- Paste options in the Paste Special dialog box include:

  All   Replaces paste area cells with all formulas, formats, and notes contained in copied cells.

  Formulas   Copies data that exists in formula bar of copied cells (the formulas). *NOTE: Relative cell references in formulas will adjust.*

  Values   Copies data as it appears in copied cells (results of formulas).

  Formats   Copies only the formats of cells.

  Notes   Copies notes cells may contain.

In this exercise, you will create a stock portfolio worksheet prepared to summarize stock transactions for the year and use a named range to print the worksheet range. To summarize stock transactions, you will use the Copy and Paste Special command to combine extracted data in a new worksheet.

EXERCISE DIRECTIONS:

1. Create ⌨ the worksheet on the right or open 💾 **35MARKET.XLS**.
2. Enter dates in the format illustrated with the current year.
3. Set width of column B to 15.
4. Freeze titles in columns A and B.
5. Find GAIN or LOSS (subtract COST from SELLING PRICE and add DIVIDENDS EARNED).
6. Copy the formula to the remaining stocks.
7. Find TOTAL SELLING PRICE.
8. Copy the total formula to COST, DIVIDENDS EARNED and GAIN or LOSS columns; format results for two decimal places.
9. Find % GAIN or LOSS (divide the GAIN or LOSS by the COST) and format the result for a two-place percent.
10. Copy the % GAIN OR LOSS formula to the remaining stocks and to the TOTALS line.
11. Create the following named ranges:
    PRINTALL   A1:J13
    STOCK   A1:B13
12. Using the range name PRINTALL, print one copy to fit on a page.
13. Save the workbook file; name it **MARKET**.
14. Extract the STOCK range from the MARKET workbook into the MKTSUM workbook:
    - Copy range named STOCK to clipboard.
    - Create a new workbook.
    - Use the **Paste Special** command to paste the values into cell A1 in the new workbook.

15. Set the width of column B to 15.

16. Save the new workbook; name it **MKTSUM**.

17. Extract the GAIN or LOSS and % GAIN or LOSS to the MKTSUM workbook:

    - Select the **MARKET** workbook.

    - Copy the GAIN or LOSS and % GAIN or LOSS columns (I1:J13) to the clipboard.

    - Select cell D1 in the **MKTSUM** workbook and paste the values.
      *NOTE: Use the **Values** paste option from the **Paste Special** dialog box.*

18. In **MKTSUM**, format % GAIN OR LOSS data for two-place percent.

19. Enter a worksheet title in **MKTSUM** (in cells B1 and B2) that reads:
    MICHAEL CRAWFORD
    SUMMARY OF STOCK TRANSACTIONS - 199-

20. Print one copy of **MKTSUM** workbook.

21. Resave **MKTSUM.**

22. Close both workbook files.

NO. OF SHARES	COMPANY NAME	SYMBOL	DATE BOUGHT	DATE SOLD	SELLING PRICE	COST	DIVIDEND EARNED	GAIN OR LOSS	% GAIN OR LOSS	
			MICHAEL CRAWFORD							
			STOCK ANALYSIS - TRANSACTIONS FOR 199-							
	← 15 →									
200	Crystal Motors	CM	1/15/96	11/5/96	6548.95	7453.76	585.50			
100	US Brands	USB	1/30/96	6/30/96	9057.43	6923.12	325.40			
50	IGM	IGM	2/17/95	4/25/95	3248.95	2576.98	0.00			
300	Microgem	MIG	2/17/96	12/5/96	3954.69	5391.23	0.00	▼	▼	
500	Consolidated Gas	CG	3/28/96	12/20/96	15487.54	14326.54	1054.50			
	TOTALS				►	►	►	►	►	

COPY AND PASTE SPECIAL (Combine Data)

Combines data copied to the paste area in the way you specify.

1. Select range of worksheet to extract.

2. Click **Edit** menu .... [Alt]+[E]

3. Click **Copy** .... [C]

To change destination workbook or worksheet:

- Select workbook and/or sheet to receive data.

4. Select upper-left cell in destination area.

5. Click **Edit** menu .... [Alt]+[E]

6. Click **Paste Special** .... [S]

7. Select **Paste** option:

   - **All** .... [A]
   - **Formulas** .... [F]
   - **Values** .... [V]
   - **Formats** .... [T]
   - **Notes** .... [N]

To prevent overwriting existing data with blank cells:

- Select ☐ **Skip Blanks** .... [B]

To change orientation of data in paste area:

- Select ☐ **Transpose** .... [E]

8. Click [OK] .... [↵]

Excel ■ Lesson 6 ■ Exercise 35   123

EXERCISE

■ Create New Workbook ■ Select Workbook
■ Copy and Paste Special (Extract and Combine Data)

36

NOTES:

Copy and Paste Special

- As described in the previous exercise, the **Paste Special** command gives you added control on how data is pasted when copied. The Operation options in the Paste Special dialog box provide a variety of ways to combine data.

- In this lesson you will use the **Add** operation option in the Paste Special dialog box to extract and combine data to the same range in another workbook. The **Add** option will allow you to add the values from each quarter to obtain a total for the three quarters.

- Operation options in the Paste Special dialog box include:

None	Replaces paste cells with copied cells (default setting).
Add	Adds numeric data in copied cells to values in paste cells.
Subtract	Subtracts numeric data in copied cells from values in paste cells.
Multiply	Multiplies numeric data in copied cells by values in paste cells.
Divide	Divides numeric data in copied cells by values in paste cells.

In this exercise, you will extract data in a named range to a new file. Then you will use the Paste Special command to combine (add) the quarterly totals (as values) in the new workbook file, thus creating a summary workbook.

EXERCISE DIRECTIONS:

1. Open ⌨ **WOOD** or open 💾 **36WOOD**.

2. Use the **Copy** and **Paste Special** commands to extract the named range EMPS to a cell A1 in a new workbook file using the **Formulas** option; save and name the new workbook **WOODSUM**.

3. Edit the second line of the **WOODSUM** workbook title to read:
   COMPENSATION SUMMARY - JANUARY-SEPTEMBER

4. Select the **WOOD** workbook.

5. Use the **Copy** and **Paste Special** commands to extract and combine the following named ranges into cell F1 of the **WOODSUM** workbook.

   JAN_MAR

   APR_JUNE

   JUL_SEPT

   IMPORTANT: *Each time you paste data to cell F1 using **Paste Special**, set the Paste option to **Values** and the Operation option to **Add**. Each quarter's values will be added to the data in the range.*

—IN COLUMN F OF WOODSUM WORKBOOK—

6. Enter the column title:

   TOTAL
   COMPENSATION

7. The combined summary data for AVERAGES, HIGHEST and LOWEST is now incorrect. To correct this information, copy the formulas for TOTALS, AVERAGES, HIGHEST and LOWEST, from the BASE SALARY column to the TOTAL COMPENSATION column.

8. Format column F to show two decimal places.
9. Adjust the column width to show all values.
10. Resave **WOODSUM** and print one copy.
11. Close both workbook files.

	A	B	C	D	E	F	G	H	I	J	K	L	M
1		WOODWORKS FURNITURE COMPANY											
2		QUARTERLY SALES AND SALARY REPORT - JANUARY-SEPTEMBER											
3													
4	EMP.			BASE		5%	JAN-MAR		5%	APR-JUN		5%	JULY-SEPT
5	NO.	NAME		SALARY	SALES	COMMISSION	SALARY	SALES	COMMISSION	SALARY	SALES	COMMISSION	SALARY
6													
7	1	ABRAMS, JUDY		1,500.00	113,456.67	5,672.83	7,172.83	114,342.90	5,717.15	7,217.15	112469.32	5,623.47	7,123.47
8	2	CHANG, PETER		1,500.00	150,654.87	7,532.74	9,032.74	143,276.70	7,163.84	8,663.84	152643.36	7,632.17	9,132.17
9	3	LINSEY, KELLY		1,500.00	234,765.36	11,738.27	13,238.27	187,956.76	9,397.84	10,897.84	215050.16	10,752.51	12,252.51
10	4	JOHNSON, LETOYA		1,500.00	89,765.43	4,488.27	5,988.27	93,984.69	4,699.23	6,199.23	98463.14	4,923.16	6,423.16
11	5	RIVERA, TONY		1,500.00	287,987.76	14,399.39	15,899.39	254,768.60	12,738.43	14,238.43	246315.19	12,315.76	13,815.76
12	6	THOMPSON, JIM		1,500.00							76451.13	3,822.56	5,322.56
13													
14		TOTALS		9,000.00	876,630.09	43,831.50	51,331.50	794,329.65	39,716.48	47,216.48	901,392.30	45,069.62	54,069.62
15		AVERAGES		1,500.00	175,326.02	8,766.30	10,266.30	158,865.93	7,943.30	9,443.30	150,232.05	7,511.60	9,011.60
16		HIGHEST		1,500.00	287,987.76	14,399.39	15,899.39	254,768.60	12,738.43	14,238.43	246,315.19	12,315.76	13,815.76
17		LOWEST		1,500.00	89,765.43	4,488.27	5,988.27	93,984.69	4,699.23	6,199.23	76,451.13	3,822.56	5,322.56
18													
19													
20													

range A1:D17 named EMPS

COPY AND PASTE SPECIAL (Combine Data)

Combines data copied to the paste area in the way you specify.

1. Select range of worksheet to extract.
2. Click **Edit** menu .... `Alt` + `E`
3. Click **Copy** .... `C`

To change destination workbook or worksheet:

- Select workbook and/or sheet to receive data.

4. Select upper-left cell in destination area.
5. Click **Edit** menu .... `Alt` + `E`
6. Click **Paste Special...** .... `S`

7. Select **Paste** option:

   - **A**ll .... `A`
   - **F**ormulas .... `F`
   - **V**alues .... `V`
   - Forma**t**s .... `T`
   - **N**otes .... `N`

To combine copied data with paste area data:

Select **Operation** option:

- **N**one .... `O`
- A**d**d .... `D`
- **S**ubtract .... `S`
- **M**ultiply .... `M`
- D**i**vide .... `I`

To prevent overwriting existing data with blank cells:

- Select ☐ **Skip Blanks** .... `B`

To change orientation of data in paste area:

- Select ☐ **Transpose** .... `E`

8. Click `OK` .... `↵`

EXERCISE

37

- ■ Copy and Paste Special (Extract and Combine Data)
- ■ Create New Workbook ■ Select Workbook
- ■ Delete Columns and Rows ■ Named Ranges ■ Replace

NOTES:

Replace

■ You may find it necessary to change a value or text entry throughout a worksheet. The **Replace** feature can replace all or some of the existing information quickly with another entry.

If you wish to confirm each replacement, you can select the Find Next option. Note the Edit, Replace dialog box below:

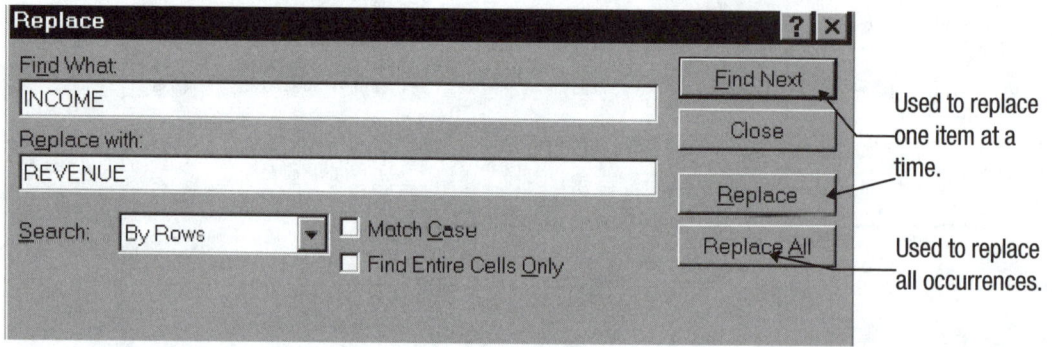

Replace dialog box showing Find What: INCOME, Replace with: REVENUE, Search: By Rows, options Match Case and Find Entire Cells Only, buttons Find Next (Used to replace one item at a time.), Close, Replace, Replace All (Used to replace all occurrences.)

> In this exercise, you will update the Green Thumb Landscape Servide worksheet to include fourth-quarter data. You will practice using the Replace feature and also create a new worksheet comparing quarterly data using the Copy, Paste Special procedure.

EXERCISE DIRECTIONS:

1. Open ⌨ **IS** or 💾 **37IS**.

2. Delete the COMBINED TOTALS column.

3. Enter fourth-quarter data indicated below, beginning in the next available column of your worksheet.

	N	O	P	Q
1				
2				
3				
4				4TH QTR.
5	OCT	NOV	DEC	TOTALS
6				
7				
8	9968.54	6235.87	5256.78	
9	1065.93	968.54	1054.32	
10				
11				
12				
13	150.00	55.00	55.00	
14	1255.00	754.65	754.65	
15	1435.62	567.87	102.54	
16	95.87	325.65	627.89	
17	25.00	25.00	25.00	
18	546.87	325.87	95.87	
19				

4. Copy formulas, where necessary, to complete the worksheet.

5. Find 4TH QTR. TOTALS.

6. Copy the formula to the remaining items.

7. Center column title labels.

8. Format numeric data for two decimal places.

9. Create the following named ranges (notice underscores) for each quarterly total column:

   _1ST_QTR

   _2ND_QTR

   _3RD_QTR

   _4TH_QTR

   ✓ *Include blank cells in column. For example, E1:E21 for _1ST_QTR.*

10. Clear the freeze on Column A titles.

11. Save the file, or *save as* **IS**.

12. Use the Copy and Paste Special commands to extract column A data, rows 1 through 21, to cell A1 in a new workbook file; save and name the new workbook **ISQTRS**.

13. In ISQTRS workbook, enter a worksheet title beginning in cell C1 that reads:

GREENTHUMB LANDSCAPE SERVICE
QUARTERLY INCOME STATEMENT COMPARISON

14. Select the IS workbook.

15. Use the Copy and Paste Special commands to copy the named range _1ST_QTR to the range beginning in C1 in the ISQTRS workbook.

HINT: Use the name box to select the named references quickly.

IMPORTANT: Set the Paste option to **Values**, Operation option to **None**, and select **Skip Blanks**.

16. Repeat step 15 for the _2ND_QTR, _3RD_QTR, and _4TH_QTR named ranges. Paste ranges in ISQTRS workbook in columns D1, E1, and F1, respectively.

—FROM ISQTRS WORKBOOK—

17. Enter title in column G:

COMBINED
TOTALS

18. Find the combined total for Service Fees INCOME.

19. Copy the formula to the remaining items.

20. Practice using the Replace feature as follows:

- Select Edit, Replace.
- Replace INCOME with REVENUE and check Match Case box.
- Click Replace All.
- ✓ *The capitalized "INCOME" words have been replaced.*
- Restore the worksheet to its original status by clicking Edit, Undo.
- Repeat this procedure using the Find Next button. (You may have to move the Replace dialog box so you can see each occurrence.)
- Replace or skip occurrences using the Find Next button until all are done.
- Restore the worksheet to its original status by clicking Edit, Undo.

21. Format all numeric values for two decimal places.

22. Adjust column widths as needed.

23. Save the **ISQTRS** workbook and print one copy.

24. Close the workbook files.

	A	B	C	D	E	F	G	H	I	J	K	L	M	N	O
1		GREEN THUMB LANDSCAPE SERVICE													
2		COMPARATIVE INCOME STATEMENT												insert 4TH QTR data	
3															
4					1ST QTR.				2ND QTR.	COMBINED				3RD QTR.	
5		JANUARY	FEBRUARY	MARCH	TOTALS	APRIL	MAY	JUNE	TOTALS	TOTALS	JULY	AUGUST	SEPT.	TOTALS	
6															
7	INCOME:														
8	Service Fees	5342.87	5543.65	6165.87	17052.39	8343.84	9862.89	10359.45	28566.18	4561857	11986.45	11050.65	10573.87	33610.97	
9	Consultations	1564.98	1654.76	1689.76	4909.50	1893.65	1498.62	1287.49	4679.76	9589.26	1343.27	1186.87	965.78	3495.92	
10	Total Income	6907.85	7198.41	7855.63	21961.89	10237.49	11361.51	11646.94	33245.94	55207.83	13329.72	12237.52	11539.65	37106.89	
11															
12	EXPENSES:														
13	Advertising	55.00	65.00	150.00	270.00	150.00	165.00	165.00	480.00	750.00	165.00	165.00	150.00	480.00	
14	Salaries	754.65	754.65	1255.55	2764.85	1255.55	1255.55	1255.55	3766.65	6531.50	1255.55	1255.55	1255.00	3766.10	
15	Supplies	154.76	245.65	589.53	989.94	769.54	965.62	1276.54	3011.70	4001.64	1887.98	1667.09	1654.98	5210.05	
16	Truck Maint.	95.00	125.54	243.98	464.52	185.87	543.51	324.65	1054.03	1518.55	486.98	245.90	327.65	1060.53	
17	Interest	25.00	25.00	25.00	75.00	25.00	25.00	25.00	75.00	150.00	25.00	25.00	25.00	75.00	
18	Other	143.43	43.54	231.65	418.62	326.43	654.65	798.43	1779.51	2198.13	674.79	543.87	476.98	1695.64	
19	Total Expenses	1227.84	1259.38	2495.71	4982.93	2712.39	3609.33	3845.17	10166.89	15149.82	4495.30	3902.41	3889.61	12287.32	
20															
21	NET INCOME	5680.01	5939.03	5359.92	16978.96	7525.10	7752.18	7801.77	23079.05	40058.01	8834.42	8335.11	7650.04	24819.57	
22															
23		extract to new file, ISQTRS													
24															
25															
26															

REPLACE

Replaces text in worksheet with specified text.

1. Select any cell to search entire worksheet.

   OR

   Select cells to search.

   OR

   Select sheets to search.

2. Click **Edit** menu .... `Alt`+`E`

3. Click **Replace**................................ `E`

4. Type characters to search for in **Find What:** [   ] ... `N`

   NOTE: You may use wildcard characters (and ?) to represent any character (?) or group of characters (*) in a search. To find data containing wildcard characters, you must type a tilde (~) before the wildcard character.*

5. a. Click in **Replace with:**
      [   ] .... `Alt`+`E`

   b. Type or edit replacement text..................*text*

   ### To set a search direction:

   a. Click **Search:**
      [⬇] .... `Alt`+`S`

   b. Click desired search direction...................... `⬆⬇` , `↵`

      Search options include:
      By Columns, By Rows, (All, Down, Up (module sheets only))

   ### To make search case specific:

   - Select ☐ **Match Case** .... `Alt`+`C`

   ### To find cells that match exactly:

   - Select ☐ **Find Entire Cells Only**............................ `Alt`+`O`

6. Click [Find Next] .... `Alt`+`F`

   Excel selects first cell meeting the search criteria.

7. Select one of the following:

   ### To globally replace cell contents:

   - Click [Replace All] .... `Alt`+`A`

      Excel replaces all matches and returns you to normal operations.

   ### To selectively replace cell contents:

   a. Click [Replace] .... `Alt`+`R`

      to replace contents of active cell and find next match.

      OR

      Click [Find Next] .... `Alt`+`F`

      to retain contents of active cell and find next match.

   b. Repeat step **a** for each item found.

   c. Click [Close] .... `Esc`

      to close Replace dialog box.

NEXT EXERCISE

EXERCISE
Use Templates (Spreadsheet Solutions)

38

NOTES:

■ Excel provides template spreadsheets (model worksheet designs) for common business tasks. The formulas, formats, print ranges, layout, etc., are pre-set so that you only need to add your data. If data is added to a template file, the Save As option should be used to prevent changing the template.

■ You can customize the template for your purposes and save it as a template file with a new filename. This will enable you to use a customized form that only requires the new variable data. You may also create your own templates by saving them as template files.

■ The template spreadsheet solutions that are available in Excel are found on the Spreadsheet Solutions page of the **File, New** dialog box. Note the illustration of the New dialog box with the Spreadsheet Solutions tab selected.

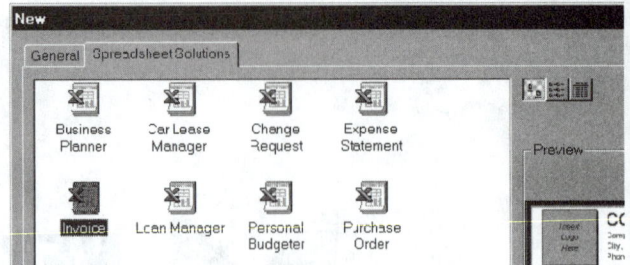

■ Each template workbook contains the **template worksheet** and a **customize worksheet** with data entry placeholders to customize the form for your use. In addition, a **template toolbar** appears on the template when it is opened. Note the illustration of the Invoice toolbar with a ToolTip displayed.

■ Several of the templates provided by Excel have a database feature that allows you to track the forms created by creating a record of the data. For the purposes of this exercise, the template will be used without the database feature.

> *In this exercise, you will explore a template and the template toolbar. You will customize the Invoice template for the Art Depot, save it as a template and create an invoice.*

EXERCISE DIRECTIONS:

1. Open a new file.

2. Switch to the Spreadsheet Solutions page in the New dialog box.

3. Double-click the Invoice template.

4. Place the mouse pointer under every button on the Invoice toolbar to view the ToolTip.

5. Press the Size to Screen/Return to Size button (top left corner) to view the template. Press the button to return to size.

6. To view a cell tip, click on the cell under the Total column heading. Place your mouse in the center of the cell and the cell tip will display.

7. Click on the [?] button to view a help screen on the invoice template. After looking at the screen, press the Close button.

8. Close the invoice toolbar.

9. Switch to the Customize Invoice sheet.

10. Make the entries as shown on the form to the right.

11. Switch to the Invoice sheet and check your input.

12. Click on the **Insert Fine Print Here** location at the bottom of the invoice and insert:

    Please check merchandise carefully upon delivery.

13. Click on the **Insert Farewell Statement Here** location and insert:

    Thank you for your order.

14. Save the file as ADINV as a template file.

    ✓ *You will be prompted to save the invoice as a database record. Click Cancel.*

15. Close ADINV.

16. Open a new workbook. Use the ADINV template.

17. Enter information to complete an invoice for Martinson Advertising as follows:

    Customer: Martinson Advertising
                     40 Scaran Road
                     Peoria, IL 62543

Phone:	402-555-1234
Order No.:	MA25
Invoice Number:	AD456
Rep:	Mary
FOB	Galesburg, IL

QTY	DESCRIPTION	UNIT PRICE
6	Toner Cartridges X-341	69.95
10	Drawing Pads JJ4356	21.95
5	Pencil sets CA65763	5.43

Payment Details: Check

18. Print a copy of the invoice.

19. Save the invoice as **MARTINSON AD**.

20. Close the file.

CUSTOMIZE YOUR INVOICE

Hover Your Pointer
HERE for a Useful Tip!

Type Company Information Here...

Company Name	Art Depot	Phone	309-555-9000
Address	1254 Miller Road	Fax	309-555-9001
City	Galesburg		
State	IL		
ZIP Code	61401		

Specify Default Invoice Information Here...

Credit Cards Accepted

1st Tax Name	IL
Rate	6.00%

☑ Apply tax on local purchases only.

Master Plan
Discovery
American Presto

2nd Tax Name	
Rate	

☐ Apply tax on local purchases only.

Shipping Charge $7.50

☐ Share invoice numbers on network.

Counter Location

Template Wizard Database d:\msoffice95\excel\library\invdb.xls

Formatted Information

Art Depot
1254 Miller Road
Galesburg, IL 61401
309-555-9000 fax 309-555-9001

USE AN EXCEL TEMPLATE

1. Click **F**ile menu .... `Alt`+`F`
2. Click **N**ew .... `N`
3. Click Spreadsheet Solutions tab.
4. Double-click on desired template.

SAVE A FILE AS A TEMPLATE

1. Click **F**ile menu .... `Alt`+`F`
2. Click Save **A**s .... `A`

   NOTE: *If you are saving from an Excel template, a message will be displayed about creating a database record. Click Cancel if the database feature will not be used.*

3. Select drive in **Save in** box.
4. Double-click folder name in documents list.
5. Repeat step 4 until folder to receive template is current.
6. Click on **File name** box .... `N`
7. Enter name of template .... *template name*
8. Click on **Save as type** box .... `T`
9. Select **Template** option .... `↓`
10. Click **S**ave .... `S`

OPEN ORIGINAL TEMPLATE FILE

1. Click **Open** button .... [icon]
   on Standard Toolbar.

   OR

   a. Click **F**ile menu .... `Alt`+`F`
   b. Click **O**pen .... `O`

2. Select Templates (*xlt) in **Files of type** .... `T`
3. Select folder containing template in **Look in** box.
4. Select template file to open.
5. Press **Shift** and click **Open**.

NEXT EXERCISE

EXERCISE

■ Original Templates ■ Arrange Workbooks ■ Link Workbooks

39

NOTES:

Original Templates

■ When you need to create several workbooks containing similar data and formulas that are not provided with the Excel program, you can create your own form and save the workbook as a template. When the file is saved as a template, it automatically saves to the Templates directory of Microsoft Office 95. Once the file is in that directory, you can move the file to the Spreadsheet Solutions folder to be able to view your template in the New dialog box as illustrated in the last exercise.

■ It is advisable to save a template file as a read-only file so that the format cannot be accidentally changed or overwritten.
  - ✓ *Template files have .XLT filename extensions.*

Arrange Workbooks

■ When working with a number of open files, you may want to use the **Arrange** command on the <u>W</u>indow menu to position the workbook windows automatically so you can easily select one or the other workbook.

Link Workbooks

■ **Linking workbooks** allows you to consolidate and merge data from several workbooks into one summary workbook. Linking allows the summary workbook to be automatically or manually updated when the linked data changes.

■ The workbooks that provide the data are referred to as **source workbooks**; the workbook that references the data is referred to as the **dependent workbook**. References to cells in other workbooks are called **external references**.

■ By default, links are set to automatic updating. Excel updates links when you open the dependent workbook and also when source data is changed while the dependent workbook is open.

■ Linking differs from combining data (Copy and Paste Special) in that the combining of data merely copies, adds, or subtracts data to the dependent file. Changes in the source workbook are not reflected in the dependent workbook except by repeating the combining procedure.

■ There are three ways to link a file:
  - The copied data from the source workbook may be pasted into the dependent workbook as a *pasted link* which automatically creates an external reference that links the workbooks.
    - ✓ *In this exercise, we will use the Paste Link method.*
  - An external reference may be typed in a formula using the following format: drive:\path\[file.xls]sheetname!reference *EXAMPLES:*

    =c:\excel\[SAM.xls]Sheet1!A1 creates a link to A1 in SAM workbook.

    =sum([sam.xls]Sheet1!A1:D1) + B3 finds sum of A1:D1 in SAM workbook and adds it to contents of B3 in current workbook.
    - ✓ *If the source file is in the same directory, you may omit the path.*
  - An external reference may be included in a formula by selecting cells in the source workbook while editing or creating a formula in the dependent workbook.

- If the cell in an external reference includes a formula, only the formula result will be brought forward.

- When possible, follow these guidelines for saving linked workbooks:

  - Save linked workbooks in the same directory.
  - Save the source workbooks before the dependent workbook.

- An illustration of the linking process appears below.

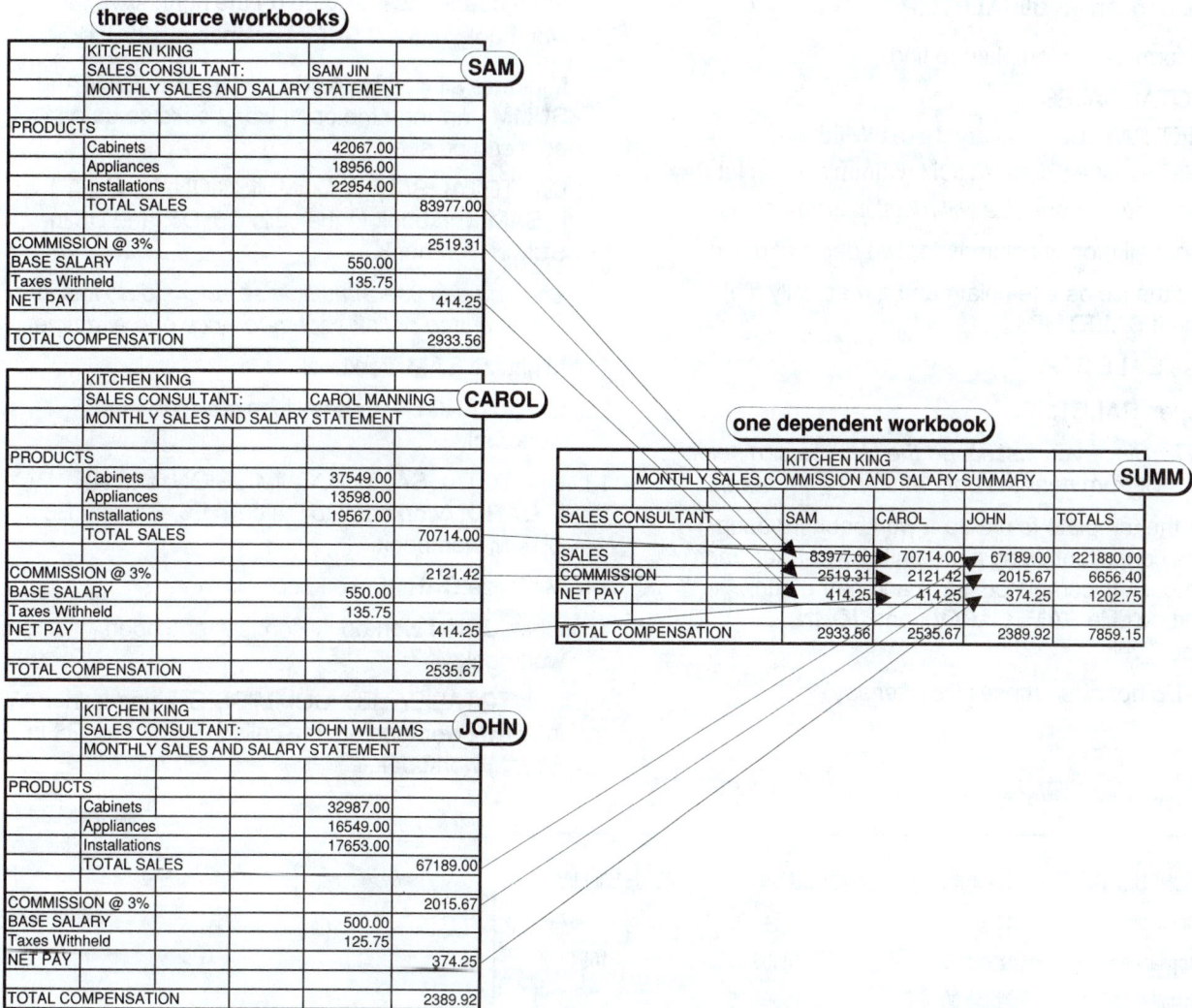

three source workbooks

SAM

KITCHEN KING				
SALES CONSULTANT:		SAM JIN		
MONTHLY SALES AND SALARY STATEMENT				
PRODUCTS				
	Cabinets		42067.00	
	Appliances		18956.00	
	Installations		22954.00	
	TOTAL SALES			83977.00
COMMISSION @ 3%				2519.31
BASE SALARY			550.00	
Taxes Withheld			135.75	
NET PAY				414.25
TOTAL COMPENSATION				2933.56

CAROL

KITCHEN KING				
SALES CONSULTANT:		CAROL MANNING		
MONTHLY SALES AND SALARY STATEMENT				
PRODUCTS				
	Cabinets		37549.00	
	Appliances		13598.00	
	Installations		19567.00	
	TOTAL SALES			70714.00
COMMISSION @ 3%				2121.42
BASE SALARY			550.00	
Taxes Withheld			135.75	
NET PAY				414.25
TOTAL COMPENSATION				2535.67

JOHN

KITCHEN KING				
SALES CONSULTANT:		JOHN WILLIAMS		
MONTHLY SALES AND SALARY STATEMENT				
PRODUCTS				
	Cabinets		32987.00	
	Appliances		16549.00	
	Installations		17653.00	
	TOTAL SALES			67189.00
COMMISSION @ 3%				2015.67
BASE SALARY			500.00	
Taxes Withheld			125.75	
NET PAY				374.25
TOTAL COMPENSATION				2389.92

one dependent workbook

SUMM

KITCHEN KING				
MONTHLY SALES, COMMISSION AND SALARY SUMMARY				
SALES CONSULTANT	SAM	CAROL	JOHN	TOTALS
SALES	83977.00	70714.00	67189.00	221880.00
COMMISSION	2519.31	2121.42	2015.67	6656.40
NET PAY	414.25	414.25	374.25	1202.75
TOTAL COMPENSATION	2933.56	2535.67	2389.92	7859.15

In this exercise, the Kitchen King Company creates a monthly sales and salary statement for each sales consultant. They would like a summary workbook consolidating the information about the consultants' sales performance. Using the Linking feature, the data on the consolidated workbook will automatically update monthly as the consultant data changes.

EXERCISE DIRECTIONS:

1. Create template workbook A, as indicated on the right, or open 💾 **39SALETMP**.

2. Add formulas to template to find:
   - TOTAL SALES
   - NET PAY (Base Salary-Taxes Withheld)
   - TOTAL COMPENSATION (Commission+Net Pay)
     - ✓ Note: Formulas will result in zero values.

3. Format all money columns for two decimal places.

4. Save the file as a template and a read-only file; name it **SALETMP**.

5. Close **SALETMP**.

6. Reopen **SALETMP**.

   HINT: Since you just saved the file, you can select it from near the bottom of the **File** menu.

7. Use the template to create a workbook for each sales consultant using the data below. After each workbook is completed, save and name each workbook file **SAM**, **CAROL**, and **JOHN**, respectively.

   - ✓ Do not close these files after saving.

8. Open a new workbook and create workbook B (dependent), as indicated on the right; save the workbook; name it **SUMM** or open 💾 **39SUMM**.

9. Minimize all workbook windows except **SAM** and **SUMM**; arrange the open workbooks so data in both can be seen.

10. Link TOTAL SALES, COMMISSION, and NET PAY in SAM workbook to the cells D6, D7, and D8 in **SUMM** workbook.

    - ✓ You can use a multiple selection to do this in one step or link each reference one at a time.

11. Minimize **SAM** workbook.

12. Open **CAROL** workbook icon; arrange open workbooks.

13. Link TOTAL SALES, COMMISSION, and NET PAY in **CAROL** workbook to the cells E6, E7, and E8 in **SUMM** workbook.

14. Minimize **CAROL** workbook.

15. Open **JOHN** workbook icon; arrange open workbooks.

16. Link TOTAL SALES, COMMISSION, and NET PAY in **JOHN** workbook to the cells G6, G7, and G8 in **SUMM** workbook.

CONSULTANT:	SAM JIN	CAROL MANNING	JOHN WILLIAMS
Cabinets	42067.00	37549.00	32987.00
Appliances	18956.00	13598.00	16549.00
Installations	22954.00	19567.00	17653.00
BASE SALARY	550.00	550.00	500.00
Taxes Withheld	135.75	135.75	125.75

17. Find all totals in **SUMM** workbook.

18. Save the **SUMM** workbook.

19. Print one copy of **SUMM** workbook.

20. Minimize all windows except **SAM** and **SUMM** so they are both visible.

21. Select **SAM** workbook and change his cabinet sales to $52067.

22. Note the updated values in the **SAM** column of the SUMM workbook and the updated totals.

23. Close all workbook files, *without* resaving.

	A	B	C	D	E	F
1		KITCHEN KING				
2		SALES CONSULTANT:				
3		MONTHLY SALES AND SALARY STATEMENT				
4						
5	PRODUCTS					
6		Cabinets				
7		Appliances				
8		Installations				
9		TOTAL SALES				0
10						
11	COMMISSION @ 3%					0
12	BASE SALARY					
13	Taxes Withheld					
14	NET PAY					0
15						
16	TOTAL COMPENSATION					0
17						
18		Workbook A -- source template file				
19						

	A	B	C	D	E	F	G
1				KITCHEN KING			
2		MONTHLY SALES,COMMISSION AND SALARY SUMMARY					
3							
4	SALES CONSULTANT			SAM	CAROL	JOHN	TOTALS
5							
6	SALES						
7	COMMISSION						
8	NET PAY						
9							
10	TOTAL COMPENSATION						
11							
12		Workbook B -- dependent file					

CREATE A TEMPLATE WORKBOOK

Saves and names the active workbook as a template file.

1. Click **File** menu .... `Alt`+`F`
2. Click **Save As** .... `A`
3. Click **Save File as Type** .... `Alt`+`T`
4. Select **Template** file type ..... `↑↓`, `↵`
5. Double-click in **File Name** ... `Alt`+`N`
6. Type filename .... *filename*
7. Click `Save` .... `↵`

ARRANGE WORKBOOK WINDOWS

1. Click **Window** menu .... `Alt`+`W`
2. Click **Arrange** .... `A`
3. Select desired **Arrange** option:
   - **Tiled** .... `T`
   - **Horizontal** .... `O`
   - **Vertical** .... `V`
   - **Cascade** .... `C`
4. Click `OK` .... `↵`

LINK WORKBOOKS USING PASTE LINK

1. Open workbooks to link.
2. Arrange workspace so both workbooks are in view.
3. Select cell(s) to reference in source workbook.
4. Click **Edit** menu .... `Alt`+`E`
5. Click **Copy** .... `C`
6. Select cell(s) to receive reference(s) in dependent workbook.
   - ✓ *If referencing more than one cell, select upper-left cell in paste cell range.*
7. Click **Edit** menu .... `Alt`+`E`
8. Click **Paste Special** .... `S`
9. Click `Paste Link` .... `Alt`+`L`
10. Press **Escape** .... `Esc` to end procedure.

SAVE FILE AS A TEMPLATE WITH READ-ONLY RECOMMENDATION

1. Click **File** menu .... `Alt`+`F`
2. Click **Save As** .... `A`
3. Click **Save File as Type** .... `Alt`+`T`
4. Select **Template** file type .... `↑↓`, `↵`
5. Double-click in **File Name** ... `Alt`+`N`
6. Type filename .... *filename*
7. Click `Options...` .... `Alt`+`O`
8. Click ☐ **Read-Only Recommended** .... `Alt`+`R`
9. Click `OK` .... `↵`
10. Click `Save` .... `↵`

EXERCISE

40

■ **Workbook Sheets** ■ **3-D Formulas** ■ **Duplicate Workbook Window**
■ **Arrange Workbooks** ■ **Select Workbook** ■ **Print Workbook**
■ **Print Worksheet on Specified Number of Pages**

NOTES:

3-D Formulas

■ A **3-D formula** uses references to values in any sheet or in a range of sheets in a workbook. This type of formula is useful, for example, if you want to summarize a group of similar worksheets on a Totals sheet. The 3-D formulas would be placed on the Totals sheet to summarize all the values in the detail sheets in that workbook.

■ In a 3-D reference:

  • Exclamation points (**!**) separate a sheet name from a cell reference.

    For example, Sheet3!A2 refers to cell A2 on Sheet 3.

  • Colons (**:**) between worksheet names indicate a range of worksheets. Use quotation marks if the worksheet name contains a space. For example, Sheet3:Sheet5!A1:D1 refers to cells A1 to D1 on Sheet3 through Sheet5.

  • Functions can be combined with 3-D references to create a formula that refers to data on different sheets. You can type a 3-D reference in a formula, or you can insert it by selecting the cells in the worksheet you wish to reference while typing or editing a formula.

    Note the examples that follow:
    =SUM(Sheet1:Sheet3!A1)

    Totals the values in A1 from Sheets 1 to 3.

    =AVERAGE(Sheet3:Sheet5!A1:D4)

    Averages the values in A1:D4 from Sheets 3 to 5.

    =Sheet1!A1+Sheet2!A1

    Adds the values from A1 on Sheets 1 and 2

    ="March Sales"!A5+"April Sales"!A5

    Adds the values from A5 on the March and April Sales sheets.

• When a formula with a 3-D reference is copied, the cell references will change relative to the new location, but the sheet names will remain constant.

Workbook Sheets

■ You can use the sheet tabs or the menu to **copy sheets** and the data they contain. You should copy a sheet when you need to create multiple sheets that contain similar or identical data arrangements.

Duplicate Workbook Window

■ You can create **duplicate workbook windows** of the active workbook to view more than one worksheet at a time.

Consider the following when working with duplicate workbook windows:

• Excel places the new workbook window in front of the active workbook window.

  NOTE: If the active workbook is maximized, you will not be able to see the new workbook.

• Duplicate workbook windows are indicated in the title bar which shows the workbook name followed by a colon and a number. For example, BOOK1:1.

• Your system memory determines the number of duplicate windows you can open.

• Closing a duplicate window will not close the workbook.

• You can add or edit data in the original or duplicate window.

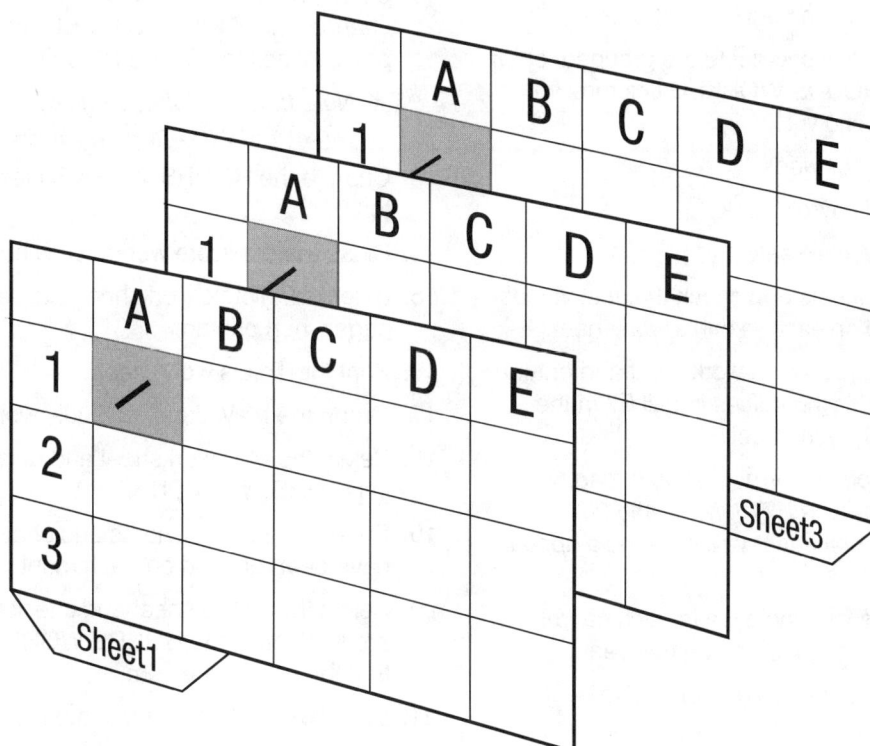

EXAMPLE: Using 3-D references to add the valucs in A1 in a range of sheets.
=SUM(**Sheet1:Sheet3!A1**) or
=**Sheet1!A1+Sheet2!A2+Sheet3!A3**

> *In this exercise, you will recall the SALNEW payroll file and add a new worksheet (Totals) to it. In the new worksheet you will enter formulas containing 3-D references to the May, June, and July worksheets. Finally, you will open a duplicate workbook window so you can view the Totals worksheet while you change test values in the May worksheet.*

EXERCISE DIRECTIONS:

1. Open 💾 **SALNEW** or 🖬 **40SALNEW.XLS**.

2. Copy the July sheet.

3. Rename July (2) sheet; name it **Totals**.

4. Move the Totals tab to the right of July.

5. Group the May, June, and July worksheets.

6. Select May and while worksheets are grouped, enter test values in the HOURS WORKED columns for each employee as shown:

10	for first payroll week
20	for second payroll week
30	for third payroll week

7. Deselect grouped sheets and check that test values have been entered on each month's worksheet.

8. Select cell E7 in the TOTALS worksheet and enter a 3-D formula that adds the values in cell E7 in the May, June, and July worksheet.

   HINT: *The completed formula should read: =May!E7+June!E7+July!E7 and 30 (the sum of the test values) should appear in the cell.*

9. Repeat step 8 for each employee in each payroll week or copy the formula to each employee.

   ✓   *The formula may be copied from E7 to each employee.*

10. Open a duplicate workbook window and select the Totals worksheet in the duplicate window.

11. Arrange workbook windows so data in both workbook windows is in view.

12. Select the May worksheet in the original window and change the HOURS WORKED test values in the first payroll week to 50 for each employee.

    ✓   *Note that the Totals worksheet in the duplicate window shows updated values.*

13. Change the HOURS WORKED test values back to 10.

14. Close the duplicate workbook window.

15. Select the Totals worksheet and set it to fit on one page when printed.

16. Print the Totals worksheet.

17. Group the May, June, and July worksheets.

18. Select the May worksheet and delete all test values in HOURS WORKED.

19. Deselect grouped sheets and check that test values have been deleted on each month's worksheet.

20. Select the Totals sheet and check that the formulas are in place in the HOURS WORKED column and that the values are zero.

21. Save **SALNEW** as a template file.

22. Close the workbook file.

COPY SHEETS WITHIN A WORKBOOK

✓ *Excel will rename sheets that you copy.*

Copy One Sheet by Dragging

- Press **Ctrl** and drag......... ⧫ Sheet # ⧸
  sheet tab to copy to desired
  sheet tab position.

  *Pointer becomes a ⬚ and black
  triangle indicates point of insertion.*

Copy Multiple Sheets by Dragging

1. Select sheets to copy.

2. Press **Ctrl** and drag selected sheet
   tabs to desired sheet tab position.

   *Pointer becomes a ⬚, and black
   triangle indicates point of insertion.*

Copy Sheets Using the Menu

1. Select sheets to copy.

2. Click **E**dit menu .... Alt + E

3. Click **M**ove or Copy Sheet .. Alt + M

4. Select location in **Before Sheet** ... ▲▼
   list to insert copied sheet.

5. Click **C**reate a Copy .... Alt + C

6. Click OK .... ↵

INSERT 3-D REFERENCE IN FORMULA

Using the mouse to select references.

1. Type initial part of formula.

2. Select sheet containing cell(s) to
   reference.

   *NOTE: When you click a sheet tab, its
   name appears in the formula
   bar.*

3. Select cell(s) to reference.

   *NOTE: When you select the cell(s), the
   complete 3-D reference
   appears in the formula bar.*

To reference a range of sheets:

- Press **Shift** and click the last
  worksheet tab to reference.

4. Type or insert remaining parts of
   formula or repeat steps 2 and 3, if
   necessary.

5. Press **Enter** .... ↵

*NOTE: When you press Enter, Excel returns
to the starting worksheet.*

TYPE A 3-D REFERENCE IN FORMULA

1. Type initial part of formula.

2. Place insertion point in formula where
   reference will be typed.

3. Type the sheet name.......... *sheetname*

   ✓ *If the sheet name contains a space,
   type single or double quotes before
   and after the sheet name.*

To type a 3-D reference for a range of worksheets:

a. Press **colon (:)**........................ :

b. Type last sheet name .. *sheet name*
   in range.

4. Press **exclamation (!)**.................. !

5. Type cell reference
   or range................................*reference*

   *EXAMPLES: Sheet1:Sheet5!A1:A5'
   'Total Sales'!A1:A5*

OPEN A DUPLICATE WORKBOOK WINDOW

*Creates a new window for active workbook
window.*

1. Click **W**indow menu............. Alt + W

2. Click **N**ew Window .... N

CLOSE A DUPLICATE WORKBOOK WINDOW

- Double-click workbook window
  control menu box........................ ▦

OR

1. Select duplicate workbook .. Ctrl + Tab

2. Press **Alt + F4** .... Alt + F4

EXERCISE

Summary

41

In this exercise, the Main Street Bakery wants to use their basic Muffin recipe to create low-fat and pumpkin muffins. They also wish to use the format to create a new workbook template for a Basic Sweet Dough Recipe. To accomplish this task, the basic muffin recipe must be revised and then saved as a template so the baker can use it to create other sweet bread recipes.

EXERCISE DIRECTIONS:

1. Open ⌨ **MUFFIN** or 💾 **41MUFFIN.XLS.**

2. Rename Sheet1; name it Basic.

3. Copy the Basic sheet twice immediately to the right of the Basic sheet.

4. Rename the new sheets Low Fat and Low Fat Pumpkin.

5. Delete all sheets except Basic, Low Fat and Low Fat Pumpkin.

6. On the Low Fat sheet, change the title to read:
   LOW FAT MUFFIN RECIPE

7. On the Low Fat Pumpkin sheet change title to read:
   LOW FAT PUMPKIN MUFFIN RECIPE

8. Select (group) the Low Fat and Low Fat Pumpkin sheets, then use the Replace feature to change the following ingredients in the selected sheets:

Replace:	With:
milk	skim milk
vegetable oil	apple sauce
egg	egg white

9. Select (group) all sheets and make the following replacements:

Replace:	With:
MEAS.	MEASUREMENT
tbl.	tablespoon
tsp.	teaspoon
AMT	AMOUNT

10. Adjust column widths to fit the longest entry where appropriate.

11. Ungroup the sheets, then make the following changes or additions to the Low Fat Pumpkin Recipe:

    - Change the skim milk amount to ½ cup.
    - Add ¾ cup pumpkin, canned.
    - Add ¼ teaspoon nutmeg.
    - Add 2 tablespoons walnut pieces.

12. Format the added whole number (2) as a fraction.

13. Copy NEW AMOUNT formula to added ingredients to complete the recipe.

14. Change the DESIRED YIELD value to 36 in all recipes.

15. Save the workbook; or save as **MUFFIN.**

16. Print one copy of the workbook.

17. Delete the Low Fat and Low Fat Pumpkin sheets.

18. Delete the data in the AMOUNT, MEASUREMENT, and INGREDIENTS columns.

    ✓ *The formulas in the NEW AMOUNT column will show zeros.*

19. Change the title to read BASIC SWEET DOUGH RECIPE.
    Add amounts and ingredients to the sweet dough recipe as follows:

AMOUNT	MEASUREMENT	INGREDIENTS
¼	ounce	yeast, dry
¼	cup	water (105-115 degrees)
3	large	eggs
½	cup	sweet butter, melted
½	cup	sour cream
½	cup	sugar
1 ½	teaspoon	SALT
1	teaspoon	vanilla
4 ½	cups	flour

20. Delete formulas (cells showing zeros) that do not have ingredients.

21. Change the YIELD for the recipe to 2 loaves.

22. Change the DESIRED YIELD to 10.

23. Spell check the worksheet.

24. Save the workbook as a template; name it **BREAD.**

25. Print one copy of the template.

26. Close all workbooks.

EXERCISE
Summary

42

Ms. McConnell administered three additional exams plus a final examination to her class. She needs to revise the worksheet she prepared earlier to include new test data and two new students. In addition, Ms. McConnell's supervisor has requested a separate worksheet showing student names and final exam averages.

EXERCISE DIRECTIONS:

✓ *Freeze row labels to facilitate data entry.*

1. Open ⌨ **TEST** or 💾 **42TEST**.

2. Insert rows in alphabetical sequence for the following two new students: Einhorn, J., ID# 211 and Hawthorne, M., ID# 212.

3. Insert the columns of data, as shown on the right, for TESTS 4, 5, and 6 after the TEST 3 column.

4. Edit the NO. TESTS TAKEN and TEST AVERAGE columns to include the new test data.

5. Enter the FINAL EXAM grades after the TEST AVERAGE column:

   Aaronson, 72; Barnett, 85; Costello, 86; Dionesios, 70; Einhorn, 69; Ellenberg, 65; Fallstaff, 91; Garcia, 71; Hamway, 89; Hawthorne, 71; Ianelli, 61; Jae Woo, 80; Kelly, 96

6. Find the FINAL AVERAGE for each student. The final exam is worth 1/3 of the final average, while the tests are worth 2/3 of the final average.

   HINT: (FINAL EXAM+TEST AVERAGE+TEST AVERAGE)/3

7. Format test averages to one decimal place and center new titles.

8. Complete the worksheet.

9. Save the workbook file, or *save as* **TEST**.

10. Using the Copy and Paste Special feature, create a separate workbook with student names in column A and Final Average data in column C.

11. Enter a three line title:

    FINAL AVERAGES

    BUSINESS MARKETING 101

    MS. ANN MC CONNELL

12. Save the new file; name it **TESTSUM**.

13. Switch to the **TEST** worksheet. Print one copy of **TEST**.

14. Close the workbook files.

	A	F	G	H
5	STUDENT NAME	TEST 4	TEST 5	TEST 6
6	Aaronson, M.	75		69
7	Barnett, F.	85	79	82
8	Costello, A.	83	84	76
9	Dionesios, A.	76	74	78
10	Einhorn, J.	52	61	70
11	Ellenberg, L.		69	52
12	Falstaff, S.	84	88	
13	Garcia, H.	72		80
14	Hamway, R.	82	85	81
15	Hawthorne, M.	41	59	57
16	Ianelli, J.	72	76	79
17	Jae Woo, K.		84	73
18	Kelly, G.	91	94	84
19				
20	NO. OF PAPERS			
21	CLASS AVERAGE			
22	HIGHEST GRADE			
23	LOWEST GRADE			
24				

NEXT LESSON

LESSON 7

ADVANCED FEATURES AND FUNCTIONS

Exercises 43-53

- Insert IF Functions
- Print Compressed Worksheet
- Auditing
- Enter a Date as Numerical Data
- Format Numerical Dates
- AutoFormat
- Color Buttons
- Insert Lookup Functions
- Copy/Paste Special
- Protect a Sheet
- Lock Cells in a Worksheet
- Hide Data
- Non-Consecutive References in a Function

EXCEL

EXERCISE

Insert an IF Function

43

NOTES:

- An **IF statement** is a logical function which sets up a conditional statement to test data. The truth or falsity of the condition will determine the results of the statement.

- The format for an IF statement is:

  =IF(CONDITION,X,Y)

  If the condition is true, the function results in X; if the condition is false, the function results in Y.

- In this exercise, the teacher uses an IF statement to determine the final grade based on the final average. The passing grade is 71. Therefore, an IF statement can be used to test whether the final average is greater than 70.9. If the condition is true that the average is greater than 70.9, the student passes and the word PASS is entered in the function location. If the condition is false, the word FAIL is entered in the function location.

Note the analysis of one of the IF statement formulas used in this problem:

function	then	otherwise

=IF(C8>70.9,"PASS","FAIL")

condition	If true,	If false,
(Is grade	"PASS"	"FAIL"
greater	will be	will be
than	entered	entered
70.9?)	in cell.	in cell.

NOTE: Since PASS and FAIL are labels, you must enclose them in quotation marks (").

- In the condition section of the function, IF statements may use the following conditional operators:

=	Equals	<=	Less than or equal to
>	Greater than	>=	Greater than or equal to
<	Less than	&	Used for linking text
<>	Not equal to		

NOTE: IF statements may be used in combination with OR, AND, and NOT statements to evaluate complex conditions.

- The IF function may be typed or entered using the Function Wizard.

In this exercise, you will calculate the FINAL GRADE and CREDITS GRANTED for Ann McConnell's class based on a 71% passing grade by using IF statements.

EXERCISE DIRECTIONS:

1. Create the worksheet on the right ⌨ or open 💾 **43TESTSM.XLS**.

2. Insert the following columns after FINAL AVERAGES:

FINAL	CREDITS
GRADE	GRANTED

3. Enter an IF statement for the first student in the FINAL GRADE column that will produce the word PASS if the final average is greater than 70.9, and FAIL if it is not.

4. Copy the formula to the other students.

5. Enter an IF statement for the first student in the CREDITS GRANTED column that will produce the number three, for three credits, if the final average is greater than 70.9, and zero if it is not.

6. Copy the formula to the other students.

7. Center all new entries.

8. Delete the row containing Number of Papers.

9. Save the workbook file; name it **TESTSUM**.

10. Print one copy of the worksheet.

11. Close the workbook file.

	A	B	C	D	E	F
1			FINAL AVERAGES			
2			BUSINESS MARKETING 101			
3			MS. ANN MC CONNELL			
4						
5			FINAL	*FINAL*	*CREDITS*	
6	STUDENT		AVERAGE	*GRADE*	*GRANTED*	
7	Aaronson, M.		77.1			
8	Barnett, F.		82.3			
9	Costello, A.		80.8			
10	Dionesios, A.		76.1			
11	Einhorn, J.		63.7			
12	Ellenberg, L.		68.9			
13	Falstaff, S.		87.4			
14	Garcia, H.		77.4			
15	Hamway, R.		83.3			
16	Hawthorne, M.		58.6			
17	Ianelli, J.		73.0			
18	Jae Woo, K.		77.8	▼	▼	
19	Kelly, G.		90.6			
20						
21	NO. OF PAPERS					
22	CLASS AVERAGE		76.7			
23	HIGHEST GRADE		91			
24	LOWEST GRADE		59			

INSERT AN IF FUNCTION USING FUNCTION WIZARD

NOTE: You can also type a function to insert it.

1. Click cell.................................. 🔢
   to receive function.

2. Click **Function Wizard** button .... *fx*
   on Standard Toolbar.

3. Select **Logical**.............................. 📈
   in **Function Category** list.

4. Select **IF**
   function...................... Alt + N , 📈
   in **Function Name** list.

5. Click [Next >].............................. ↵

6. Type condition...................... *condition*
   in **logical test** box.
   NOTE: You can click cells in worksheet to insert cell references.

7. Click **value_if_true** box .... [Tab]

8. Type the argument ....*argument*
   if condition is true.

9. Click **value_if_false** box............... [Tab]

10. Type the argument ....*argument*
    if condition is false.

11. Click [Finish]...........................↵

INSERT IF FUNCTION USING KEYBOARD AND MOUSE

1. Click cell to receive function........ 🔢

2. Type =**IF** .... 🔢

3. Press **(** (open parenthesis) .... (

4. Type condition...................... *condition*

5. Press **,** (comma) .... ,

6. Type action if condition
   is true ....*true action*

7. Press **,** (comma) .... ,

8. Type action if condition
   is false............................... *false action*

9. Press **)** (close parenthesis) ....)

10. Press **Enter** .... ↵

EXERCISE

■ IF Function ■ Print Compressed Worksheet

NOTES:

IF Function

■ An IF statement may be created to perform one calculation if the condition is true, and perform another calculation if the condition is false.

■ When creating a condition using the **greater than** operator (>), care must be taken to use the correct value. In this problem, when testing if the sales are over $500,000, it is necessary to use >499,999 or >=500,000 in the formula so that a value of 500,000 is interpreted as a true condition.

Print Compressed Worksheet

■ The Page Setup, Scaling option is used to print a worksheet larger or smaller than its actual size. Note the illustration of the scaling option in the Page Setup dialog box below:

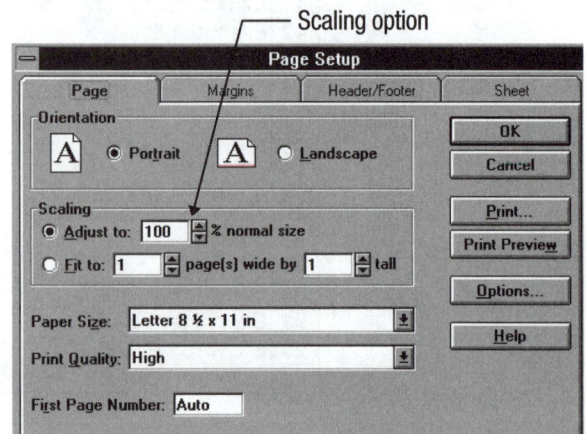

> In this exercise, you will find the commission on sales for sales personnel working at Smiling Sammy's Cars. Sammy will give a .5% (half of one percent) bonus to agents who exceed $500,000 in sales.

EXERCISE DIRECTIONS:

1. Create the worksheet on the right ⌨ or open 💾 **44CAR.XLS.** Set column widths for A-C to AutoFit.

2. Find COMM. (commission).

3. Copy the formula to the remaining employees.

4. Using an IF statement, find the BONUS for those agents who exceed $500,000 in sales.

    HINT: If SALES are greater than or equal to $500,000, compute a .5% bonus on SALES; otherwise, enter zero.

5. Find TOTAL COMPENSATION.

6. Copy the formula to the remaining employees.

7. Format all money columns for currency with no decimal places.

8. Total all money columns.

9. Set column widths, as necessary.

10. Save the workbook file; name it **CAR**.

11. Print one copy compressed to 50% of its actual size.

12. Close the workbook file.

	A	B	C	D	E	F	G	H
1			SMILING SAMMY'S CARS					
2			COMMISSION REPORT FOR SALES PERSONNEL					
3								
4				COMM.			TOTAL	
5	NAME	LOCATION	SALES	RATE	COMM.	BONUS	COMPENSATION	
6								
7	R. BUICK	ELMHURST	640000	4.00%				
8	M. CADDY	JAMAICA	450000	3.00%				
9	J. DODGE	ELMHURST	125000	3.00%				
10	O. FORD	JAMAICA	745000	4.00%				
11	W. HONDA	MASPETH	0	3.00%				
12	V. JAGUAR	ELMHURST	550000	4.00%				
13	A. LEXUS	JAMAICA	210000	3.00%				
14	E. LINCOLN	MASPETH	435000	4.00%	▼	▼	▼	
15	B. NISSAN	MASPETH	745000	4.00%				
16								
17	TOTALS		▶		▶	▶	▶	
18								

CHANGE SCALE OF PRINTED DATA

1. Click **File** menu .... `Alt`+`F`
2. Click **Page Setup** .... `U`
3. Click **Page** tab .... `Ctrl`+`Tab`

To reduce or enlarge data on printed sheet:

a. Double–click [☐] **%**
   normal size .... `Alt`+`A`

b. Type percentage (10-400) ..*number*

NOTE: *You can also click the increment box arrows to select a percentage.*

4. Click [OK] .... `↵`

Excel ■ Lesson 7 ■ Exercise 44   149

EXERCISE
■ IF Function ■ Audit Formulas

45

NOTES:

Audit Formulas

- If you are using a worksheet created by another person or if you have an error in a formula, you may wish to audit or trace the formulas. When the Auditing feature is selected on the Tools menu, a list of options appears along with the option to Show the Auditing Toolbar. The toolbar, as shown below, contains icons to trace the **precedents** or **dependents** of a cell in a formula.

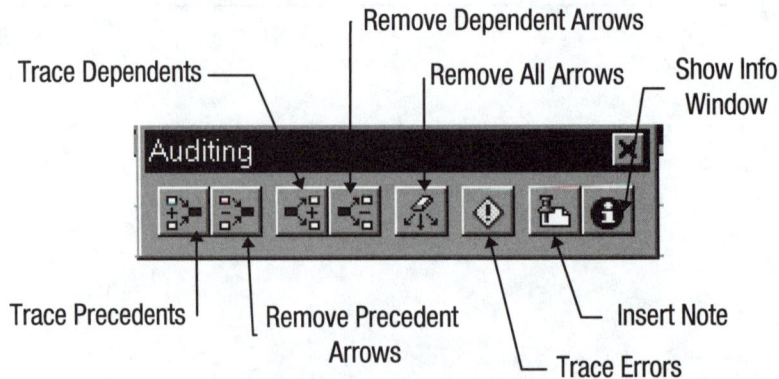

AUDITING TOOLBAR

- The **precedents** are the cells that are referred to by the formula in the cell you wish to audit. For example, if you select a formula cell and click Trace Precedents, arrows will appear showing the cells used in the formula.

- The **dependents** are the cells that contain formulas that refer to the cell you wish to audit. For example, if you select a cell that is used in a formula and click Trace Dependents, arrows will appear showing the cell with the formula that refers to the active cell.

- In order for the Trace Error icon to work, an error message must be displayed.

- The Attach Note button provides another way to access the Cell Notes feature discussed in an earlier exercise. The Info Window for the formula will display the cell address, formula, and cell note.

The Martinson Manufacturing Company has decided to change its policy and give salary increases based on seniority. Employees who have more than five years of service will receive a 7.25% raise; otherwise, they will receive a 4.5% raise.

You will do a salary analysis by comparing the amount of SALARY and % INCREASE each employee received this year over last year and then compute the new raise and salary. Auditing will be used to check formulas.

EXERCISE DIRECTIONS:

1. Create the worksheet on the right exactly as shown or open 💾 **45INCR.XLS.**

2. Freeze titles vertically at column E.

3. Find:
   - RAISE 1996 (from 1995 to 1996)
   - 1996% INCREASE (based on 1995 salary)

4. Copy the formula to the remaining employees.

5. Using YEARS OF SENIORITY as a condition, create an IF statement to enter the percent of the raise (7.25% or 4.5%) in the 1997% INCREASE column.

   HINT: If YEARS OF SENIORITY is greater than five, .0725; otherwise, .045.

6. Find RAISE 1997 by using the 1997% INCREASE and SALARY 1996.

7. Format all money columns for two decimal places and all percent columns for two-place percents.

8. Find SALARY 1997.

   HINT: 1996 salary + 1997 raise

9. Copy the formula to the remaining employees.

10. Total all money columns.

11. Set column widths, as necessary.

12. Clear the freeze.

13. Select Tools, Auditing and show the Auditing Toolbar.

14. Select the Raise 1996 formula in F8 and Trace Precedents.

    NOTE: Arrows to the cells referenced in the formula display.

15. Remove the precedents arrows.

16. Select the Salary 1996 figure in E8 and Trace Dependents.

    NOTE: Arrows to the formula cells that use E8 display.

17. Remove the dependents arrows.

18. Select several other formula or data locations and trace precedents or dependents.

19. Remove all arrows.

20. Select the Raise 1997 formula in I8 and attach the following note:

    Raise is computed at 7.25% for employees with more than five years of service.

    Employees with less than five years receive a 4.5% raise.

21. Click the Show Info Window icon and view the Cell I8 Info Window.

22. Use the Windows menu to return to the worksheet.

23. Save the file; name it **INCR.**

24. Print one copy to fit on a page.

25. Close the file.

	A	B	C	D	E	F	G	H	I	J
1				MARTINSON MANUFACTURING COMPANY						
2				ANALYSIS OF SALARY INCREASES						
3										
4										
5			YEARS OF	SALARY	SALARY	RAISE	1996 %	1997 %	RAISE	SALARY
6	EMPLOYEE		SENIORITY	1995	1996	1996	INCREASE	INCREASE	1997	1997
7										
8	Miller, John		15	45500.00	49000.00					
9	Vantnor, Link		11	32300.00	35000.00					
10	Barrow, Wilson		5	16500.00	17500.00					
11	Abrahams, Larry		3	18500.00	20000.00					
12	Nunex, Maria		7	21000.00	23000.00					
13	Tse, Sandra		4	25600.00	27000.00					
14	D'Agostino, Joe		8	28500.00	30000.00					
15	Harrison, Reggie		9	33000.00	35000.00					
16	Wingate, George		6	25400.00	27000.00	▼	▼	▼	▼	▼
17	Ingold, Terry		10	38000.00	41500.00					
18										
19	TOTALS				▶	▶			▶	▶

AUDIT WORKSHEET

These audit tools can be used to debug worksheet formulas. Tracer arrows are not saved with the workbook.

SHOW AUDITING TOOLBAR

1. Click **Tools** menu .... `Alt`+`T`
2. Click **Auditing** .... `T`
3. Click **Show Auditing** Toolbar........ `S`

TRACE DEPENDENT FORMULAS

1. Select cell containing data used by a formula.
2. Click **Trace Dependents**
    button..
    on Auditing Toolbar.

    NOTE: If tracer arrows do not appear, deselect the Hide All option on the View sheet in the Tools, Options dialog box.

REMOVE DEPENDENT TRACER ARROWS

1. Select cell containing data used by a formula.
2. Click **Remove Dependent**
    Arrows button............................
    on Auditing Toolbar.

TRACE PRECEDENT DATA AND FORMULAS

1. Select cell containing formula.
2. Click **Trace Precedents**
    button ....
    on Auditing Toolbar.

REMOVE PRECEDENT TRACER ARROWS

1. Select cell containing formula.
2. Click **Remove Precedent**
    Arrows button............................
    on Auditing Toolbar.

REMOVE ALL TRACER ARROWS

•   Click **Remove All Arrows**
    button ....
    on Auditing Toolbar.

ATTACH NOTE TO A FORMULA

1. Select cell to receive note.
2. Enter **Note in Text Note** box......... *note*
3. Click `OK` ....

SHOW INFO WINDOW

1. Select cell with info window.
2. Click **Show Info Window**
    button ....
    on Auditing Toolbar.

NEXT EXERCISE

EXERCISE

■ Enter Dates as Numerical Data ■ Format Numerical Dates

46

NOTES:

Enter Dates as Numerical Data

- Excel recognizes the number format you desire based on your data entry. For example, if you enter 25%, the entry is recognized as a value with a percent format. Similarly, if you enter 12/24/97 without a label prefix, the entry is recognized as numerical data in date format.

- Dates can be entered as label data (with a label prefix); but, when there is a need to add or subtract dates, they must be entered as numerical data (without a label prefix).

- Dates entered in one of the standard formats are automatically recognized as dates and assigned a **serial value**. The serial value is the number of days the date represents counting from January 1, 1900. Therefore, 1/1/1900, is given a serial value of 1 and 1/30/1900 is given a serial value of 30.

This system allows you to add or subtract dates and obtain the correct valuation.

- The current date can be entered on any worksheet by pressing Ctrl+; (semicolon).

Format Numerical Dates

- Once you enter a date as a numerical value, you may change the date format by using the **Format, Cells, Number** commands. Illustrated below are the standard date formats that Excel recognizes as numerical date values. Any date entry may be formatted using the formats from this dialog box. To view a serial value for a date, you can format the date as a number. Note the table of examples that shows the format, your entry, what shows on the formula bar and the numerical value of the date.

Your Entry	Formula Bar	Format	Displays	Numerical Value
12/24/00	12/24/1900	Mar-95	Dec-00	359
25-Jul	07/25/95	4-Mar-95	25-Jul-95	34905
7/25/95 6:30	07/25/95 2:30 PM	3/4/95 13:30	7/25/95 14:30	34905
12/24/2000	12/24/2000	March 4, 1995	December 24, 2000	36884

In this exercise, you will make modifications to the stock analysis worksheet prepared earlier to find how many days each stock was held. You will then be able to determine the annual rate of return on each stock. In addition, you will modify the named range, PRINTALL, to include the larger worksheet.

EXERCISE DIRECTIONS:

1. Open ⌨ **MARKET** or open 💾 **46MARKET.XLS**.

2. Edit the title to include the current year.

3. Set column width to ten for DATE BOUGHT and DATE SOLD columns.

4. Edit dates so they are entered as numerical data (remove label prefix and add year, if necessary).

5. Format the dates to D-MMM-YY or 04-Mar-95 format.

6. Insert a column entitled DAYS HELD between DATE SOLD and SELLING PRICE columns.

7. Find DAYS HELD.

   HINT: DATE SOLD-DATE BOUGHT (Format column F to General number format.)

8. Insert a column, entitled ANNUAL YIELD, between DIVIDENDS EARNED and GAIN OR LOSS.

9. Center all column titles.

10. Based on a 365-day year, find the ANNUAL YIELD.

    HINT: ((DIVIDENDS EARNED/COST)/DAYS HELD)*365

11. Format the ANNUAL YIELD for a two-place percent.

12. Copy the formula to the remaining stocks.

13. Edit the named range PRINTALL to include the entire worksheet.

14. Save the file; name it **MARKET**.

15. Print one copy to fit on a page using the range PRINTALL.

16. Close the workbook file.

	A	B	C	D	E	F	G	H	I	J	K	L	M
1				MICHAEL CRAWFORD									
2				STOCK ANALYSIS - TRANSACTIONS FOR 199-									
3													
4	NO. OF	COMPANY		DATE	DATE	DAYS	SELLING		DIVIDENDS	ANNUAL	GAIN OR	% GAIN OR	
5	SHARES	NAME	SYMBOL	BOUGHT	SOLD	HELD	PRICE	COST	EARNED	YIELD	LOSS	LOSS	
6													
7	200	Crystal Motors	CM	15-Jan-96	05-Nov-96		6548.95	7453.76	585.50		-319.31	-4.28%	
8	100	US Brands	USB	30-Jan-96	30-Jun-96		9057.43	6923.12	325.40		2459.71	35.53%	
9	50	IGM	IGM	17-Feb-96	25-Apr-96		3248.95	2576.98	0.00		671.97	26.08%	
10	300	Microgem	MIG	17-Feb-96	05-Dec-96		3954.69	5391.23	0.00		-1436.54	-26.65%	
11	500	Consolidated Gas	CG	28-Mar-96	20-Dec-96		15487.54	14326.54	1054.50		2215.50	15.46%	
12													
13		TOTALS		▶ 10	▶ 10		38297.56	36671.63	1965.40		3591.33	9.79%	
14													
15													
16													
17													

Edit dates so they are entered as numerical dates as shown.

ENTER A DATE AS NUMERICAL DATA

NOTE. Dates, entered as numerical data, are right–aligned and can be calculated.

1. Select cell to receive date.

   To enter current date:

   • Press **Ctrl** + ; (semicolon).................. [Ctrl] + [;]

   To enter a specific date:

   • Type date .... date in valid format.

You may use the following formats:

   • m/d/yy.................... (e.g. 6/24/96)
   • d-mmm.................... (e.g. 24-Jun)
   • d-mmm-yy.........(e.g. 24-Jun-96)
   • mmm-yy.................. (e.g. Jun-96)

2. Press **Enter** .... [↵]

NOTE: If Excel displays number signs (######), the column is not wide enough to display the date. To see the entry, double–click the right border of the column heading.

FORMAT NUMERICAL DATES

1. Select cells containing numerical dates to format.

2. a. Click **Format** menu ...... [Alt] + [O]

   b. Click **Cells** .... [E]

   OR

   a. Right–click any selected cell.

   b. Click **Format Cells**

3. Click **Number** tab ....[Ctrl] + [Tab]

4. Select **Date** .... [Alt] + [C], [↕] in **Category** list.

5. Select desired format .... [↕]

6. Click [OK] .... [↵]

EXERCISE

■ IF Function ■ Numerical Date Formats ■ Numerical Dates
■ AutoFormat ■ Color Buttons

47

NOTES:

AutoFormat

■ Excel provides built-in formats which can be applied to a range of data. These formats, **AutoFormats**, include number formats, fonts, borders, patterns, colors, alignments, row heights, and column widths. They give the worksheet a professional, organized appearance.

■ The AutoFormat dialog box provides a selection of table formats that may be applied to a range of data. (See the illustration below.) Any of the AutoFormats may be customized through the Options dialog box.

Color Buttons

■ The Color buttons on the Formatting Toolbar provide a palette of colors that can be used to color the foreground area or the text in a selected cell. (See the illustration below.)

■ If you do not have a color printer, your AutoFormat or color settings may not print properly.

■ Accounts Receivable are records for customers who owe money to a company. Aging of accounts receivable is done to determine how many days the customers' payments are overdue.

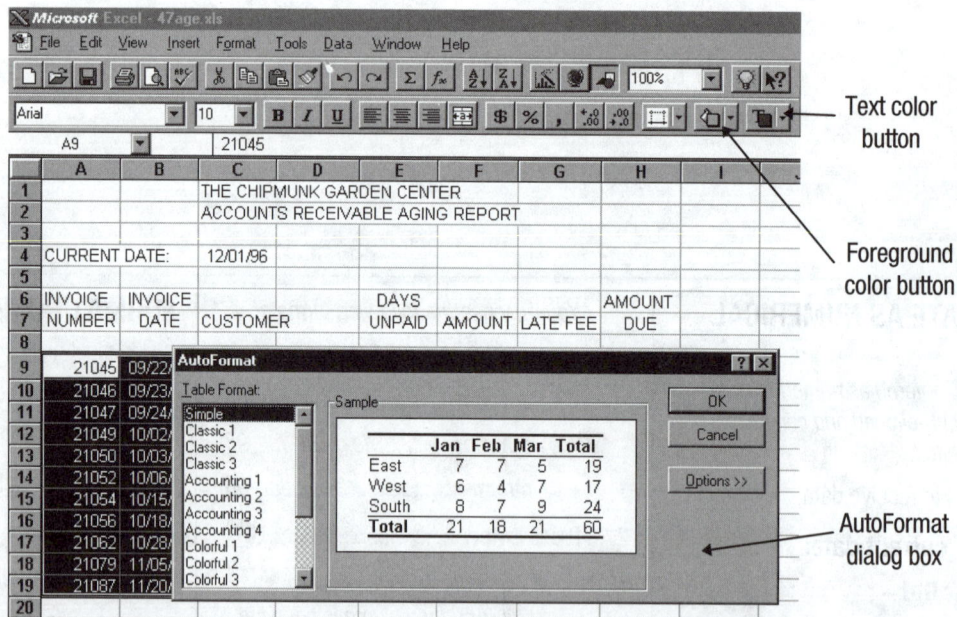

Text color button

Foreground color button

AutoFormat dialog box

In this exercise, your supervisor has asked you to determine how many days, as of today (December 1, 1996), the accounts receivable invoices have been unpaid. In addition, she wants you to calculate a late fee of 1% on unpaid amounts that are outstanding for more than 30 days.

EXERCISE DIRECTIONS:

1. Create the worksheet below, or open 💾 **47AGE**.

2. Find the DAYS UNPAID.

   HINT: DAYS UNPAID = CURRENT DATE-
   INVOICE DATE

   ✓ *The reference to the current date should be an*
   absolute reference.

3. Use an IF statement to find a 1% LATE FEE only if
   the days unpaid are greater than 30.

4. Copy the formula to the remaining invoices.

5. Find AMOUNT DUE and copy to all invoices.

6. Total all money columns. Set money columns to two
   decimal places.

7. Select column D and delete the column to prepare
   for AutoFormat.

   ✓ *As you highlight each table format, an example*
   of the style appears in the Sample box.

8. Select the heading range A1 to H4 and do
   the following:

   • Format the text for bold type.

   • Change the background color to dark navy.

   • Change the text color to white.

9. Save the file; name it **AGE**.

10. Print one copy so that it all fits on one page.

11. Close the workbook file.

	A	B	C	D	E	F	G	H
1			THE CHIPMUNK GARDEN CENTER					
2			ACCOUNTS RECEIVABLE AGING REPORT					
3								
4	CURRENT DATE:		12/01/96					
5								
6	INVOICE	INVOICE			DAYS			AMOUNT
7	NUMBER	DATE	CUSTOMER		UNPAID	AMOUNT	LATE FEE	DUE
8								
9	21045	09/22/96	BROWN BROTHERS			475.43		
10	21046	09/23/96	REDLY FARMS			321.43		
11	21047	09/24/96	BROWN BROTHERS			543.98		
12	21049	10/02/96	PINKSTON CORP.			32.45		
13	21050	10/03/96	J.J. BURGUNDY			1324.32		
14	21052	10/06/96	REDLY FARMS			124.98		
15	21054	10/15/96	BLUETOWN CO.			564.12		
16	21056	10/18/96	PINKSTON CORP.			187.65		
17	21062	10/28/96	J.J. BURGUNDY			454.56		
18	21079	11/05/96	M. MAROON			308.21		
19	21087	11/20/96	REDLY FARMS		▼	163.28	▼	▼
20								
21	TOTALS					▶	▶	
22								

APPLY AUTOFORMAT

1. Select range of data to be formatted.

2. Click **Format** menu .... `Alt`+`O`

3. Click **AutoFormat** .... `A`

4. Select desired format.

5. Click `OK` .... `↵`

APPLY COLOR TO CELL FOREGROUND

1. Select object or range of cells.

2. Click on **Foreground Color** Button
   arrows.

3. Select color.

OR

1. Select object or range of cells.

2. Click **Format** menu .... `Alt`+`O`

3. Click **Cells** .... `E`

4. Select **Patterns** tab .... `Ctrl`+`Tab`

5. Click **Color** .... `Alt`+`C`

6. Select color.

7. Click `OK` .... `↵`

APPLY COLOR TO TEXT

1. Select range of data.

2. Click on **Text Color** Button arrows.

3. Select color.

OR

1. Select object or range of cells.

2. Click **Format** menu .... `Alt`+`O`

3. Click **Cells** .... `E`

4. Select **Font** .... `↹`

5. Click **Color** .... `Alt`+`C`

6. Select color.

7. Click `OK` .... `↵`

EXERCISE

Insert Lookup Functions

48

NOTES:

Insert Lookup Functions

- The **lookup functions** (VLOOKUP and HLOOKUP) select an appropriate value from a table and enter it into a location on the worksheet. For example, the VLOOKUP function may be used to look up taxes on a tax table to create a payroll, or to look up postage rates to complete a bill of sale.

- The table containing the data to be looked up must be created in a blank or empty location on the worksheet. The mortgage payment table below, created in Exercise 27, may be used as the table for a lookup function.

	A	B	C	D	E	F	G	H	I
1			MORTGAGE PAYMENT TABLE AT 9%						
2									
3				TERM IN YEARS					
4			15	20	25	30			
5	PRINCIPAL	100000	1014.27	899.73	839.20	804.62		table range	
6		105000	1064.98	944.71	881.16	844.85		B5:F12	
7		110000	1115.69	989.70	923.12	885.08			
8		115000	1166.41	1034.68	965.08	925.32			
9		120000	1217.12	1079.67	1007.04	965.55			
10		125000	1267.83	1124.66	1049.00	1005.78			
11		130000	1318.55	1169.64	1090.96	1046.01			
12		135000	1369.26	1214.63	1132.92	1086.24			
13		1	2	3	4	5		column positions	
14									

- As with all formulas, the lookup function is entered in the location on the worksheet that requires an answer from a table.

- There are two ways to look up data, depending on the way the data is arranged: **vertically** or **horizontally**.

  - **VLOOKUP** (vertical lookup) looks up data in a particular *column* in the table, while

  - **HLOOKUP** (horizontal lookup) looks up data in a particular *row* in the table.

- The VLOOKUP function uses the following format and contains three arguments (parts), defined below:

  =VLOOKUP(*item,table-range,column-position*)

  - **ITEM** is text, a value, or a cell reference of the item you are looking for (*search item*) and should be in the first column of the VLOOKUP table. Numerical search items should be listed in ascending order.

  - **TABLE-RANGE** is the range reference or range name of the lookup table in which the search is to be made. If the lookup function is to be copied, the range should be expressed as an absolute reference.

  - **COLUMN-POSITION** is the column number in the table from which the matching value should be returned. The far left column has a position number of one; the second column has a position number of two, etc.

  - NOTE: *Column positions are counted from the left column in the range, not from the left column of the worksheet.*

- For example, note the outlined lookup table on the left. To look up the mortgage payment for a mortgage amount of $105,000 for 25 years at 9%, a lookup formula would be created as follows:

  | item | table range | column position |

  =VLOOKUP(105000,B5:F12,4)

- In looking up numeric data, the lookup function returns to the formula location:

  - The value from the table (in this case 881.16), or

  - The largest value less than or equal to the search item.

- If you need to look up more than one item and to copy the lookup formula, the formula should use the cell reference (not the value) as the search item. In addition, the range should be absolute so that the table range remains constant.

EXAMPLE:

$$\text{=VLOOKUP(E6,\$B\$5:\$F\$12,4)}$$

with labels: item, table range, column position

In this exercise, you will retrieve the mortgage table created earlier and create a worksheet for the Mortgage Money Store to calculate the mortgage amount and the customer's monthly mortgage payment for 25 or 30 years. Use the VLOOKUP function to enter mortgage payments depending upon the mortgage amount.

EXERCISE DIRECTIONS:

1. Open ⌨ **TABLE** or open 💾 **48TABLE.XLS**.

   REMINDER: The values in cells B4, B15, and B16 are needed to compute the values in the table. Do not delete or change these values.

2. Create the MORTGAGE MONEY STORE worksheet below MORTGAGE PAYMENT TABLE, as indicated.

3. Center all column titles and set column widths to AutoFit.

4. Find MORTGAGE AMOUNT by subtracting the DOWN PAYMENT from the CONTRACT PRICE.

5. Copy the formula to the remaining customers.

6. Using the VLOOKUP function, find the monthly payment for the first customer (for 25 years) based on the amount to be mortgaged.

   ✓ *Note the outlined range and column position which have been illustrated.*

7. Format the result for two decimal places.

8. Copy the formula to the remaining customers.

9. Using the VLOOKUP function, find the monthly payment for the first customer (for 30 years) based on the amount to be mortgaged.

   ✓ *Note the range and column position illustrated.*

10. Format the result for two decimal places.

11. Copy the formula to the remaining customers.

12. Select the Mortgage Money Store title and column headings. Do the following:

    - Set the color to yellow.
    - Set the font color to black.
    - Bold the text.

13. Save the file; name it **HOME**.

14. Select the MORTGAGE MONEY STORE portion of the worksheet.

15. Print one copy of the selection to fit on one page.

16. Close the workbook file.

	A	B	C	D	E	F	G	H	I
1			MORTGAGE PAYMENT TABLE AT 9%						
2									
3				TERM IN YEARS					
4		1014.27	15	20	25	30	table range		
5	PRINCIPAL	100000	1014.27	899.73	839.20	804.62	B5:F12		
6		105000	1064.98	944.71	881.16	844.85			
7		110000	1115.69	989.70	923.12	885.08			
8		115000	1166.41	1034.68	965.08	925.32			
9		120000	1217.12	1079.67	1007.04	965.55			
10		125000	1267.83	1124.66	1049.00	1005.78			
11		130000	1318.55	1169.64	1090.96	1046.01			
12		135000	1369.26	1214.63	1132.92	1086.24			
13		1	2	3	4	5	column positions		
14	Input cells								
15	column:	100000							
16	row:	15							
17							VLOOKUP functions		
18			MORTGAGE MONEY STORE						
19							MONTHLY	MONTHLY	
20			CONTRACT	DOWN	MORTGAGE		PAYMENT	PAYMENT	
21	CUSTOMER		PRICE	PAYMENT	AMOUNT		25 YEARS	30 YEARS	
22									
23	JACKSON, R.		185000	80000					
24	NELSON, G.		255000	120000					
25	PINCHOT, T.		320000	200000					
26	SANCHEZ, J.		195000	80000					
27	TIMMERMAN, F.		215000	105000					

INSERT A VLOOKUP OR HLOOKUP FUNCTION USING FUNCTION WIZARD

NOTE: *You can also type a function to insert it.*

1. Click cell..................................... ⬚
    to receive function.

2. Click **Function Wizard** button..... *fx*
    on Standard toolbar.

3. Select **Lookup &**
    Reference................. Alt + C , ⬚
    in **Function Category** list.

4. Select **VLOOKUP** or
    HLOOKUP .... Alt + N , ⬚
    in **Function Name** list.

5. Click ⬚ Next > .... ⬚

6. Type item.................................... *item*
    in **lookup-value** box.

    NOTE: *Item can be an actual column*
    item or a reference to a cell
    containing the column item.
    You can click cell in worksheet
    to insert cell reference.

7. Click **table_array** box.................. Tab

8. Type reference .... *reference*
    to table range.

    NOTE: *You can select range in*
    worksheet to insert
    cell references.

9. Click **col_index_num** box............ Tab

10. Type the column
    position .... *column number*

11. Click ⬚ Finish .... ⬚

NEXT EXERCISE

EXERCISE 49

■ Vertical Lookup Function (VLOOKUP) ■ Copy/Paste Special

NOTES:

- In Exercise 48, you created lookup formulas using the cell references of the table range. It is possible to use a named range rather than the cell reference of the table. When you copy a formula containing a named range, the reference will not change, that is, it will always refer to the original table location. An absolute reference is not required if a named range is used in a lookup formula.

- When the items in a lookup table are not in ascending order (A-Z), you must add the FALSE argument to the VLOOKUP function. Otherwise, VLOOKUP may return inaccurate results.

  EXAMPLE: =VLOOKUP(*A1,table,2,*FALSE)

  The FALSE argument requires VLOOKUP to find an exact match in the first column of the lookup table. If an exact match is not found, VLOOKUP returns the #VALUE! error message.

In this exercise, you will create an inventory valuation for Pringle Auto Repair Shop. On March 1, Pringle did an inventory of the parts they had on hand. These parts were listed by item number only. Use the VLOOKUP function to find the item name and the unit cost from a table created from a previously saved worksheet. You may either use a named table range or a range reference with absolute references in your formula.

EXERCISE DIRECTIONS:

1. Open ⌨ **PARTS** or open 💾 **49PARTS.XLS**.

2. Edit the title as shown.

3. Create the top portion of the worksheet indicated by inserting rows to accommodate the new data.

   NOTE: Item numbers should be entered as label data.

4. Format all column titles appropriately.

5. Name the range A21:G29, ITEM.

6. Using the VLOOKUP function and the range name ITEM, find the ITEM NAME based on the item number.

   NOTE: Since the item numbers in the ITEM table are not in ascending order, you must include the FALSE argument in each VLOOKUP function.

7. Copy the formula to the remaining items.

8. Using the VLOOKUP function, find the UNIT COST based on the item number.

9. Copy the formula to the remaining items.

10. Find:
    - VALUE and copy the formula to the remaining items.
    - TOTAL of the VALUE column (format for two decimal places).

11. Select the top portion of the worksheet and copy it to a new worksheet using the Paste Special, Values option.

12. In the new worksheet, select the three-line title and column headings and set to bold.

13. Right align the Unit Cost, Quan, and Value column headings.

14. Since formats do not copy, format the Unit Cost and Value columns for two decimal places.

15. Save the workbook file, name it **VALUE**.

16. Print one copy of **VALUE**.

17. Close the workbook file.

18. Close **PARTS** without saving the file.

	A	B	C	D	E	F	G	H
1			PRINGLE AUTO REPAIR SHOP					
2			*INVENTORY VALUATION*					
3			*MARCH 1, 199-*					
4								
5	*ITEM*	*ITEM*			*UNIT*			
6	*NUMBER*	*NAME*			*COST*	*QUAN*	*VALUE*	
7								
8	*093*					*14*		
9	*142*					*5*		
10	*175*					*4*		
11	*321*					*72*		
12	*932*					*25*		
13								
14	*TOTAL*							
15								
16								
17								
18	ITEM			UNIT	SELLING			
19	NUMBER	ITEM		COST	PRICE	MARKUP	% MARKUP	
20								
21	142	carburetor		120.00	168.00	48.00	40.00%	
22	321	spark plugs		2.00	3.00	1.00	50.00%	
23	093	tires		55.00	77.00	22.00	40.00%	
24	393	brakes		60.00	84.00	24.00	40.00%	
25	659	alarm		125.00	195.00	70.00	56.00%	
26	572	mats		45.00	63.00	18.00	40.00%	
27	175	battery		45.00	70.00	25.00	55.56%	
28	421	radio		185.00	265.00	80.00	43.24%	
29	932	fan belt		15.00	28.00	13.00	86.67%	
30								
31	AVERAGES			72.44	105.89	33.44	50.16%	
32	HIGHEST VALUE			185.00	265.00	80.00	86.67%	
33	LOWEST VALUE			2.00	3.00	1.00	40.00%	
34								
35	1	2	3	4	5	6	7	

EXERCISE 50

- ■ **Horizontal Lookup Function (HLOOKUP)** ■ **Protect a Sheet**
- ■ **Lock Cells in a Worksheet** ■ **AutoFormat**

NOTES:

Horizontal Lookup Function

- While VLOOKUP looks up data in a particular *column* in the table, HLOOKUP looks up data in a particular *row* in the table.

- The HLOOKUP function uses the same format and contains the same three arguments (parts) as VLOOKUP.

  =HLOOKUP(item,table-range,row-position)

- **ITEM** is text, a value, or a cell reference of the item you are looking for (**search Item**) and should be in the first row of the (HLOOKUP) table. Numerical search items should be listed in ascending order.

- **TABLE-RANGE** is the range reference or range name of the lookup table in which the search is made.

- **ROW-POSITION** is the row number in the table from which the matching value should be returned. The top row has a position number of one; the second row has a position number of two, and so forth.

Protect a Sheet

- It is possible to **protect**, or **lock**, an entire worksheet, individual cells, or a range of cells from accidental changes or unauthorized use. By default, all cells are locked in a worksheet, The locked status of cells becomes enabled when you **protect the worksheet.**

- If you need to keep certain cells accessible in a protected worksheet, these cells must be unlocked *before* the worksheet is protected.

- When you protect a worksheet, you can assign a password so that others cannot unprotect the worksheet without supplying the password.

  IMPORTANT: If you set a password when protecting a worksheet and you forget the password, you will not be able to make changes to locked cells in the worksheet.

- When a workbook is protected, the message **Locked cells cannot be changed** will appear when you try to change the contents of a locked cell. When protection is on, Excel will let you copy, but not move, locked cells to an unlocked area of the worksheet. Locked cells cannot receive moved or copied cells.

In this exercise, you will create a worksheet listing daily sales for a mail order firm. As an employee of the J.J. Barney Catalog Sales company, you are to compute the sales tax and shipping charges for all orders. Using HLOOKUP, you will compute the postage and sales tax required, depending on the zone to which the package is being shipped.

EXERCISE DIRECTIONS:

1. Create the worksheet as shown, or open 📁 **50ZONE.XLS.**

2. Create a series to enter the order numbers.

3. Name the postage rates range, C21:H23, RATES.

4. Using HLOOKUP, find POSTAGE (based on the zone.) Be sure to use the name RATES in the function.

5. Copy the function to the remaining items.

6. Using HLOOKUP, find TAX RATE (based on the zones.) Be sure to use the name RATES in the function.

7. Copy the function to the remaining items.

8. Find:
   - SALES TAX

     HINT: *Sales tax is not charged on postage.*
   - TOTAL SALE (including postage and sales tax)

9. Copy formulas to the remaining items.

10. Format all money columns for two-place decimals.

11. Center column headings.

12. Bold worksheet titles.

13. Select the column headings and the data without the lookup table. Use AutoFormat to apply the Colorful 2 format.

14. Change the background color and font color of the title range A1:G3 to match the column headings.

15. **To protect the lookup table**:
    - Unlock the range A1:G18.
    - Protect the worksheet; do not set a password.

16. To test protection:
    - Try to edit an entry in the rate table.
    - Try to copy a value to the rate table.
    - Try to edit an entry in the PRICE column.

    NOTE: *Since the price column was unlocked the edit should have been successful. Undo the last edit.*

17. Print one copy of the top portion of the worksheet.

18. Save the workbook file; name it **ZONE**.

19. Close the workbook file.

	A	B	C	D	E	F	G	H
1			J. J. BARNEY CATALOG SALES					
2			JUNE 20, 199-					
3								
4					TAX	SALES	TOTAL	
5	CAT.NO.	PRICE	ZONE	POSTAGE	RATE	TAX	SALE	
6								
7	J43256	59.95	1					
8	J43257	65.49	3					
9	J43258	29.95	2					
10	J43259	43.98	4					
11	J43260	16.89	5					
12	J43261	98.78	6					
13	J43262	35.89	5					
14	J43263	54.99	3					
15	J43264	36.67	6					
16	J43265	89.67	1					
17	J43266	29.95	4	▼	▼	▼	▼	
18	J43267	43.65	3					
19								
20			POSTAGE AND SALES TAX RATES					
21	ZONE		1	2	3	4	5	6
22	POSTAGE		4	4.5	5	5.5	6	6.5
23	SALES TAX RATE		0.08	0.06	0	0.04	0.05	0.07
24								

PROTECT A SHEET

Prevents changes to locked cells, graphic objects, embedded charts in a worksheet or chart items in a chart sheet.

1. Lock or unlock cells as desired.
    NOTE: By default, all cells and objects in a worksheet are locked.

2. Click **Tools** menu .... `Alt`+`T`

3. Click **Protection** .... `P`

4. Click **Protect Sheet** .... `P`

To password protect sheet:

*   Type password .... *password* in **Password (optional)** text box.

To protect cell contents and chart items:

*   Select ☐ **Contents** ..... `Alt`+`C`

To protect graphic objects:

*   Select ☐ **Objects** .... `Alt`+`O`

To protect scenarios:

*   Select ☐ **Scenarios** ... `Alt`+`S`

5. Click [OK] .... `↵`

If a password was typed:

a. Retype password .... *password* in text box.

b. Click [OK] .... `↵`

UNPROTECT A SHEET

1. Click **Tools** menu .... `Alt`+`T`

2. Click **Protection** .... `P`

3. Click **Unprotect Sheet** .... `P`

If sheet is password protected:

a. Type password .... *password* in **Password** text box.

b. Click [OK] .... `↵`

LOCK/UNLOCK CELLS IN A WORKSHEET

Locks or unlocks specific cells. By default, all cells in a worksheet are locked. Locking takes effect when a worksheet is protected.

1. If necessary, unprotect worksheet.
    NOTE: You cannot lock or unlock cells if the worksheet is protected.

2. Select cell(s) to unlock or lock.

3. Click **Format** menu .... `Alt`+`O`

4. Click **Cells** .... `E`
    *NOTE: Press **Ctrl + 1** to access **Format** options quickly.*

5. Click **Protection** tab .... `Ctrl`+`Tab`

6. Deselect or
    select ☐ **Locked** .... `Alt`+`L`
    NOTE: A gray check box indicates the current cell selection contains mixed (locked/unlocked) settings.

7. Click [OK] .... `↵`

8. Repeat steps for each cell or object to lock or unlock.

9. Protect worksheet to enable locking.

NEXT EXERCISE

EXERCISE

■ Hide Data ■ Non-Consecutive References in a Function

51

NOTES:

■ There are two ways to hide data in a worksheet, **Hide Cell Contents** and **Hide Columns**.

Hide Cell Contents

• You may hide data to make a cell or a range appear blank.

• When you make a hidden cell active or edit the cell's contents, the data it contains appears in the formula bar.

• The contents of hidden cells do not print. Therefore, this feature may be used to print *selected, non-consecutive columns* of data in a worksheet.

• If hidden cell data is moved or copied, it remains hidden in the new location.

Hide Columns

• You may hide one or more columns to make them disappear from the display.

• Hidden columns may be redisplayed at any time.

• The worksheet border does not display the column letters of hidden columns.

• A column must be unhidden to view or edit data in a hidden column.

Non-Consecutive References in a Function

■ When using functions whose arguments (parts) are from *non-consecutive columns*, you cannot use a range in your formula. Instead, you must specify the individual cells to be calculated using commas (,) to separate the cells.

EXAMPLE: =MAX(G16,J16,M16)

In this exercise, Woodworks Furniture Company would like a simplified report showing only quarterly salaries of employees. To accomplish this, you will hide columns, find total salaries for January through September, and print desired data.

EXERCISE DIRECTIONS:

1. Open ⌨ **WOOD** or open 🖫 **51WOOD.XLS**.

2. Hide columns D, E, F, H, I, K and L.

3. Edit the second title to read:
   QUARTERLY SALARY SUMMARY - JANUARY-SEPTEMBER

4. Insert a new, centered column title in column N:
   JAN-SEPT
   SALARY

5. In column N, find total JAN-SEPT SALARY using the non-consecutive columns format in your formula.

6. Copy formula for the remaining employees.

7. Copy formulas for TOTALS, AVERAGES, HIGHEST and LOWEST to column N. (Be sure to use JULY-SEPT formulas which include the new employee.)

8. Format columns for two decimal places with commas.

9. Reset column width, as necessary.

10. Save as a new file; name it **WOODQTR**.

11. Select the range A1:N17 and print the selection.

12. Redisplay hidden columns.

13. Hide column N.

14. Hide cells containing employee names.

15. Re-edit the second title to read:
    QUARTERLY SALARY SUMMARY - JANUARY-SEPTEMBER

16. Resave **WOODQTR**.

17. Close the workbook file.

	A	B	C	D	E	F	G	H	I	J	K	L	M
1				WOODWORKS FURNITURE COMPANY									
2		QUARTERLY SALES AND SALARY REPORT - JANUARY-SEPTEMBER											
3		QUARTERLY SALARY SUMMARY											
4	EMP.			BASE		5%	JAN-MAR		5%	APR-JUNE		5%	JULY-SEPT
5	NO.	NAME		SALARY	SALES	COMMISSION	SALARY	SALES	COMMISSION	SALARY	SALES	COMMISSION	SALARY
6													
7	1	ABRAMS, JUDY		1,500.00	113,456.67	5,672.83	7,172.83	114,342.87	5,717.14	7,217.14	112,469.32	5,623.47	7,123.47
8	2	CHANG, PETER		1,500.00	150,654.87	7,532.74	9,032.74	143,276.65	7,163.83	8,663.83	152,643.36	7,632.17	9,132.17
9	3	LINSEY, KELLY		1,500.00	234,765.36	11,738.27	13,238.27	187,956.76	9,397.84	10,897.84	215,050.16	10,752.51	12,252.51
10	4	JOHNSON, LETOYA		1,500.00	89,765.43	4,488.27	5,988.27	93,984.69	4,699.23	6,199.23	98,463.14	4,923.16	6,423.16
11	5	RIVERA, TONY		1,500.00	287,987.76	14,399.39	15,899.39	254,768.64	12,738.43	14,238.43	246,315.19	12,315.76	13,815.76
12	6	THOMPSON, JIM		1,500.00							76,451.13	3,822.56	5,322.56
13													
14		TOTALS		9,000.00	876,630.09	43,831.50	51,331.50	794,329.61	39,716.48	47,216.48	901,392.30	45,069.62	54,069.62
15		AVERAGES		1,500.00	175,326.02	8,766.30	10,266.30	158,865.92	7,943.30	9,443.30	150,232.05	7,511.60	9,011.60
16		HIGHEST		1,500.00	287,987.76	14,399.39	15,899.39	254,768.64	12,738.43	14,238.43	246,315.19	12,315.76	13,815.76
17		LOWEST		1,500.00	89,765.43	4,488.27	5,988.27	93,984.69	4,699.23	6,199.23	76,451.13	3,822.56	5,322.56
18													
19													
20						hide				hide			hide
21													
22													
23													
24													

HIDE CONTENTS OF CELL

1. Select cells containing data to hide.

2. a. Click **Format** menu ...... Alt + O

   b. Click **Cells** .... E

   OR

   a. Right–click selection.

   b. Click **Format Cells**.

3. Click **Number** tab .... Ctrl + Tab

4. Select **Custom** .... [↑↓]
   in **Category** list box.

5. Double-click in
   Type : [_____] .... Alt + T

6. Type ;;; (three
   semicolons) .... [;] [;] [;]

7. Click [OK] .... [↵]

REDISPLAY HIDDEN CELL

1. Repeat steps 1-3 in **HIDE CONTENTS OF CELL**.

2. Select desired format .... [↑↓]
   in **Category** list box.

3. Click [OK] .... [↵]

HIDE COLUMNS USING THE MENU

1. Select any cells in column(s) to hide.

2. Click **Format** menu .... Alt + O

3. Click **Column** C

4. Click **Hide** .... H
   A bolded column heading border appears where a column is hidden.

HIDE COLUMNS BY DRAGGING

Hide One Column

1. Point to *right border* of column heading.
   Pointer becomes a ↔.

2. Drag ↔ left to column's left border.
   Excel displays a bolded column heading border where a column is hidden.

Hide Multiple Columns

1. Select columns.

2. Point to *right border* of any selected column heading.
   Pointer becomes a ↔.

3. Drag ↔ left to column's left border.
   Excel displays a bolded column heading border where a column is hidden.

SHOW HIDDEN COLUMNS BY DRAGGING

1. Point *just right of* bolded column heading border.
   Pointer becomes a ↔.

2. Drag ↔ right.

SHOW HIDDEN COLUMNS USING THE MENU

1. Select surrounding columns.

2. Click **Format** menu .... Alt + O

3. Click **Column** C

4. Click **Unhide** .... U

EXERCISE

Summary

52

> *The Chipmunk Garden Center is updating its accounts receivable aging report as of 2/1/97. Paid invoices will be deleted from this new report, and new invoices that have not been paid will be added.*
>
> *In addition, The Chipmunk Garden Center has changed its late fee policy. It will now determine late fees based on the number of days the account is unpaid. The late fee will be determined using a Lookup formula.*

EXERCISE DIRECTIONS:

1. Open ⌨ **AGE** or 💾 **52AGE.XLS**.

2. Delete rows for invoices shown on right.

3. Insert rows below remaining invoices and enter the following new invoices:

INVOICE NUMBER	INVOICE DATE	CUSTOMER		DAYS UNPAID	AMOUNT
21093	12/10/96	YELLOW BROS.			168.42
21106	12/16/96	PINKSTON CORP.			396.16
21142	12/29/96	REDLY FARMS			84.96
21179	1/4/97	GREENBERG BROS.			1490.14
21205	1/10/97	BLUETOWN CO.			354.75
21246	1/25/97	PINKSTON CORP.			742.15

4. Change the CURRENT DATE to 2/1/97.

5. Copy the DAYS UNPAID formula for the new data.

6. Create the LATE FEE TABLE below the worksheet.

7. Name the range in LATE FEE TABLE containing days and interest values LATETABLE.

8. Insert a column between AMOUNT and LATE FEE, and enter the label INTEREST RATE.

9. Delete values in the LATE FEE and AMOUNT DUE columns.

10. Format INTEREST RATE column for three decimal places.

11. Protect the LATE FEE TABLE:
    - Unlock all cells in entire worksheet.
    - Select cells in LATE FEE TABLE and lock them.
    - Turn worksheet protection on.

12. Using VLOOKUP, find INTEREST RATE (based on the days unpaid).

13. Copy the function to the remaining items.

    NOTE: If you did not use the LATETABLE range name in the function, you must set the table range to absolute before copying.

14. Find:
    - LATE FEE
    - AMOUNT DUE

15. Copy formulas to the remaining items.

16. Disable worksheet protection.

17. Format all remaining money columns for two decimal places.

18. Center column titles.

19. Edit the TOTAL formulas.

20. Change the interest rate for one unpaid day to be 0.005.

21. Protect the worksheet.

22. Print one copy of the top portion of the worksheet.

23. Resave the workbook file.

24. Save and close the file; name it **AGE**.

	A	B	C	D	E	F	G	H	I
1			THE CHIPMUNK GARDEN CENTER						
2			ACCOUNTS RECEIVABLE AGING REPORT						
3									
4	CURRENT DATE:		~~12/01/96~~ →	2/1/97					
5									
6	INVOICE	INVOICE		DAYS			AMOUNT		
7	NUMBER	DATE	CUSTOMER	UNPAID	AMOUNT	LATE FEE	DUE	Insert INTEREST RATE column	
8									
9	21045	09/22/96	BROWN BROTHERS	70	475.43	4.75	480.18		
10	~~21046~~	~~09/23/96~~	~~REDLY FARMS~~	~~60~~	~~321.43~~	~~3.21~~	~~324.64~~		
11	~~21047~~	~~09/24/96~~	~~BROWN BROTHERS~~	~~68~~	~~543.98~~	~~5.44~~	~~549.42~~		
12	~~21049~~	~~10/02/96~~	~~PINKSTON CORP.~~	~~60~~	~~92.45~~	~~0.92~~	~~93.77~~		
13	~~21050~~	~~10/03/96~~	~~J.J. BURGUNDY~~	~~59~~	~~1324.32~~	~~13.24~~	~~1337.56~~		
14	~~21052~~	~~10/06/96~~	~~REDLY FARMS~~	~~56~~	~~124.98~~	~~1.25~~	~~126.23~~		
15	~~21054~~	~~10/15/96~~	~~BLUETOWN CO.~~	~~47~~	~~564.12~~	~~5.64~~	~~569.76~~		
16	~~21056~~	~~10/18/96~~	~~PINKSTON CORP.~~	~~44~~	~~187.65~~	~~1.88~~	~~189.53~~		
17	~~21062~~	~~10/29/96~~	~~J.J. BURGUNDY~~	~~34~~	~~454.56~~	~~4.55~~	~~459.11~~		
18	21079	11/05/96	M. MAROON	26	308.21	0.00	308.21		
19	21087	11/20/96	REDLY FARMS	11	163.28	0.00	163.28		
20									
21	TOTALS				4500.41	40.29	4540.70		
22									
23									
24	LATE FEE TABLE								
25									
26	UNPAID								
27	DAYS	INTEREST							
28	1	0.000							
29	30	0.010							
30	60	0.015	◄ name range LATETABLE						
31	90	0.020							
32	120	0.025							
33	150	0.030							

EXERCISE

Summary

53

As the manager of the Heavy Metal Import Company, you are responsible for deciding from which country to buy various metals like copper, iron, ore, etc. To determine which country can offer you the best price, you must convert the price quotes to U.S. dollars.

EXERCISE DIRECTIONS:

1. Create the worksheet and table below or open 💾 **53METAL.XLS**.

2. Globally format the worksheet to set column width at 12.

3. Using VLOOKUP, find the CURRENCY each country uses.

4. Using VLOOKUP, find the CONVERSION FACTOR for each country.

5. Format appropriately.

6. Find U.S. PRICE PER UNIT.

7. Find the LOWEST UNIT PRICE IN U.S. DOLLARS using the MIN function.

8. Save the workbook file; name it **METAL**.

9. Use the Copy, Paste Special feature to copy the top portion of this worksheet to a new workbook.

10. Format the Conversion factor to a four-place decimal.

11. Format the U.S. Price to two-place decimals.

12. Use the AutoFormat feature and select a style for the worksheet.

13. Adjust column widths, if necessary.

14. Save the workbook file; name it **IRON**.

15. Print one copy of IRON.

16. Close all workbooks.

	A	B	C	D	E	F
1			HEAVY METAL IMPORT CO.			
2			ITEM: IRON ORE			
3						
4			FOREIGN			U.S.
5	BIDDING		PRICE		CONVERSION	PRICE PER
6	COUNTRY		PER UNIT	CURRENCY	FACTOR	UNIT
7						
8	AUSTRALIA		135			
9	BRAZIL		420			
10	CANADA		110			
11	GERMANY		160			
12	INDIA		1680			
13	ITALY		125000			
14						
15	LOWEST UNIT PRICE IN U.S. DOLLARS					
16						
17						
18	CONVERSION TABLE FOR FOREIGN CURRENCY					
19			FACTOR	FOREIGN UNITS		
20			(DOLLAR VAL	THAT EQUAL		
21			OF ONE	ONE DOLLAR		
22	COUNTRY	CURRENCY	FOR'N UNIT)			
23						
24	AUSTRALIA	DOLLARS	0.7789	1.2839		
25	BRAZIL	CRUZEIROS	0.2310	4.3290		
26	BRITAIN	POUNDS	1.8106	0.5523		
27	CANADA	DOLLARS	0.8803	1.1360		
28	FRANCE	FRANCS	0.1861	5.3735		
29	GERMANY	MARKS	0.6363	1.5716		
30	INDIA	RUPEES	0.0600	16.6667		
31	ITALY	LIRA	0.0008	1250.0000		
32	JAPAN	YEN	0.0078	128.2051		

LESSON 8

CHART AND MAP DATA

Exercises 54-64

- Create and Edit Charts

  Pie

  Column

  Stacked Bar

  Line

  Area

  Combination

  Open-High-Low-Close

  3-D charts

- Chart Sheets and Embedded Charts

- Print Charts

- Change Data Orientation

- Change Colors and Patterns

- Add Chart Text

- Edit Linked Text

- Data Map

EXERCISE

■ Create Column, Line and Pie Charts ■ Change Chart Type
■ Select and Size Embedded Chart ■ Enable Chart Editing
■ Edit Chart Text

54

NOTES:

- **Charts** are a way of presenting and comparing data in a graphic format.

- You can create **embedded charts** or **chart sheets**.

  • When you create an embedded chart, the chart exists as an *object* in the worksheet alongside the data.

  • When you create a chart sheet, the chart exists on a separate sheet in the workbook. Excel names chart sheets Chart1, Chart2 etc. You can change these sheet names to better describe the chart.

- All charts are linked to the data they plot. When you change data in the plotted area of the worksheet, the chart also changes.

- To create a chart, you must first select the data to plot. Here are some guidelines for selecting data to chart:

  • The selection should be rectangular.

  • The selection should not contain blank columns or rows.

  • Non-adjacent selection is used to plot data separated by other data or blank columns or rows.

  • Hide columns you do not wish to plot.

  • The blank cell in the upper-left corner of a selection tells Excel the data below and to

the right of the blank cell contains labels for the values to plot.

• The selection determines the orientation (in columns or rows) of the data series. However, orientation may be changed as desired.

- The illustration below shows two selections that would result in the same displayed chart. Both selections are rectangular and contain a blank cell (outlined) in the upper-left corner. The second selection (B) contains non-adjacent ranges which are required because of the blank column between the data. To make a non-adjacent selection, you must hold down the Control key between selections.

- Typically the selection of worksheet data will include these parts of a chart that are identified using the illustration below and on page 176.

data series	Values the chart represents. (Income values)
series labels	Labels identifying the charted values. These labels appear in the chart **legend** which identifies each data series in the chart. (Labels for Years 1 and 2)
category labels	Labels identifying each data series shown on the horizontal or x-axis. (Quarter labels)

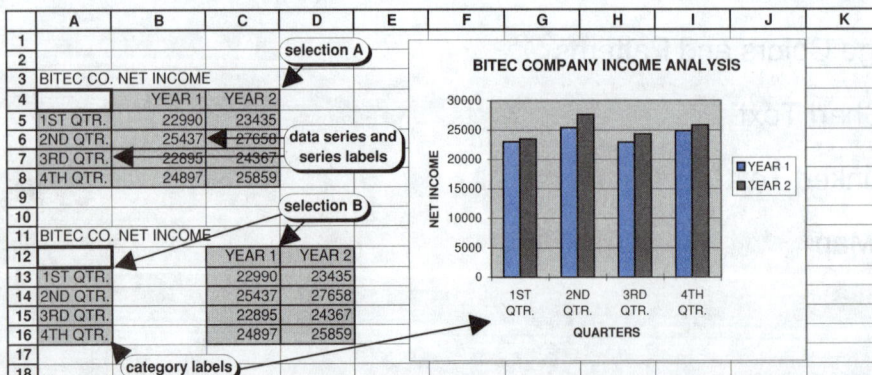

- For charts which use axes (all except pie charts):

  - The **y-axis** typically represents the vertical scale. The scale values are entered automatically, based on the values being charted. (See illustration on next page.)

  - The **x-axis** is the horizontal scale and typically represents the data series categories.

  - The **x-axis title** describes the x-axis (horizontal) data. (QUARTERS in the illustration on the previous page.)

  - The **y-axis title** describes the y-axis (vertical) data. (NET INCOME in the illustration on previous page.)

- The basic steps to creating a chart are:

  1. Select the worksheet data to chart.

  2. Select **Chart** from the **Insert** menu, then select **On This Sheet** (for an embedded chart) or **As New Sheet**.

  *NOTE: You can also create an embedded chart by clicking the **ChartWizard** button on the Standard Toolbar.*

  3. If creating an embedded chart, indicate desired size and position in the worksheet.

  4. Follow the ChartWizard prompts to select desired chart type and other chart characteristics.

Change Chart Types

- Excel provides many chart types. In this exercise we will discuss and explore three of them (*illustrated below*):

  - **Column charts** compare individual or sets of values. The height of each bar is proportional to its corresponding value in the worksheet.

  - **Pie charts** are circular graphs used to show the relationship of each value in a data range to the entire data range. The size of each wedge represents the percentage each value contributes to the total.

    Only one numerical data range may be used in a pie chart to indicate the values to be represented as pie slices.

    Pie charts may be formatted to indicate the percentage each piece of the pie represents of the whole.

  - **Line charts** are another way of presenting data graphically. Line charts are especially useful when plotting trends since lines connect points of data and show changes over time effectively.

- Charts can be copied and then edited to produce a different chart that uses the same worksheet data.

  NOTE: The contents of clipboard remain unchanged until another item is copied. Therefore, you can paste a copied chart more than once.

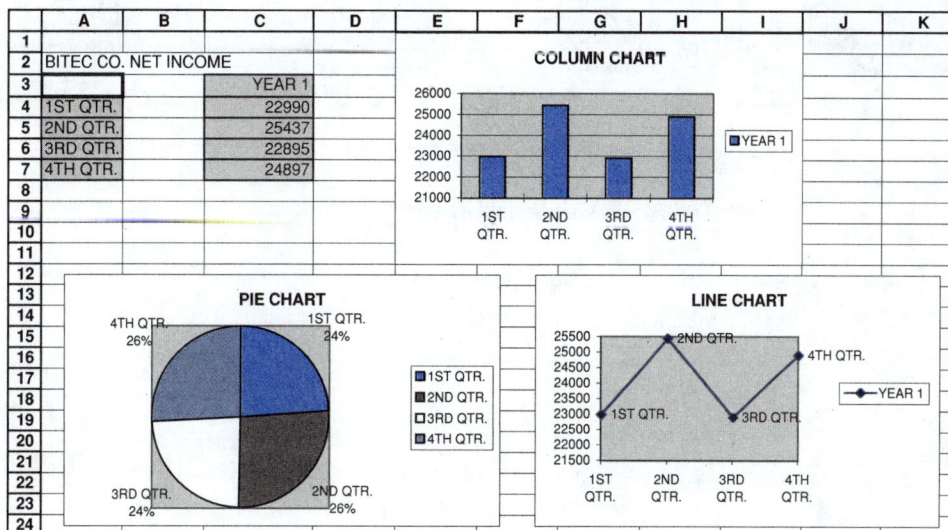

Select and Size Embedded Charts

- Two ways of working with embedded charts are:

  - You can click an embedded chart once to format it as an *object*. When you click it, **handles** (small squares) appear around its border. When selected in this way, you can size, move and copy it, for example.

  - You can double–click an embedded chart to edit it as a *chart*. When you double–click it, a thick border with handles appears or, if the entire chart was not displayed on the sheet, the chart appears in a window.

Enable Chart Editing

- To edit a chart sheet, just click the sheet tab of the chart you want to change.

- All chart items, such as the **legend** and **data markers** (*illustrated below*), can be changed and enhanced. Chart items may be changed by clicking them and making changes. Double–clicking some chart items opens a dialog box for entry changes. When you right–click chart items, Excel displays a shortcut menu containing relevant commands.

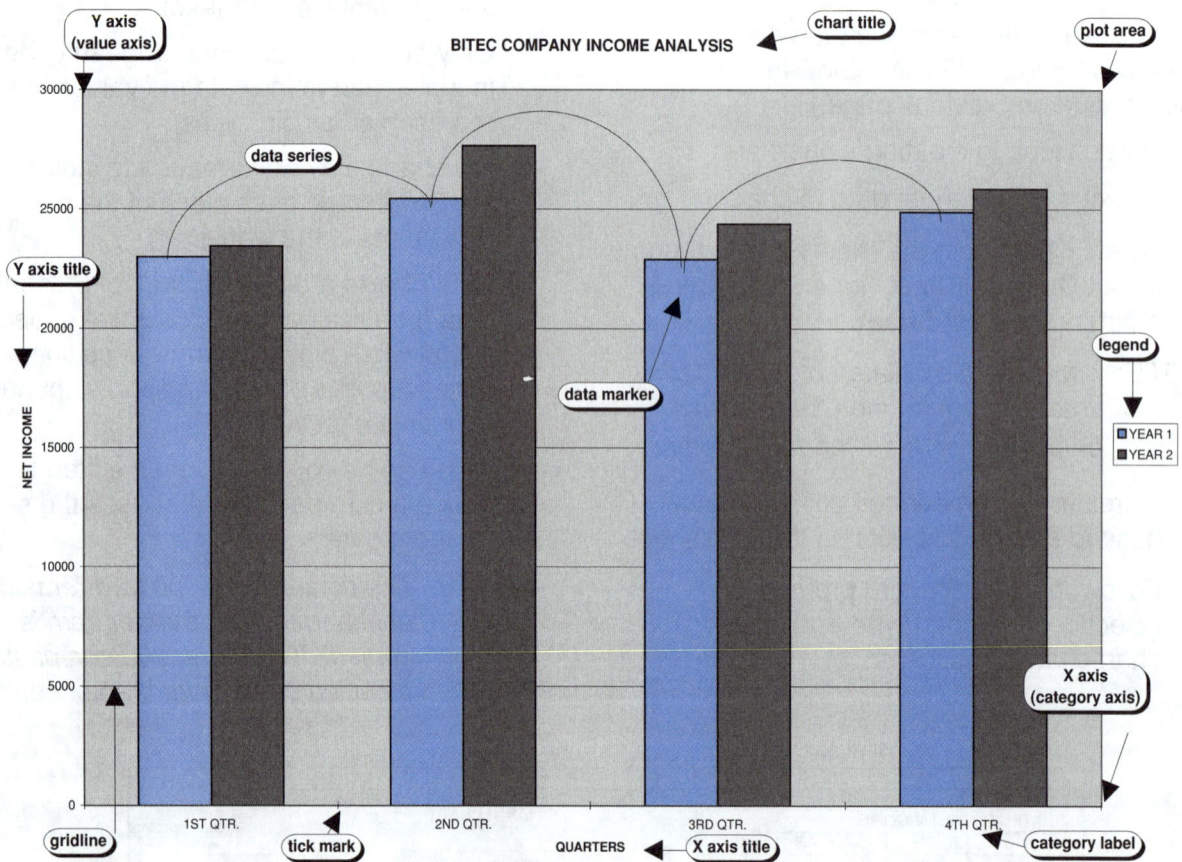

COLUMN CHART

- When editing is enabled, Excel provides the following tools for editing:

  - **Menu bar options**

    Excel modifies the menu bar so options specific to the chart type and selected chart item are available. For example:

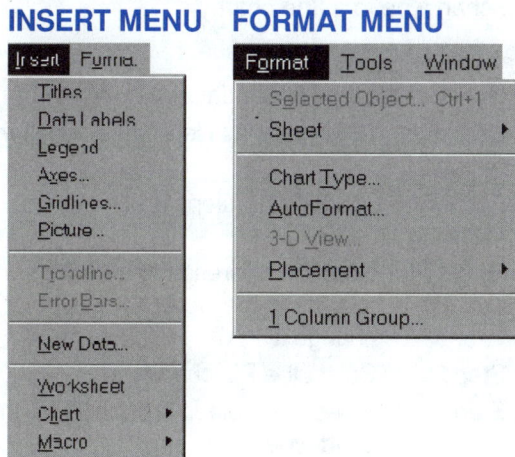

    INSERT MENU   **FORMAT MENU**

Insert	Forma.
Titles	
Data Labels	
Legend	
Axes...	
Gridlines...	
Picture ..	
Trendline..	
Error Bars...	
New Data...	
Worksheet	
Chart	►
Macro	►

Format	Tools	Window
Selected Object... Ctrl+1		
Sheet		►
Chart Type...		
AutoFormat...		
3-D View...		
Placement		►
1 Column Group...		

- **Shortcut menu options**

  When you select any part of the chart and right-click with the mouse, appropriate shortcut menu options appear. Some of these are:

  Clear

  Insert: Axes, Data Labels, Error Bars, Gridlines, Titles, Trendline

  Format: Axis, Axis Title, Chart Area, Chart Title, Data Labels, Data Point, Data Series, Error Bars, Gridlines, Legend, Legend Entry, Legend Key, Trendline

  Chart Type

  Autoformat

  3-D View

  Format Chart Type Group

- **Name box**

  Displays the selected chart item.

In this exercise, you will create a column chart, a line chart and a pie chart with labels showing quarterly Income data for the Bitec Company.

EXERCISE DIRECTIONS:

1. Create the worksheet as shown below.

2. Create an embedded chart to show the Net Income by quarter:

   - Select the non-adjacent ranges indicated by the shaded cells in the worksheet.
   - Click the ChartWizard button and place the chart in the range B10:G24.
   - Follow the ChartWizard steps and make the following selections:

     Step 1:   Note the reference to the range of data to chart from the worksheet. Do not change it.

     Step 2:   Note the default chart type (**Column**). Do not change it.

     Step 3:   Note the default format (**6**) for the column chart type. Do not change it.

     Step 4:   Note the orientation of the data series is set to **Columns**. Do not change it.

     Step 5:   • Remove the legend.
               Note the changes in the sample chart.

               • Add the legend.

               • Add the chart title:
                 BITEC COMPANY INCOME ANALYSIS

               • Add the following axis titles:
                 Category (X): QUARTERS
                 Value (Y):   NET INCOME

3. Size the chart so that the category labels (QTR. labels) fit on one line.

4. Copy the embedded chart to the worksheet range beginning at B26.

5. Enable chart editing for the copied chart and change the chart type to a **line** chart.

6. To create a pie chart on a sheet:

   - Reselect the worksheet data.
   - Use Insert, Chart, and As New Sheet to insert a **pie** chart.
   - Follow the ChartWizard steps and make the following selections:

     Step 1:   Note the reference to the range of data to chart in the worksheet. Do not change it.

     Step 2:   Select the Pie chart type.

     Step 3:   Select the default format (7) for the pie chart type.

     Step 4:   Note, but do not change, the settings for ChartWizard step 4.

     Step 5:   • Add a legend.
               • Add the chart title:
                 BITEC COMPANY

7. With the chart sheet selected, edit the chart title to add a second line:
   INCOME ANALYSIS

8. Preview the pie chart on the chart sheet.

   ✓ *The chart will print on its own sheet.*

9. Select Sheet1 and deselect the worksheet data.

10. Preview Sheet1.

    ✓ *The column and line charts will print with the worksheet data.*

11. Close the Preview screen.

12. Save the workbook file; name it **INCOME**.

13. Close the workbook file.

	A	B	C	D
1	BITEC CO. NET INCOME			
2				
3			YEAR 1	
4	1ST QTR.		22990	
5	2ND QTR.		25437	
6	3RD QTR.		22895	
7	4TH QTR.		24897	
8				

SELECT NON-ADJACENT CELLS USING THE MOUSE

1. Click first cell.
2. Press **Ctrl** and click each additional cell.

   AND/OR

   Press **Ctrl** and drag through cells until desired cell ranges are highlighted.

SELECT NON-ADJACENT CELLS USING THE KEYBOARD

1. Select first cell in range............... [↑↓←→]
2. Select first range of cells .... [Shift] + [↑↓←→]
3. Press **Shift + F8** .... [Shift] + [F8] to begin ADD mode.
4. Move active cell .... [↑↓←→] to first cell in next range to select.
5. Select cells in range .... [Shift] + [↑↓←→]
6. Repeat steps 2–4 for each additional range to select.

CREATE A CHART FROM WORKSHEET DATA

1. Select cells containing data to plot.
2. a. Click **I**nsert menu .... [Alt] + [I]

   b. Click **C**hart .... [H]

   c. Click **O**n This Sheet .... [O]

   OR

   Click **A**s New Sheet .... [A]

   NOTE: You can click the ChartWizard button [📊] *on the Standard Toolbar to create an embedded chart on the worksheet.*

   If **O**n This Sheet was selected:

   Pointer becomes a [+📊].

   • Drag chart outline to desired size.

   NOTE: To create a square chart, press Shift while dragging chart outline. To align chart with cell structure, press Alt while dragging chart outline.

—CHARTWIZARD – STEP 1 OF 5—

3. If necessary, select cells in worksheet to plot.

   OR

   Type reference ....*reference* to cells to plot in **Range** text box.
4. Click [Next >] .... [↵]

—CHARTWIZARD – STEP 2 OF 5—

5. Select desired chart type .... [↔/↘]

   Chart types include: *Area, Bar, Column, Line, Pie, Doughnut, Radar, XY (Scatter), Combination, 3-D Area, 3-D Bar, 3-D Column, 3-D Line, 3-D Pie, 3-D Surface*
6. Click [Next >] .... [↵]

—CHARTWIZARD – STEP 3 OF 5—

7. Select desired chart format.

   NOTE: Available formats depend upon the selected chart type.

—CHARTWIZARD – STEP 4 OF 5—

8. Select desired chart options:

   To change orientation of data series:

   • Select ○ **R**ows .... [Alt] + [R]

   OR

   Select ○ **C**olumns ..... [Alt] + [C]

   Excel shows the result of your selections in a sample chart.

   To specify rows or columns to use for axis labels, legend text or chart title:

   • Select number of rows/columns ..... [Alt] + [U], [↕/↗] in **Use First** increment box.

   NOTE: Options depend upon the selected chart type. To plot values in first row or column (not use them as labels), select 0 (zero).
9. Click [Next >] .... [↵]

—CHARTWIZARD – STEP 5 OF 5—

10. Select desired chart options:

   To add or remove legend:

   • Select ○ **Y**es .... [Alt] + [E]

   OR

   Select ○ **N**o .... [Alt] + [N]

To add a chart title:

a. Click **C**hart Title: [_____] ..... [Alt] + [C]

b. Type desired chart title. .*chart title*

To add axis titles:

• Type titles in provided **Axis Titles** text boxes.

   NOTE: Options depend upon the selected chart type.

11. Click [Finish] .... [↵]

ENABLE CHART EDITING

Embedded Chart

• Double–click embedded chart.

   The chart is surrounded by a thick border with handles or, if the entire chart was not displayed on the sheet, the chart appears in a window.

Chart Sheet

• Select chart sheet.

   A Chart toolbar may appear with these chart buttons:

   [📊] **Chart Type**

   [📊] **Default Chart**

   [📊] **ChartWizard**

   [📊] **Horizontal Gridlines**

   [📋] **Legend**

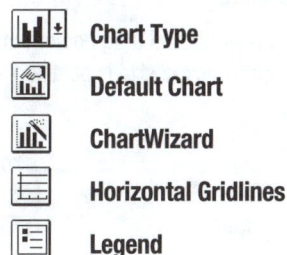

DISABLE CHART EDITING

Embedded Chart

• Click any cell in worksheet.

   NOTE: The chart remains selected as an object. Click any cell again to deselect the chart object.

Chart Sheet

• Click another sheet tab.

SELECT EMBEDDED CHART AS AN OBJECT

- If chart editing is enabled, click any cell in worksheet.

  OR

  Click anywhere on embedded chart.
  Handles (black squares) appear on chart border

SIZE EMBEDDED CHARTS

1. Select chart.
2. Point to handle on side of border to size.

   Pointer becomes a ↙ ↕ ↘ ↔ when positioned correctly.
   NOTE: To size object proportionally, point to corner handle.

To size object without constraints:

- Drag border outline until desired size is obtained.

To size object and align to gridlines:

- Press **Alt** and drag border outline until desired size is obtained.

CHANGE CHART TYPE FOR ENTIRE CHART

1. Enable chart editing.
2. Click **Format** menu .... `Alt` + `O`
3. Click **Chart Type** .... `T`
4. Select ◯ **Entire Chart** .... `Alt` + `E`
5. Select ◯ **2-D** .... `Alt` + `2`

   OR

   Select ◯ **3-D** .... `Alt` + `3`
6. Select desired chart type .... `Tab` , `↵`
7. Click `    OK    ` .... `↵`

EDIT CHART TEXT IN CHART

Edits unlinked chart text (such as axis and chart titles, text boxes, and trendline labels) and some linked text (data labels and tick mark labels).
NOTE: When you edit linked text in a chart, Excel removes the link to the worksheet data.

1. Enable chart editing.

2. Click chart item containing text.

To replace existing text with new text:

a. Type desired text .... *text*
   Text appears in formula bar.

b. Press **Enter** .... `↵`

To edit existing text:

a. Click desired character position in chart text.

b. Insert and delete characters as desired.
   *NOTE: To insert a line break, press **Enter**.*

c. Click anywhere outside of chart text.

NEXT EXERCISE

EXERCISE

■ **Change Chart Types and Subtypes** ■ **Create an Area Chart**
■ **Delete an Embedded Chart** ■ **Select Chart Items**
■ **Change Legend Position**

55

NOTES:

Chart Types and Subtypes

■ When you create a chart, you select a chart type and format that best presents the worksheet data. Worksheet data may be charted using one of fifteen chart types: Area, Bar, Column, Line, Pie, Doughnut, Radar, XY (Scatter), Combination, 3-D Area, 3-D Bar, 3-D Column, 3-D Line, 3-D Pie, 3-D Surface.

■ Excel also provides **chart subtypes** or formats which are variations on the selected chart type. In ChartWizard, after you select one of the fifteen chart types, you are asked to select a format or subtype for that chart type. However, if you wish to change a chart format in edit mode, you must use the Options button on the Format, Chart Type dialog box.

■ The **stacked column chart** is a chart subtype of the Column chart. This chart is often used to show the total effect of several sets of data. Each bar consists of sections representing values in a range. For example, in the illustration below, the 1ST QTR. bar has two sections representing Year 1 and Year 2 values.

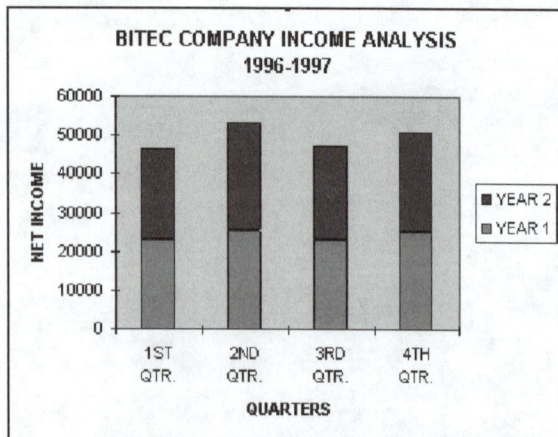

STACKED COLUMN CHART

Select Chart Items

■ Any item in a chart may be selected and changed when chart editing is enabled. Selected items are marked with squares, and the name of the selected item is displayed in the name box.

Create a Combination Chart

■ The **combination chart** is a special chart type that lets you plot each data series as a different chart type. For example, in the illustration below, the line chart type is used to plot the Year 1 net income which can be compared to the column chart type showing Year 2 net income. A combination chart may be selected from the ChartWizard or, if a column chart is already embedded, one data series may be selected and formatted for a line chart type using the Format, Chart Type, Selected Series options.

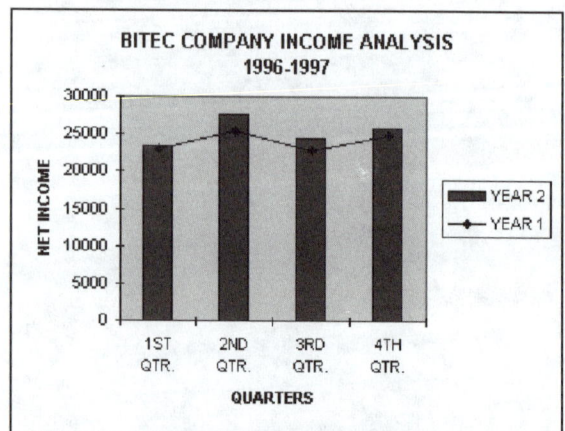

COMBINATION CHART

Change Legend Position

■ A chart **legend** is usually created automatically when the data is charted. Legend placement and labels may be changed or edited by clicking on the legend in chart edit mode, right-clicking the mouse, and selecting Format Legend.

In this exercise, you will retrieve the Bitec Company Net Income statistics, include additional data and prepare several graphs. The Accounting Department wants to compare the quarterly income data from two years.

EXERCISE DIRECTIONS:

1. Open 🖮 **INCOME** or open 💾 **55INCOME.**

2. Enter new data in column D, as illustrated.

3. Delete all embedded charts on Sheet1.

4. Rename Sheet1; name it DATA.

5. To create an embedded **column** chart showing Year 1 and Year 2 data, in the DATA sheet:

   - Select the non-adjacent ranges indicated by the shaded cells in the worksheet.
   - Click the Chart Wizard button on the Standard Toolbar.
   - Place the chart in the range B10:G28.
   - Select the default chart type (**Column**) and format (**6**), the default format or subtype.
   - Add the chart title:
     BITEC COMPANY INCOME ANALYSIS
   - Create axis titles as follows:
     Category (X): QUARTERS
     Value (Y):   NET INCOME

6. Size the chart as needed.

7. Change legend placement to the bottom of the chart (under the x-axis category label).

8. Edit the chart and add a second line to the chart title:
   1996-1997

9. Select the chart as an object and cut it to the clipboard.

10. In Sheet2, select cell A1 and paste the chart stored in the clipboard.

11. Select cell A20 and paste the chart stored in the clipboard again.

12. Edit the chart pasted to cell A20 and change it to a **line** chart.

13. In Sheet2, select cell A40 and paste the chart stored in the clipboard.

14. To change the subtype of this chart to **stacked column:**

    - Double-click on the chart.
    - Select Format, Chart Type, Options.
    - Select the Subtype tab.
    - Select the stacked column subtype.

15. Change legend placement to the right side of chart.

16. To create a combination chart:

    - Select the column chart (first chart on Sheet2) as an object.
    - Copy and paste it to A60.
    - Enable chart editing.
    - Select the Year 1 data series.
    - Use Format, Chart Type, Selected Series to change the chart type for Year 1 to line.

17. Rename Sheet2; name it EMBEDDED CHARTS.

18. Rename Chart1; name it PIE CHART.

19. To preview the embedded charts:

    - Select EMBEDDED CHARTS sheet.
    - Set it to print on one page.
    - Preview the worksheet.

20. Select the DATA sheet and resave the workbook file, or save as **INCOME**.

21. Close the workbook file.

	A	B	C	D	E
1	BITEC CO. NET INCOME				
2					
3			YEAR 1	YEAR 2	
4	1ST QTR.		22990	23435	
5	2ND QTR.		25437	27658	
6	3RD QTR.		22895	24367	
7	4TH QTR.		24897	25859	
8					

DELETE AN EMBEDDED CHART

1. Select embedded chart as an object.
2. Press **Delete**................................. `Del`

CHANGE CHART SUBTYPE

1. Enable chart editing.
2. Click **Format** menu ....`Alt`+`O`
3. Click **Chart Type**........................... `T`
4. Click `Options` ....`Alt`+`O`
5. Click **Subtype** tab...............`Ctrl`+`Tab`
6. Select desired style ....`Alt`+`S`, `↹` in **Subtype** group.
7. Click `OK` ....`↵`

CREATE A COMBINATION CHART

Change chart type for specified data series.

1. Enable chart editing.
2. Select data series for which a new chart type will be selected.
3. Click **Format** menu ....`Alt`+`O`
4. Click **Chart Type**........................... `T`
5. Select ◯ **Selected Series** ..`Alt`+`S`
6. Select ◯ **2-D** ....`Alt`+`2`

    OR

    Select ◯ **3-D** ....`Alt`+`3`
7. Select desired chart type.... `Tab`, `↹`
8. Click `OK` ....`↵`

POSITION LEGEND IN CHART

1. Enable chart editing.
2. Right–click legend.
3. Click **Format Legend** ....`↓`, `↵`
4. Click **Placement** tab............`Ctrl`+`Tab`
5. Select desired position:

    • **Bottom**........................`Alt`+`B`
    • **Corner**........................`Alt`+`C`
    • **Top**.............................`Alt`+`T`
    • **Right**..........................`Alt`+`R`
    • **Left**............................`Alt`+`L`
6. Click `OK` ....`↵`

SELECT CHART ITEMS

Select chart items (such as the legend or a data series) prior to selecting commands to change the item in some way.

NOTE: Excel marks the currently selected chart item with squares, and displays its name in the name box.

• Enable chart editing.

To select next or previous class of chart items:

• Press **up** or **down**............... `↑↓`

To select next or previous item for selected chart class:

• Press **left** or **right**............... `↔`

To select a specific item with the mouse:

• Click chart item.

To select a data series:

• Click any data marker in data series.

To select a data marker:

a. Click any data marker in data series.
b. Click data marker in selected series.

To select the chart area:

• Click any blank area outside plot area.

To select the plot area:

• Click any blank area inside plot area.

To select the legend or legend items:

NOTE: Legend items are the legend entry and key.

a. Click legend.
b. Click item in legend.

To deselect a selected chart item:

• Press **Escape**........................ `Esc`

NEXT EXERCISE

EXERCISE

■ **Edit Linked Chart Text** ■ **Series Labels for Pie Charts**
■ **Move an Embedded Chart** ■ **Change Chart Colors and Patterns**
■ **Insert Chart Titles and Axis Labels**

56

NOTES:

Edit Linked Chart Text

■ Chart text or labels linked to the worksheet, such as category labels and legend entries, are automatically created from the data in the worksheet selection.

If you edit linked chart text in the worksheet, Excel automatically updates the chart.

Insert Chart Titles and Axis Labels

■ You can add unlinked text (such as chart titles, axis labels, and the legend) at any time using the Insert menu that appears when chart editing is enabled.

Series Labels for Pie Charts

■ In a **pie** chart, all the wedges make up the data series and each wedge represents a data point in the series. To identify the wedges in the pie chart, a label range should be selected as series labels. See the selection for pie chart data on the next page.

Move Embedded Chart

■ You can move an embedded chart when chart editing is enabled or when the chart is selected as an object (*see page 176*).

Change Chart Colors and Patterns

■ Charts may be customized by changing the colors or patterns that automatically appear to differentiate data markers. A different pattern and/or color (area format) may be specified for data. For example, you may wish to change the color of the bars or lines for a color presentation, or you may wish to change the colors to a black and white pattern for a crisper copy on your non-color printer. To change colors or patterns:

• Select the chart item while chart editing is enabled.

• Press Ctrl+1

or

Right-click and select Format Data Series

or

Click Format, Selected Data Series

• Make the changes in the Format Data Series dialog box.

■ The Format Data Series dialog box contains five tabs including the Patterns tab sheet illustrated below:

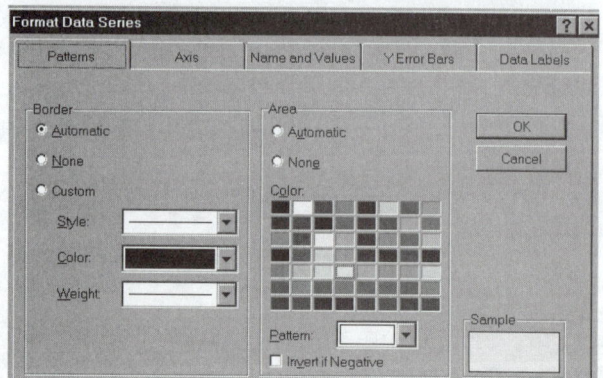

		selection for pie chart			COMBINED	
	1ST QTR.	2ND QTR.	3RD QTR.	4TH QTR.	TOTALS	series labels
INCOME:						
Service Fees	17052.39	28566.18	33610.97	21461.19	100690.73	
Consultations	4909.50	4679.76	3495.92	3088.79	16173.97	
Total Income	21961.89	33245.94	37106.89	24549.98	116864.70	
EXPENSES:						
Advertising	270	480	480	260	1490.00	
Salaries	2764.85	3766.65	3766.1	2764.3	13061.90	
Supplies	989.94	3011.7	5210.05	2106.03	11317.72	
Truck Maint.	464.52	1054.03	1060.53	1049.41	3628.49	
Interest	75	75	75	75	300.00	
Other	418.62	1779.51	1695.64	968.61	4862.38	
Total Expenses	4982.93	10166.89	12287.32	7223.35	34660.49	
NET INCOME	16978.96	23079.05	24819.57	17326.63	82204.21	data

		selection for column chart			COMBINED	
	1ST QTR.	2ND QTR.	3RD QTR.	4TH QTR.	TOTALS	series labels
INCOME:						
Service Fees	17052.39	28566.18	33610.97	21461.19	100690.73	
Consultations	4909.50	4679.76	3495.92	3088.79	16173.97	
Total Income	21961.89	33245.94	37106.89	24549.98	116864.70	
EXPENSES:						
Advertising	270.00	480.00	480.00	260.00	1490.00	
Salaries	2764.85	3766.65	3766.10	2764.30	13061.90	
Supplies	989.94	3011.70	5210.05	2106.03	11317.72	data
Truck Maint.	464.52	1054.03	1060.53	1049.41	3628.49	
Interest	75.00	75.00	75.00	75.00	300.00	
Other	418.62	1779.51	1695.64	968.61	4862.38	
Total Expenses	4982.93	10166.89	12287.32	7223.35	34660.49	
NET INCOME	16978.96	23079.05	24819.57	17326.63	82204.21	

In this exercise, you will retrieve the Greenthumb Landscape Service's quarterly income statement comparison worksheet and prepare and modify several charts to present the data graphically.

EXERCISE DIRECTIONS:

1. Open 🖳 **ISQTRS** or open 💾 **56ISQTRS.**

2. Create an embedded **pie** chart, comparing 1ST, 2ND, 3RD and 4TH QUARTER NET INCOME:

   - Make a non-adjacent selection that includes a blank cell.

     NOTE: When selecting worksheet data to chart, the selection area must be rectangular and a blank cell should be included in the selection. In each illustration on the previous page the non-adjacent selections (shaded) include a blank cell. The selection of a blank cell helps Excel correctly identify the labels for the data series.

   - Omit blank column in the selection.
   - Place the chart in the range B24:H38.

     —FROM CHARTWIZARD—

   - Select option (**5**) for the **pie** chart format.
   - Do not add chart titles or a legend when creating the chart.

3. Edit the **pie** chart and insert a chart title.

   GREENTHUMB LANDSCAPE SERVICE
   QUARTERLY NET INCOME

   ✓ *Excel uses the NET INCOME label; highlight the label and enter the new data.*

4. Insert a chart legend.

   ✓ *Excel uses worksheet labels to identify each data series. The legend entries are:*

   1ST QTR., 2ND QTR., 3RD QTR., and 4TH QTR.

5. In the worksheet, change 1ST QTR. label to read:

   JAN-MAR

   ✓ *Linked text changes in chart legend and label.*

6. Change the label back to 1ST QTR.

7. Select the 1ST QTR. Pie slice and change the color.

8. Create an embedded **column** chart comparing EXPENSES for the four quarters:

   - Omit blank columns in the selection.
   - Do not include TOTAL EXPENSES column or TOTALS row.
   - Omit blank column B.
   - Place chart in the range B41:H55.

   —FROM CHARTWIZARD—

   - Select default chart type and format.
   - Data series should be in columns.
   - Include a legend.
   - Do not add a chart title or axis titles when creating the chart. You will add them later.

9. Edit the chart and insert the following chart titles:

   - Chart Title
   - Value (Y) Axis
   - Category (X) Axis

     NOTE: Excel inserts default titles in chart.

10. Edit the chart titles to read:

    Title: GREENTHUMB LANDSCAPE SERVICE EXPENSES

    Y: DOLLARS

    X: EXPENSES

11. Using the same data and titles as those for the **column** chart, create a **stacked column** chart.

12. Place the **stacked column** chart in the range B58:H72.

13. Select each of the quarterly data series items and change the format so that the columns use different patterns instead of colors.

14. Using the same data and titles as those for the **column** chart, create a **line** chart.

15. Place the **line** chart in the range B74:H89.

16. Edit the **pie** chart and edit the second line of the chart title to read:

    NET INCOME COMPARISON

17. If necessary, move and size charts to align them.

18. Set worksheet to print on one page.

19. Use Print Preview to view your work.

20. Save and close the workbook file; name it **ISQTRS.**

	A	B	C	D	E	F	G
1			GREENTHUMB LANDSCAPE SERVICE				
2			QUARTERLY INCOME STATEMENT COMPARISON				
3							
4							
5							COMBINED
6			1ST QTR.	2ND QTR.	3RD QTR.	4TH QTR.	TOTALS
7	INCOME:						
8	Service Fees		17052.39	28566.18	33610.97	21461.19	100690.73
9	Consultations		4909.50	4679.76	3495.92	3088.79	16173.97
10	Total Income		21961.89	33245.94	37106.89	24549.98	116864.70
11							
12	EXPENSES:						
13	Advertising		270.00	480.00	480.00	260.00	1490.00
14	Salaries		2764.85	3766.65	3766.10	2764.30	13061.90
15	Supplies		989.94	3011.70	5210.05	2106.03	11317.72
16	Truck Maint.		464.52	1054.03	1060.53	1049.41	3628.49
17	Interest		75.00	75.00	75.00	75.00	300.00
18	Other		418.62	1779.51	1695.64	968.61	4862.38
19	Total Expenses		4982.93	10166.89	12287.32	7223.35	34660.49
20							
21	NET INCOME		16978.96	23079.05	24819.57	17326.63	82204.21

EDIT LINKED CHART TEXT IN WORKSHEET

When you edit linked text (legend entries, data labels [values or text], and tick mark labels) in the worksheet, Excel automatically updates the chart.

1. Select worksheet containing chart data to edit.

2. Edit cell containing data label or value.

MOVE AN EMBEDDED CHART

1. Select chart.

2. Point to chart border.
   Pointer becomes a ⬚ when positioned correctly.

3. Drag border outline to desired position.

   OR

   Press **Alt** and drag border outline to align object to gridlines.

INSERT A CHART LEGEND

1. Enable chart editing.

2. Click **I**nsert menu .... `Alt` + `I`

3. Click **L**egend .... `L`

INSERT CHART TITLE AND AXIS LABELS

1. Enable chart editing.

2. Click **I**nsert menu .... `Alt` + `I`

3. Click **T**itles .... `T`

4. Select desired **Attach Text to** options:
   NOTE: Available options depend upon selected chart type.

   • **Chart Title** .... `T`

   • **V**alue (Y) Axis .... `V`

   • **C**ategory (X) Axis .... `C`

   • Second Value (**Y**) Axis .... `Y`

   • Second Category (**X**) Axis .... `X`

5. Click `OK` .... `↵`

NOTE: Chart titles and axis labels are not linked to worksheet data, and they can be edited in the chart.

EXERCISE

■ Print Charts ■ Print Preview Charts ■ Print Embedded Chart
■ Use Non-color Printers ■ Add Data to a Chart

57

NOTES:

Print Charts

■ Charts can be printed with the worksheet or as separate sheets. You can select an embedded chart to print it apart from the worksheet.

Print Preview Charts

■ You can use Print Preview to see how a worksheet or chart will print.

From Print Preview, you can also:

• View the previous or next page when more than one page will be printed.

• Change the page margins by dragging the handles that appear when you select the Margins button.

• Click the Setup button to access the Page Setup dialog box from which you can change many page print settings such as scaling.

• Print the chart or worksheet.

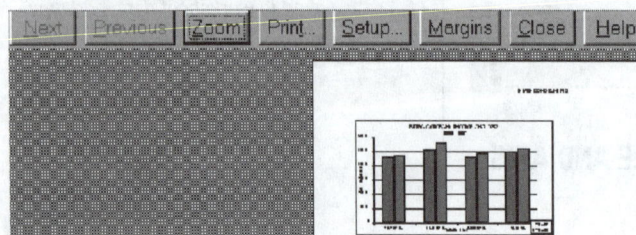

PRINT PREVIEW SCREEN

Print Embedded Chart

■ An embedded chart may be printed as part of the worksheet or, if it is selected, as a separate chart. When printing a selected embedded chart or a chart sheet:

• Excel selects the page orientation (**Portrait** or **Landscape**) that best matches the shape of the chart. You can change the page orientation from the Page tab in the Page Setup dialog box.

• The Sheet tab becomes a Chart tab in the Page Setup dialog box. You can set chart print options such as **Printing Quality** and **Printed Chart Size** from the Chart tab.

Use Non-color Printers

■ If your computer equipment includes a color monitor, the chart components will be shown in different colors. When you print these charts using a black and white printer, the colored text and lines are printed in black; the colored areas are printed in shades of gray; and the background color is ignored.

Add Data to a Chart

■ You may need to add an additional series of data to a chart to update the information. For example, you may want to add information about another division or add another year's information. To add data to an embedded chart on the same worksheet, select the new data and drag it onto the chart. On a chart sheet or separate worksheet, use the Copy and Paste commands to add the information.

In this exercise, you will add information for Year 3 and print the charts you created for the BITEC CO.

EXERCISE DIRECTIONS:

1. Open 🖰 **INCOME** or 💾 **57INCOME.**

2. Enter the new information for YEAR 3 in the worksheet as shown below.

3. Copy the new column, select EMBEDDED CHARTS sheet, select the column chart and paste the data.

4. Repeat this process for all charts on the worksheet.

5. Adjust size and location of chart elements, if necessary.

6. Print Preview the embedded chart in the worksheet.

7. From the Print Preview window, select the Setup button.

　　　—FROM PAGE SETUP DIALOG BOX—

8. Select the Sheet tab, and turn printing of gridlines off.

9. Select the Page tab, and set worksheet scale to one page wide by one page tall.

10. Return to the Preview screen and print the worksheet.

11. Enable chart editing on the **line** chart, then select Print Preview.

　　✓　*Only the line chart appears.*

12. Select the Setup button.

13. Select the Chart tab, and set the **Printed Chart Size** to Scale to Fit the Page; set print quality to draft.

14. Return to Print Preview and print the chart.

15. Select the PIE CHART sheet.

16. Preview the chart sheet and note the page orientation.

17. Click the Setup button and change the orientation of the page (**Landscape** or **Portrait**).

18. Close the dialog box and preview the chart sheet.

19. If the page orientation is set to portrait, change it back to landscape.

20. Print the chart sheet from the Print Preview window.

21. Save and close the workbook file; name it **INCOME.**

	A	B	C	D	E	F	G	H	I
1	BITEC CO.	NET INCOME							
2									
3			YEAR 1	YEAR 2	YEAR 3				
4	1ST QTR.		22990	23435	24547				
5	2ND QTR.		25437	27658	28343				
6	3RD QTR.		22895	24367	27543				
7	4TH QTR.		24897	25859	26598				
8									
9									
10									
11									
12									
13									
14									
15									

Income57.xls

PIE CHART / DATA / EMBEDDED CHARTS / Sheet3

INCOME WORKBOOK WITH DATA SHEET SELECTED

PRINT CHARTS

Prints chart sheet or embedded chart as part of the worksheet.

1. Select worksheet or chart sheet containing chart to print.

2. Follow steps to **PRINT A WORKSHEET**, page 53.

PRINT EMBEDDED CHART SEPARATELY

1. Enable chart editing for chart to print.

2. Follow steps to **PRINT A WORKSHEET**, page 53.

SET CHART PRINT OPTIONS

—*FROM PRINT PREVIEW*—

1. Click `Setup...` .... `Alt`+`S`

   OR

   —*FROM WORKSHEET OR CHART SHEET*—

   a. Click **File** menu ....`Alt`+`F`

   b. Click **Page Setup** .... `U`

2. Click **Chart** tab .... `Ctrl`+`Tab`

   NOTE: *Available options depend upon the currently selected printer.*

To set printed chart size:

Select desired **Printed Chart Size** option:

- **Use Full Page** .... `Alt`+`U`
- **Scale to Fit Page** .... `Alt`+`F`
- **Custom** .... `Alt`+`C`

  NOTE: *With **Custom** selected, you can center the chart on the page from the **Margins** tab.*

To set print quality of chart:

- Select ☐ **Draft Quality** .... `Alt`+`Q`

To print chart in black and white:

- Select ☐ **Print in Black and White** .... `Alt`+`B`

3. Click `OK` .... `↵`

   to return to sheet or Print Preview.

SET PAGE ORIENTATION OF PRINTED PAGE

—*FROM PRINT PREVIEW*—

1. Click `Setup...` .... `Alt`+`S`

   OR

   —*FROM WORKSHEET OR CHART SHEET*—

   a. Click **File** menu ....`Alt`+`F`

   b. Click **Page Setup** .... `U`

2. Click **Page** tab .... `Ctrl`+`Tab`

3. Select ○ **Portrait** .... `Alt`+`T`

   OR

   Select ○ **Landscape** .... `Alt`+`L`

4. Click `OK` .... `↵`

   to return to sheet or Print Preview.

ADD DATA SERIES TO A CHART

1. Select column or row of data.

2. Click **Edit** menu .... `Alt`+`E`

3. Click **Copy** .... `C`

4. Select chart to receive data.

5. Click **Paste** .... `P`

NEXT EXERCISE

EXERCISE 58

■ **Change Orientation of Data Series and Chart Text**
■ **Change Angle of First Slice in a Pie Chart**

NOTES:

Change Orientation of Data Series

■ For charts that use axes (all except pie charts), Excel automatically determines if the selected data range(s) will be plotted **by row** or **by column** layout. When you are creating a chart, ChartWizard proposes the orientation of the data series and allows you to make a change. You can also change the orientation of the data series after creating the chart, by making the change in ChartWizard, while in chart edit mode.

■ ChartWizard proposes how to plot the data series based on your selection.

If selection contains more columns than rows:

• ChartWizard proposes to plot the data series in rows.

• Column labels are used as x-axis labels.

• Row labels are used as legend labels.

If selection contains more rows than columns:

• ChartWizard proposes to plot the data series in columns.

• Row labels are used as x-axis labels.

• Column labels are used as legend labels.

If selection contains an equal number of rows and columns:

• ChartWizard proposes to plot the data series in rows.

■ You can change the orientation of the data series as shown in Illustration A on the next page.

Change Orientation of Chart Text

■ Chart text, such as axis labels or titles, can be arranged vertically facing left, vertically facing right, vertically, or horizontally. The text should be selected in chart edit mode and formatted using the Format, Selected text dialog box. An illustration of the formats are displayed in the dialog box.

Change Angle of First Slice in a Pie Chart

■ **Pie** charts are used to chart a single data series as shown in Illustration B on the next page. You can change the angle of the first pie slice, as shown below, by clicking the Format menu, selecting the chart type group, and setting the angle by degrees on the Options tab dialog box.

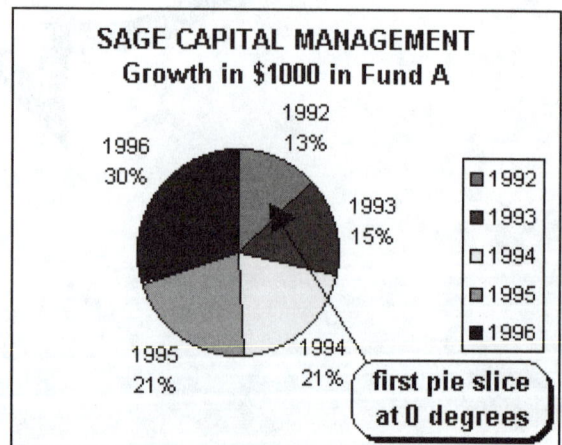

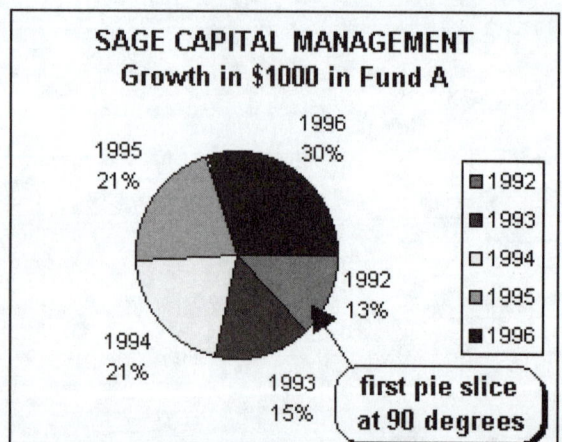

SAGE CAPITAL MANAGEMENT
Growth of $1000

		FUND A	FUND B
	1992	1024.00	1050.00
	1993	1199.10	1183.35
	1994	1598.41	1462.62
	1995	1627.18	1807.80
	1996	2328.49	1921.69

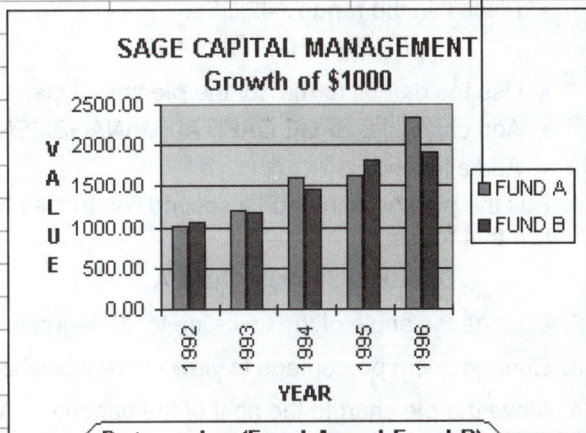

SAGE CAPITAL MANAGEMENT
Growth of $1000

Data series (Fund A and Fund B) plotted in column layout.

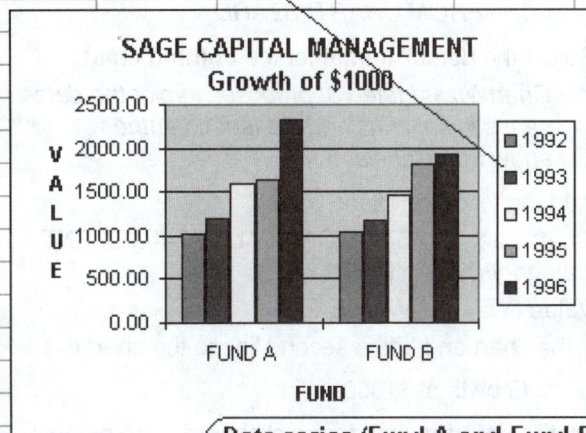

SAGE CAPITAL MANAGEMENT
Growth of $1000

Data series (Fund A and Fund B) plotted in row layout.

ILLUSTRATION A

SAGE CAPITAL MANAGEMENT
Growth of $1000

		FUND A	FUND B
	1992	1024.00	1050.00
	1993	1199.10	1183.35
	1994	1598.41	1462.62
	1995	1627.18	1807.80
	1996	2328.49	1921.69

Pie chart
(A single data series)

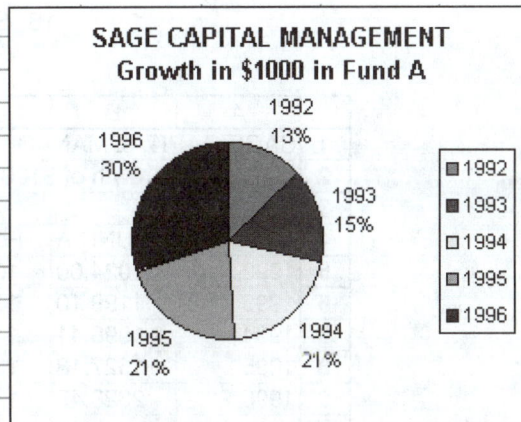

SAGE CAPITAL MANAGEMENT
Growth in $1000 in Fund A

1992 13%
1993 15%
1994 21%
1995 21%
1996 30%

ILLUSTRATION B

In this exercise, you will create several charts comparing the growth and performance of an investment in Fund A to one in Fund B, for Sage Capital Management, for a five-year period.

EXERCISE DIRECTIONS:

1. Create the worksheet as shown below, or open 💾 **58FUND.**

   NOTE: The row labels should be formatted as label data.

2. Create an embedded **column** chart comparing Fund A to Fund B for 1992-1996, by using the Chart Wizard button.

   • Place the chart in the range A11:E25.

      —FROM CHARTWIZARD—

   • Select the default format for the **column** chart.

      ✓ ChartWizard (step 3) proposes to plot the data series in columns and the legend entries show Fund labels.

   • Add the following titles:
      Chart Title: SAGE CAPITAL MANAGEMENT
      Category (X):   YEAR
      Value (Y):   VALUE

3. Edit the chart and add a second line to the chart title:

      Growth of $1000

4. Copy the **column** chart to the clipboard, then paste it to the range starting at G11.

5. Change the plot orientation to rows.

   ✓ Note changes to the legend entries and x-axis labels.

6. Edit the X-Axis title to FUND.

7. Edit both **column** charts and change the alignment of the y-axis label to vertical orientation, (one letter under the other.)

8. Place another copy of the **column** chart in the range starting at A27.

9. Change the chart type to a **bar** chart.

10. Create an embedded **pie** chart that shows the values of Fund A for 1992-1996.

    • Place it in the range A42:D54.

       —FROM CHARTWIZARD—

    • Use the default format for the **pie** chart type.
    • Add chart title: SAGE CAPITAL MANAGEMENT
    • Add a legend.

11. Edit the **pie** chart and add a second line to the chart title that reads:

       Growth of $1000 in Fund A

12. Change the angle of the first slice to 90 degrees.

13. Change zoom percentage to view entire worksheet.

14. Move the **pie** chart to the right of the bar chart. Align charts (size and move them) as needed.

15. Change colors of bars in the column and bar charts so that each chart is different.

16. Print Preview the sheet.

17. Print the worksheet so that the data and charts fit on one page.

18. Save the workbook file; name it **FUND.**

	A	B	C	D
1	SAGE CAPITAL MANAGEMENT			
2		Growth of $1000		
3				
4		FUND A	FUND B	
5	1992	1024.00	1050.00	
6	1993	1199.10	1183.35	
7	1994	1598.41	1462.62	
8	1995	1627.18	1807.80	
9	1996	2328.49	1921.69	
10				

CHANGE ORIENTATION OF DATA SERIES

1. Enable chart editing.

2. Click **ChartWizard** button .... [icon] on Standard Toolbar.

3. Click [Next >] .... [↵]

4. Select ◯ **Rows** .... [Alt]+[R]

   OR

   Select ◯ **Columns** .... [Alt]+[C]

5. Click [OK] .... [↵]

CHANGE ORIENTATION OF CHART TEXT

NOTE: *You cannot change orientation of text in a legend.*

1. Enable chart editing.

2. Double–click chart text.

   OR

   a. Click text to change.

   b. Click **Format** menu ...... [Alt]+[O]

   c. Click **Selected** .... [E]
   NOTE: *Menu item changes to describe selected item.*

3. Click **Alignment** tab .... [Ctrl]+[Tab]

4. Click desired **Orientation** option .... [Alt]+[O], [↗]

5. Click [OK] .... [↵]

SET FORMAT OPTIONS FOR A CHART TYPE GROUP

NOTE: *Most charts (except combination charts) contain a single chart type group in which each data series is pre-formatted. For example, in a pie chart the angle of the first pie slice is set to zero degrees. This procedure changes the formats specific to the active chart type.*

1. Enable chart editing.

2. Click **Format** menu .... [Alt]+[O]

3. Click numbered chart type group *number* at bottom of menu.

4. Click **Options** tab .... [Ctrl]+[Tab]

5. Select desired format options .... [Alt]+*letter* for chart type group.
   NOTE: *Available options depend upon selected chart type.*

   Format options include: *Angle of First Slice, Chart Depth (3-D), Doughnut Hole Size, Drop Lines, High-Low Lines, Gap Depth (3-D), Overlap, Gap Width, Radar Axis Labels, Series Lines, Up-Down Bars, Vary Colors By Point/Slice (2-D and 3-D)*

6. Click [OK] .... [↵]

EXERCISE

- Create an Open-High-Low-Close Chart
- Format Data Markers in a Line Chart ■ Set Scale of Value Axis

59

NOTES:

Create an Open-High-Low-Close Chart

- **Open-High-Low-Close** charts are used to track changes in data during a particular time period, and are a subtype of the **line** chart. This chart is commonly used to show the opening, high, low and closing stock prices, usually on a daily basis.

Format Data Markers

- For each day, the opening, high, low and closing values are represented by a unique data marker. Excel lets you format the shape and color of the data markers. You can choose a shape that relates to the meaning of the marker—a circle for open, for example.

Set Scale of Value Axis

- Excel determines the scale used on the value axis from the range of data plotted. This scale can be changed. For example, you can set the display of the minimum and maximum values and the major and minor units of values on the y-axis.

  NOTE: When selecting chart items such as a data series or y-axis, look at the chart item name in the name box to confirm that the correct chart item is selected.

- When you right–click a selected chart item, Excel displays a shortcut menu appropriate to the selected item. This method can help you get your work done faster.

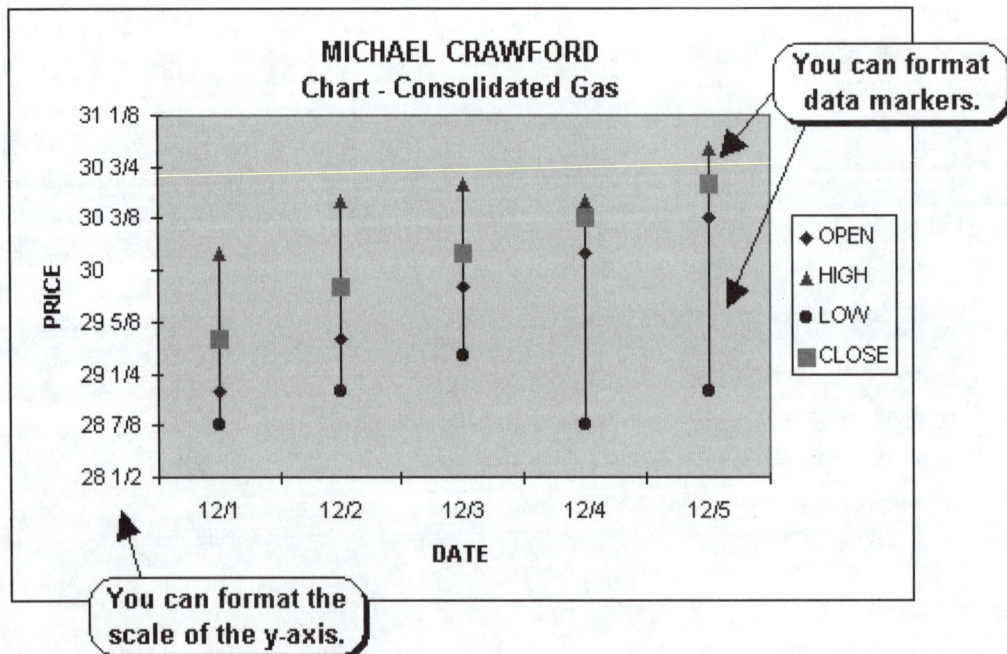

MICHAEL CRAWFORD
Chart - Consolidated Gas

You can format data markers.

You can format the scale of the y-axis.

In this exercise, you will prepare an Open-High-Low-Close chart for Michael Crawford. He is considering the sale of his Consolidated Gas stock and needs to evaluate the stock's performance for the week.

EXERCISE DIRECTIONS:

1. Create the worksheet as shown below, or open 🖫 **59CHART.**

   NOTE: Format the dates in column A as label data and enter the values as mixed numbers.

2. Create an **Open-High-Low-Close** chart on a separate sheet using the Insert, Chart, As New Sheet method.

   - Place the chart below the worksheet data.
     —FROM CHARTWIZARD—

   - Select a **line** chart type and choose format (**7**) (Open-High-Low-Close) as the subtype.

   Chart titles should be as follows:

   Chart Title: MICHAEL CRAWFORD
   Category (X):   DATE
   Value (Y):   PRICE

3. Edit the chart and add to second line of chart title:

   CHART - CONSOLIDATED GAS

4. Select the y-axis chart item and format its scale as follows:

Minimum:	28.5
Maximum:	31.125
Major Unit:	.375
Minor Unit:	.125

5. Select each data series in turn and format the styles of the markers as follows:

   OPEN (Series 1)   Style of marker: diamond
                      Foreground and
                      Background: black
   HIGH (Series 2)   Style of marker: triangle
                      Foreground and
                      Background: red
   LOW (Series 3)   Style of marker: circle
                      Foreground and
                      Background: blue
   CLOSE (Series 4)   Style of marker: square
                      Foreground and
                      Background: bright green

6. Size the chart to increase space between markers.

7. Rename the Chart1 sheet, CHART.

8. Rename the Sheet1 sheet, DATA.

9. Save the workbook file; name it **CHART**.

10. Print the CHART sheet.

11. Close the workbook file.

	A	B	C	D	E	F
1		MICHAEL CRAWFORD				
2		CHART - CONSOLIDATED GAS				
3						
4		OPEN	HIGH	LOW	CLOSE	
5	12/1	29 1/8	30 1/8	28 7/8	29 1/2	
6	12/2	29 1/2	30 1/2	29 1/8	29 7/8	
7	12/3	29 7/8	30 5/8	29 3/8	30 1/8	
8	12/4	30 1/8	30 1/2	28 7/8	30 3/8	
9	12/5	30 3/8	30 7/8	29 1/8	30 5/8	
10						

SET SCALE OF VALUE AXIS

1. Enable chart editing.
2. Double–click value axis to format.

   OR

   a. Right–click value axis.

   b. Click **Format**

   Axis........................... 🔲 , ↵
3. Click **Scale** tab .... Ctrl + Tab
4. a. Select scale options to change:

   Mi̲nimum .... Alt + N

   Ma̲ximum .... Alt + X

   Ma̲jor Unit.................... Alt + A

   Mi̲nor Unit .... Alt + I

   Category (X) Axis

   C̲rosses at .... Alt + C

   b. Type desired value .... *number* for selected item in text box.
5. Repeat step 4 for each scale option to change.
6. Click ⬛ OK .... ↵

FORMAT DATA MARKERS IN A LINE CHART

1. Enable chart editing.
2. Double–click any data marker in series to format.

   OR

   a. Select data series to format. *Name box shows number of selected series (S1 or S2 . . .).*

   b. Click **F̲ormat** menu...... Alt + O

   c. Click **S̲elected Data Series**... E
3. Click **Patterns** tab .... Ctrl + Tab
4. Select desired **Marker** options:

   • **A̲utomatic**.................. Alt + U

   • **N̲one**........................... Alt + O

To change style of marker:

a. Click **Sty̲le** .... Alt + L

b. Select a marker style.................. 🔲 , Alt + ↑

To change foreground color of marker:

a. Click **F̲oreground** .... Alt + F

b. Select a foreground color.................. 🔲 , Alt + ↑

To change background color of marker:

a. Click **B̲ackground** .... Alt + B

b. Select a background color.................. 🔲 , Alt + ↑

5. Click ⬛ OK .... ↵

NEXT EXERCISE

EXERCISE
60

- **Insert Data Labels in a Chart** ■ **AutoFormat a Chart**
- **Size Plot Area or Legend in a Chart** ■ **Move a Chart Item**
- **Create Exploded Pie Chart** ■ **Create Area Chart**

NOTES:

Create Exploded Pie Chart

■ An exploded pie chart has one or more wedges of the pie separated from the circle for emphasis. To create an exploded chart effect, you can move any selected wedge (data point) by dragging it away from the center of the pie.

NOTE: When you drag a slice, the associated labels move with it.

AutoFormat a Chart

■ The **AutoFormat** feature lets you select a built-in format for the current chart type.

IMPORTANT: When you use AutoFormat any custom formats you have applied are lost.

✓ *The illustration below shows the available AutoFormats for a pie chart.*

- The letters (ABC) in formats 2, 5 and 7 indicate that these formats include **data labels**.

- Format 3 will set your pie chart to show the first pie slice exploded while format 4 sets your chart to show all the pie slices exploded.

- The percent signs (%) in formats 6 and 7 indicate that a percentage will appear next to each slice if you select any of these formats.

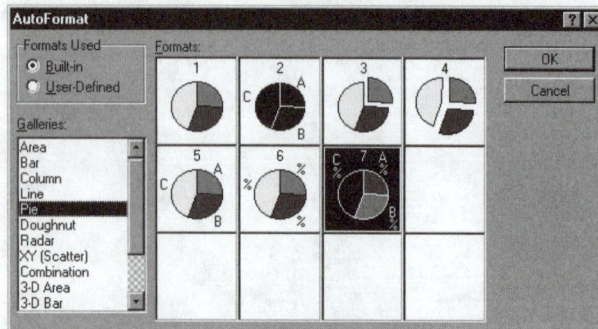

AUTOFORMATS FOR PIE CHART

Insert Data Labels in a Chart

■ Since a pie chart has only one data series, data labels can be used effectively to identify the numeric values instead of a legend. Data labels may be inserted, if desired, by using the Insert menu.

Size Plot Area or Legend in a Chart

■ After adding data labels to a chart, you may want to move or size the plot area of the chart. When you do this, the data labels adjust with the plot area. When the plot area is selected, **plot** appears in the name box. Note the illustration of a pie chart with plot area selected below.

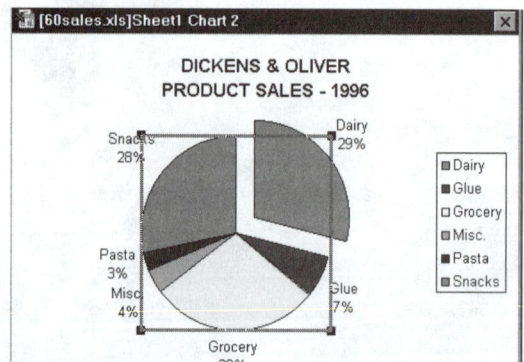

Create an Area Chart

■ A two-dimensional area chart can be described as a stacked bar and line chart combined. The data series are stacked, but a trendline is drawn between the data points. An illustration of an area chart is shown below:

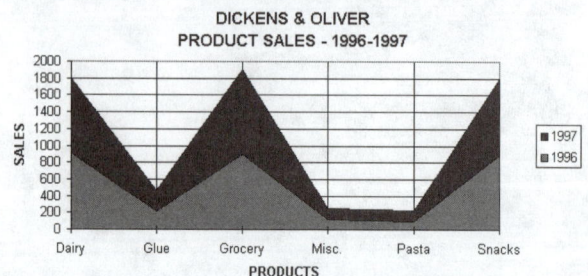

AREA CHART

In this exercise, you will create a worksheet for Dickens & Oliver, a diversified food products company. They want to compare sales for all products for each year by creating pie charts and compare both years by creating an area chart.

EXERCISE DIRECTIONS:

1. Create the worksheet as shown on the next page, or open 💾 **60SALES.**

2. Create an embedded **pie** chart illustrating 1996 sales, using ChartWizard and a nonadjacent selection of data:

   - Place chart in the range A13:F26.
        —FROM CHARTWIZARD—

   - Select format (**3**) for the pie chart format—it contains one exploded pie slice.
   - Add a legend.
   - Add the first line of the chart title to read:
        DICKENS & OLIVER

3. Edit the chart and add a second line to chart title to read:
        PRODUCT SALES - 1996

4. Select chart data and use Insert menu to include data labels in the chart. Set the labels to show label and percent.

   NOTE: When the name box displays S1, the series is selected.

5. Select the plot area of chart, and size and move it as desired. Try to enlarge the pie portion of the chart.

6. Create an embedded **pie** chart illustrating 1997 sales using ChartWizard and a nonadjacent selection of data:

   - Place chart in the range A27:F40.
        —FROM CHARTWIZARD—

   - Select format (**5**) for the pie chart format—no exploded pie slices.
   - Add a legend.
   - Add the first line of the chart title to read:
        DICKENS & OLIVER

7. Edit the chart and add a second line to chart title to read:
        PRODUCT SALES - 1997

8. Select chart data and insert data labels in the new chart. Set the labels to show label and percent.

   NOTE: When the name box displays S1, the series is selected.

9. Select the plot area of chart, and size and move it as desired.

10. Use AutoFormat to change the format of the second pie chart to format (**5**) (no exploded slices).

    NOTE: Your custom format is lost—data labels no longer contain percentages.

11. Select the DAIRY data marker and format this data point as follows:

    NOTE: When the name box displays SIP1, the correct slice (data point) is selected.

    Settings from the Patterns tab:
    - Color: black
    - Pattern: horizontal stripes

    Settings from the Data Labels tab:
    - Data label to show label and percent

12. With the DAIRY marker selected, move it to the right to explode the pie slice.

    NOTE: If you move the wrong item, select **Undo** from the **Edit** menu.

13. Create an embedded **area** chart illustrating 1996 and 1997 sales. Include the year labels and use ChartWizard and a non-adjacent selection of data:

    - Place chart in the range A42:H55.
         —FROM CHARTWIZARD—

    - Select an area chart.
    - Add a legend.
    - Add titles as follows:
         Chart title: DICKENS & OLIVER
         X-Axis title: PRODUCTS
         Y-Axis title: SALES

14. Edit the chart and add a second line to chart title to read:
         PRODUCT SALES - 1996 1997

15. With the worksheet selected, set entire worksheet to print on one page.

16. Save the workbook file; name it **SALES**.

17. Close the workbook file.

	A	B	C	D	E	F
1		DICKENS & OLIVER				
2		PRODUCT SALES				
3						
4				1996	1997	
5						
6	Dairy			906	895	
7	Glue			215	250	
8	Grocery			901	1003	
9	Misc.			122	125	
10	Pasta			94	135	
11	Snacks			888	912	
12		(IN THOUSANDS OF DOLLARS)				
13						

INSERT DATA LABELS IN A CHART

Adds data labels to a specific data marker, data series, or all data series.

1. Enable chart editing.
2. Select appropriate chart item:

   To add labels to a specific series:
   - Select desired series.

   To add labels to a specific data marker:
   - Select desired data marker.

   To add labels to all markers in all data series:
   - Select chart or plot area.
     NOTE: The name box displays currently selected chart item.

3. Click **Insert** menu .... `Alt` + `I`
4. Click **Data Labels** .... `D`
5. Select desired **Data Labels** option:
   - **None** .... `Alt` + `N`
     to remove existing data label.
   - **Show Value** .... `Alt` + `V`
     to show value of data point.
   - **Show Percent** .... `Alt` + `P`
     to show percentage of part to whole for pie and doughnut charts.
   - **Show Label** .... `Alt` + `L`
     to show category or series name.
   - **Show Label and Percent** .... `Alt` + `A`
     to show category or series name and percentage of part to whole for pie and doughnut charts.

   To display legend keys next to data labels:
   - Select ☐ **Show Legend Key** .... `Alt` + `K`

6. Click `OK` .... `↵`

NOTE: Data labels are linked to worksheet data and they can be edited in the worksheet or in the chart.

AUTOFORMAT A CHART

Applies a built-in or custom-made format to chart.

NOTE: When you select an AutoFormat, all custom formats are lost.

1. Enable chart editing.
2. Click **Format** menu .... `Alt` + `O`
3. Click **AutoFormat** .... `A`
4. Select ◯ **Built-in** .... `Alt` + `B`

   OR

   Select ◯ **User-Defined** ..... `Alt` + `U`

To change chart type:

- Select chart type .... `⊡`
  in **Galleries** or **Formats** list box.

  Galleries list items include:
  Area, Bar, Column, Line, Pie, Doughnut, Radar, XY (Scatter), Combination, 3-D Area, 3-D Bar, 3-D Column, 3-D Line, 3-D Pie, 3-D Surface

  Formats list items include:
  custom names defined by user

5. Select a format .... `Alt` + `F`, `⊡`
   in **Formats** list box.
6. Click `OK` .... `↵`

SIZE PLOT AREA OR LEGEND IN A CHART

1. Enable chart editing.
2. Select plot area or legend.
   Handles appear on border of item.
3. Point to handle on side of item to size.
   Pointer becomes a ⤢ ↕ ⤡ ↔ .
4. Drag item outline in direction to size.

MOVE A CHART ITEM

NOTE: *You can move the plot area, legend, chart title, data labels, pie slices and axes labels.*

1. Enable chart editing.
2. Select chart item to move.
3. Drag chart item outline to desired position.

CHANGE AREA FORMAT OF A DATA SERIES OR DATA POINT

1. Enable chart editing.
2. Select appropriate chart item:

To format a specific series:

a. Select desired series.

b. Click **Format** menu ...... `Alt`+`O`

c. Click **Selected Data Series** ... `E`

To format a specific data point:

a. Select desired data marker.

b. Click **Format** menu ...... `Alt`+`O`

c. Click **Selected Data Point** ..... `E`

   NOTE: *The name box displays currently selected chart item.*

3. Click **Patterns** tab .... `Ctrl`+`Tab`

4. Select desired **Area** options:

- **Automatic** .... `Alt`+`U`
- **None** .... `Alt`+`O`

To change area color:

- Select a color ..... `Alt`+`C`, `↕` in **Color** group.

To change area pattern:

a. Click **Pattern**

   `[            ▼]` .... `Alt`+`P`

b. Select desired pattern .... `↕`, `Alt`+`↑`

5. Click `OK` .... `↵`

UNDO LAST CHANGE

1. Click **Edit** menu .... `Alt`+`E`

2. Click **Undo** .... `U`

   NOTE: *Complete name of **Undo** menu item depends on last action.*

EXERCISE

■ Create a 3-D Chart ■ Enter Line Breaks in a Cell Entry
■ Set View Options for a 3-D Chart ■ Add Chart Text and Gridlines

61

NOTES:

Enter Line Breaks in a Cell Entry

■ When you select worksheet text to chart, Excel uses the labels in individual cells to identify markers and sometimes axes in the chart.

■ When your worksheet labels are in more than one row, you should combine the text so it is contained in a single cell, as shown below. Use F2 to edit the cell and press Alt+Enter, which inserts a line break in the contents of the cell. The row height adjusts automatically to show multiple lines of text.

	A	B	C	D
1				
2				
3				
4	NO. OF SHARES	COMPANY NAME	SYMBOL	DATE BOUGHT
5				
6				

Add Chart Text and Gridlines

■ You can add unlinked text to a chart and position it as desired to add information to a chart. Linked chart text includes a reference to a worksheet cell which displays the cell's contents in the chart. A linked cell requires the entry of a complete worksheet reference, including the sheet name, or the cell may be selected from the worksheet. Chart text that is linked in this way will change when the contents of the referenced cell changes.

■ You can add **gridlines** to some charts to further clarify where data points fall on the chart. These lines may be added to or removed from any axis.

Create a 3-D Chart

■ You can select a **3-D Chart** format to add interest and emphasize the data you want to compare.

Changing a 2-D chart to 3-D adds a **z-axis** which becomes the value axis.

You may change the view of a 3-D chart by using the following 3-D format options:

• increase or decrease elevation

• rotate chart left or right

• increase or decrease perspective

• lock axes at right angles

Note the illustration of the Format 3-D View dialog box:

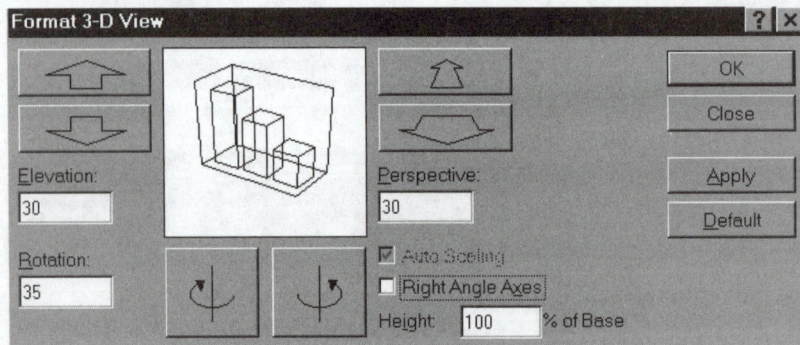

FORMAT 3-D VIEW DIALOG BOX

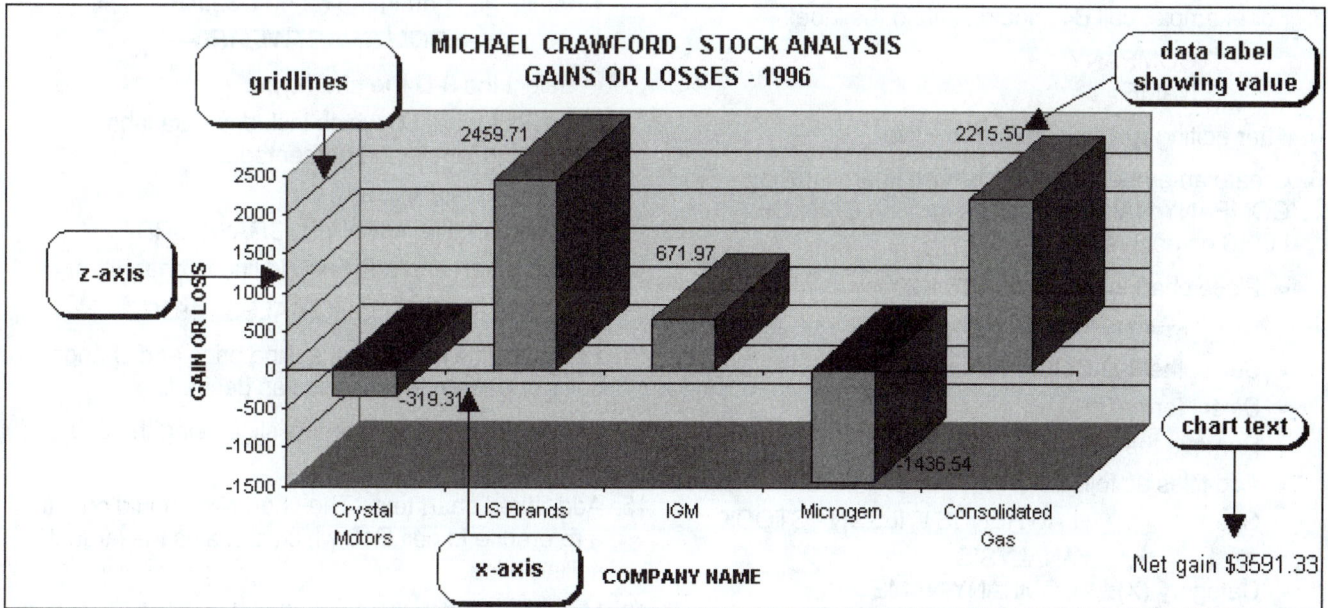

MICHAEL CRAWFORD - STOCK ANALYSIS
GAINS OR LOSSES - 1996

gridlines

data label showing value

z-axis

x-axis

chart text

2459.71

671.97

2215.50

-319.31

-1436.54

GAIN OR LOSS

Crystal Motors   US Brands   IGM   Microgem   Consolidated Gas

COMPANY NAME

Net gain $3591.33

ILLUSTRATION OF 3-D CHART

In this exercise, you will retrieve Michael Crawford's stock analysis data and create enhanced charts to present his gain and loss for the year. In addition, you will chart the percent that each stock's selling price represents of his total stock portfolio sales using a pie chart.

EXERCISE DIRECTIONS:

1. Open ⌨ **MARKET** or open 💾 **61MARKET.**

2. Unfreeze window panes.

3. Edit row four so the contents of each cell contains the text now found in row four and five. Most cells will then contain two lines of text.

    For example, cell B4 should contain the label:

    > COMPANY
    > NAME

4. After editing row four, delete row five.

5. Create an embedded **3-D column** chart showing COMPANY NAMES of stocks and the GAIN OR LOSS on each stock:

    - Place chart in the range B15:K29.
      —*FROM CHARTWIZARD*—

    - Select the **3-D Column** chart type.
    - Select format (**1**).
    - Remove the legend
    - Add titles as follows:
Chart:	LAWRENCE WILSON - STOCK ANALYSIS
Category (X):	COMPANY NAME
Value (Z):	GAIN OR LOSS

6. Edit the chart and add a second line to the chart title:

    > GAINS OR LOSSES - 1996

7. Insert data labels showing values next to each data marker in the series.

8. Insert major gridlines for the value axis, which is now the z-axis.

9. Select the data area and format the 3-D view using the controls in the Format, 3-D View dialog box.

    - change the elevation
    - change the rotation of the chart
    - click OK to view the chart
    - re-select the data and 3-D View dialog box
    - deselect the Right Angle Axes box
    - change the perspective
    - move dialog box so chart is visible
    - click Default to return to default settings

10. Add unlinked chart text to the corner of the chart as follows:

    > Net gain $3591.33

11. Create a **3-D pie** chart showing company names and SELLING PRICE data:

    - Place the chart in the range D32:I46.
      —*FROM CHARTWIZARD*—

    - Select the **3-D Pie** chart type.
    - Select format (**7**) which includes data labels showing labels and percentages.
    - Do not add a legend.
    - Add chart title: MICHAEL CRAWFORD

12. Edit the chart and add second line to chart title:

    > STOCK PORTFOLIO SALES - 1996

13. Explode slice for highest selling price and change color or pattern for this slice as desired.

14. Change the angle of the first slice using the 3-D View dialog box.

15. Add linked chart text. The chart text should contain a reference to cell G10 which contains the largest selling price.

16. Move linked chart text onto the slice to which it belongs.

17. Select the worksheet and set it to print on one page.

18. Print the worksheet.

19. Resave the workbook and close the file.

	A	B	C	D	E	F	G	H	I	J	K	L
1					MICHAEL CRAWFORD							
2				STOCK ANALYSIS - TRANSACTIONS FOR 199-								
3												
4	NO. OF SHARES	COMPANY NAME	SYMBOL	DATE BOUGHT	DATE SOLD	DAYS HELD	SELLING PRICE	COST	DIVIDENDS EARNED	ANNUAL YIELD	GAIN OR LOSS	% GAIN OR LOSS
5	SHARES	NAME	SYMBOL	BOUGHT	SOLD	HELD	PRICE	COST	EARNED	YIELD	LOSS	LOSS
6												
7	200	Crystal Motors	CM	15-Jan-96	05-Nov-96	295	6548.95	7453.76	585.50	9.72%	-319.31	-4.28%
8	100	US Brands	USB	30-Jan-96	30-Jun-96	152	9057.43	6923.12	325.40	11.29%	2459.71	35.53%
9	50	IGM	IGM	17-Feb-96	25-Apr-96	68	3248.95	2576.98	0.00	0.00%	671.97	26.08%
10	300	Microgem	MIG	17-Feb-96	05-Dec-96	292	3954.69	5391.23	0.00	0.00%	-1436.54	-26.65%
11	500	Consolidated Gas	CG	28-Mar-96	20-Dec-96	267	15487.54	14326.54	1054.50	10.06%	2215.50	15.46%
12												
13		TOTALS				1074	38297.56	36671.63	1965.40		3591.33	182.73%
14												

Add second line to cell labels as shown, then delete row 5.

ENTER LINE BREAKS IN A CELL ENTRY

1. Double–click cell to edit.

   OR

   a. Select cell to edit.

   b. Press **F2** .... `F2`

2. Place insertion point .... `⟷` where line break will be inserted.

3. Press **Alt + Enter** .... `Alt`+`↵`

4. Type text as needed .... *text*

INSERT OR REMOVE GRIDLINES

1. Enable chart editing.

2. Click **Insert** menu .... `Alt`+`I`

3. Click **Gridlines** .... `Alt`+`G`

4. Select or deselect (X/Y/Z) axis options:

   NOTE: Available options depend upon selected chart type.

   • **Major Gridlines** .... `Alt`+*letter*

   • **Minor Gridlines** .... `Alt`+*letter*

5. Click [OK] .... `↵`

ADD CHART TEXT

1. Enable chart editing.

2. Click formula bar.

   OR

   Press **F2** .... `F2`

   ### To add unlinked text:

   • Type text .... *text*

   ### To add linked text:

   a. Press **Equal** .... `=`

   b. Select desired cell in worksheet.

      OR

      Type reference to desired cell .... *reference*

3. Press **Enter** .... `↵`

4. Move text box, if necessary.

SET VIEW OPTIONS FOR A 3-D CHART (Change Rotation and Elevation)

1. Enable chart editing.

2. Click **Format** menu .... `Alt`+`O`

3. Click **3-D View** .... `V`

   ### To increase or decrease elevation:

   • Click **Elevation** button `⬆` or `⬇`

   OR

   a. Select desired **Elevation** button .... `Tab`

   b. Press **Space** .... `Space` until desired elevation is obtained.

   ### To rotate chart left or right:

   • Click **Rotation** button .... `↺` or `↻`

   OR

   a. Select desired **Rotation** button .... `Tab`

   b. Press **Space** .... `Space` until desired rotation is obtained.

To increase or decrease perspective:

*NOTE: This option is not available if **Right Angle Axes** is selected.*

- Click **Perspective** button .. `⬭` or `⬆`

OR

a. Select desired **Perspective** button .... `Tab`

b. Press **Space** .... `Space` until desired perspective is obtained.

To lock axes at right angles:

- Select `☐` **Right Angle Axes** .... `Alt`+`X`

To scale chart to fill window:
*NOTE: This option is available if **Right Angle Axes** is selected.*

- Select `☐` **Auto Scaling** .... `Alt`+`S`

To set height in relation to base of chart:

a. Click **Height:** `[        ]` **%** of **Base** .... `Alt`+`I`

b. Type number (5-500) .... *number*

To preview chart in sheet with current settings:

a. Move dialog box so chart is visible.

b. Click `Apply` .... `Alt`+`A`

To return chart to default settings:

- Click `Default` .... `Alt`+`D`

4. Click `OK` .... `↵`

NEXT EXERCISE

EXERCISE

■ Use Data Map Feature ■ Edit Map and Legend ■ Data Map Toolbar

62

NOTES:

Use Data Map Feature

■ Excel 7.0 has a new mapping feature that will display geographic data, such as information about countries or states, on the appropriate map. To use the map feature, select the range of cells to be mapped, including the geographic data, and click the Map button 🌐 on the Standard Toolbar. Excel then provides the cross hair + mouse symbol to drag and size the map and finds the map that relates to the data selected. (If you do not have the map icon on your toolbar, rerun the Setup program to install the mapping feature.)

■ This exercise will demonstrate several options in the data mapping feature.

Edit Map

■ As with charts, to edit the map when in worksheet mode, you must double-click on the displayed map. When the map is first created, you are in edit mode which includes a border around the map, a menu bar that includes map commands, and the Data Map toolbar which replaces the Standard and Formatting toolbars. Note the illustration below of the data map menus, toolbars and the Data Map Control Box.

■ The Data Map Control Box may be hidden or displayed. It is displayed when the map is created and may be used to format items on the map. The format buttons may be dragged onto the box area to change the format of the map. The Data Map Control box may be closed with the Close button or by clicking the Show/Hide Data Map Control Box icon on the Map toolbar.

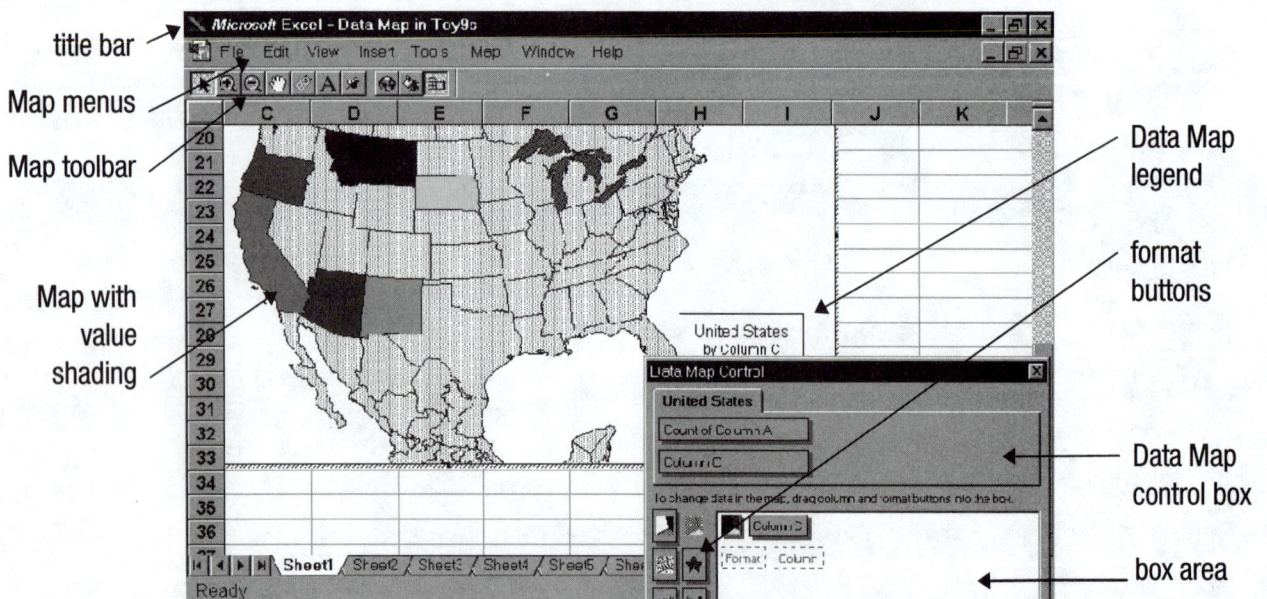

212

Data Map Toolbar

- The Data Map Toolbar contains icons that enable you to edit the map and change map views. Note the illustration of the Data Map Toolbar below:

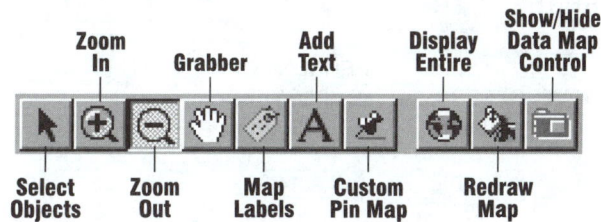

DATA MAP TOOLBAR

In this exercise, you will use the Palmer Toy Manufacturing Co. worksheet to apply the map feature. The map and the legend will be edited, data labels will be added, and the map will be sized and moved for better appearance. Use the illustration of the solution to assist you in creating the desired result.

EXERCISE DIRECTIONS:

1. Open ⌨ **TOYS** or 💾 **62TOYS**.

2. Select the range to map, including the state names and the number of employees.

3. Click on the Map button 🔲 on Standard Toolbar.

4. Place the map in the range A16.I30.

5. Select the United States map from the Multiple Maps Available box.

   ✓ *The default map will appear with a legend, a Data Map Control box and the map menus and toolbar.*

6. Explore the Data Map Control box by moving the pointer over the format buttons to see the ToolTips.

   ✓ *The chart is using Value Shading.*

7. Change the chart to Category Shading by clicking and dragging the Category Shading button into the box.

   ✓ *The shading changes to colors.*

8. Close the Data Map Control box.

9. Double-click the map to change to the edit map mode.

10. To hide the North America heading:

   - Double-click on the NORTH AMERICA title box.
   - Right-click and select **Hide** from the shortcut menu.

11. To edit the legend:

   - Double-click on the legend box.
   - Right-click and select **Edit** from the shortcut menu.
   - Check that **Use compact format** is deselected and that **Show legend** is selected.
   - Change the titles and fonts as follows:

   Palmer Toy Manufacturing Co. (Bookman Old Style, 11 pt.)
   Employees by State (Bookman Old Style, 9 pt.)

12. To label the map with state names and data:

   - Click the Map Labels icon on the Map toolbar (in edit mode).
   - In the Map Labels dialog box, select **Map Feature Names** for state labels.
   - Point to each state that has data. You will note that the name of the state appears. Place the label in the topmost position within each state. Click to insert the label.
   - Click the Map Labels icon on the Map toolbar.
   - In the Map Labels dialog box, select the **Values from** option and note that Column C or the column with the values is selected.
   - Point to each state and click to enter the value below the state name.

13. To change colors of the states:

   - Select the **Map, Category Shading Options** from the map menu bar.
   - Go to the values for Arizona (1060 - Red) and change it to white.
   - Go to the values for Montana (450 - Blue) and change it to gray.

14. To move the map into view:

   - Use the Zoom In icon to bring it closer for easier viewing.
   - Use the Grabber icon to move the map to the left of the map area.
   - Move the legend box to the bottom right corner of the map.

     (Use the illustration of the solution as a guide for moving the elements of the map.)

15. Print a copy of the worksheet.

16. Close and save the workbook file, or save as **TOYS**.

	A	B	C	D	E	F	G	H	I
1	PALMER TOY MANUFACTURING CO.								
2	EMPLOYEES BY STATE								
3									
4					PERCENT OF				
5	STATE		EMPLOYEES		EMPLOYEES				
6	Arizona		1060		33.81%				
7	California		120		3.83%				
8	Montana		450		14.35%				
9	New Mexico		695		22.17%				
10	Oregon		543		17.32%				
11	South Dakota		267		8.52%				
12									
13	Total Employees		3135		100.00%				
14									

Map showing: Oregon 543, Montana 450, South Dakota 267, California 120, Arizona 1060, New Mexico 695.

Palmer Toy Manufacturing
Employees by State

- 1,060 (1)
- 120 (1)
- 267 (1)
- 450 (1)
- 543 (1)
- 695 (1)

INSERT AND USE A DATA MAP

1. Select cells containing geographic data.

2. Click **Map** button.........................

   OR

   a. Click **Insert** menu......... Alt + I

   b. Click **Map** .... M

      Pointer becomes a +.

3. Drag rectangle to define map area.

4. a. If prompted, select desired map in list.

   b. Click [OK] .... ⏎

ENABLE MAP EDITING

- Double-click data map...........*data map*
  The Data Map Control window opens and the Data Map Toolbar appears below the menu bar.

CHANGE CATEGORY SHADING

1. Select **Map** .... Alt + M

2. Select **Category Shading Options** .... E

3. Select **Categories** C

4. Select category .... ↓

5. Select **Color** C

6. Select new color .... ↓

7. Click [OK] .... ⏎

NEXT EXERCISE

EXERCISE

Summary

63

As an employee of the United States Labor Department, you have been asked to analyze employment trends in the state of New Jersey using data from the 1980 and 1990 censuses.

You will create a worksheet using the data below and create several graphs as directed.

Employment in Selected Industries

	1980	1990	Change
Agriculture, etc.	24,447	40,161	64.3%
Mfg., nondurable	414,416	347,224	-16.2%
Mfg., durable	405,728	306,212	-24.5%
Finance, real estate	231,953	346,037	49.2%

EXERCISE DIRECTIONS:

1. Create a worksheet using the data above, or open 💾 **63NJDATA**.

2. Format appropriately and set column widths where needed.

3. Create an embedded **column** graph comparing 1980 and 1990 trends.

4. Include appropriate titles and legends, as well as horizontal gridlines.

5. Using the same data and titles above, create **line** and **combination** charts.

6. Create a **3-D column** chart showing changes in each industry.

7. Include appropriate titles, horizontal and vertical gridlines, and data labels.

8. Create an **area** chart comparing the 1980 and 1990 data.

9. Include appropriate titles, a legend and data labels.

10. Create an embedded **pie** chart of 1990 data. Format the pie sections for different patterns, and explode a section of the pie representing the largest employment area in the state.

11. Include appropriate titles and data labels.

12. Use **Edit**, **Cut** and **Edit**, **Paste** to move each chart to a separate worksheet.

13. Rename each sheet containing a chart as follows:

    COLUMN CHART

    LINE CHART

    COMBINATION CHART

    3-D COLUMN CHART

    AREA CHART

    PIE CHART

14. Rename Sheet1; name it DATA.

15. NEW: Select the PIE CHART sheet. Copy the pie chart to a new location on the sheet and change the chart type to the doughnut format.

16. Save the workbook file; name it **NJDATA**.

17. Close the workbook.

EXERCISE

Summary

64

As an employee of the Woodworks Furniture Company, you have been asked to chart sales and commission data for the first three quarters of the year from a previously saved worksheet.

EXERCISE DIRECTIONS:

1. Open ⌨ **WOOD** or open 💾 **64WOOD**.

2. Edit row 5 titles so each cell contains the entire title (insert a line break).

   HINT: Add EMP and a line break to cell A5.

   EMP.
   NO.

3. Delete NAME title in cell B5.

   NOTE: This blank cell will be selected when you create the chart.

4. Delete row 4.

5. Create an embedded **3-D column** chart comparing quarterly salary data for each employee.

6. Include appropriate titles, a legend, horizontal and vertical gridlines.

7. Create an embedded **line** chart comparing quarterly sales data for each employee.

8. Include appropriate titles, a legend and horizontal gridlines.

9. In the worksheet, edit titles in indicated cells as follows:

   E4: JAN-MAR
   SALES

   H4: APR-JUNE
   SALES

   K5: JULY-SEPT
   SALES

NOTE: Since legend text is linked to these worksheet cells, the legend entries in the line chart should change as well.

10. Using the same data, titles and enhancements as in the **line** chart, create an embedded **stacked column** chart.

11. Print a copy of the entire worksheet on one page.

12. Save the workbook file; name it **WOOD**.

13. Open ⌨ **WOODQTR** or open 💾 **64WODQTR**.

14. Create a **pie** chart displaying total compensation for each employee. Use an appropriate two-line heading. Use a pattern on the section of the pie representing the highest compensation. Enter a data label on the largest pie section and explode the section.

15. Print a copy of only the pie chart.

16. Save the workbook file; name it **WOODQTR**.

17. Close the workbook.

NEXT LESSON

LESSON 9

ENHANCING THE WORKSHEET

Exercises 65-74

- Change Font and Font Size
- Change Font Attributes
- Change Cell Colors and Patterns
- Hide Worksheet Gridlines
- Format Painter
- Set Styles
- Change Cell Borders
- Print Multiple Copies
- Change Print Margins
- Print in Portrait/Landscape Orientation
- Center Titles Over Selected Range
- Edit Cell Formats
- Enlarge the Printout
- Add and Format Graphic Objects
- Use Drawing Toolbar
- Change the Row Height
- Enhance a Worksheet and Chart
- Add a Text Box
- Format a Text Box

EXCEL

EXERCISE
- Change Font and Font Size
- Change Font Attributes (Bold, Italics and Underscore)

65

NOTES:

- Excel lets you apply desktop publishing features to create a more attractive screen view and printout. In Exercise 47, a worksheet was formatted using AutoFormat which provides sets of styles to enhance your worksheet. In this lesson, customized styles and enhancements are discussed so that you may get exactly the presentation you require. Your printer and monitor must be able to support these features.

Change Font and Font Size

- Worksheet enhancements, such as changing the font and font size, can be accomplished using the toolbar.

- A **font** is a set of characters that share a design and name. Since Windows TrueType fonts are scalable, a single TrueType font can be set to a variety of sizes. The current font name (usually Arial) is displayed in the Font box and the current font size is displayed in the Font Size box.

- You can change the default or standard font Excel uses. To do this, select **Options** from the **Tools** menu. Then, from the General tab in the Options dialog box, set the standard font and font size.

- The **font size** is an attribute that sets the height of characters in a scalable font. This size is measured in **points**. A point is $1/_{72}$ of an inch. When the size of a font is changed, Excel automatically adjusts the row height but does not adjust the column width.

- The easiest way to apply a new font or font size is to select the cells to format, then select the font or font size in the **Font** or **Font Size box** on the Formatting Toolbar. (See the illustration below.) When a font and font size are selected, Excel immediately formats the text in the selected cells.

- Another way to apply new fonts or font sizes is to use the **Format, Cells** commands or Ctrl+1, which display the Format Cells dialog box. The illustration on the right shows the Format tab in the dialog box.

Change Font Attributes

- The Bold, Italics and Underline styles were discussed in Exercise 15 and may be used with font and font size changes to further enhance the worksheet. These attributes may be set using the Formatting Toolbar buttons, as shown earlier, or using the settings in the Format Cells, Font tab dialog box as shown on the right.

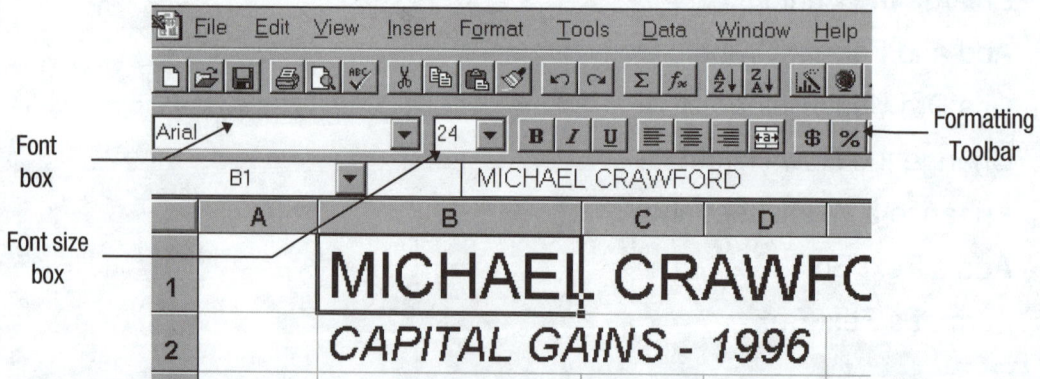

USING THE FORMATTING TOOLBAR TO CHANGE FONT AND FONT SIZE.

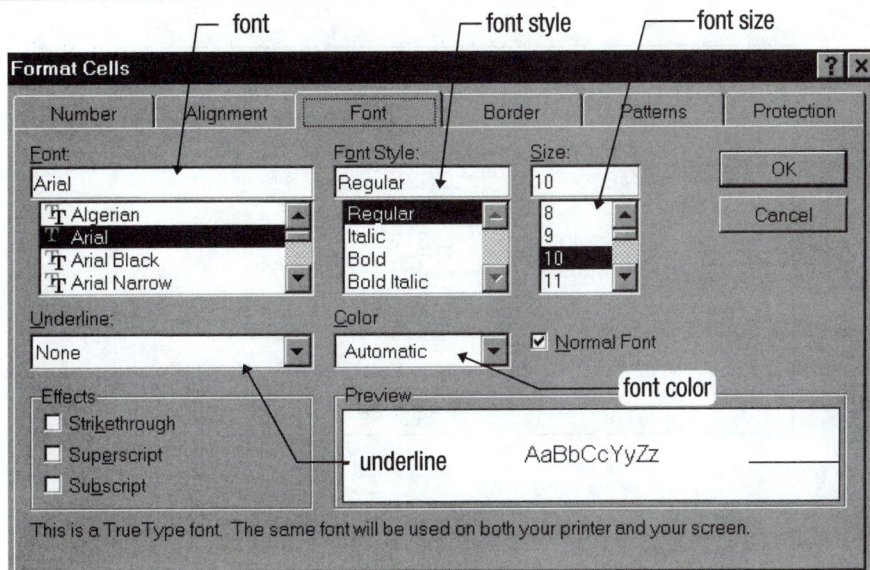

font — font style — font size

FORMAT CELLS DIALOG BOX

In this exercise, you will enhance the MKTSUM worksheet by changing fonts, font sizes and text style for selected parts.

EXERCISE DIRECTIONS:

1. Open ⌨ **MKTSUM** or open 💾 **65MKTSUM**.

    • In the illustrations on the next page, compare MKTSUM with the enhanced version below it.

2. Edit the subtitle, which should be in cell B2, to read:

    CAPITAL GAINS - 1996.

    NOTE: Move the subtitle, if necessary.

3. Make the font changes indicated below using the Format Cells dialog box:

    • Main title: Arial 22 point, Bold Italic
    • Secondary titles: Arial 16 point, Bold
    • Column titles: Arial 14 point, Italic
    • Data in rows 7–11: MS Serif 9.5 point
    • TOTALS row: Arial 12 point, Bold

    NOTE: If your system does not have these fonts, choose a font that best matches the illustration on the next page..

4. Adjust column widths to view complete labels and values in each column.

5. Make the font changes indicated below using the Formatting Toolbar:

    • Main title: Arial 24 point, Bold
    • Secondary titles: Arial 18 point, Bold Italics
    • Column titles: Arial 14 point, Bold
    • Data in rows 7–11: MS Serif 10 point
    • TOTALS row: Arial 12 point, Bold, Underline

6. Adjust column widths to view complete labels and values in each column.

7. Center the data in column A.

8. Move main and secondary titles to Column A.

9. Preview the worksheet.

10. Print one copy of the worksheet.

11. Save the workbook file; name it **MKTSUM**.

12. Close the workbook file.

MICHAEL CRAWFORD				
SUMMARY OF STOCK TRANSACTIONS - 199-				
NO. OF	COMPANY	GAIN OR	% GAIN OR	
SHARES	NAME	LOSS	LOSS	
200	Crystal Motors	-319.31	-4.28%	
100	US Brands	2459.71	35.53%	
50	IGM	671.97	26.08%	
300	Microgem	-1436.54	-26.65%	
500	Consolidated Gas	2215.50	15.46%	
	TOTALS	3591.33	9.79%	

MICHAEL CRAWFORD

CAPITAL GAINS - 1996

NO. OF SHARES	COMPANY NAME	GAIN OR LOSS	% GAIN OR LOSS	
200	Crystal Motors	-319.31	-4.28%	
100	US Brands	2459.71	35.53%	
50	IGM	671.97	26.08%	
300	Microgem	-1436.54	-26.65%	
500	Consolidated Gas	2215.50	15.46%	
	TOTALS	**3591.33**	**9.79%**	

CHANGE FONT USING THE FONT BOX

1. Select cells or characters in cells to format.
2. Click **Font** box drop-down arrow
   `Arial` `±`
   on Formatting Toolbar.
3. Select desired font .... `↕↲` , `⏎`

CHANGE FONT SIZE USING THE FONT SIZE BOX

1. Select cells or characters in cells to format.
2. a. Click **Font Size** box
      drop-down arrow `10` `±`
      on Formatting Toolbar.
   b. Select a number in
      list .... `↕↲` , `⏎`

   OR

   a. Click **Font Size**
      box `10` `±`
      on Formatting Toolbar.
   b. Enter desired
      number .... *number*, `⏎`

CHANGE FONT, FONT SIZE, AND FONT STYLE USING THE MENU

1. Press **Ctrl+1** .... `Ctrl` + `1`

   OR

   a. Click **Format** menu .... `Alt` + `O`
   b. Click **Cells** .... `E`

2. Select **Font** tab .... `Ctrl` + `Tab`
3. To set font:
   a. Click **Font** .... `Alt` + `F`
   b. Select desired font .... `↕↲`
4. To set font style:
   a. Click **Font Style** .... `Alt` + `O`
   b. Select desired style .... `↕↲`
5. To set font size:
   a. Click **Size** .... `Alt` + `S`
   b. Select desired font size .... `↕↲`
6. To set underline:
   • Click **Underline** .... `Alt` + `U`

EXERCISE

66

■ Change Cell Colors and Patterns ■ Hide Worksheet Gridlines
■ Copy Formats Using Format Painter ■ Set Styles

NOTES:

Change Cell Colors and Patterns

■ Cells in a worksheet may be filled with a **pattern** and/or **color**. The color buttons on the Formatting Toolbar were discussed in Exercise 47. However, you may make color and pattern settings using the Format cells dialog box, as shown on the Patterns tab sheet in the illustration below. The settings on the Patterns sheet are for the cell background.

To set font color, settings must be made on the Font sheet. It is more efficient to use the color buttons on the Formatting Toolbar. It is possible to display and print data in white against a black (or color) background. This is sometimes called **reverse type**.

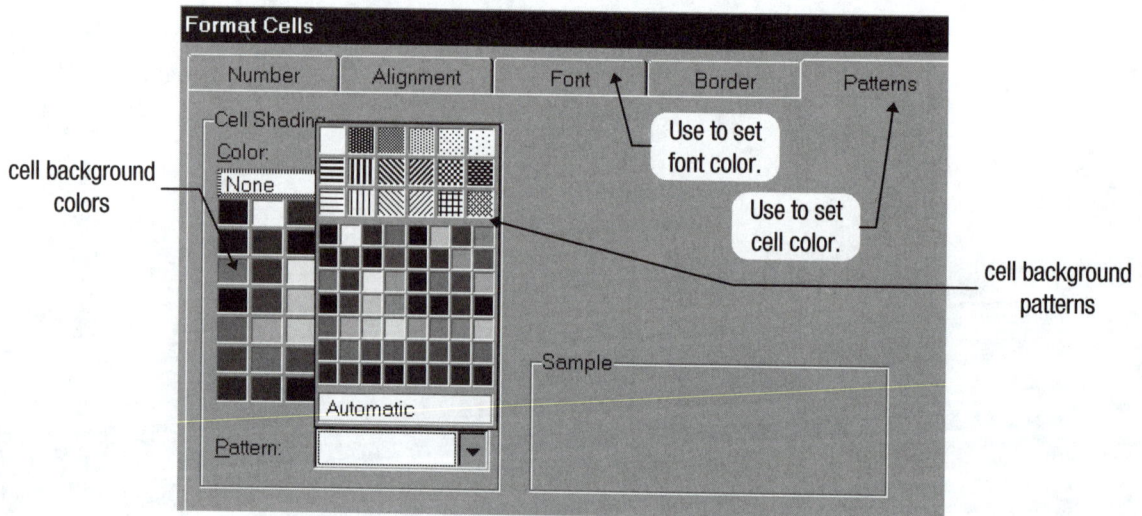

FORMAT CELLS PATTERNS SHEET

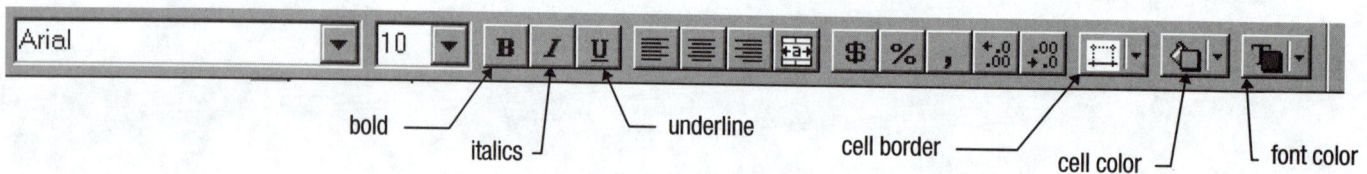

FORMATTING TOOLBAR

Hide Worksheet Gridlines

- You can further enhance a worksheet by adding or removing the gridlines. For printing purposes, the gridlines can be added or removed using the File, Page Setup, Sheet tab. The default setting is for hidden gridlines. For display purposes, gridlines may be removed using the Tools, Options, View preferences procedure.

Format Painter

- Once you make a series of settings, you may need to reproduce them for other data on the worksheet. Custom formats can be reused with Format Painter or by defining the settings as a style.

- The **Format Painter** button on the Standard Toolbar, allows you to copy all the formats from one cell to another in one step. By clicking the cell with the desired format, clicking Format Painter and then clicking the cell to be formatted, all the formats are copied to the new location. If you wish to use the Format Painter button on several different cells, you should double-click Format Painter to enable it for multiple applications.

Set Styles

- The second method of reusing formats is to set and name a style that can be invoked when needed. This is useful if your company uses the same formats for headings or totals for all reports. To set a style, select the cell with your custom formatting, then use the **Format, Style** commands to give the style a name. Once the style has a name, it can be applied to any cell using the same menu commands to select the style name.

> *In this exercise, you will enhance the salary report for Martinson Manufacturing Company using Format Painter, colors, patterns and styles.*

EXERCISE DIRECTIONS:

1. Open ⌨ **INCR** or open 💾 **66INCR.**

   - In the illustration, compare **INCR** with the enhanced version below it.

2. Change the worksheet so it looks like the enhanced version:

   - Main title: Arial 18 point bold
   - Subtitle: Arial 14 point bold
   - Main and Subtitle area (A1:J3): Color background to yellow (Row 1, Box 6), cell borders to underline.
   - ✓ *Row and box numbers refer to location of color in color palette.*
   - Column titles: Bold and color background to light blue (Row 3, Box 8).
   - Use Format Painter to copy format from column titles to Totals line.
   - SALARY 1996 column data: Color to light gray (Row 5, Box 8).
   - RAISE 1997: Use Format Painter to copy color format from SALARY 1996.
   - SALARY 1997: Font color white and cell color black for reverse type.
   - TOTALS data: Select numbers and set underline for Double Accounting style using the Format cells dialog box, Font tab sheet.

3. Set gridlines off for worksheet.

4. Preview the worksheet.

5. To set a style for total numbers:

   - Select the numbers on the TOTALS line.
   - Click **Format, Style** and name the style Total Numbers.

6. To test and apply the style:

   Select George Wingate's salary for 1996.

   Click **Format, Style** and use the Style Name list box to select Total numbers. Click OK.

   ✓ *The number will take on the totals style.*

   Use Format Painter to return the salary number to its original style.

7. Set the worksheet to print on one page, then print the worksheet.

8. Save the workbook file; name it **INCR.**

	A	B	C	D	E	F	G	H	I	J
1				MARTINSON MANUFACTURING COMPANY						
2				ANALYSIS OF SALARY INCREASES						
3										
4										
5			YEARS OF	SALARY	SALARY	RAISE	1996 %	1997 %	RAISE	SALARY
6	EMPLOYEE		SENIORITY	1995	1996	1996	INCREASE	INCREASE	1997	1997
7										
8	Miller, John		15	45500.00	49000.00	3500.00	7.69%	7.25%	3552.50	52552.50
9	Vantnor, Link		11	32300.00	35000.00	2700.00	8.36%	7.25%	2537.50	37537.50
10	Barrow, Wilson		5	16500.00	17500.00	1000.00	6.06%	4.50%	787.50	18287.50
11	Abrahams, Larry		3	18500.00	20000.00	1500.00	8.11%	4.50%	900.00	20900.00
12	Nunex, Maria		7	21000.00	23000.00	2000.00	9.52%	7.25%	1667.50	24667.50
13	Tse, Sandra		4	25600.00	27000.00	1400.00	5.47%	4.50%	1215.00	28215.00
14	D'Agostino, Joe		8	28500.00	30000.00	1500.00	5.26%	7.25%	2175.00	32175.00
15	Harrison, Reggie		9	33000.00	35000.00	2000.00	6.06%	7.25%	2537.50	37537.50
16	Wingate, George		6	25400.00	27000.00	1600.00	6.30%	7.25%	1957.50	28957.50
17	Ingold, Terry		10	38000.00	41500.00	3500.00	9.21%	7.25%	3008.75	44508.75
18										
19	TOTALS			284300.00	305000.00	20700.00			20338.75	325338.75

MARTINSON MANUFACTURING COMPANY

ANALYSIS OF SALARY INCREASES

EMPLOYEE	YEARS OF SENIORITY	SALARY 1995	SALARY 1996	RAISE 1996	1996 % INCREASE	1997 % INCREASE	RAISE 1997	SALARY 1997
Miller, John	15	45500.00	49000.00	3500.00	7.69%	7.25%	3552.50	52552.50
Vantnor, Link	11	32300.00	35000.00	2700.00	8.36%	7.25%	2537.50	37537.50
Barrow, Wilson	5	16500.00	17500.00	1000.00	6.06%	4.50%	787.50	18287.50
Abrahams, Larry	3	18500.00	20000.00	1500.00	8.11%	4.50%	900.00	20900.00
Nunex, Maria	7	21000.00	23000.00	2000.00	9.52%	7.25%	1667.50	24667.50
Tse, Sandra	4	25600.00	27000.00	1400.00	5.47%	4.50%	1215.00	28215.00
D'Agostino, Joe	8	28500.00	30000.00	1500.00	5.26%	7.25%	2175.00	32175.00
Harrison, Reggie	9	33000.00	35000.00	2000.00	6.06%	7.25%	2537.50	37537.50
Wingate, George	6	25400.00	27000.00	1600.00	6.30%	7.25%	1957.50	28957.50
Ingold, Terry	10	38000.00	41500.00	3500.00	9.21%	7.25%	3008.75	44508.75
TOTALS		284300.00	305000.00	20700.00			20338.75	325338.75

BOLD, ITALICIZE OR UNDERLINE DATA USING THE TOOLBAR

1. Select cells or characters in cells to format.

   —FROM FORMATTING TOOLBAR—

2. Click **Bold** button......................... **B**

   AND/OR

   Click **Italic** button........................ *I*

   AND/OR

   Click **Underline** button .... **U**

To remove font style:

- Click format button again.

CHANGE FONT COLOR USING THE TOOLBAR

1. Select cells or characters in cells to format.

2. Click color option on

   Font Color button...................
   to apply it to selection.

   OR

   a. Click **Font Color** button

   drop-down arrow.............
   Excel displays a color palette.
   NOTE: To apply several colors,
   drag color palette off the
   toolbar to keep the color
   palette open.

   b. Click desired color on palette.

HIDE WORKSHEET GRIDLINES

(See SET VIEW PREFERENCES, page 14.)
(See SET PRINT OPTIONS FOR
WORKSHEETS, page 80.)

COPY FORMATS USING FORMAT PAINTER

- Select cell(s) containing formats to copy.

To copy formats only once:

   a. Click **Format Painter**

   button................................
   on Standard Toolbar.
   Pointer changes to a ⊕🖌.

   b. Select cell or range of cells where you want to apply the formats.

To copy formats several times:

   a. Double–click **Format**

   Painter button ....
   on Standard Toolbar.
   Pointer changes to a ⊕🖌.

   b. Select destination cell(s).

   c. Repeat step b, as desired.

   d. Click **Format Painter**

   button again.......................
   to end copying.

SET FONT AND FONT ATTRIBUTES USING THE MENU

Changes font, font attributes, font size and
font color. Underlines and sets special effects
for data in cells.

1. Select cells or characters in cells to format.

2. Click **Format** menu .... `Alt`+`O`

3. Click **Cells** .... `E`

   OR

   a. Right-click any selected cell.

   b. Click **Format Cells**.

4. Click **Font** tab .... `Ctrl`+`Tab`

To change font:

- Select a font

   name .... `Alt`+`F`, 🔽
   in **Font** list box.

To change font style:

- Select a font

   style.................. `Alt`+`O`, 🔽
   in **Font Style** list box.

   Font Style list items include:
   Regular, Italic, Bold, Bold Italic

To change font size:

- Select a point

   size .... `Alt`+`S`, 🔽
   in **Size** list box.

To select underline style:

   a. Click **Underline**

   .... `Alt`+`U`

   b. Select an underline

   style .... 🔽, `Alt`+`↑`

   Underline list items include:
   None, Single, Double, Single
   Accounting, Double Accounting

To apply special effects:

- Select desired **Effects** options:

   Strikethrough .... `Alt`+`K`

   Superscript................. `Alt`+`E`

   Subscript .... `Alt`+`B`

To set font to normal font style:

- Select ☐ **Normal**

   Font .... `Alt`+`N`

To set font color:

   a. Click **Color**

   .... `Alt`+`C`

   b. Select a color .... 🔽, ↵

5. Click [OK] ....↵

CHANGE COLOR OF CELLS USING THE TOOLBAR

1. Select cell(s) to format.

2. Click color option on

   Color button ....
   to apply it to selection.

   OR

   a. Click **Color** button

   drop-down arrow ....
   Excel displays a color palette.
   NOTE: To apply several colors,
   drag color palette off the
   toolbar to keep the color
   palette open.

   b. Click desired color on palette.

CHANGE COLOR AND/OR PATTERN OF CELLS USING THE MENU

1. Select cell(s) to format.
2. Click **Format** menu .... `Alt`+`O`
3. Click **Cells** .... `E`

   OR

   a. Right-click any selected cell.
   b. Click **Format Cells**.
4. Click **Patterns** tab .... `Ctrl`+`Tab`

To select a color for cells:

- Click desired
  color .... `Alt`+`C`, `↕`
  in **Color** palette.

To select a pattern for cells:

a. Click **Pattern**

   .... `Alt`+`P`

b. Select a
   pattern .... `↕`, `Alt`+`↑`

c. Click **Pattern**

   .... `Alt`+`P`

d. Select a color for
   pattern .... `↕`, `Alt`+`↑`

5. Click `OK` .... `↵`

SET STYLES BY EXAMPLE

1. Select cell containing desired formats.
2. Click **Format** menu .... `Alt`+`O`
3. Click **Style** .... `S`

4. Type **Style Name** in text box.
   Excel displays the style's formats in Style Includes box.

To exclude format categories from style:

- Deselect desired **Style Includes** options.

5. Click `OK` .... `↵`

APPLY STYLES

1. Select cell to be formatted.
2. Click **Format** menu .... `Alt`+`O`
3. Click **Style** .... `S`
4. Select desired **Style Name** .... `↕`
5. Click `OK` .... `↵`

EXERCISE

Change Cell Borders

67

NOTES:

Change Cell Borders

■ To outline or separate data, you can include a variety of line styles bordering the edge of a cell or range of cells. You can add, remove or change lines to the left, right, top, bottom or any combination of these sides. Borders are set using either the Format Cells dialog box, the Border tab or by using the Borders button on the Formatting Toolbar. Note the illustrations below:

■ When you clear cell contents, the border format does not change; therefore, the border must be cleared separately. Excel provides a keyboard shortcut (**Ctrl** + **Shift** + **-**) that quickly removes all borders from selected cells.

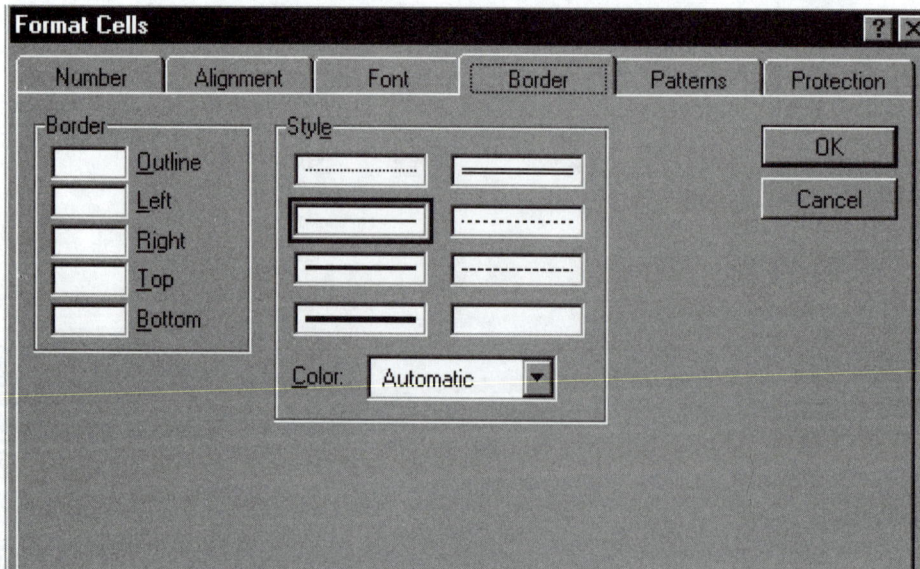

FORMAT CELLS DIALOG BOX WITH BORDER TAB SELECTED

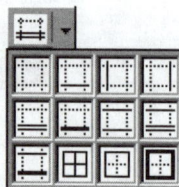

BORDERS BUTTON ON THE FORMATTING TOOLBAR

EXERCISE DIRECTIONS:

1. Open ⌨ **CAR** or open 💾 **67CAR**.
   - In the illustration, compare **CAR** with the enhanced version below it.
2. Make the changes to your worksheet as indicated below:
   - Insert a row above the titles.
   - Titles: Move the main title to column C.

     Edit subtitle to COMMISSION REPORT.

     Set Arial 16 point, Bold for both titles.
   - Title and subtitle: Outline - use the Border button.
   - Column titles: Arial 12 point, Bold.
   - Column title cells: Thick top and bottom borders. Set the top and bottom borders separately using the Format Cells dialog box.
   - Titles and column titles: Color cell pale green (Row 5, Box 3).
   - Column A and B data: Pale green color (Row 5, Box 3).
   - Column B data: Italicize font.
   - Column E data: Pale yellow color (Row 5, Box 4).
   - Column F data: Next darker shade of yellow (Row 4, Box 3).
   - Column G data: Pale green color (Row 5, Box 3).
   - Column C data: Medium width line to right side of cells.
   - Last row of data: Medium width line to bottom of cells.
   - TOTALS data: Double-line across bottom of cells.
   - TOTALS lines: Pale green color (Row 5, Box 3).
3. Widen columns, as necessary, to view complete labels and values.
4. Set gridlines off for worksheet.
5. Set worksheet to print on one page and preview the worksheet.
6. Print the worksheet.
7. Save the workbook file; name it **CAR.**

NAME	LOCATION	SALES	COMM. RATE	COMM.	BONUS	TOTAL COMPENSATION
		SMILING SAMMY'S CARS				
	COMMISSION REPORT FOR SALES PERSONNEL					
R. BUICK	ELMHURST	$640,000	4.00%	$25,600	$3,200	$28,800
M. CADDY	JAMAICA	$450,000	3.00%	$13,500	$0	$13,500
J. DODGE	ELMHURST	$125,000	3.00%	$3,750	$0	$3,750
O. FORD	JAMAICA	$745,000	4.00%	$29,800	$3,725	$33,525
W. HONDA	MASPETH	$0	3.00%	$0	$0	$0
V. JAGUAR	ELMHURST	$550,000	4.00%	$22,000	$2,750	$24,750
A. LEXUS	JAMAICA	$210,000	3.00%	$6,300	$0	$6,300
E. LINCOLN	MASPETH	$435,000	4.00%	$17,400	$0	$17,400
B. NISSAN	MASPETH	$745,000	4.00%	$29,800	$3,725	$33,525
TOTALS		$3,900,000		$148,150	$13,400	$161,550

SMILING SAMMY'S CARS
COMMISSION REPORT

NAME	LOCATION	SALES	COMM. RATE	COMM.	BONUS	TOTAL COMPENSATION
R. BUICK	ELMHURST	$640,000	4.00%	$25,600	$3,200	$28,800
M. CADDY	JAMAICA	$450,000	3.00%	$13,500	$0	$13,500
J. DODGE	ELMHURST	$125,000	3.00%	$3,750	$0	$3,750
O. FORD	JAMAICA	$745,000	4.00%	$29,800	$3,725	$33,525
W. HONDA	MASPETH	$0	3.00%	$0	$0	$0
V. JAGUAR	ELMHURST	$550,000	4.00%	$22,000	$2,750	$24,750
A. LEXUS	JAMAICA	$210,000	3.00%	$6,300	$0	$6,300
E. LINCOLN	MASPETH	$435,000	4.00%	$17,400	$0	$17,400
B. NISSAN	MASPETH	$745,000	4.00%	$29,800	$3,725	$33,525
TOTALS		$3,900,000		$148,150	$13,400	$161,550

CHANGE CELL BORDERS USING THE TOOLBAR

1. Select cell(s) to format.

2. Click border option on

   Borders button .... [⊞]▾
   to apply it to selected cells.

   OR

   a. Click **Borders** button

      drop-down arrow.............. [⊞]▾
      Excel displays a border palette.
      NOTE: To apply several border
      styles, drag border palette
      off the toolbar to keep the
      border palette open.

   b. Click desired border on palette.

ADD CUSTOM BORDERS TO CELLS

Applies or removes borders from cells.

1. Select cell(s) to format.

2. Click **Format** menu .... [Alt]+[O]

3. Click **Cells** .... [E]

   OR

   a. Right–click any selected cell.

   b. Click **Format Cells**.

4. Click **Border** tab .... [Ctrl]+[Tab]

5. Select a style
   for border.................. [Alt]+[E], [↕]
   in **Style** group.

6. Select border to apply style to in
   Border group:

   • **O**utline .... [Alt]+[O]

   • **L**eft.............................. [Alt]+[L]

   • **R**ight .... [Alt]+[R]

   • **T**op.............................. [Alt]+[T]

   • **B**ottom........................ [Alt]+[B]

To remove border:

• Follow steps to apply border
  again.

To change border color:

   a. Click **C**olor:

      [   ]▾ .... [Alt]+[C]

   b. Select desired
      color............................. [↔], [↵]

7. Repeat steps 5 and 6 for each border.

8. Click [OK] .... [↵]

REMOVE ALL BORDERS FROM CELLS

1. Select cells with borders to remove.

2. Press **Ctrl** +
   Shift + - .... [Ctrl]+[Shift]+[-]

NEXT EXERCISE

EXERCISE

■ Print Multiple Copies ■ Change Print Margins
■ Print in Portrait/Landscape Orientation ■ Edit Cell Formats
■ Center Titles Over Selected Range

68

NOTES:

Print Options

■ You can set a variety of print options from the tabs in the Page Setup dialog box.

Page tab:

- Reduce or enlarge data on printed sheet.

- Set first page number.

- Set page orientation.

- Set paper size.

- Set print quality.

- Set sheet(s) to fit on a specific number of pages.

Margins tab:

- Set header and footer margins.

- Set how data is aligned on page.

- Set page margins.

Header/Footer tab:

- Customize header or footer.

- Select a built-in footer.

- Select a built-in header.

Sheet tab:

- Set columns as repeating print titles.

- Set page order when printing.

- Set print area.

- Set printing of gridlines.

- Set printing of notes.

- Set printing of row and column headings.

- Set printing to black and white.

- Set printing to draft quality.

- Set rows as repeating print titles.

OR

Chart tab:

- Set printed chart size.

- Set printed quality of chart.

- Set printing to black and white.

■ You can access the Page Setup dialog in three ways:

- From the **File** menu select **Page Setup**.

- From the Print dialog box, select the Page Setup button.

- From Print Preview, select the Setup button.

- NOTE: All worksheet exercises in this book have been illustrated using gridlines. The gridlines may be cleared when desired.

■ Excel lets you set print margins in two ways:

- From Print Preview, where you can drag margin handles to approximate positions, or

- From the Margins tab in the Page Setup dialog box, where you can indicate exact margins in inches.

■ As with charts, a worksheet can be printed with either a **portrait** (vertical) or **landscape** (horizontal) paper orientation. Landscape orientation must be supported by the available printer. Note examples below:

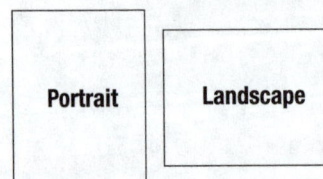

| Portrait | Landscape |

Center Titles Over Selected Range

- A title can be realigned so it is centered over a range of cells. You can do this by selecting the title and extending the selection to include the cells in which the title should be centered. Excel will center the title when you click the **Center Across Columns** button .

- Centering across columns changes where data appears — it does not change the original location of the data.

Edit Cell Formats

- Cell formats may be cleared or reset using the Format Cells dialog box. Formats that have been set using the Font tab, such as underline, must be cleared on that sheet, in the dialog box.

- If you are uncertain as to which color or pattern you had previously set, you may select a cell in that color and check the Patterns tab in the Format Cells dialog box.

In *this exercise, you will edit a worksheet for presentation. After making changes to the worksheet, including centering titles, you will test the effectiveness of the presentation by printing the worksheet in portrait orientation using the default margin settings and comparing it to a second printing in landscape orientation with wider margins.*

EXERCISE DIRECTIONS:

1. Open ⌨ **INCR** or open 💾 **68INCR**.

   - In the illustration, compare **INCR** with the enhanced version on next page.

2. Make the changes to your worksheet indicated below:

   - Remove cell borders from rows 1 and 2.
   - Move title and subtitle to Column A.
   - Center title and subtitle over columns A-J.
   - Column heading rows: Use top and bottom borders.
   - Columns A-C: Color same as column heading area, pale blue.
   - Column C: Center data. Cell border at the right of the cells.
   - Row 17: Bottom border across worksheet.
   - Columns D-I: Color pale yellow (Row 5, Box 4).
   - Column J: Font black, background pale blue, cell border at the left.
   - Totals rows 18 and 19: Color pale blue.

   - Row 19: Remove font format for double accounting underline. Insert cell border for double lines across bottom of worksheet.
   - Format money columns for commas.
   - Adjust column widths, if necessary.

3. Set worksheet to fit on one page.

4. Preview the worksheet.

5. Print one copy of the worksheet with portrait orientation.

6. Change top, bottom, right and left margins to 1".

7. Print one copy of the worksheet.

8. Change the page orientation to landscape.

9. Preview the worksheet.

   —FROM PRINT PREVIEW—

10. Adjust margins as desired.

11. Print two copies of the worksheet.

12. Save and close the workbook file; name it **INCR**.

13. Decide which worksheet would be better for the presentation.

MARTINSON MANUFACTURING COMPANY
ANALYSIS OF SALARY INCREASES

EMPLOYEE	YEARS OF SENIORITY	SALARY 1995	SALARY 1996	RAISE 1996	1996 % INCREASE	1997 % INCREASE	RAISE 1997	SALARY 1997
Miller, John	15	45500.00	49000.00	3500.00	7.69%	7.25%	3552.50	52552.50
Vantnor, Link	11	32300.00	35000.00	2700.00	8.36%	7.25%	2537.50	37537.50
Barrow, Wilson	5	16500.00	17500.00	1000.00	6.06%	4.50%	787.50	18287.50
Abrahams, Larry	3	18500.00	20000.00	1500.00	8.11%	4.50%	900.00	20900.00
Nunex, Maria	7	21000.00	23000.00	2000.00	9.52%	7.25%	1667.50	24667.50
Tse, Sandra	4	25600.00	27000.00	1400.00	5.47%	4.50%	1215.00	28215.00
D'Agostino, Joe	8	28500.00	30000.00	1500.00	5.26%	7.25%	2175.00	32175.00
Harrison, Reggie	9	33000.00	35000.00	2000.00	6.06%	7.25%	2537.50	37537.50
Wingate, George	6	25400.00	27000.00	1600.00	6.30%	7.25%	1957.50	28957.50
Ingold, Terry	10	38000.00	41500.00	3500.00	9.21%	7.25%	3008.75	44508.75
TOTALS		284300.00	305000.00	20700.00			20338.75	325338.75

MARTINSON MANUFACTURING COMPANY
ANALYSIS OF SALARY INCREASES

EMPLOYEE	YEARS OF SENIORITY	SALARY 1995	SALARY 1996	RAISE 1996	1996 % INCREASE	1997 % INCREASE	RAISE 1997	SALARY 1997
Miller, John	15	45,500.00	49,000.00	3,500.00	7.69%	7.25%	3,552.50	52,552.50
Vantnor, Link	11	32,300.00	35,000.00	2,700.00	8.36%	7.25%	2,537.50	37,537.50
Barrow, Wilson	5	16,500.00	17,500.00	1,000.00	6.06%	4.50%	787.50	18,287.50
Abrahams, Larry	3	18,500.00	20,000.00	1,500.00	8.11%	4.50%	900.00	20,900.00
Nunex, Maria	7	21,000.00	23,000.00	2,000.00	9.52%	7.25%	1,667.50	24,667.50
Tse, Sandra	4	25,600.00	27,000.00	1,400.00	5.47%	4.50%	1,215.00	28,215.00
D'Agostino, Joe	8	28,500.00	30,000.00	1,500.00	5.26%	7.25%	2,175.00	32,175.00
Harrison, Reggie	9	33,000.00	35,000.00	2,000.00	6.06%	7.25%	2,537.50	37,537.50
Wingate, George	6	25,400.00	27,000.00	1,600.00	6.30%	7.25%	1,957.50	28,957.50
Ingold, Terry	10	38,000.00	41,500.00	3,500.00	9.21%	7.25%	3,008.75	44,508.75
TOTALS		284,300.00	305,000.00	20,700.00			20,338.75	325,338.75

CHANGE PRINT MARGINS

—FROM PRINT PREVIEW—

1. Click `Setup...` .... `Alt` + `S`

   OR

   —FROM WORKSHEET OR CHART SHEET—

   a. Click **File** menu .... `Alt` + `F`

   b. Click **Page Setup** .... `U`

2. Click **Margins** tab .... `Ctrl` + `Tab`

To set page margins:

a. Select margin to change:

   Top .... `Alt` + `T`

   Bottom .... `Alt` + `B`

   Left .... `Alt` + `L`

   Right .... `Alt` + `R`

b. Type or select number .....*number* in margin increment box.

c. Repeat steps a and b as needed.

To set header and footer margins:

NOTE: To prevent data from overlapping, these settings should be less than the top and bottom margin settings.

a. Select margin to change:

   Header .... `Alt` + `A`

   Footer .... `Alt` + `F`

b. Type or select number .....*number* in margin increment box.

c. Repeat steps a and b as needed.

To center data within margins:

- Select ☐ **Horizontally** `Alt` + `Z`

   AND/OR

   Select ☐ **Vertically** .... `Alt` + `V`

   *NOTE: For chart sheets, you must first select **Custom** from the Chart tab to enable these options.*

3. Click `OK` .... `↵`

   to return to sheet or Print Preview.

CHANGE PRINT MARGINS BY DRAGGING MARGIN HANDLES

—FROM PRINT PREVIEW—

1. Click `Margins` .... `Alt` + `M`

   Excel displays margin and column handles.

2. Drag margin handle to desired position.

   NOTE: Status bar displays size as you drag handle.

CHANGE PAGE ORIENTATION

1. Click **File** menu .... `Alt` + `F`

2. Click **Page Setup** .... `Alt` + `U`

3. Click **Page** tab .... `Ctrl` + `Tab`

4. Select ◯ **Portrait** .... `T`

   OR

   Select ◯ **Landscape** .... `L`

5. Click `OK` .... `↵`

SPECIFY NUMBER OF COPIES TO PRINT

Prints worksheet data using the current page settings a specified number of times.

1. Click **File** menu .... `Alt` + `F`

2. Click **Print** .... `P`

3. Select desired **Print What** option:

   - **Selection** .... `Alt` + `N`

   - **Selected Sheet(s)** .... `Alt` + `D`

   - **Entire Workbook** .... `Alt` + `E`

4. Click **Copies:** ☐ ⇳ .... `Alt` + `C`

5. Type number of copies .... *number*

6. Click `OK` .... `↵`

CENTER TITLES OVER SELECTED RANGE

1. Select cells in which data will be centered.

2. Click **Center Across Columns** button .... 🔳 on Formatting Toolbar.

   OR

   a. Click **Format** menu ...... `Alt` + `O`

   b. Click **Cells** .... `E`

   c. Click **Alignment** .... `Ctrl` + `Tab`

   d. Select ☐ **Center across selection** .... `Alt` + `A`

EXERCISE

■ Enlarge the Printout ■ Add and Size Graphic Objects

69

NOTES:

Enlarge the Printout

■ In the last exercise, the worksheet was reduced so a large print range would fit on one page. It is possible, however, to expand a small worksheet printout to fill the page, thus enlarging the worksheet data.

Add and Size Graphic Objects

■ You may add graphic objects to your worksheet to enhance its appearance. The objects may be from clip art files you own or from Microsoft ClipArt Gallery. When **Insert, Object** is selected, the Object dialog box appears. When Microsoft ClipArt Gallery is selected, you can select an object from a variety of clip art categories and styles.

NOTE: If Microsoft ClipArt Gallery is not on your ObjectType list, you need to modify your installation of Excel.

■ When an object is inserted into a worksheet, it may have to be sized or moved for proper placement. Selecting the object creates a frame and handles which are used to move and size it as you did with chart objects.

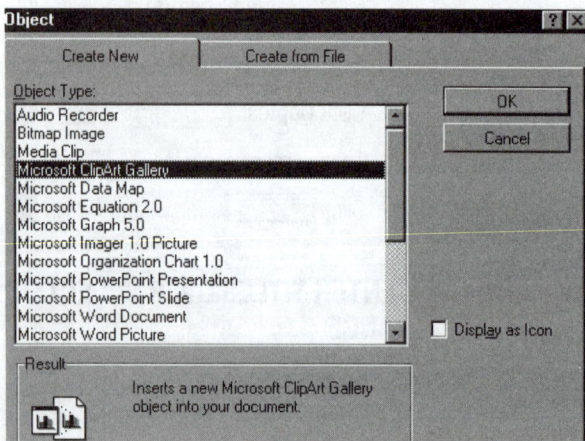

In this exercise, Smiling Sammy's Cars wants you to enhance its commission report by adding a graphic, hiding the location column, moving the title lines, and expanding the size of the print range.

EXERCISE DIRECTIONS:

1. Open ⌨ **CAR** or open 💾 **69CAR**.
   - In the illustration, compare **CAR** with the enhanced version below it.
2. Make the changes to your worksheet indicated below:

   - Move title and subtitle to column D.
   - Insert a row under the subtitle.
   - Add a third line: AUGUST in column D. Format for Arial, 14 point.
   - Adjust color and border for the new title.
   - Center the titles within the outlined area.

- Hide the LOCATION column.
- Insert, Object, Microsoft ClipArt, Transportation category, Car.
- Size and move the object into place as per the illustration.
- Change TOTAL COMPENSATION to TOTAL DUE.
- Adjust column width of the last column so that titles and column data fit.
- R. Buick row: Color pale green.
- M. Caddy row: Color white.
- Use Format Painter to copy striped format from first two rows to all the other rows of data.
- Include a cell border as a line under all data across the worksheet.

3. • Change the page setup to scale the output to 120%.
   • From the Margins tab, center the page between margins horizontally.
4. Preview the worksheet. It should fit on one page in portrait orientation.
5. Print one copy with this setting.
6. Save and close the workbook file; name it **CAR.**

SMILING SAMMY'S CARS COMMISSION REPORT

NAME	LOCATION	SALES	COMM. RATE	COMM.	BONUS	TOTAL COMPENSATION
R. BUICK	ELMHURST	$640,000	4.00%	$25,600	$3,200	$28,800
M. CADDY	JAMAICA	$450,000	3.00%	$13,500	$0	$13,500
J. DODGE	ELMHURST	$125,000	3.00%	$3,750	$0	$3,750
O. FORD	JAMAICA	$745,000	4.00%	$29,800	$3,725	$33,525
W. HONDA	MASPETH	$0	3.00%	$0	$0	$0
V. JAGUAR	ELMHURST	$550,000	4.00%	$22,000	$2,750	$24,750
A. LEXUS	JAMAICA	$210,000	3.00%	$6,300	$0	$6,300
E. LINCOLN	MASPETH	$435,000	4.00%	$17,400	$0	$17,400
B. NISSAN	MASPETH	$745,000	4.00%	$29,800	$3,725	$33,525
TOTALS		$3,900,000		$148,150	$13,400	$161,550

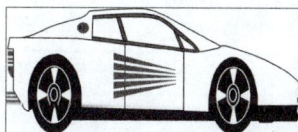

SMILING SAMMY'S CARS COMMISSION REPORT
AUGUST

NAME	SALES	COMM. RATE	COMM.	BONUS	TOTAL DUE
R. BUICK	$640,000	4.00%	$25,600	$3,200	$28,800
M. CADDY	$450,000	3.00%	$13,500	$0	$13,500
J. DODGE	$125,000	3.00%	$3,750	$0	$3,750
O. FORD	$745,000	4.00%	$29,800	$3,725	$33,525
W. HONDA	$0	3.00%	$0	$0	$0
V. JAGUAR	$550,000	4.00%	$22,000	$2,750	$24,750
A. LEXUS	$210,000	3.00%	$6,300	$0	$6,300
E. LINCOLN	$435,000	4.00%	$17,400	$0	$17,400
B. NISSAN	$745,000	4.00%	$29,800	$3,725	$33,525
TOTALS	$3,900,000		$148,150	$13,400	$161,550

INSERT CLIP ART OBJECT INTO WORKSHEET

1. Select cell where object will be inserted.

2. Click **Insert** menu................. `Alt` + `I`

3. Click **Object**................................... `O`

4. Click **Create New** tab.......... `Ctrl` + `Tab`

5. Select source application in Object Type list.

6. Click `OK` .... `↵`

To insert clip art from Microsoft ClipArt Gallery 2.0:

1. Click **Categories** .... `Alt` + `G`

2. Select category............................ `↕↕`

3. Click **Pictures** .... `Alt` + `P`

4. Select picture .... `↕↕`

5. Select **Insert** .... `I`

SIZE AND MOVE CLIP ART OBJECTS

• Double-click object.

To size object:

1. Select object border.
   Handles appear on the item's border.

2. Point to handle on side of item to size.

3. Drag item outline in direction to size.

To move object:

• Drag object item outline.

CHANGE SCALE OF PRINTED DATA

1. Click **File** menu.................... `Alt` + `F`

2. Click **Page Setup**... .... `U`

3. Click **Page** tab .... `Ctrl` + `Tab`

4. Double–click `☐` `⬍`
   % normal size .... `Alt` + `A`

5. Type percentage (10-400) .... *number*
   NOTE: *You can also click the increment box arrows to select a percentage.*

6. Click `OK` .... `↵`

NEXT EXERCISE

EXERCISE

■ **Use Drawing Toolbar** ■ **Change Row Height**
■ **Add and Format Graphic Objects**

70

NOTES:

Use Drawing Toolbar

■ If you wish to add **graphic objects** that are not provided in clip art files, you may create a customized object by using the Drawing Toolbar. You can draw lines, arcs, arrows, rectangles, ellipses, polygons, or freehand graphics on any area of a worksheet or chart.

Use the **View, Toolbars** commands, or the Drawing button on the Standard Toolbar, to

select the Drawing Toolbar for display. The Toolbar, which may be docked anywhere on the screen, is illustrated below.

■ Select the desired button to draw the object. Use the buttons for a filled rectangle, ellipse, arc or freeform for opaque objects. The arrow button will enable the mouse to draw an arrow that may be dragged to the required size.

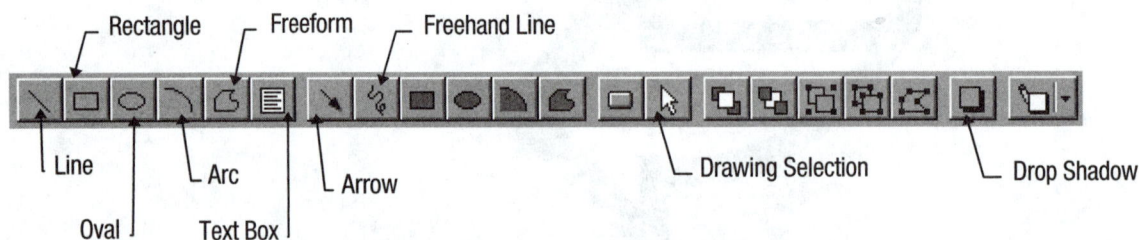

DRAWING TOOLBAR

Format Objects

■ Drawn graphic objects can be rotated, sized, moved, copied and deleted. They can also have various background and border attributes. When a transparent (default) background is selected, the underlying data will not be obscured. Object borders or fill

patterns, including shadows and rounded corners, may be formatted by selecting the object and clicking on the **Format, Object** commands or by pressing Ctrl+1. The Format Object dialog box that appears is shown below:

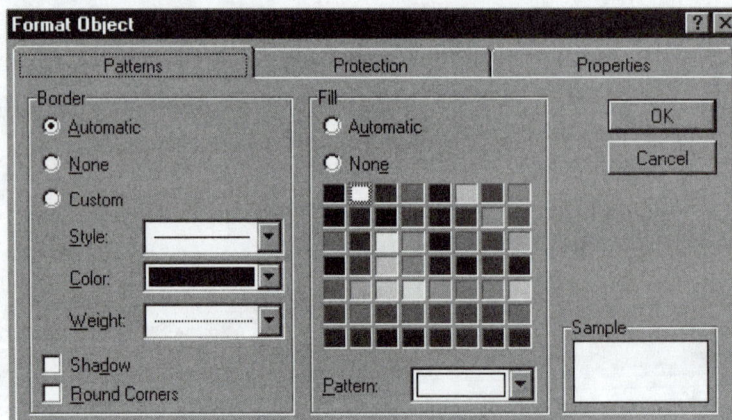

FORMAT OBJECT DIALOG BOX

Increase Row Height

- **Row height** is determined (by default) by the point size of the typeface used. However, you may increase or decrease the row height, as desired, by selecting **Format, Row, Height.** If you increase the row height, you may then select the alignment of the text within the row, as you would column data. For example, text may be placed at the top, center or bottom (default) of a row that has been increased in height.

In this exercise, the Heavy Metal Company would like to include a logo on its report by using the Drawing Toolbar and a clip art object. The worksheet will be enhanced by increasing the row height and by using other previously learned techniques

---

EXERCISE DIRECTIONS:

1. Open ⌨ **METAL** or open 💾 **70METAL**.
   - In the illustration, compare **METAL** with the enhanced version on the next page.
2. Make the changes to your worksheet indicated below:
   - Insert a row above and below the titles.
   - Main title: Move to D2, Century Gothic, 16 pt. (If you do not have this font, use a sans serif, or plain font.)
   - Subtitle: Move to D4, Century Gothic, 12 pt.
   - Make the Drawing Toolbar active.
   - Use the Filled Arc drawing tool to fill in area to the left of the titles.
   - Format arc border to custom weight, third level of intensity.
   - Insert object from the MS Clipart Gallery, representing a distribution design, in the location shown in the illustration.
   - Format the color of the arc the same color as the clip art circle, (Row 2 Box 2).
   - Format cell borders, as illustrated, above and below the column heading rows.

   - Column headings: Bold headings. Change the row height of the titles to 18 points. Vertically center all column titles. Left-align BIDDING COUNTRY and CURRENCY labels and right-align all other titles.
   - Color all white areas in title and column heading areas pale yellow, (Row 5, Box 4).
   - Insert an underscore under U.S. Price Per Unit.
   - Insert double lines under Lowest Price in US $.
   - Draw an arrow pointing to the price as illustrated.
   - Select and format the arrow line for the heaviest weight provided.
   - Color the Lowest Price line pale yellow.
   - Insert a single line as shown one line below the total.
3. Set print area for the top portion of worksheet, excluding the conversion table.
4. Preview the worksheet.
5. If necessary, turn printing of gridlines off.
6. Save and close the file; name it **METAL.**

	A	B	C	D	E	F
1			HEAVY METAL IMPORT CO.			
2			ITEM: IRON ORE			
3						
4			FOREIGN			U.S.
5	BIDDING		PRICE		CONVERSION	PRICE PER
6	COUNTRY		PER UNIT	CURRENCY	FACTOR	UNIT
7						
8	AUSTRALIA		135	DOLLARS	0.7789	105.15
9	BRAZIL		420	CRUZEIROS	0.2310	97.02
10	CANADA		110	DOLLARS	0.8803	96.83
11	GERMANY		160	MARKS	0.6363	101.81
12	INDIA		1680	RUPEES	0.0600	100.80
13	ITALY		125000	LIRA	0.0008	100.00
14						
15	LOWEST UNIT PRICE IN U.S. DOLLARS					96.83

HEAVY METAL IMPORT CO.
ITEM: IRON ORE

BIDDING COUNTRY	FOREIGN PRICE PER UNIT	CURRENCY	CONVERSION FACTOR	U.S. PRICE PER UNIT
AUSTRALIA	135	DOLLARS	0.7789	105.15
BRAZIL	420	CRUZEIROS	0.2310	97.02
CANADA	110	DOLLARS	0.8803	96.83
GERMANY	160	MARKS	0.6363	101.81
INDIA	1680	RUPEES	0.0600	100.80
ITALY	125000	LIRA	0.0008	100.00

LOWEST UNIT PRICE IN U.S. DOLLARS ⟶ 96.83

CHANGE ROW HEIGHT USING THE MENU

Sets row height to a specific size.

1. Select any cell in row(s) to size.

2. Click **Format** menu .... `Alt` + `O`

3. Click **Row** .... `R`

4. Click **Height** .... `E`

5. Type number (0-409) .... *number* in **Row Height** text box.

   NOTE: Number represents height in points.

6. Click `OK` .... `↵`

CHANGE ROW HEIGHT USING THE MOUSE

Change One Row Height

1. Point to bottom border of row heading.

   Pointer becomes a ↕.

2. Drag ↕ up or down.
   Excel displays height on left side of formula bar.

Change Several Row Heights

1. Select rows to format.

   NOTE: Click Select All button ☐ to change all rows.

2. Point to bottom border of any selected row heading.

   Pointer becomes a ↕.

3. Drag ↕ up or down.
   Excel displays height on left side of formula bar.

Set Row Height to Fit Tallest Entry

• Double–click row headings bottom border.

DRAW GRAPHIC OBJECTS

Draws objects such as rectangles, lines, arrows and ellipses.

1. Click **Drawing** button.................. 🖼

   on Standard Toolbar to show Drawing Toolbar.

2. Click desired drawing tool on Drawing Toolbar.
   Pointer becomes a ┼ and the status bar displays instructions.

3. Point to an area where a corner or end of object will begin.

4. Drag object's outline until desired size and shape is obtained.

   NOTE: You can use the SHIFT, ALT and CTRL keys to constrain the objects you draw. For example, if you hold SHIFT while drawing an ellipse, you will draw a perfect circle.

SET WEIGHT OF AN OBJECT'S BORDER OR LINE

Sets weight (thickness) of border or line.

1. Click object to format.
   Excel marks object with a selection outline and handles.

2. Click **Format** menu .... `Alt` + `O`

3. Click **Object** .... `E`

4. Click **Patterns** tab .... `Ctrl` + `Tab`

5. Click **Weight:**

   `▼` .... `Alt` + `W`

6. Select desired line or border

   thickness.................. `↗↓` , `Alt` + `↑`

7. Click `OK` .... `↵`

FORMAT GRAPHIC OBJECTS (Summary)

1. Double–click object to access format options quickly.

   NOTE: You can also click the object to select it, then select Object or Selected Object from the Format menu.

2. Click **Patterns** .... `Ctrl` + `Tab`

To change line or border style:

• Select desired **Line** or **Border** options:

   Automatic—to return object to default setting.

   None— to make selection invisible.

   Custom—to allow for custom formatting such as Style, Color and Weight.

   Shadow— to add shadow to rectangles, ellipses, charts or text boxes.

   Round Corners—to round corners of rectangles, charts and text boxes.

To change or add an arrow style to a line:

• Select **Arrowhead** options:

   Style, Width, Length

   NOTE: To add an arrow to a line, you must first select an arrow style before selecting a width or length.

To fill object with color or pattern:

• Select desired **Fill** options:

   Automatic— to return object to default setting.

   None—to remove fill.

   Color palette— to add fills to rectangles, ellipses, charts or text boxes.

   Pattern—to add a pattern to selection. To color the pattern, select Pattern again.

3. Click `OK` .... `↵`

EXERCISE

■ **Enhance a Worksheet and Chart** ■ **Add a Text Box**
■ **Format a Text Box**

71

NOTES:

Add a Text Box

■ It is possible to add a text box object, in paragraph form, to both a worksheet and a chart. The text box tool is on the Drawing Toolbar and it allows you to drag out the shape of the box to be created. Text in a text box object can be enhanced using the same font options as those used for cell data.

Format a Text Box

■ As with any object, text boxes can be formatted. The border and background of the text box can be cleared so that the text box cannot be seen. A text box can also be enhanced by adding a drop shadow and/or rounded corners. Adding an arrow to the text box creates a data label.

In this exercise, you will enhance the Quarterly Income Statement Comparison worksheet and chart, and add explanatory paragraphs.

EXERCISE DIRECTIONS:

1. Open ⌨ **ISQTRS,** or 💾 **71ISQTRS.**

   • In the illustration, compare **ISQTRS** with the enhanced version below it.

2. Move all charts except the column chart to Sheet2 of the workbook. Rename Sheet2, CHARTS.

3. Move the column chart directly below the worksheet data. Rename Sheet1, EXPENSE ANALYSIS.

4. Make the changes to your worksheet indicated below:

   • Insert two rows above the title of the worksheet.
   • Move title and subtitle to column A.
   • Delete column B.
   • Adjust the width of column A to a little beyond the longest entry.
   • Include double lines above and below the title and the subtitle as shown.
   • Worksheet titles: Set to 12pt and center titles over columns A-F. Color the font white and the cell blue, (Row 1, Box 5).
   • Column titles: Bold. Adjust column widths to allow more space between data columns. Enter a line below titles. Color cells gray, (Row 5, Box 8).
   • Bold the labels INCOME, EXPENSES and NET INCOME.

   • Include a single line above the Total Income and Total Expenses data, and a double line *below* NET INCOME data.
   • 3RD QTR. Supplies cell: Outline with a wide line.
   • Worksheet text box: Create a text box containing the explanatory note, as shown in the illustration. Size the text box so it fits in the range G16:H23. Set the text box text to 8 pt. Italics. Format the text box and remove the border and set the color to none on the text box object.
   • Turn worksheet gridlines off.
   • Move the column chart to fit the range A25:H38.
   • Move the chart legend to below the chart.
   • Chart text box: Create and enter the text as shown in the chart illustration. Center the text box text. Format the text box for drop shadow and rounded corners. Draw an arrow from the text box to the highest Supplies column.

4. Set the left and right print margins to .2".

5. Preview the worksheet.

6. Print a copy to fit on one page.

7. Save and close the file; name it **ISQTRS.**

	A	B	C	D	E	F	G
1			GREENTHUMB LANDSCAPE SERVICE				
2			QUARTERLY INCOME STATEMENT COMPARISON				
3							
4			1ST QTR.	2ND QTR.	3RD QTR.	4TH QTR.	COMBINED
5			TOTALS	TOTALS	TOTALS	TOTALS	TOTALS
6							
7	INCOME						
8	Service Fees		17052.39	28566.18	33610.97	21461.19	100690.73
9	Consultations		4909.50	4679.76	3495.92	3088.79	16173.97
10	Total Income		21961.89	33245.94	37106.89	24549.98	116864.70
11							
12	EXPENSES:						
13	Advertising		270.00	480.00	480.00	260.00	1490.00
14	Salaries		2764.85	3766.65	3766.10	2764.30	13061.90
15	Supplies		989.94	3011.70	5210.05	2106.03	11317.72
16	Truck Maint.		464.52	1054.03	1060.53	1049.41	3628.49
17	Interest		75.00	75.00	75.00	75.00	300.00
18	Other		418.62	1779.51	1695.64	968.61	4862.38
19	Total Expenses		4982.93	10166.89	12287.32	7223.35	34660.49
20							
21	NET INCOME		16978.96	23079.05	24819.57	17326.63	82204.21

GREENTHUMB LANDSCAPE SERVICE
QUARTERLY INCOME STATEMENT COMPARISON

	1ST QTR.	2ND QTR.	3RD QTR.	4TH QTR.	COMBINED TOTALS
INCOME					
Service Fees	17052.39	28566.18	33610.97	21461.19	100690.73
Consultations	4909.50	4679.76	3495.92	3088.79	16173.97
Total Income	21961.89	33245.94	37106.89	24549.98	116864.70
EXPENSES:					
Advertising	270.00	480.00	480.00	260.00	1490.00
Salaries	2764.85	3766.65	3766.10	2764.30	13061.90
Supplies	989.94	3011.70	5210.05	2106.03	11317.72
Truck Maint.	464.52	1054.03	1060.53	1049.41	3628.49
Interest	75.00	75.00	75.00	75.00	300.00
Other	418.62	1779.51	1695.64	968.61	4862.38
Total Expenses	4982.93	10166.89	12287.32	7223.35	34660.49
NET INCOME	16978.96	23079.05	24819.57	17326.63	82204.21

The expenses for Supplies in the third quarter exceeded expectations and resulted in the implementation of a new inventory and cost control system.

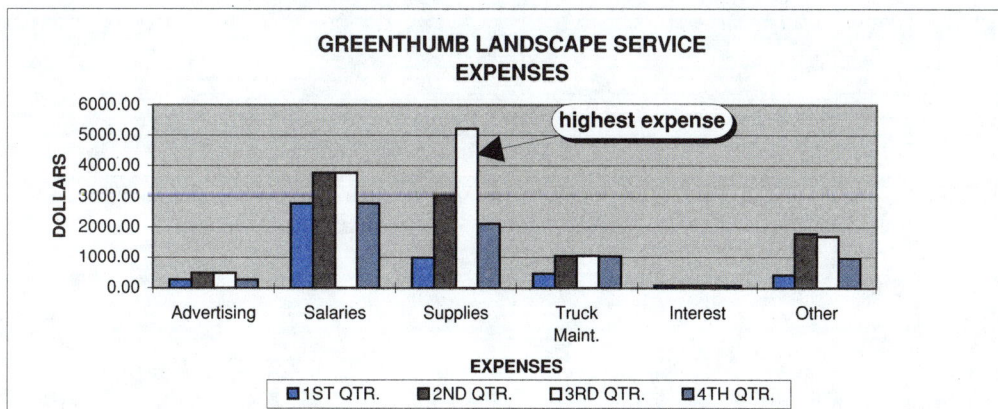

GREENTHUMB LANDSCAPE SERVICE
EXPENSES

highest expense

CREATE A TEXT BOX

1. Click **Text Box** button................. 🔲
   on Drawing Toolbar.
   Pointer becomes a ╋.

2. Position ╋ where corner of box
   will be.

To create a box without constraints:

- Drag box outline until desired size
  is obtained.

To create a square box:

- Press **Shift** and drag box outline
  until desired size is obtained.

To create a box and align it to gridlines:

- Press **Alt** and drag box outline
  until desired size is obtained.

3. Type text...*text*
   as desired.

4. Click outside text box to return to
   normal operations.

FORMAT TEXT BOX OBJECT

1. Select object to be formatted.

2. To format text:

- Select text and format for font,
  size, and style using Formatting
  Toolbar.

3. To format box:

   a. Press **Ctrl+1** .... Ctrl + 1

      OR

      - Click **Format**
        menu .... Alt + O

      - Click **Object**.................. E

   b. Select **Patterns** tab .... Ctrl + Tab

   c. Select Border and Fill settings.

   d. Click [OK] .... ↵

NEXT EXERCISE

EXERCISE
Summary

72

You have been asked to enhance the Woodworks Furniture Company quarterly sales and salary report worksheet.

EXERCISE DIRECTIONS:

1. Open ⌨ **WOOD** or open 💾 **72WOOD**.

2. Delete the **line** chart.

3. Place **3-D column** and **stack** charts side-by-side below the worksheet. Allow space for a note between the charts. The **3-D column** chart should be to the left of the **stack** chart and both charts should be equal in size and fit within the width of the worksheet.

4. Include a text box object between the two charts. Set the text to italics and create a shadow on the box. Size and place the box between the charts. Enter the following text:

   Tony Rivera was awarded "highest sales" awards for each quarter. Kelly Linsey won the "most-improved sales" award for the third quarter.

5. Enhance the worksheet and chart as desired or follow the suggestions listed at the right:

- Move the titles to column A.
- Set titles to Bookman Old Style font (or a serif font), 16 point, bold.
- Center titles over the width of the worksheet.
- Color the top three rows pale lavender.
- Bold column headings.
- Adjust column width as necessary.
- Color column headings pale yellow.
- Color remaining worksheet, including chart area, a pale gray.

6. Print a copy of the file in landscape orientation to fit on one page.

7. Save and close the workbook file; name the file **WOOD**.

EXERCISE

Summary

73

You work in the accounting department of the Shirley Micro Company, a computer firm. Each year, you create a balance sheet showing the total assets, liabilities and capital of your company.

Your supervisor, Mr. Martin Harold, has asked you to create a balance sheet comparing 1994, 1995 and 1996 data, including charts. The worksheet and charts should be enhanced so the report is ready to be presented to the bank officers.

EXERCISE DIRECTIONS:

1. Create the worksheet on the next page as shown, or open 🖫 **73BAL**. Format data and set column widths, as necessary. Include the indicated cell borders.

2. Find:
   - Total Assets for each year.
   - Total Liabilities for each year.
   - CAPITAL (Total Assets - Total Liabilities).
   - TOTAL LIABILITIES AND CAPITAL.

3. Create an embedded **3-D column** chart (subtype 5) below the worksheet comparing asset items (not totals) for 1994, 1995 and 1996. Place the chart in A24:F40. Include an appropriate heading, axis labels and titles, and a legend.

4. Create an embedded **3-D column** chart (subtype 4) comparing liability items (not totals) for 1994, 1995 and 1996. Place the chart in A42:F58. Include an appropriate heading, axis labels and titles, and a legend.

5. Include the following text in a text box next to the Asset chart:

   There has been a significant increase in Accounts Receivable due to the economic downturn.

6. Add a drop shadow to the text box and insert an arrow pointing to the column showing the increase in Accounts Receivable.

7. Include the following text in a text box next to the Liability chart:

   The decrease in Loans Payable was due to the payment of a long-term note due in September.

8. Add a drop shadow to the text box and insert an arrow pointing to the decrease in Loans Payable.

9. Enhance the worksheet and charts, as desired, or follow the suggestions listed below:

   - Set first two titles for Arial, 14 point, bold.
   - Set third title for Arial, 12 point, bold.
   - Color three line title area pale ivory.
   - Add a graphic at the right side of the title area.
   - Bold ASSETS, LIABILITIES and CAPITAL section titles.
   - Color worksheet pale gray.

10. Print a copy of the worksheet to fit on one page.

11. Save and close the workbook file; name it **BAL**.

	A	B	C	D	E	F	G
1	SHIRLEY MICRO COMPANY						
2	COMPARATIVE BALANCE SHEET						
3	December 31, 1996						
4							
5	**ASSETS**				1994	1995	1996
6		Cash			789,650	806,460	797,950
7		Investments			465,888	370,700	613,000
8		Accounts Receivable			1,321,700	1,342,690	1,545,500
9		Inventories			876,450	892,600	991,300
10		Other Assets			535,000	529,700	639,700
11	TOTAL ASSETS						
12							
13	**LIABILITIES**						
14		Accounts Payable			598,600	654,900	785,600
15		Loans Payable			623,800	793,500	384,500
16		Income Taxes Payable			276,000	287,050	345,200
17	Total Liabilities						
18							
19	**CAPITAL**						
20		Martin Harold, Capital					
21	TOTAL LIABILITIES AND CAPITAL						

LESSON 10

ANALYZING DATA

Exercises 74-89

- Database Lists

    Create a List

    Add Records and Fields to a List

    Wrap Text

    Use a Data Form to Manage Records in a List

    Name Lists

    Sort Records in a List

    Update Database

    Advanced Filter

    Database (List) Functions

    Subtotals Feature

- Pivot Tables
- Consolidate Data

EXCEL

EXERCISE
74

■ Create a List/Database ■ Add Records and Fields to a List ■ Wrap Text

NOTES:

Create a List/Database

■ While Excel is known mainly as spreadsheet software, it also has database capabilities that can help you organize, manage and locate information in a list. Data from external sources, such as database files, may be brought into Excel, or lists may be exported from Excel to a database program for analysis. We will limit our discussion to creating and using the database functions provided in Excel.

■ A **list** (or database) is a collection of related information.

■ Excel automatically recognizes a labeled series of rows containing a set of data as a list. As shown in the illustration below, in a list:

- Each row is a complete **record**, which could be information about one person in the database.

- Column labels are **field names**, or the name of a part of a record.

- Columns of data are **fields**, which are parts of records.

Fields are categories of information in a list. For example, the last name of the employee would be the data in the LAST field.

■ When creating a list, keep the following guidelines in mind:

Column Labels (Field Names)

- Type unique column labels in the first row of the list. The Excel List feature utilizes these names to find and organize the data.

- The column label format (font, alignment, cell borders, etc.) should be different from the record data.

- If a column label is wider than the column, use word wrap or insert a line break in the column label.

- The data you enter in a field should be either all numbers or all text if you intend to sort the list by that field at a later time.

- A formula or function can be used to determine field data.

Do not insert a blank row between column labels and the records in the list.

Row Data (Records)

- Do not include blank rows in a list.

Location of List

- If you need to store more than one list in a workbook, it is best to store each on a separate sheet.

- Do not store other data in cells adjacent to the list data.

- Avoid storing data to the left or right of a list because it may become hidden when you filter the records (see Exercise 80, page 274).

Add Records and Fields to a List

- A field (column of data) may be added in a list to the right of the last field, or you may insert a column and enter data.

- A record may be added in a list below the last record, or you may insert a row and enter data.

Wrap Text

- Word wrap will allow you to keep a longer column title or field name within one cell. This is necessary in a database list since the field name must be in the cell above the data for the field. Use the **Format, Cells** commands and the Alignment tab to wrap text.

In this exercise, you will create a database of Cyber Shop employees located in three cities. You will format field data, add records, add a field, and calculate values for the new field.

EXERCISE DIRECTIONS:

1. Create the list as shown in the worksheet below, or open 🖫 **74SHOP**.

2. Format the WKSAL field data for two decimal places.

3. Align column labels as shown and set them for bold type.

4. Set the STORE LOCATION cell for word wrap and size column to show label on two lines as shown.

5. Add the following employee records to the end of the list:

6. To include an annual salary field, enter the field name ANNSAL in column F.

7. Enter a formula to calculate the annual salary.

8. Format the ANNSAL column for two decimal places.

9. Save the workbook; name it **SHOP**.

10. Print one copy.

11. Close the workbook file.

LAST	FIRST	STORE LOCATION	IDNO	WKSAL
Gregonis	Dimitri	LA	14395	275.00
Hopkins	George	NY	14396	310.00
Seltzer	Al K.	CHI	14931	255.00
Restivo	Mary	CHI	14932	295.00

	A	B	C	D	E	F
1	LAST	FIRST	STORE LOCATION	IDNO	WKSAL	ANNSAL
2	Carson	Larry	NY	14356	235.45	
3	Palmeri	Marie	CHI	14367	276.50	
4	Lee	Chin	LA	13254	345.00	
5	Baez	Franco	NY	14236	268.50	
6	Martino	John	LA	14289	342.90	
7	Carson	George	NY	14078	389.76	
8	Sawyer	Harriet	CHI	13290	358.60	
9	Samtanai	Perkash	LA	14354	215.45	
10	Tommei	Lori	NY	13852	376.00	
11	Watterson	Cathy	LA	14269	325.75	
12	Lee	Randy	CHI	13298	365.80	
13	Rogers	Jane	NY	14024	310.89	
14	Naidle	Adam	LA	14321	243.50	
15	Lee	Michael	CHI	14295	276.00	

CREATE A LIST (Database Table)

Excel automatically recognizes a labeled series of rows containing a set of data as a list. Many database operations, such as sorting and filtering records, can be done to a list.

1. Type field names
   (column labels) .... *field names*
   in adjacent cells in top row.
   *NOTE: If a label does not fit in a
   column, turn word wrap on in
   the cell or insert a line break.*

2. Enter data....................................*data*
   for first record below field names.

3. Enter data....................................*data*
   for each record in remaining rows.
   *NOTES: Do not leave empty rows
   between records.*

   *The row containing the field names
   must be the first row of the range.*

4. Format column labels as desired.

ADD A RECORD TO A LIST

- Enter data ....*data*
  for each field in row below last record
  in list.

OR

1. Insert a row where record will be
   entered in the list.

2. Enter field data ....*data*
   in row.

ADD A FIELD TO A LIST

1. Type field name
   (column label) ....*field name*

   in adjacent cell in top row of list.

2. Enter data ....*data*
   for each record below field name.

OR

1. Insert a column where field will be
   entered in the list.

2. Type field
   name (column label) ....*field name*
   in first row of list in column.

3. Enter data .... *data*
   for each record below field name.

WRAP TEXT IN CELLS

*Wraps text to fit in cell. The row height
changes to accommodate the text.*

1. Select cell(s) containing text to wrap.

2. Click **Format** menu.............. `Alt`+`O`

3. Click **Cells** .... `E`

4. Click **Alignment** tab .... `Ctrl`+`Tab`

5. Select ☐ **Wrap Text** .... `Alt`+`W`

6. Click `OK` .... `↵`

NEXT EXERCISE

EXERCISE

■ Use a Data Form ■ Name Lists

75

NOTES:

Use a Data Form

■ You can manage records in a list or with a **data form.** When using a list, you can view all the records at once. However, using a data form allows you to work with one record at a time. You can create multiple lists in a workbook, and you can use a data form with any list.

■ From a data form you can:

- Browse or find records.

- Edit records.

- Add (append) new records.

- Delete records.

- Find records that match a criteria you specify.

■ Data forms are used in customer service applications since the data is clearly organized and easy to read. Note the illustration of a data form below:

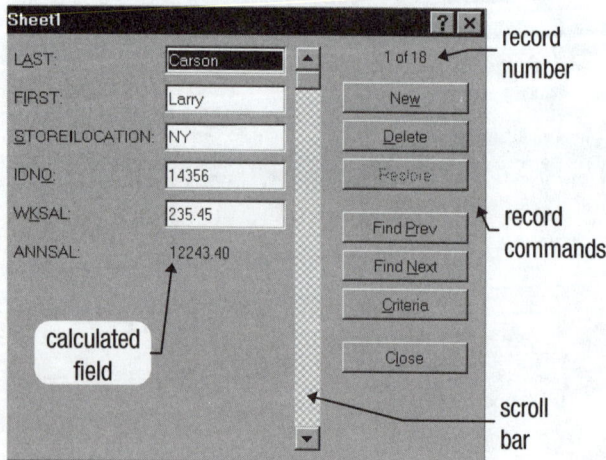

■ In a data form, calculated fields cannot be edited. However, Excel shows the contents of a calculated field and automatically adds the formula to the calculated field when you add a new record.

■ Use the following keys to work within a data form:

Tab	Positions insertion point in next field.
Shift + **Tab**	Positions insertion point in previous field.
Enter	Displays next record or inserts a new blank record.

■ To cancel changes made to data in a data form, press the Esc key or use the close button in the top right corner.

Name Lists

■ If you name a range containing a list, and then add or delete records, the name will no longer accurately reference the list data. However, if you name a list DATABASE, the range will adjust when you add or delete records from a data form. The named range for a database list should include the field names.

NOTE: You can name only one range DATABASE in a worksheet.

In this exercise, you will use a data form to view and add records to the Cyber Shop employee list.

EXERCISE DIRECTIONS:

1. Open ⌨ **SHOP** or open 💾 **75SHOP.**
2. Display a data form for the list.
3. Use the Find <u>N</u>ext and Find <u>P</u>rev buttons to view each record in the list.
4. Use the scroll box to move to the top and bottom of the list.
5. Close the data form.
6. Name the employee list (A1:F19) DATABASE.
7. Display a Ne<u>w</u> data form for the list and add the following records:

LAST	FIRST	STORE LOCATION	IDNO	WKSAL
Valdez	Lina	NY	14385	265.00
Accosta	Anthony	LA	13929	375.55
Graham	Holly	NY	14402	285.00
Esther	Polly	CHI	14235	286.50

8. Close the data form.

    NOTE: *Excel automatically added formulas for the new records to the calculated field ANNSAL.*

9. In the name box, select the DATABASE range.

    ✓ *Note the range includes the new records.*

10. Reformat the database of employees:
    - Center the column labels and data in columns C, D and E.
    - Right–align the ANNSAL column label.
11. Print the worksheet containing the list.
12. Save the workbook file; name it **SHOP**.
13. Close the workbook file.

OPEN A DATA FORM FOR A LIST

Displays data in a list one record at a time.

1. Select any cell in list.
2. Click **Data** menu .... `Alt`+`D`
3. Click **Form** .... `Alt`+`O`
4. Select from available options.
5. Click `Close` .... `Alt`+`L`

DISPLAY RECORDS USING A DATA FORM

—FROM DATA FORM—

View Next Record

- Click down scroll arrow .... `↓`

  OR

  Click `Find Next` .... `Alt`+`N`

View Previous Record

- Click up scroll arrow .... `↑`

  OR

  Click `Find Prev` .... `Alt`+`P`

Scroll to Record

- Drag scroll box .... `☐`

Move Forward Ten Records

- Click below scroll box.

Move Back Ten Records

- Click above scroll box.

ADD RECORDS TO A LIST USING A DATA FORM

—FROM DATA FORM—

1. Click `New` .... `Alt`+`W`
2. Type data in each record field.
   NOTE: *Press Tab to move to next field.*

To add additional records:

- Repeat steps 1 and 2 for each record to add.

EDIT RECORD IN A LIST USING A DATA FORM

—FROM DATA FORM—

1. Display record to edit.
2. Select field to edit .... `Tab`
3. Edit data as desired.
   NOTE: *Do not press Enter after typing data in field.*
4. Repeat steps 2 and 3 for each field to change.

To cancel changes made to current record:

- Click `Restore` .... `Alt`+`R`
  NOTE: *You must restore changes before moving to another record.*

  OR

  Press **Esc** .... `Esc`

EXERCISE

■ **Sort Records in a List** ■ **Undo a Sort**

76

NOTES:

Sort Records in a List

■ Records in a list may be rearranged or sorted in a variety of ways, depending on what type of information is needed.

For example, you can sort a list to find information arranged:

- In alphabetical or numerical order.

- Into groups (for example, all people in the list living in New York City or Chicago.)

- In reverse alphabetical or numerical order.

■ You can sort records in a list in two ways:

- Using the **Data** menu **Sort** command.

- Using the Sort Ascending or Sort Descending buttons on the Standard Toolbar (quick sort).

■ Using the **Sort** command from the **Data** menu (Note the illustration of the Sort dialog box below):

- You must first select any cell in the list. This tells Excel which list you want to sort. By default, when you sort a list, Excel will not sort the column labels.

- From the Sort dialog box, indicate the field(s) you wish to sort and the sort order. Excel will propose the Sort By field selected in the worksheet or the last field the list was sorted by.

- You must indicate whether you want the list sorted in ascending or descending order. **Ascending** arranges labels alphabetically, values from the smallest to the largest, dates from the oldest to the most recent, and time from the earliest to the latest. **Descending** reverses this order.

- You can sort records in a list by more than one field.

For example, you could sort the employee list using LAST name (as the Sort By field) and FIRST name (as the Then By field). This would result in employees with the same last names arranged in alphabetical first name order.

- To sort by more than three fields, first sort the list using the least important columns. Then, repeat the sort using the most important columns.

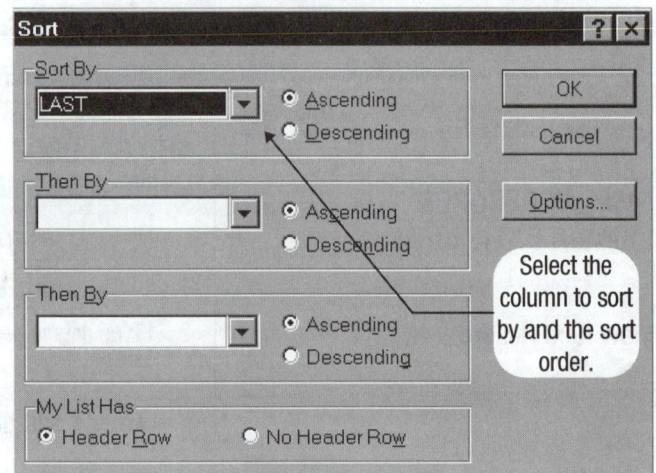

Select the column to sort by and the sort order.

SORT DIALOG BOX

- The Options button in the Sort dialog box displays the dialog box below and contains the following:

  First Key Sort Order   Select a custom sort order, such as days of the week, or months in the year.

  Case Sensitive   Select to arrange duplicate items in case order.

  Orientation   Select to change the sort orientation from columns to rows.

- Using the sort buttons from the Standard Toolbar:

  Sort Ascending

  Sort Descending

- You must first select any data cell in the *column* you wish to sort by.

- You can sort by only one column at a time. You can repeat the sort command on other columns (sorting least important columns first) to arrange records by more than one column.

- The sort buttons will apply any special options you have previously set from the Sort dialog box, such as Case Sensitive *(see left)*.

Undo a Sort

- To undo a sort, Excel provides a one level **Edit**, **Undo Sort** option. This option must be used *immediately* after the sort.

- Sort permanently changes the record order if the **Edit**, **Undo Sort** option is not used. If you want to keep both the original order version and the sorted version, you can copy the original version to another sheet.

In this exercise, you will sort the SHOP file in a variety of ways. The three sorts are shown in the illustration below and on the next page.

EXERCISE DIRECTIONS:

1. Open ⌨ **SHOP** or open 💾 **76SHOP**.

2. Use the Sort Ascending button, with the cursor in the IDNO column, to create **SORT A** shown below.

3. Use the Sort Descending button to sort the records by the ANNSAL column.

   ❷ Which employee earned the highest annual salary?

   ❷ Which earned the lowest annual salary?

4. Use the **Sort** command on the **Data** menu to create **SORT B** shown below.

   • Sort the records by two fields: Use LAST name as the **Sort By** field in ascending order. Use FIRST name as the **Then By** field in ascending order.

5. Print one copy of the records showing the results of **SORT B**.

6. Use the **Sort** command on the **Data** menu to create **SORT C** shown below.

   • Sort the data by three fields: Use STORE LOCATION as the **Sort By** field in descending order. Use LAST as the **Then By** field in ascending order. Use FIRST as the next **Then By** field in ascending order.

7. Undo the last sort so the records remain in Last/First name alphabetical order (**SORT B**).

8. Save and close the workbook file; name it **SHOP**.

LAST	FIRST	STORE LOCATION	IDNO	WKSAL	ANNSAL	Sort by IDNO
Lee	Chin	LA	13254	345.00	17940.00	
Sawyer	Harriet	CHI	13290	358.60	18647.20	
Lee	Randy	CHI	13298	365.80	19021.60	
Tommei	Lori	NY	13852	376.00	19552.00	
Accosta	Anthony	LA	13929	375.55	19528.60	
Rogers	Jane	NY	14024	310.89	16166.28	
Carson	George	NY	14078	389.76	20267.52	
Esther	Polly	CHI	14235	286.50	14898.00	
Baez	Franco	NY	14236	268.50	13962.00	
Watterson	Cathy	LA	14269	325.75	16939.00	
Martino	John	LA	14289	342.90	17830.80	
Lee	Michael	CHI	14295	276.00	14352.00	
Naidle	Adam	LA	14321	243.50	12662.00	
Samtanai	Perkash	LA	14354	215.45	11203.40	
Carson	Larry	NY	14356	235.45	12243.40	
Palmeri	Marie	CHI	14367	276.50	14378.00	
Valdez	Lina	NY	14385	265.00	13780.00	
Gregonis	Dimitri	LA	14395	275.00	14300.00	
Hopkins	George	NY	14396	275.00	14300.00	
Graham	Holly	NY	14402	285.00	14820.00	
Seltzer	Al K.	CHI	14931	255.00	13260.00	
Restivo	Mary	CHI	14932	295.00	15340.00	

SORT A

LAST ◄	FIRST ◄	STORE LOCATION	IDNO	WKSAL	ANNSAL	Sort by LAST, then by FIRST.	
Accosta	Anthony	LA	13929	375.55	19528.60		
Baez	Franco	NY	14236	268.50	13962.00		
Carson	George	NY	14078	389.76	20267.52		
Carson	Larry	NY	14356	235.45	12243.40		
Esther	Polly	CHI	14235	286.50	14898.00		
Graham	Holly	NY	14402	285.00	14820.00		
Gregonis	Dimitri	LA	14395	275.00	14300.00		
Hopkins	George	NY	14396	275.00	14300.00		
Lee	Chin	LA	13254	345.00	17940.00		
Lee	Michael	CHI	14295	276.00	14352.00		
Lee	Randy	CHI	13298	365.80	19021.60		
Martino	John	LA	14289	342.90	17830.80		
Naidle	Adam	LA	14321	243.50	12662.00		
Palmeri	Marie	CHI	14367	276.50	14378.00		
Restivo	Mary	CHI	14932	295.00	15340.00		
Rogers	Jane	NY	14024	310.89	16166.28		
Samtanai	Perkash	LA	14354	215.45	11203.40		
Sawyer	Harriet	CHI	13290	358.60	18647.20		
Seltzer	Al K.	CHI	14931	255.00	13260.00		
Tommei	Lori	NY	13852	376.00	19552.00		
Valdez	Lina	NY	14385	265.00	13780.00		
Watterson	Cathy	LA	14269	325.75	16939.00		

SORT B

LAST	FIRST	STORE LOCATION ◄	IDNO	WKSAL	ANNSAL	Sort by STORE LOCATION, then by LAST, then by FIRST.	
Esther	Polly	CHI	14235	286.50	14898.00		
Lee	Michael	CHI	14295	276.00	14352.00		
Lee	Randy	CHI	13298	365.80	19021.60		
Palmeri	Marie	CHI	14367	276.50	14378.00		
Restivo	Mary	CHI	14932	295.00	15340.00		
Sawyer	Harriet	CHI	13290	358.60	18647.20		
Seltzer	Al K.	CHI	14931	255.00	13260.00		
Accosta	Anthony	LA	13929	375.55	19528.60		
Gregonis	Dimitri	LA	14395	275.00	14300.00		
Lee	Chin	LA	13254	345.00	17940.00		
Martino	John	LA	14289	342.90	17830.80		
Naidle	Adam	LA	14321	243.50	12662.00		
Samtanai	Perkash	LA	14354	215.45	11203.40		
Watterson	Cathy	LA	14269	325.75	16939.00		
Baez	Franco	NY	14236	268.50	13962.00		
Carson	George	NY	14078	389.76	20267.52		
Carson	Larry	NY	14356	235.45	12243.40		
Graham	Holly	NY	14402	285.00	14820.00		
Hopkins	George	NY	14396	275.00	14300.00		
Rogers	Jane	NY	14024	310.89	16166.28		
Tommei	Lori	NY	13852	376.00	19552.00		
Valdez	Lina	NY	14385	265.00	13780.00		

SORT C

SORT A LIST USING THE MENU

1. Select any cell in list to sort.
2. Click **Data** menu .... `Alt`+`D`
3. Click **Sort** .... `S`

To set the first key sort order:

a. Click **Sort By:**

    [_____▼] .... `Alt`+`S`

b. Select field
   name .... `↑↓`, `Alt`+`↑`

c. Select ◯ **Ascending** .. `Alt`+`A`

   OR

   Select ◯ **Descending** `Alt`+`D`

To set second key sort order:

a. Click **Then By:**

    [_____▼] .... `Alt`+`T`

b. Select field
   name .... `↑↓`, `Alt`+`↑`

c. Select ◯ **Ascending** .. `Alt`+`C`

   OR

   Select ◯ **Descending** `Alt`+`N`

To set third key sort order:

a. Click **Then By:**

    [_____▼] .... `Alt`+`B`

b. Select field
   name .... `↑↓`, `Alt`+`↑`

c. Select ◯ **Ascending** .. `Alt`+`I`

   OR

   Select ◯ **Descending** `Alt`+`G`

To include or exclude header row from sort:

- Select ◯ **No Header Row** .... `Alt`+`W`

  OR

  Select ◯ **Header Row** .... `Alt`+`R`

To select a custom sort order for first key:

a. Click [Options] .... `Alt`+`O`

b. Click **First Key Sort Order:**

    [_____▼] .. .. `Alt`+`F`

c. Select desired
   order .... `↑↓`, `Alt`+`↑`

d. Click [OK] .... `↵`

To change orientation of sort (columns to rows):

a. Click [Options] .... `Alt`+`O`

b. Select ◯ **Sort Left to Right** .... `Alt`+`L`

c. Click [OK] .... `↵`

To set a case sensitive sort:

a. Click [Options] .... `Alt`+`O`

b. Select ☐ **Case Sensitive** .... `Alt`+`C`

c. Click [OK] .... `↵`

4. Click [OK] .... `↵`

SORT A LIST USING THE TOOLBAR

1. Select cell in column to sort by in the list.

   NOTES: Excel applies settings made in a previous sort, if one was made.

   The active cell determines the column Excel will sort by.

2. Click **Sort Ascending** button ...... `A/Z↓`
   on Standard Toolbar.

   OR

   Click **Sort Descending** button .... `Z/A↓`
   on Standard Toolbar.

UNDO A SORT

NOTE: To successfully undo a sort, you must undo it immediately.

1. Click **Edit** menu .... `Alt`+`E`
2. Click **Undo Sort** .... `Alt`+`U`

NEXT EXERCISE

EXERCISE

■ Create a List/Database ■ Add Records to a List ■ Use Data Form
■ Name Lists ■ Sort Records in a List ■ Default Sort Order

77

NOTES:

Default Sort Order

■ The default order for sorting data is as follows:

- Data is arranged according to the underlying value, not the data format.

- When a sort is in ascending order, Excel uses the following order:

  Numbers from the smallest negative to largest positive number.

  Dates and times are sorted chronologically.

Text and text that includes numbers, such as addresses, are sorted as follows:

0 1 2 3 4 5 6 7 8 9 (space) ! " # $ % & ' ( ) * + , - . / : ; < = > ? @ [\ ] ^ _ ` { | } ~ A B C D E F G H I J K L M N O P Q R S T U V W X Y Z

- **Blank cells** appear last whether the sort is in ascending or descending order.

In this exercise, you will use the procedures discussed in earlier exercises to create, modify and add to a database, in list or data form format. The DreamHouse Real Estate Company will also require the sorting of the data list.

EXERCISE DIRECTIONS:

1. Create the list as shown on the right, or open 🖫 **77REAL**.

2. Set column widths as follows:
   - Column A: 20
   - Column F: 12
   - ✓ *Adjust other column widths so that data can be fully viewed.*

3. Format the money column data for currency with two decimal places.

4. Open a data form and add the following data to the database list:

5. Use the Find <u>N</u>ext and Find <u>P</u>rev buttons to view each record in the list.

6. Use the scroll box to move to the top and bottom of the list of forms. Return to the list.

7. Use the quick sort buttons to sort the list by PRICE in descending order.
   - ❓ Which house is the most expensive?
   - ❓ Which house is the least expensive?

8. Print one copy of this sort.

ADDRESS	TOWN	AVAIL	TYPE	ROOMS	PRICE
321 Englewood Drive	Totten	3/1/97	Townhouse	9	$279,000
89 Kingsley Street	Annadale	3/15/97	Colonial	11	$375,000
607 Miller Street	Springville	2/1/97	Townhouse	7	$210,000
90 Camden Road	Annadale	2/15/97	Split	8	$245,000
805 Nardino Road	New Dorp	3/15/97	Split	7	$180,000

9. Use the **Data, Sort** method to sort the list by TOWN in ascending order, then by type in ascending order, then by PRICE in descending order.

   ❷ Which town has the most Townhouse-type homes?

   ❷ Which town has the most homes for sale?

   ❷ Which townhouse is the least expensive in Springville?

10. Print one copy of this sort.

11. Sort the list so that the AVAIL dates are in ascending order.

    ❷ Your client can't move in until February 15, 1997. How many homes are available after that date?

12. Print one copy of this sort.

13. Save and close the file; name it **REAL.**

	A	B	C	D	E	F
1		DREAMHOUSE REAL ESTATE COMPANY				
2			CURRENT LISTINGS			
3						
4	ADDRESS	TOWN	AVAIL	TYPE	ROOMS	PRICE
5	45 Mintum Road	Arrochar	12/1/96	Colonial	10	$ 345,000.00
6	125 Kelly Boulevard	Springville	1/1/96	Townhouse	7	$ 185,000.00
7	670 Circle Loop	Sunset Hill	12/1/96	Split	10	$ 450,000.00
8	89 Alberta Lane	New Dorp	2/2/96	Ranch	7	$ 195,000.00
9	345 Jacques Avenue	Totten	1/1/97	Colonial	7	$ 190,000.00
10	5 Flagg Terrace	New Dorp	2/1/97	Townhouse	6	$ 165,000.00
11	29 Club Road	Sunset Hill	3/1/97	Colonial	8	$ 245,000.00
12	914 Sand Lane	Totten	2/1/97	Ranch	7	$ 192,000.00
13	823 Barrow Road	Springville	3/1/97	Split	7	$ 188,000.00
14	92 Vellum Drive	New Dorp	2/1/97	Colonial	9	$ 287,500.00
15	621 Blait Road	Arrochar	4/1/97	Ranch	8	$ 225,500.00
16						

EXERCISE

■ Add a Field to a List ■ Maintain Original Record Order

78

NOTES:

Add a Field to a List

■ Fields may be added to a list by inserting a column or field in the desired location. Column headings must be contained within one cell to qualify as a field name. After a field or column is added, it will appear in the form view of the record.

Maintain Original Record Order

■ Once a set of records is sorted, the original order of the records is no longer intact.

To retain the original order, you may create a record number field and enter sequential numbers in that field. By using the field that contains these numbers as the Sort By field, you may re-sort the records and return them to their original order.

■ If a sort result is not what you expected, check that the data in the Sort By column does not contain both values and text. Consider adding an apostrophe (') to numbers if this is the case.

In this exercise, you modify a worksheet to use as a database list. A series is used to number the records in the list. New data is added and the list sorted in various ways to produce several sales and shipping reports for J.J. Barney Catalog Sales. Once the reports are completed, you will return the list to its original order by sorting on the record numbers.

EXERCISE DIRECTIONS:

1. Open 🖳 **ZONE** or open 💾 **78ZONE**.

2. Unprotect the worksheet, if it is protected, and clear the print range.

3. Rename Sheet2; name it Postage Rates.

4. Use cut and paste to move the POSTAGE AND SALES TAX RATES table and title to A1 in the Postage Rates sheet.

   NOTE: Since the HLOOKUP function references the table by name (RATES), the move should not produce errors.

5. In Sheet1, delete the blank row, row 6.

6. Rename Sheet1; name it Sales List.

7. Insert a column at column A.

8. Add the label REC NO. to row 5 in column A.

9. Using the procedure to create a series, enter sequential numbers starting with one and stepping by one to number all the catalog item records.

10. Use Format Painter to format the new column to match the colors in the rest of the worksheet.

11. Since field names in a list must be in one cell, delete first line of titles and word wrap column labels in columns F, G, and H, in row 5, so that both lines of each column title are contained in one cell.

12. Add the following sales to the list, using fill handles to create numbers in series:

REC. NO.	ORDER NO.	PRICE	ZONE
13	J43268	92.54	4
14	J43269	21.43	2
15	J43270	52.45	5
16	J43271	63.29	3
17	J43272	42.18	6
18	J43273	76.42	1
19	J43274	35.87	3
20	J43275	17.25	4

13. Copy the POSTAGE, TAX RATE, SALES TAX, and TOTAL SALES formulas down for the new sales.

14. Switch to form view to note new field for REC. NO.

15. In list view, move the worksheet titles to column C. Correct cell colors.

16. Sort on ZONE in ascending order.

    ❷ Which zone received the most shipments?

17. Print one copy of the list.

18. Sort on TOTAL SALE in descending order.

    ❷ What was the highest sale?

    ❷ What was the lowest sale?

19. Sort on ZONE (Sort By field) in ascending order and on TOTAL SALE (Then By field) in ascending order.

    ❷ What was the highest sale in Zone 1? Zone 5?

20. Print one copy of the list.

21. Re-sort the list back to its original order.

    NOTE: Use the REC. NO. field as the Sort By field.

22. Save and close the workbook file; name it **ZONE.**

	A	B	C	D	E	F	G	H	I
1			J. J. BARNEY CATALOG SALES						
2			JUNE 20, 199-			Edit and use word wrap			
3						so that each label is in one cell.			
4		Insert a column for REC. NO.							
5	REC. NO	ORDER NO.	PRICE	ZONE	POSTAGE	TAX RATE	SALES TAX	TOTAL SALE	
6									
7	1	J43256	59.95	1	4.00	0.08	4.80	68.75	
8	2	J43257	65.49	3	5.00	0	0.00	70.49	
9	3	J43258	29.95	2	4.50	0.06	1.80	36.25	
10	4	J43259	43.98	4	5.50	0.04	1.76	51.24	
11	5	J43260	16.89	5	6.00	0.05	0.84	23.73	
12	6	J43261	98.78	6	6.50	0.07	6.91	112.19	
13	7	J43262	35.89	5	6.00	0.05	1.79	43.68	
14	8	J43263	54.99	3	5.00	0	0.00	59.99	
15	9	J43264	36.67	6	6.50	0.07	2.57	45.74	
16	10	J43265	89.67	1	4.00	0.08	7.17	100.84	
17	11	J43266	29.95	4	5.50	0.04	1.20	36.65	
18	12	J43267	43.65	3	5.00	0	0.00	48.65	
19									

EXERCISE
Update Database (Find, Delete and Modify Records Using a Data Form)

79

NOTES:

Update Database

- The accuracy of a database of records depends on maintaining and updating information. From a data form, you can search a list for records based on specified criteria. These records, once located, can be viewed, edited or deleted.

- Search criteria are clues about field data used to search for a specific record or group of records. When you click the Criteria button in a data form, these options will appear:

Clear	Clears the current criteria.
Restore	Restores a cleared criteria.
Find Prev	Shows previous record meeting specified criteria. When the first record is reached, Excel sounds a beep.
Find Next	Shows next record meeting specified criteria. When the last record is reached, Excel sounds a beep.
Form	Returns form to show original options without using criteria. (When you select the Find Prev or Find Next button, the Form button becomes the Criteria button.)

- After selecting the Criteria button from the data form, you can select a field upon which to base the search, set the condition (operator) of the search (=, >, >=, <, <=, <>), and the data value(s) to search for. If no operator is typed, the search condition is set to find records that begin with the data value you typed. When you browse the records that match the search criteria, you can edit or delete them.

- A **wildcard** is a symbol used in a search value to substitute for unknown characters. The use of wildcards is particularly useful when working with large databases.

There are two wildcard symbols available:

- An **asterisk** (*), used to indicate an unknown group of characters.

  For example, if you were searching a list for a particular employee and you are certain only of the first two letters of the last name, you would indicate the search value for the LAST name field as *Pa**. This criteria will find all records in which the last name begins with *Pa*.

- A **question mark** (?), used to substitute for an unknown single character.

  For example, if you were searching for a particular employee but were uncertain of one character in the name, the search value would be entered as *Na?dle*. This criteria will find all records with any letter in the question mark location.

- When you delete a record, Excel removes the entire row in the worksheet and the record cannot be restored. From a data form, you can click **Delete** to remove a record from a list.

- To remove or change the criteria, click the Criteria button again and select from available options.

In this exercise, you will retrieve the SHOP database, and search and update it to reflect personnel changes within the company.

EXERCISE DIRECTIONS:

1. Open ⌨ **SHOP** or open 💾 **79SHOP**.

2. Include two new fields and data, as shown in the worksheet below:

   - Insert two columns between columns D and E.
   - Enter the field names HIRED and DEPT.
   - Enter the data as shown below.
     - ✓ AutoComplete will allow you to enter the DEPT. after typing the first few letters. See Exercise 21.
   - Format columns E and F to center data.
   - Using a data form, enter new employee records.

   IMPORTANT: Since the list was named DATABASE, Excel will include the new records in the list only if entered from a data form. If you want to add records directly to the worksheet, delete the name DATABASE before doing so.

3. Close the data form.

4. Select DATABASE from the name box to check that all records and the field names are selected. Then deselect the range.

5. From a data form:

   - Find all the records of employees whose last name is Carson. Change the first name of Larry Carson to Laurence.
   - Find all records that match Cars?n, and check that all are spelled Carson. Change any incorrect records.
   - Find the records for employees whose last name begin with the letter P.
     - ❓ How many employees fall into this category?
   - Find the records of all employees hired before 01/03/94.
     - ❓ How many employees fall into this category?

     HINT: Use < (less than) as the search operator. Do not type a space between operator and data value.

   - Delete Franco Baez because he has left the company.

6. Close the data form.

7. Re-sort the records on LAST name (Sort By field) and FIRST name (Then By field) to place names in alphabetical order.

8. Print a copy of the list to fit on one page.

9. Save and close the workbook file; name it **SHOP.**

LAST	FIRST	STORE LOCATION	IDNO	HIRED	DEPT.	WKSAL	ANNSAL
Accosta	Anthony	LA	13929	10/30/96	Sales	375.55	19528.60
Baez	Franco	NY	14236	11/1/93	Stock	268.50	13962.00
Carson	George	NY	14078	4/1/93	Admin.	389.76	20267.52
Carson	Larry	NY	14356	9/30/94	Stock	235.45	12243.40
Esther	Polly	CHI	14235	11/15/96	Admin.	286.50	14898.00
Graham	Holly	NY	14402	11/1/96	Sales	285.00	14820.00
Gregonis	Dimitri	LA	14395	5/25/96	Admin.	275.00	14300.00
Hopkins	George	NY	14396	6/10/96	Stock	275.00	14300.00
Lee	Chin	LA	13254	5/15/92	Sales	345.00	17940.00
Lee	Michael	CHI	14295	3/5/94	Stock	276.00	14352.00
Lee	Randy	CHI	13298	7/25/94	Stock	365.80	19021.60
Martino	John	LA	14289	11/1/94	Admin.	342.90	17830.80
Naidle	Adam	LA	14321	2/15/94	Sales	243.50	12662.00
Palmeri	Marie	CHI	14367	9/1/94	Stock	276.50	14378.00
Restivo	Mary	CHI	14932	10/1/96	Sales	295.00	15340.00
Rogers	Jane	NY	14024	5/18/95	Sales	310.89	16166.28
Samtanai	Perkash	LA	14354	11/25/95	Sales	215.45	11203.40
Sawyer	Harriet	CHI	13290	2/13/96	Admin.	358.60	18647.20
Seltzer	Al K.	CHI	14931	7/25/96	Stock	255.00	13260.00
Tommei	Lori	NY	13852	8/25/95	Admin.	376.00	19552.00
Valdez	Lina	NY	14385	10/15/96	Stock	265.00	13780.00
Watterson	Cathy	LA	14269	12/15/95	Sales	325.75	16939.00
Jackson	Martin	LA	14397	10/25/96	Stock	275.00	
Parsons	Lyle	NY	14398	10/31/96	Admin.	285.50	
Carsen	Penn	CHI	14399	11/5/96	Sales	225.75	

FIND SPECIFIC RECORDS IN A LIST USING A DATA FORM

1. Select any cell in list.

2. Click **Data** menu .... `Alt`+`D`

3. Click **Form**..................................... `O`

4. Click `Criteria` .... `Alt`+`C`

5. Select text box............................. `Tab`
   of field to search.

6. Type a criterion........................*criterion*
   NOTE: *Wildcard characters (? or *) may be used to stand for one (?) or more (*) characters in the position of the wildcard character. To find an actual ? or *, precede ? or * character with a tilde (~).*

EXAMPLES:

Type pau *or* pau* *in a text field to find records beginning with pau, such as Paul or Paula.*

Type >=1/1/89 *in a date field to find records containing dates on or after 1/1/89.*

Type (718) ???-???? *in a character field to find phone numbers that have a 718 area code.*

Type * Shaw *in a character field to find records that have* **any** *first name and Shaw as a last name.*

7. To add criteria to additional fields, repeat steps **5** and **6**.

8. Click `Find Next` .... `Alt`+`N`

   OR

   Click `Find Prev` .... `Alt`+`P`

9. Repeat step **8** for each matching record to find.

To obtain access to entire list:

a. Click `Criteria` .... `Alt`+`C`

b. Click `Clear` .... `Alt`+`C`

c. Click `Form` .... `Alt`+`F`

10. Click `Close` .... `Alt`+`L`
    to return to worksheet.

DELETE RECORDS IN A LIST USING A DATA FORM

CAUTION: Deleted records cannot be restored.

—FROM DATA FORM—

1. Display record to delete.

2. Click `Delete` .... `Alt`+`D`

3. Click `OK` .... `↵`

Excel deletes records in list, and moves them up to close the space left by the deletion.

To delete additional records:

- Repeat steps **1–3** for each record to delete.

NEXT EXERCISE

EXERCISE

AutoFilter a List

80

NOTES:

- **AutoFilter**, which is selected from the **Data, Filter** menu commands, provides another way to find and work with records in a list. With AutoFilter you can show only the records from the list that meet a selected criteria. For example, you might want to show only records for employees in LA, as shown in the illustration below.

- When you start AutoFilter, Excel adds a drop-down arrow to each field name. You can then set a **filter criterion** (specify which records to show) for any field by clicking a drop-down arrow and making a selection.

  From any field name drop-down list you can select:

  [All]   to end filtering for a field.

  A specific data value, such as LA or NY.

  [Custom...]   to specify a condition such as records within a range of dates or records containing two data values in a field.

  [Blanks]   to show records with blanks (no data) in the field.

  [NonBlanks] to show records with any data in the field.

- You can select or set a filter criterion in more than one column to find subsets of the records. For example, you can show only the records of Sales DEPT. employees in NY.

- Removing criterion without ending AutoFilter:

  - To remove a filter criterion for a single field, select **[All]** from the drop-down list for that field.

  - To remove all filter criteria, select **Filter, Show All** from the **Data** menu.

- When you filter a list, Excel hides the data of the records that do not meet the criteria. This does not move or delete the records from the list.

drop-down arrow

LOCATION

	A	B	STORE					
1	LAST	FIRST	STORE LOCATIO	IDNO	HIRED	DEPT	WKSA	ANNSA
2	Accosta	Anthony	(All) (Top 10...) (Custom...) CHI LA NY (Blanks) (NonBlanks)	13929	10/30/96	Sales	375.55	19528.60
8	Gregonis	Dimitri		14395	05/25/96	Admin.	275.00	14300.00
10	Jackson	Martin		14397	10/25/96	Stock	275.00	14300.00
11	Lee	Chin		13254	05/15/92	Sales	345.00	17940.00
14	Martino	John		14289	11/01/94	Admin.	342.90	17830.80
15	Naidle	Adam		14321	02/15/94	Sales	243.50	12662.00
20	Samtanai	Perkash	LA	14354	11/25/95	Sales	215.45	11203.40
25	Watterson	Cathy	LA	14269	12/15/95	Sales	325.75	16939.00
26								
27								

filter criterion

In this exercise, you will use the AutoFilter feature to show specific records in the database list. You will then print these filtered records for your supervisor.

EXERCISE DIRECTIONS:

1. Open ⌨ **SHOP** or open 💾 **80SHOP**.
2. Use AutoFilter to show only employees who work in LA.
3. Print a copy of the list to fit on one page.
4. Filter the list to show employees who work in the sales department of the LA store.
5. Change the filter criterion for the DEPT. field to show only administrators (Admin.) in the LA store.
6. Print a copy of the list to fit on one page.
7. Remove all filter criteria.
8. Filter the employee list to show only records for employees with an annual salary that is greater than or equal (>=) to 17000.
9. Print a copy of the filtered records.
10. Remove all filter criteria.
11. Filter records to produce a list of employees hired after 1/1/95 who work in the Stock department.
12. Print a copy of all filtered records.
13. Remove all filter criteria.

    ❷ Using filters, determine how many employees earn more than $300 per week and were hired after 1/1/95.

14. End AutoFilter.
15. Close the workbook file. You do not need to save the changes.

FILTER A LIST AUTOMATICALLY

NOTES: You can use **AutoFilter** with one list in a worksheet at a time and the list must have column labels.
If you select criterion from more than one drop-down list, Excel will show only records meeting the criteria specified by both filters.

1. Select any cell in list to filter all fields.
   OR
   Select cells containing field names in list to filter only the selected fields.
2. Click **Data** menu .... `Alt`+`D`
3. Click **Filter** .... `F`
4. Click **AutoFilter** .... `F`
   Excel adds drop-down list arrows next to column labels.
5. Click drop-down arrow .... `▼` of field you want to filter.
6. Select item from list .... `⤢`, `↵`
   In addition to a specific item you can select:

   (All) — to end filtering for the field.
   (Blanks) — to show only records that have no data in the column.

(NonBlanks) — to show only records that have data in the column.

(Custom...) — to specify up to two comparison criteria for data in the column.

If **Custom** was selected:
a. Click first [____▼] .... `Tab`,`↓`
b. Select a column item .... `⤢`, `Alt`+`↑`
c. Click first [____▼] .... `Tab`,`↓`
d. Select desired item operator .... `⤢`, `Alt`+`↑`

To specify another criterion for column:
a. Select ◯ **And** .... `Alt`+`A`
   OR
   Select ◯ **Or** .... `Alt`+`O`
b. Click second [____▼] .... `Tab`,`↓`

c. Select a column item .... `⤢`, `Alt`+`↑`
d. Click second [____▼] .... `Tab`
e. Select desired item operator .... `⤢`, `Alt`+`↑`

SHOW ALL RECORDS IN A FILTERED LIST

1. Click **Data** menu .... `Alt`+`D`
2. Click **Filter** .... `F`
3. Click **Show All** .... `S`

END AUTOFILTER

1. Click **Data** menu .... `Alt`+`D`
2. Click **Filter** .... `F`
3. Click **AutoFilter** .... `F`
   to deselect it.

EXERCISE
Advanced Filter

81

NOTES:

Advanced Filter

■ Like AutoFilter, **Advanced Filter** lets you filter records in a list. Advanced Filter has the characteristics listed below:

- The criteria are typed in the worksheet, which allows for more complex filters.

- The field names, in the list, will not contain drop-down arrows as in AutoFilter.

- Records may be filtered in two ways:

  The records that do not meet the criteria are hidden in the list (in-place filtering).

  OR

  The records that meet the criteria are copied (extracted) to a worksheet range.

■ Guidelines for using Advanced Filter:

- You must type the criteria in a range away from the data (above or below the list) in the worksheet. Note the illustration on page 279.

- From the Advanced Filter dialog box you must specify:

  The action (to filter the list in-place or copy the result list to another location).

  The range containing the list.

  The worksheet cells containing the criteria range.

  The worksheet range to copy the results to, if the action requires it.

NOTE: The range can be the beginning cell or a range of cells for the result list. You cannot specify another worksheet, but you can copy the result there later. The ranges may be selected at each point in the dialog box, or they may be keyed into each location. See the illustration of the Advanced Filter dialog box below showing the areas to be specified which relate to the illustrated worksheet on page 279.

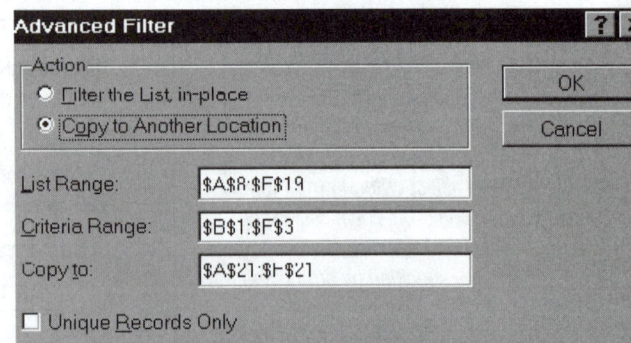

Advanced Filter	? >
Action	
○ Filter the List, in-place	OK
● Copy to Another Location	Cancel
List Range: $A$8:$F$19	
Criteria Range: $B$1:$F$3	
Copy to: $A$21:$F$21	
☐ Unique Records Only	

■ Guidelines for setting up a simple criteria range:

- You can copy the field names (column labels) to ensure that the labels in the criteria range are identical to the field names in the list.

- Type the criteria below the criteria labels.

- If the records must match the criteria, you can omit the = (equal sign) operator and just type the value.

- The criteria range, specified in the Advanced Filter dialog box, cannot contain empty columns.

- If more than one criteria is specified on one line, as in the illustration, the search will locate only records that match all criteria.

- The advantages of copying the results of a filter to another location are:

  - Records that meet the specified criteria are listed together.

  - Records in the result list can be sorted, filtered again and formatted.

  - Records can be changed without affecting the records in the original list.

  - You can delete fields in the result list that you are not interested in.

  - The result list can be printed separately as a report.

- To end in-place filtering, use the **Filter, Show All** command from the **Data** menu.

- Result lists can be moved or copied to any worksheet. Column widths used by result lists are those that are current in the worksheet.

In this exercise, you will use and add to the list for the Dreamhouse Real Estate Company. Advanced filter will be used to create alternate lists for clients who wish to purchase a particular type of house.

EXERCISE DIRECTIONS:

1. Open ⌨ **REAL** or open 💾 **81REAL**.

2. Additional homes have been listed by our agency. Add the following to the **REAL** database:

ADDRESS	TOWN	AVAIL	TYPE	ROOMS	PRICE
45 Point Road	Sunset Hill	4/1/97	Split	10	$448,500
16 Beverly Circle	Arrochar	4/15/97	Colonial	8	$325,000
71 Regis Avenue	Totten	3/15/97	Ranch	7	$175,000
87 Anthony Street	Springville	3/1/97	Townhouse	7	$155,000
236 Eighth Street	New Dorp	4/1/97	Colonial	8	$210,000
624 Clarke Road	Sunset Hill	4/30/97	Ranch	8	$255,000
90 Shore Road	Totten	5/1/97	Townhouse	6	$155,000

3. Sort the list by Price in descending order.

4. Use Advanced Filter to filter the records:
   - Insert three rows above the list and titles, and copy the field names (column headings) as shown in the illustration on page 279.
   - Type a criterion to list houses located in New Dorp:
     - B1: TOWN
     - B2: New Dorp
   - Select option to filter list in-place.
   - Specify the cells containing the criterion B1:B2.
     ❓ How many houses are available in New Dorp?

5. Show all records in the list (end in-place filtering).

6. Use Advanced Filter to filter the real estate list:
   - Select option to copy to another location.
   - Specify the criteria range (B1:B2).
   - Copy the result list to A35.

7. Print one copy of the range containing the result of the filter.

8. Delete the result list.

9. Use Advanced Filter to filter the real estate list:
   - Type a criterion to list all ranch houses:
     - D1: TYPE
     - D2: Ranch
   - Select option to copy to another location.
   - Specify the criteria range (D1:D2)
   - Copy the result list to A35.
     ❓ How many Ranch-style homes are available?

10. Use Advanced Filter to further filter the result list:

- Type a criterion to list houses that cost less than $200,000.
  - F1: PRICE
  - F2: <200000
- Select option to copy to another location.
- Specify range of the result list as the list range.
- Specify criteria range (F1:F2).
- Copy filtered list to A45.
- Type a heading on each result list that describe the contents, such as: RANCH-STYLE HOMES, RANCH-STYLE HOMES UNDER $200,000.

11. Print one copy of the range containing both result lists.

12. Delete all result lists and all criteria entries.

13. Use Advanced Filter to filter the real estate list to find all Townhouse homes that cost less than $170,000. Copy the filtered list to A35.

    HINT: Enter both criteria on one line, as shown in the illustration, and use the entire area as the criteria range.

14. Enter an appropriate heading above the result list and print one copy of the townhouses that cost less than $170,000.

15. Delete result list and criteria entries.

16. Use Advanced Filter to filter the real estate list to find all New Dorp Ranches. Copy the filtered list to A35.
    ❓ How many ranches are available in New Dorp?

17. Delete results and criteria entries.

18. Save the workbook file; name it **REAL**.

	A	B	C	D	E	F	G	H
1		TOWN	AVAIL	TYPE	ROOMS	PRICE		
2		New Dorp		Ranch			criteria	
3	Criteria labels							
4	entered away	DREAMHOUSE REAL ESTATE COMPANY						
5	from data.		CURRENT LISTINGS					
6								
7	ADDRESS	TOWN	AVAIL	TYPE	ROOMS	PRICE	list range	
8	45 Mintum Road	Arrochar	12/1/96	Colonial	10	$ 345,000.00		
9	125 Kelly Boulevard	Springville	1/1/96	Townhouse	7	$ 185,000.00		
10	670 Circle Loop	Sunset Hill	12/1/96	Split	10	$ 450,000.00		
11	89 Alberta Lane	New Dorp	2/2/96	Ranch	7	$ 195,000.00		
12	345 Jacques Avenue	Totten	1/1/97	Colonial	7	$ 190,000.00		
13	5 Flagg Terrace	New Dorp	2/1/97	Townhouse	6	$ 165,000.00		
14	29 Club Road	Sunset Hill	3/1/97	Colonial	8	$ 245,000.00		
15	914 Sand Lane	Totten	2/1/97	Ranch	7	$ 192,000.00		
16	823 Barrow Road	Springville	3/1/97	Split	7	$ 188,000.00		
17	92 Vellum Drive	New Dorp	2/1/97	Colonial	9	$ 287,500.00		
18	621 Blait Road	Arrochar	4/1/97	Ranch	8	$ 225,500.00		
19								
20	ADDRESS	TOWN	AVAIL	TYPE	ROOMS	PRICE	Results	
21	89 Alberta Lane	New Dorp	2/2/96	Ranch	7	$ 195,000.00	copied	
22							to another	
23							location.	
24								

FILTER A LIST WITH ADVANCED FILTERING

NOTE: List must have column labels.

1. Set up criteria range *(see right)*.
2. Select any cell in list to filter.
3. Click **Data** menu .... `Alt`+`D`
4. Click **Filter**..................................... `F`
5. Click **Advanced Filter**................... `A`

To change proposed list range:

- Select range to filter in worksheet.

   OR

   Type reference ....*reference* of list to filter in **List Range** text box.

6. Click **Criteria Range:**

   ◻ ....`Alt`+`C`

7. Select criteria range in worksheet.

   OR

   Type criteria range ....*reference*
   NOTE: Include the criteria label(s) with the criteria.

8. Select ◯ **Filter the List, in-place**.............................`Alt`+`F`

   OR

   a. Select ◯ **Copy to Another Location** ....`Alt`+`O`

   b. Click **Copy to:**

      ◻ ....`Alt`+`T`

   c. Select destination range for result list in worksheet.

      OR

      Type destination reference ....*reference* for result list.

   CAUTION: If you indicate a single cell, Excel copies the filtered results to cells below and to the right of the cell, overwriting existing data without warning.

To hide duplicate records:

- Select ◻ **Unique Records Only**............. `Alt`+`R`

9. Click `OK` .... `↵`

SET UP A CRITERIA RANGE

Tells Excel how to filter a list, prior to using Advanced Filtering.

1. If necessary, insert blank rows above the list you want to filter.

2. Type or copy desired field names........................*field names* to a blank row above list.
   *These labels are called **criteria labels** and must be identical to the column labels in the list you want to filter.*

3. Enter criteria .... *criteria* in row(s) below criteria labels.

To show only records (rows) matching a value, date, or text:

- Enter text, number, date or logical value..........................*data* to find in column.

   EXAMPLE:
   *Below **Town**, type **New Dorp**.*
   *NOTE: When you enter text, Excel will find all items beginning with the text criteria. For example, if you enter **Sam**, Excel will include records such as **Samuel** and **Sammy**.*

   EXAMPLES:
   To find:

   An exact text match ....="=text to find"

   Any character in a specific position.............................Topic?

   Consecutive characters in a specific position....................Sa*y

   An actual question mark, asterisk, or tilde (~)............. What is that~?

   A value greater than a specified number..............................>1000

To show items that compare to a specified value:

- Use one of the following comparison operators before a value, date or text criterion.

   = ...(equal to or matches)
   <> ....(not equal to)
   > ....(greater than)
   < ....(less than)
   >= .... (greater than or equal to)
   <= .... (less than or equal to)

   EXAMPLE: Enter <170000 below the Price criteria label to show only records containing values less than 170000 for that column.

4. Filter list with Advanced Filtering *(see left)* to show results of criteria.

SHOW ALL RECORDS IN A FILTERED LIST

1. Click **Data** menu.................. `Alt`+`D`
2. Click **Filter** .... `F`
3. Click **Show All**.............................. `S`

NEXT EXERCISE

EXERCISE

■ Extract Records Using Advanced Filter ■ Edit Result List

82

NOTES:

Extract Records Using Advanced Filter

■ When you use Advanced Filter to extract records to another location in the worksheet, the extracted records are not linked to the original list. Therefore, if you need to edit the records, do so prior to using Advanced Filter.

Edit Result List

■ To meet requirements for a report, irrelevant fields may be deleted from a result list. As noted earlier, you can edit any list from a data form or from the list itself. Data forms may be used to edit the original list or the result list.

In this exercise, you will create a supplies inventory list for Great Maple Community College. Your supervisor wants reports extracted from this inventory to show specific sets of records.

EXERCISE DIRECTIONS:

1. Create the list shown on the right, or open 📁 **82SUPPLY**.

   • Set column widths A to 11 and B and C to 20.
   • Format the money column for two decimal places.
   • Left-align the date column entries.
   • Right-align the PRICE and TOTAL column labels.
   • Find the total cost of each item in the list. Format the results for two decimal places.

2. Sort VENDOR (Sort By field) in ascending order and DESCRIPTION (Then By field) in ascending order.

3. Print a copy.

4. Use Advanced Filter to extract to A30 items that are purchased in Package format. (We hope to purchase in larger units in the future.) Use cells in rows 1–2 for the criteria range (A1:G2).

5. In the result list, clear the UNIT data and label.

   NOTE: Delete the cells, do not clear them. When prompted, select Shift Cells Left, to move remaining columns in the result list.

6. Enter a two-line heading above the result list:

   GREAT MAPLE COMMUNITY COLLEGE
   SUPPLIES PURCHASED BY PACKAGE

7. Use the menu to sort the result list data by DESCRIPTION in ascending order.

8. Print a copy of the report.

9. Delete the result list and criteria, but not the result list title.

10. Edit the September 2 record to correct the vendor from Forest Stationery to Treehouse Paper.

11. Use Advanced Filter to extract to A30 all Paper City purchases that were received in a Box format.

12. In the result list, delete the columns containing VENDOR and UNIT data and label. Use the same method as suggested above.

13. Adjust column widths as necessary.

14. Move the report titles left one column.

15. Edit the report's subheading to:

    BOX UNIT PURCHASES FROM PAPER CITY

16. Print a copy of the report.

17. Delete the result list and criteria, but not the result list title.

18. Adjust column width in the database list.

19. Select a cell in the database list and use a data form and the Find procedures to change the (8.5 X 11) entries in the Description column to (Letter) and the (8.5 x 14) entries to (Legal).

20. Use Advanced Filter to extract to A30 all box unit purchases from School Central, Inc.

21. Edit the report's subheading to:

    BOX UNIT PURCHASES FROM SCHOOL CENTRAL, INC.

22. In the result list, delete the columns containing VENDOR and UNIT data and label. Adjust column widths as necessary.

23. Print one copy of the report.

24. Delete the result list, the related headings, and criteria.

25. Adjust column widths as necessary.

26. Save and close the workbook; name it **SUPPLY**.

DATE	DESCRIPTION	VENDOR	UNIT	QUANTITY	PRICE	TOTAL
	criteria labels			Type criteria below criteria labels as needed.		
		GREAT MAPLE COMMUNITY COLLEGE				
		SCHOOL STORE - SUPPLIES INVENTORY				
DATE	DESCRIPTION	VENDOR	UNIT	QUANTITY	PRICE	TOTAL
15-May-96	Folders (8.5x11)	Paper City	Box	4	12.50	
15-May-96	Folders (8.5x14)	Paper City	Box	2	18.65	
15-May-96	Paper (8.5x11)	Paper City	Case	10	45.00	
15-May-96	Paper (8.5x14)	Paper City	Case	4	49.60	
12-Jul-96	Index cards (3x5)	Treehouse Paper	Box	3	32.86	
14-Jul-96	Binders - Large	School Central, Inc.	Box	8	53.79	
19-Jul-96	Binders - Small	School Central, Inc.	Box	5	47.89	
22-Jul-96	Adhesive notes	Stickum Bros.	Package	15	5.49	
22-Jul-96	Adhesive tape	Stickum Bros.	Box	5	23.50	
10-Aug-96	Pens - Speedroll	J & J Discount	Box	20	15.75	
15-Aug-96	Pencils - #2	J & J Discount	Box	16	12.95	
25-Aug-96	Pads (5x8)	Treehouse Paper	Package	6	8.49	
2-Sep-96	Envelopes #10	Forest Stationery	Box	5	3.49	
6-Sep-96	Looseleaf - large	School Central, Inc.	Package	200	2.49	
6-Sep-96	Looseleaf - small	School Central, Inc.	Package	125	2.10	
10-Sep-96	Paper (Bond)	Paper City	Box	85	6.89	

EXERCISE
Filter a List with Multiple Criteria
83

NOTES:

- In the previous exercises, you filtered a list to find records that met criteria for two or more conditions. This meant that only records that met all the criteria were filtered. It is often necessary to open a search to find records that meet any of a series of criteria or one criteria or another.

- When filtering data, you may need to find records that meet *all* or *any* criteria as described below.

    All This is often referred to as an AND condition. That is, the records must meet the first criteria (condition) *and* the second condition. The AND condition was used in previous exercises when two items were entered on the same line in the criteria range.

    Any This is often referred to as an OR condition. That is, the records can meet the first *or* the second criteria.

- In a criteria range you tell Excel the records must meet **all** the criteria by typing the criteria in the *same row*.

EXAMPLE: This results in all New Dorp ranches.

TOWN	TYPE
New Dorp	Ranch

If the records can meet either (**any**) condition, type the criteria in *separate rows*.

EXAMPLE: This results in any homes in New Dorp and any Ranches from the entire list.

TOWN	TYPE
New Dorp	
	Ranch

If the records can meet different criteria for the same column, set up duplicate criteria labels.

EXAMPLE: This results in any Ranches or Townhouses from the list.

TYPE	TYPE
Ranch	
	Townhouse

If the records can meet different criteria within the same field, you must repeat the field that is required.

EXAMPLE: This results in any Townhouses or Ranches in Springville.

TOWN	TYPE
Springville	Townhouse
Springville	Ranch

- **Comparison operators** can be used to set individual criterion:

SYMBOL (CONDITION)		EXAMPLE	WILL PRODUCE A LISTING OF
=	(equal to)	=Ranch or Ranch	Ranch style houses.
<>	(not equal)	<>Townhouse	House types except townhouses.
>	(greater than)	>200000	Houses priced greater than $200,000.
<	(less than)	<200000	Houses priced less than $200,000.
<=	(less than or equal to)	<=200000	Houses that are $200,000 and higher.
>=	(greater than or equal to)	>=200000	Houses that are $200,000 and lower.

In this exercise, you will search the Dreamhouse Real Estate Company's listings to answer clients' requests.

EXERCISE DIRECTIONS:

1. Open ⌨ **REAL** or open 💾 **83REAL**.

2. Center the field names in the list.

3. Add an additional row to the criteria range, for "Any/or" conditions, as illustrated.

   *NOTE: Use **Advanced Filter** to do all of the filtering operations that follow. Determine if the filter requires an AND condition (criteria in one row) or an ANY condition (criteria in separate rows.)*

4. Filter the list in-place to show homes that are Split type.

   ❷ How many such listings exist?

5. End in-place filtering (show all records in the list).

6. Filter the list in-place to show Townhouses in Springville or New Dorp.

   HINT: The TOWN and TYPE criteria labels will each have two entries below them.

   ❷ How many such listings exist?

7. End in-place filtering for the list.

8. Filter the list in-place to show all houses in New Dorp *except* Townhouses.

   ❷ How many such listings exist?

9. End in-place filtering for the list.

10. Filter the list in-place to show Ranch style houses less than $200,000 that will become available on or after February 1, 1997.

    ❷ How many such listings exist?

11. Filter the list and extract (copy) to A36 all the Townhouse or Ranch style houses.

    ❷ How many such listings exist?

12. Filter the list and extract to A50 all the Townhouse or Ranch style houses that are located in New Dorp. Compare the result list created in step 12 with this result list.

    ❷ How many such listings exist?

    HINT: The TOWN and TYPE criteria labels will each have two entries below them.

13. Filter the list and extract to A56 all Ranch or Colonial style houses under $250,000.

    ❷ How many such listings exist?

14. Sort the records in *each* result list in ascending PRICE order.

15. Add appropriate titles for each of the result lists.

16. Print all the result lists on one page.

17. Save and close the workbook file; name it **REAL**.

	A	B	C	D	E	F
1	Criteria for Ranch or Townhouses in New Dorp.	TOWN	AVAIL	TYPE	ROOMS	PRICE
2		New Dorp		Ranch		
3		New Dorp		Townhouse		
4						
5		DREAMHOUSE REAL ESTATE COMPANY				
6			CURRENT LISTINGS			
7						
8	ADDRESS	TOWN	AVAIL	TYPE	ROOMS	PRICE
9	45 Mintum Road	Arrochar	12/1/96	Colonial	10	$ 345,000.00
10	125 Kelly Boulevard	Springville	1/1/96	Townhouse	7	$ 185,000.00
11	670 Circle Loop	Sunset Hill	12/1/96	Split	10	$ 450,000.00
12	89 Alberta Lane	New Dorp	2/2/96	Ranch	7	$ 195,000.00
13	345 Jacques Avenue	Totten	1/1/97	Colonial	7	$ 190,000.00
14	5 Flagg Terrace	New Dorp	2/1/97	Townhouse	6	$ 165,000.00
15	29 Club Road	Sunset Hill	3/1/97	Colonial	8	$ 245,000.00
16	914 Sand Lane	Totten	2/1/97	Ranch	7	$ 192,000.00
17	823 Barrow Road	Springville	3/1/97	Split	7	$ 188,000.00
18	92 Vellum Drive	New Dorp	2/1/97	Colonial	9	$ 287,500.00
19	621 Blait Road	Arrochar	4/1/97	Ranch	8	$ 225,500.00
20	45 Point Road	Sunset Hill	4/1/97	Split	10	$448,500.00
21	16 Beverly Circle	Arrochar	4/15/97	Colonial	8	$325,000.00
22	71 Regis Avenue	Totten	3/15/97	Ranch	7	$175,000.00
23	87 Anthony Street	Springville	3/1/97	Townhouse	7	$155,000.00
24	236 Eighth Street	New Dorp	4/1/97	Colonial	8	$210,000.00
25	624 Clarke Road	Sunset Hill	4/30/97	Ranch	8	$255,000.00
26	90 Shore Road	Totten	5/1/97	Townhouse	6	$155,000.00
27						
28	Result list					
29						
30						
31	ADDRESS	TOWN	AVAIL	TYPE	ROOMS	PRICE
32	89 Alberta Lane	New Dorp	2/2/96	Ranch	7	$ 195,000.00
33	5 Flagg Terrace	New Dorp	2/1/97	Townhouse	6	$ 165,000.00

Excel ■ Lesson 10 ■ Exercise 83   285

EXERCISE
Use Database (List) Functions

84

NOTES:

Use Database (List) Functions

- Entries in a list are the same as any entries in a worksheet. Therefore, regular functions and formulas may be used on list data. However, by using Excel's **database functions**, you can, in one step, select records that meet a certain criteria and perform calculations on those records.

- Excel contains twelve database functions that have the following format:

  =Dfunction name(*list range,field,criteria***)**

  - The **list range** argument is the range that identifies the entire list. It can be a named list or a reference to the range containing the list.

  - The **field** argument, is the field whose entries are involved in the function calculation. You may click on the field label (which will enter the cell address of the field label) or substitute the field number, which is the position of the field in the list. The first field number is 1, the second field number is 2, etc.

  - The **criteria** argument is the range that contains the typed criteria. Criteria for database functions are set up just as for Advanced Filter.

  NOTE: As with all formulas, Excel adjusts all relative cell references when a function is copied to a new location. If you plan to copy these functions, make the references in the functions absolute, or name the references that will be retained in the copied function.

- When you use a database function, the result is linked to the list and criteria range data. Therefore, if you edit a criteria, it changes the results in functions that reference it.

To prevent this, create duplicate criteria labels when setting up additional criteria for the same field name. Note the illustration on the next page.

- Excel provides the following functions that can be applied to any list:

DAVERAGE	Finds average value in field for records meeting criteria.
DCOUNT	Counts cells in field for records meeting criteria.
DCOUNTA	Counts only nonblank cells in field for records meeting criteria.
DGET	Returns value for a single record in field for records meeting criteria. Returns #NUM! if more than one record meets criteria.
DMAX	Finds maximum value in field for records meeting criteria.
DMIN	Finds minimum value in field for records meeting criteria.
DPRODUCT	Multiplies the values in a field for records meeting criteria.
DSTDEV	Estimates the standard deviation of a population based on a sample for values in a field for records meeting criteria.
DSTDEVP	Calculates the standard deviation based on the entire population for values in a field for records meeting criteria.
DSUM	Finds sum of values in a field for records meeting criteria.
DVAR	Estimates variance based on a sample for values in a field for records meeting criteria.
DVARP	Calculates variance based on the entire population for values in a field for records meeting criteria.

	A	B	C	D	E	F	G	H	I	J
1	DATE	DESCRIPTION	VENDOR	ITEMS PER	UNIT	QUANTITY	PRICE	TOTAL	ITEM PRICE	VENDOR
2										
3	Copy criteria labels as needed above the list.								Add duplicate	
4									criteria labels	
5			GREAT MAPLE COMMUNITY COLLEGE						as needed.	
6			SCHOOL STORE - SUPPLIES INVENTORY							
7										
8	DATE	DESCRIPTION	VENDOR	ITEMS PER	UNIT	QUANTITY	PRICE	TOTAL	ITEM PRICE	
9	2-Sep-96	Envelopes #10	Treehouse Paper	500	Box	5	3.49	17.45		
10	15-Aug-96	Pencils - #2	J & J Discount	200	Box	16	12.95	207.20		
11	10-Aug-96	Pens - Speedroll	J & J Discount	100	Box	20	15.75	315.00		
12	15-May-96	Folders (Letter)	Paper City	500	Box	4	12.50	50.00		
13	15-May-96	Folders (Legal)	Paper City	500	Box	2	18.65	37.30		
14	15-May-96	Paper (Letter)	Paper City	10	Case	10	45.00	450.00		
15	15-May-96	Paper (Legal)	Paper City	10	Case	4	49.60	198.40		
16	10-Sep-96	Paper (Bond)	Paper City	1	Box	85	6.89	585.65		
17	14-Jul-96	Binders - Large	School Central, Inc.	12	Box	8	53.79	430.32		
18	19-Jul-96	Binders - Small	School Central, Inc.	12	Box	5	47.89	239.45		
19	6-Sep-96	Looseleaf - large	School Central, Inc.	1	Package	200	2.49	498.00		
20	6-Sep-96	Looseleaf - small	School Central, Inc.	1	Package	125	2.10	262.50		
21	22-Jul-96	Adhesive notes	Stickum Bros.	1	Package	15	5.49	82.35		
22	22-Jul-96	Adhesive tape	Stickum Bros.	12	Box	5	23.50	117.50		
23	12-Jul-96	Index cards (3x5)	Treehouse Paper	12	Box	3	32.86	98.58		
24	25-Aug-96	Pads (5x8)	Treehouse Paper	6	Package	6	8.49	50.94		
25	15-Oct-96	Adhesive notes	Stickum Bros	6	Box	1	28.95			
26	15-Oct-96	Pads (5x8)	Treehouse Paper	60	Box	1	75.95			
27	20-Oct-96	Folders (Letter)	Paper City	2500	Case	1	60.95			
28	20-Oct-96	Folders (Legal)	Paper City	2500	Case	1	75.95			
29	20-Oct-96	Looseleaf - large	School Central, Inc.	10	Box	3	22.50			
30										
31	Average Price Per Item									
32	Total Items Purchased									
33										
34	Total Purchases from School Central, Inc.									
35	Average Purchases from School Central, Inc.									
36										
37	Total Purchases from Paper City									
38	Average Purchases from Paper City									
39										
40		CASE SUMMARY DATA								
41	Number of cases in inventory.									
42	Number of products packaged in cases.									
43	Highest value of case item.									
44	Lowest value of case item.									

Callouts in illustration:
- "Database or list range"
- "Use database functions to complete this area."

In this exercise, you will use database functions to obtain information about the supplies inventory for Great Maple Community College.

EXERCISE DIRECTIONS:

1. Open ⌨ **SUPPLY** or open 💾 **84SUPPLY**.

2. Add the additional columns illustrated for ITEMS PER and ITEM PRICE.

3. Enter the number of items in each box, package or case as shown in the illustration.

4. Enter a formula to find the ITEM PRICE.

   HINT: TOTAL/(ITEM PER*QUANTITY)

5. Format the results for two decimal places.

6. Add the data below for additional supplies purchased:

DATE	DESCRIPTION	VENDOR	ITEMS PER	UNIT	QUANTITY	PRICE
15-Oct-96	Adhesive notes	Stickum Bros	6	Box	1	28.95
15-Oct-96	Pads (5 x 8)	Treehouse Paper	60	Box	1	75.95
20-Oct-96	Folders (Letter)	Paper City	2500	Case	1	60.95
20-Oct-96	Folders (Legal)	Paper City	2500	Case	1	75.95
20-Oct-96	Looseleaf - large	School Central, Inc.	10	Box	3	22.50

7. Find the TOTAL and ITEM PRICE for each new item on the list.

8. Name the database range INPUT, as outlined in the illustration.

9. Set up all criteria labels in row one.

10. Find the Average Price per item.

   ✓ *Since this average is of all the data, and does not require a criteria filter, a regular formula may be used.*

11. Find the Total Items Purchased. (See note above.)

12. To find Total Purchases from School Central, Inc.

   • Type a criteria to show School Central, Inc., in the VENDOR field.

   • Using the DSUM function in the appropriate cell, enter the INPUT list range, the VENDOR field label address, and the criteria range.

   • Format the result for two decimal places.

13. Using the DAVERAGE function in the appropriate cell, find the average purchases from School Central, Inc. Format the results for two decimal places.

14. To find Total Purchases from Paper City, repeat step 12 for Paper City in the appropriate cell.

   HINT: *Create a second criteria label for VENDOR to the right of the criteria labels and change the criteria range. If you change the first criteria label, the School Central, Inc., result will also change.*

15. Find the average purchase for Paper City by repeating step 13 in the appropriate cell.

16. Print a copy of the information determined by steps 10-15.

17. Delete rows 31–38.

18. Find CASE SUMMARY DATA:

   • Create a formula in the appropriate cell to find the number of cases in inventory. Format the result for no decimal places.

     HINT: *Set up a criteria range for the UNIT field, then use the DSUM function to total values in the QUANTITY column meeting the criteria set up for the UNIT field.*

   • Create a formula to find the number of products packaged in cases.

     HINT: *Use the DCOUNT function to find total values in the QUANTITY column meeting a criteria set up for the UNIT field.*

   • Create a formula to find the highest value of a case item.

     HINT: *Use DMAX function to find highest value in the PRICE column meeting a criteria set up for the UNIT field.*

   • Create a formula to find the lowest value of a case item.

     HINT: *Use DMIN function to find lowest value in the PRICE column meeting a criteria set up for the UNIT field.*

19. To find the same information as found in step 18 for purchased boxed items:

   • Copy the labels used for the CASE SUMMARY DATA, leaving a blank row between the sections.

   • Edit the heading to read BOX SUMMARY DATA; edit labels to include boxes rather than cases.

     Set up and use a new criteria range, then apply the function to find answers for boxes.

20. Print a copy of the CASE SUMMARY DATA and the BOX SUMMARY DATA on one page.

21. Save and close the workbook file; name it **SUPPLY**.

INSERT A DATABASE FUNCTION USING FUNCTION WIZARD

NOTE: You can also type a function to insert it.

1. Set up criteria range in worksheet.

   NOTE: The criteria range is a location in the worksheet containing one or more criteria labels below which you must type data values that indicate a condition that must be met. Guidelines for setting up a criteria range were discussed in **Exercises 82** and **84**.

2. Select cell to receive function.

3. Click **Function Wizard** button ..... f_x on Standard Toolbar.

4. Select **Database** .... ⬛ in **Function Category** list.

5. Select desired database function .... Alt + ⬛ in **Function Name** list.

6. Click ⬛ Next > .... ⏎

7. Type reference or name of list range .... *list range* in **database** box.

   OR

   Select cells in worksheet containing field labels and list data.

8. Click **field** box .... Tab

9. Type field name .... *field name* containing data the function will calculate.

   OR

   Select cell in worksheet containing desired field label.

10. Click **criteria** box......................... Tab

11. Type reference or name of criteria range .... *criteria range*

12. Click ⬛ Finish .... ⏎

EXERCISE

Use the Subtotals Feature to Summarize a List

85

NOTES:

Subtotals Feature

■ Excel provides a **Subtotals** feature which lets you quickly summarize sorted data in a list. This feature may be used instead of Database functions to summarize specific groups of data.

The Subtotals feature automatically:

• Calculates and inserts subtotals below grouped fields.

• Calculates and inserts grand totals.

• Labels the calculated values.

• Outlines the data families in the list.

■ Follow these guidelines when using the Subtotals feature:

• First, sort the list so the fields for which you want subtotals are grouped together.

• Select **Subtotals** from the **Data** menu, then the following, as illustrated in the dialog box below:

At Each Change in: Select a field name.

Use Function: Select a function.

Add Subtotals to: Select one or more fields to calculate.

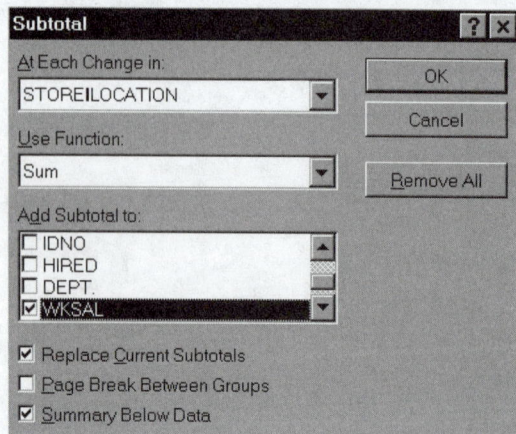

■ You can also use the Subtotals command on a filtered list. When you do so, Excel only calculates the values that are visible in the filtered list.

■ If you change the details in a list, the subtotals and grand totals will also change.

Nested Subtotals

■ You can find subtotals within subtotals (nested subtotals) if you do the following:

• Sort the list by both fields you want subtotals for.

   EXAMPLE: *Sort By DEPT., then by STORE LOCATION.*

• Find subtotal for first field you sorted by.

• From the Subtotal dialog box, deselect the Replace Current Subtotals option, then find subtotals for second field you sorted by.

Remove Subtotals

■ You can remove subtotals in three ways:

• Select Remove All button from the Subtotal dialog box.

• Replace existing subtotals by selecting new subtotal options, then select Replace Current Subtotals from the Subtotal dialog box.

• Select **Undo Subtotals** from the **Edit** menu.

Copy Subtotals

■ If you want to copy a subtotal result, use the Copy and Paste Special commands. Be sure to paste the result as a value.

Hide or Show Details

■ You can use the **outline controls** to hide or show the **details** (families of records) in the subtotaled list. Note the illustration of a subtotaled worksheet. You could then print or chart only the visible cells — just the subtotals, for example.

1 2 3		A	B	C STORE LOCATION	D IDNO	E HIRED	F DEPT.	G WKSAL	H ANNSAL
	1	LAST	FIRST	STORE LOCATION	IDNO	HIRED	DEPT.	WKSAL	ANNSAL
	2	Carson	Penn	CHI	14399	11/05/96	Sales	225.75	11739.00
	3	Esther	Polly	CHI	14235	11/15/96	Admin.	286.50	14898.00
	4	Lee	Michael	CHI	14295	03/05/94	Stock	276.00	14352.00
	5	Lee	Randy	CHI	13298	07/25/94	Stock	365.80	19021.60
	6	Palmeri	Marie	CHI	14367	09/01/94	Stock	276.50	14378.00
	7	Restivo	Mary	CHI	14932	10/01/96	Sales	295.00	15340.00
	8	Sawyer	Harriet	CHI	13290	02/13/96	Admin.	358.60	18647.20
	9	Seltzer	Al K.	CHI	14931	07/25/96	Stock	255.00	13260.00
	10			CHI Total				2339.15	
	11	Accosta	Anthony	LA	13929	10/30/96	Sales	375.55	19528.60
	12	Gregonis	Dimitri	LA	14395	05/25/96	Admin.	275.00	14300.00
	13	Jackson	Martin	LA	14397	10/25/96	Stock	275.00	14300.00
		Lee	Chin	LA	13254	05/15/92	Sales	345.00	17940.00
				LA	14289	11/01/94	Admin.	342.90	17830.80
				LA	14321	02/15/94	Sales	243.50	12662.00
				LA	14354	11/25/95	Sales	215.45	11203.40
				LA	14269	12/15/95	Sales	325.75	16939.00
				LA Total				2398.15	
				NY	14078	04/01/93	Admin.	389.76	20267.52
				NY	14356	09/30/94	Stock	235.45	12243.40
				NY	14402	11/01/96	Sales	285.00	14820.00
				NY	14396	06/10/96	Stock	275.00	14300.00
				NY	14398	10/31/96	Admin.	285.50	14846.00
				NY	14024	05/18/95	Sales	310.89	16166.28
				NY	13852	08/25/95	Admin.	376.00	19552.00
		Valdez	Lina	NY	14385	10/15/96	Stock	265.00	13780.00
	28			NY Total				2422.60	
	29			Grand Total				7159.90	

outline controls

Subtotal [?] [X]

At Each Change in:
STORE LOCATION ▼

Use Function:
Sum ▼

Add Subtotal to:
☐ HIRED
☐ DEPT.
☑ WKSAL

☑ Replace Current Subtotals
☐ Page Break Between Groups
☑ Summary Below Data

[OK]
[Cancel]
[Remove All]

subtotals

grand total

THE RESULTS OF SAMPLE SETTINGS IN THE SUBTOTAL DIALOG BOX

In this exercise, you will retrieve the SHOP workbook and use the Subtotals feature to analyze the data.

EXERCISE DIRECTIONS:

1. Open ⌨ **SHOP** or open 💾 **85SHOP**.

2. Add summary label data below the list as shown on page 293.

3. Boldface the SUMMARY DATA heading labels.

4. Make sure the list is sorted by LAST (Sort By field) and FIRST (Then By field) in ascending order as shown.

5. Find the answers for the SUMMARY DATA - ADMINISTRATION DEPARTMENT:

   a. Since you want subtotals for the ADMINISTRATION DEPARTMENT, sort the DEPT. field in ascending order.

   b. • Use the Subtotals command to find the total weekly salary paid to members of each department.

      HINT: From Subtotal dialog box, set:
      At Each Change in: DEPT.
      Use Function: Sum
      Add Subtotal to: WKSAL

      • Click the row level 2 outline symbol to hide all rows except the subtotals rows and the Grand Total row.

      • Use Copy and Paste Special to copy the Admin. subtotal to the appropriate cells in the summary area as a value.

      • Remove all subtotals from the list.

   c. Repeat step b using the Average function.

   d. Format the copied values to show two decimal places.

6. Find the answers for the SUMMARY DATA - LOS ANGELES STORE area:

   a. Since you want subtotals for the Los Angeles locations, sort the STORE LOCATION field in ascending order.

   b. Use Sum, Average, Min and Count functions as needed to answer each question:

      • Use the row level 2 outline symbol to hide details.

      • Use Copy and Paste Special command to copy LA subtotal to the appropriate cell as a value.

      • Remove all subtotals after each calculation.

      NOTE: You can also select Replace Current Subtotals when performing the next subtotal command to reduce the number of steps.

   c. Format each copied result in the summary area for the appropriate number of decimal places.

7. Find the answers for SUMMARY DATA - LOS ANGELES ADMINISTRATION DEPARTMENT:

   a. Since you want subtotals for a subgroup (Administration for Los Angeles stores), sort the records by DEPT., then by STORE LOCATION.

   b. • Use two Subtotals commands to find each summary answer for the Los Angeles Administration subgroup.

      HINT: To find total weekly salaries:
      Find sum for WKSAL on each change in DEPT. Select Subtotals again, deselect Replace Current Subtotals, and find sum for WKSAL on each change in STORE LOCATION.

      • Use the row level 2 outline symbol to hide details.

      • Use Copy and Paste Special commands to copy the appropriate subtotal result to the summary area as a value.

      • Remove all subtotals before repeating step b.

   c. Format copied results in the summary area as needed.

8. Remove subtotals in the list.

9. Print a copy of entire worksheet to fit on one page.

10. Save and close the workbook file; name it **SHOP**.

	A	B	C	D	E	F	G	H
1	LAST	FIRST	STORE LOCATION	IDNO	HIRED	DEPT.	WKSAL	ANNSAL
2	Accosta	Anthony	LA	13929	10/30/96	Sales	375.55	19528.60
3	Carson	George	NY	14078	04/01/93	Admin.	389.76	20267.52
4	Carson	Laurence	NY	14356	09/30/94	Stock	235.45	12243.40
5	Carson	Penn	CHI	14399	11/05/96	Sales	225.75	11739.00
6	Esther	Polly	CHI	14235	11/15/96	Admin.	286.50	14898.00
7	Graham	Holly	NY	14402	11/01/96	Sales	285.00	14820.00
8	Gregonis	Dimitri	LA	14395	05/25/96	Admin.	275.00	14300.00
9	Hopkins	George	NY	14396	06/10/96	Stock	275.00	14300.00
10	Jackson	Martin	LA	14397	10/25/96	Stock	275.00	14300.00
11	Lee	Chin	LA	13254	05/15/92	Sales	345.00	17940.00
12	Lee	Michael	CHI	14295	03/05/94	Stock	276.00	14352.00
13	Lee	Randy	CHI	13298	07/25/94	Stock	365.80	19021.60
14	Martino	John	LA	14289	11/01/94	Admin.	342.90	17830.80
15	Naidle	Adam	LA	14321	02/15/94	Sales	243.50	12662.00
16	Palmeri	Marie	CHI	14367	09/01/94	Stock	276.50	14378.00
17	Parsons	Lyle	NY	14398	10/31/96	Admin.	285.50	14846.00
18	Restivo	Mary	CHI	14932	10/01/96	Sales	295.00	15340.00
19	Rogers	Jane	NY	14024	05/18/95	Sales	310.89	16166.28
20	Samtanai	Perkash	LA	14354	11/25/95	Sales	215.45	11203.40
21	Sawyer	Harriet	CHI	13290	02/13/96	Admin.	358.60	18647.20
22	Seltzer	Al K.	CHI	14931	07/25/96	Stock	255.00	13260.00
23	Tommei	Lori	NY	13852	08/25/95	Admin.	376.00	19552.00
24	Valdez	Lina	NY	14385	10/15/96	Stock	265.00	13780.00
25	Watterson	Cathy	LA	14269	12/15/95	Sales	325.75	16939.00
26								
27	SUMMARY DATA - ADMINISTRATION DEPARTMENT				◄			
28	Total weekly salaries							
29	Average weekly salaries							
30								
31	SUMMARY DATA - LOS ANGELES STORE							
32	Total weekly salaries							
33	Average weekly salaries							
34	Highest weekly salary							
35	Lowest weekly salary							
36	Number of employees							
37								
38	SUMMARY DATA - LOS ANGELES ADMINISTRATION DEPARTMENT							
39	Total weekly salaries							
40	Average weekly salaries							
41	Highest weekly salary							
42	Lowest weekly salary							
43	Number of employees							

Type summary information here.

SUBTOTAL A LIST AUTOMATICALLY

Creates subtotals for groups of data in specified columns, and a grand total at the bottom of the list. Excel automatically applies outlining to the resulting list.

NOTE: You can also subtotal a filtered list.

1. Sort column(s) in list to subtotal.
   NOTE: List must contain labeled columns in its first row. Items to subtotal should be grouped together.

2. Select any cell in list.

3. Click **D**ata menu .... `Alt`+`D`

4. Click Su**b**totals .... `B`

5. Click **A**t Each Change in:
   [_____ ▼] .... `Alt`+`A`

6. Select field .... `↕`, `Alt`+`↑`
   containing groups to subtotal.

7. Click **U**se Function:
   [_____ ▼] .... `Alt`+`U`

8. Select desired
   function .... `↕`, `Alt`+`↑`

9. Select A**d**d Subtotal to:
   [_____ ▼] .... `Alt`+`D`

10. Click fields .... `↕`, `Space`
    containing values to calculate.

11. Repeat steps **9** and **10** for each field to calculate.

To replace current subtotals:

- Select ☐ **Replace**
  Current Subtotals ..... `Alt`+`C`

To force page breaks between subtotaled groups:

- Select ☐ **Page Break**
  Between Groups... ..... `Alt`+`P`

To place subtotals and grand totals above data:

- Deselect ☐ **Summary**
  Below Data .... `Alt`+`S`

12. Click [OK] .... `↵`

REMOVE ALL AUTOMATIC SUBTOTALS IN A LIST

1. Select any cell in subtotaled list.

2. Click **D**ata menu .... `Alt`+`D`

3. Click Su**b**totals .... `B`

4. Click [**R**emove All] .... `Alt`+`R`

CREATE A SUBTOTAL WITHIN A SUBTOTALED GROUP IN A LIST

1. Sort all columns in list to subtotal.

2. Subtotal first group in list.

3. Follow steps to subtotal second group in list.

4. Deselect ☐ **Replace**
   Current Subtotals .... `Alt`+`C`

5. Click [OK] .... `↵`

SHOW OR HIDE OUTLINE GROUPS AND LEVELS USING OUTLINE SYMBOLS

Show Group Details

- Click show detail symbol .... `+`
  of group to expand.

Hide Group Details

- Click hide detail symbol .... `-`
  of group to hide.

Show All Outline Groups for a Level

- Click row level symbol .... `1` `2` `3`
  for lowest level to show.

NEXT EXERCISE

EXERCISE
Use a Pivot Table to Summarize List Data
86

NOTES:

Pivot Tables

■ Excel provides a powerful tool for summarizing data in a list called a **pivot table**.

This exercise will provide an introduction to pivot tables.

With a pivot table you can:

- Use functions to summarize data fields.

- Show only the fields you specify.

- Hide or show details in the pivot table.

- Change (pivot) label orientation to rows or columns.

- Filter the results to summarize only the records you specify.

■ Guidelines for creating a pivot table:

- Select any cell in a list. The list must have labeled columns (field names).

- Determine how you want to summarize the list.

- Select the **PivotTable** command from the **Data** menu.

- Follow the prompts provided by the PivotTable Wizard:

    Step 1 of 4: Indicate source of data. In this case it is a Microsoft Excel list.

    Step 2 of 4: Change or accept proposed range that contains the data.

    Step 3 of 4: Drag field buttons onto appropriate part of layout area and assign a function to summarize fields placed in the DATA area.

    Step 4 of 4: Specify where to place the pivot table (the starting cell).

NOTE: Excel places the pivot table on a new worksheet if you do not specify the starting cell for the pivot table.

■ The Step 3 of 4 Pivot Table Wizard screen is illustrated below and is used to drag each field button to a layout area as follows:

PAGE area — Provides a drop-down list of fields from which you can select data to display in the pivot table (filter the pivot table).

ROW area — Creates row labels for each unique item in field.

COLUMN area — Creates column labels for each unique item in field.

DATA area — Specifies field to summarize.

NOTE: You must include at least one field in the DATA area. You can drag more than one field button into a layout area, but it's best to limit the number of fields when starting out.

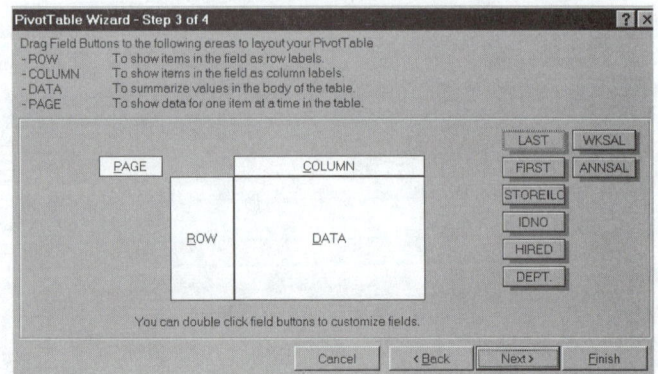

- When you create a pivot table, you may wish to display the **Query and Pivot Toolbar**. This toolbar provides buttons you can use to customize the pivot table.

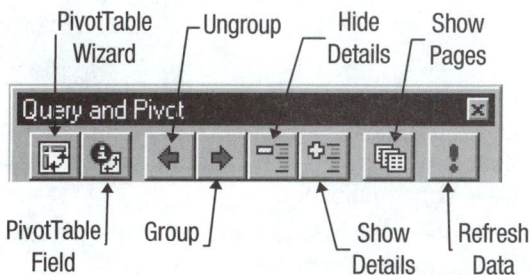

PivotTable Wizard — Ungroup — Hide Details — Show Pages
Query and Pivot
PivotTable Field — Group — Show Details — Refresh Data

QUERY AND PIVOT TOOLBAR

IMPORTANT: *Be sure to understand what a command does before trying it. For example, if you click the **Show Pages** button, Excel will create a new pivot table for each Page Field item on a separate worksheet.*

- In a pivot table, you can drag the field buttons to change their position and, thus, the view of your data. For example, you can drag a row field button to the column or page position. When you drag the button, the pointer changes to show the result of dropping the button in various areas of the pivot table.

  - Move field to column...........................
  - Move field to row..............................
  - Move field to page ....
  - Remove field from pivot table ....

- When you change a pivot table or refresh the data in it, the resulting cells will *not* retain the formatting you may have applied to it.

- You can undo the last pivot table change by selecting **Undo PivotTable** from the **Edit** menu.

	A	B	C	D	E	F	G	H
1	LAST	FIRST	STORE LOCATION	IDNO	HIRED	DEPT.	WKSAL	ANNSAL
2	Esther	Polly	CHI	14235	11/15/96	Admin.	286.50	14898.00
3	Sawyer	Harriet	CHI	13290	02/13/96	Admin.	358.60	18647.20
4	Gregonis	Dimitri	LA	14395	05/25/96	Admin.	275.00	14300.00
5	Martino	John	LA	14289	11/01/94	Admin.	342.90	17830.80
6	Carson							
7	Parsons							
8	Tommei							
9	Carson							
10	Restivo							
11	Accosta							
12	Lee							
13	Naidle							
14	Samtanai							
15	Wattersun							
16	Graham							
17	Rogers							
18	Lee							
19	Lee							
20	Palmeri							
21	Seltzer							
22	Jackson							
23	Carson							
24	Hopkins							
25	Valdez							
26								
27								
28	STORE LOCATION	(All)						
29								
30		DEPT.						
31	Data	Admin.	Sales	Stock	Grand Total			
32	Sum of ANNSAL	120341.52	136338.28	115635.00	372314.80			
33	Average of ANNSAL2	17191.65	15148.70	14454.38	15513.12			

PivotTable Wizard - Step 3 of 4

Drag Field Buttons to the following areas to layout your PivotTable
- ROW   To show items in the field as row labels.
- COLUMN   To show items in the field as column labels.
- DATA   To summarize values in the body of the table.
- PAGE   To show data for one item at a time in the table.

STORE LOCATION PAGE
DEPT. COLUMN
Sum of ANNSAL
Average of ANNSAL
ROW   DATA

LAST   WKSAL
FIRST   ANNSAL
STORE LOCATION
IDNO
HIRED
DEPT.

You can double click field buttons to customize fields.

Cancel   < Back   Next >   Finish

In this exercise, you will create pivot tables that summarize salary data for New York, Chicago, and Los Angeles employees. You will place each pivot table on a separate sheet tab.

EXERCISE DIRECTIONS:

1. Open ⌨ **SHOP** or open 💾 **86SHOP**.

2. Delete summary data below the employee list and remove subtotals if any exist.

3. Create a pivot table to summarize weekly salaries for each department for employees in Los Angeles:

   - Design the layout, dragging the field buttons, as follows:

     P̲AGE area: STORE LOCATION
     R̲OW area: blank
     C̲OLUMN area: DEPT.
     D̲ATA area: Sum of WKSAL

     NOTE: Sum is the default function for a field containing values.

   - Pivot table starting cell: Sheet2!A1

   - Go to the Pivot table. Use the page field (Store Location) drop-down button in the pivot table to show totals for Los Angeles employees.

   - Format the totals to show two decimal places and size columns as needed.

4. Modify the pivot table in Sheet2 so that it also displays average weekly salaries for Los Angeles employees:

   - Select any cell in the Pivot table.
   - Click the Pivot Table Wizard button.
   - Add a second WKSAL to the D̲ATA area.

   NOTE: Excel names it Sum of WKSAL2.

   - Change the function used by WKSAL2 to Average and select the F̲inish button. (Double–click the Sum of WKSAL2 button and make changes.)
   - Format the totals as currency and size columns as needed.
   - Name the sheet LA Dept. Salaries.
   - Print one copy of the pivot table.

5. Create a new pivot table to summarize the salary data for NY employees as you did for LA employees.

   - Select Sheet1 and any cell in the list.
   - From the PivotTable Wizard, design the layout as you did for the LA Dept. Salaries including the average of Weekly Salaries.

   - Place the pivot table in cell A1 in Sheet3.
   - Use the page field (Store Location) drop-down button in the pivot table to show summary data for New York employees.
   - Format the totals to show two decimal places.
   - Name the sheet NY Dept. Salaries.
   - Print one copy of this pivot table.

6. Create a new pivot table to summarize the salary data for Chicago employees and place on Sheet4. Format as necessary. Name the sheet Chi Dept. Salaries. Print one copy of this table.

7. Create a new pivot table to summarize employees for all store locations by department.

   - Design the layout as follows:

     D̲ATA area: Average of ANNSAL
                        Max of ANNSAL
                        Min of ANNSAL
                        Count of ANNSAL
     R̲OW area: DEPT.

   - Place the pivot table in cell A1 on Sheet5.
   - Edit the data labels in the pivot table as follows:

     Average Annual salary
     Highest Annual salary
     Lowest Annual salary
     Number of employees

     NOTE: To edit an item in a pivot table, press **F2** or click in the formula bar. You cannot double–click a cell to edit in a pivot table.

   - Format dollar values as currency.
   - Format remaining totals to show appropriate decimal places and size columns as needed.
   - Name the sheet Dept. Salary Data.
   - Print one copy of this pivot table.

8. Rename Sheet1; name it Employee List.

9. Save and close the workbook file; name it **SHOP**.

	A	B	C	D	E	F	G	H	I
1	LAST	FIRST	STORE LOCATION	IDNO	HIRED	DEPT.	WKSAL	ANNSAL	
2	Esther	Polly	CHI	14235	11/15/96	Admin.	286.50	14898.00	
3	Sawyer	Harriet	CHI	13290	02/13/96	Admin.	358.60	18647.20	
4	Gregonis	Dimitri	LA	14395	05/25/96	Admin.	275.00	14300.00	
5	Martino	John	LA	14289	11/01/94	Admin.	342.90	17830.80	
6	Carson	George	NY	14078	04/01/93	Admin.	389.76	20267.52	
7	Parsons	Lyle	NY	14398	10/31/96	Admin.	285.50	14846.00	
8	Tommei	Lori	NY	13852	08/25/95	Admin.	376.00	19552.00	
9	Carson	Penn	CHI	14399	11/05/96	Sales	225.75	11739.00	
10	Restivo	Mary	CHI	14932	10/01/96	Sales	295.00	15340.00	
11	Accosta	Anthony	LA	13929	10/30/96	Sales	375.55	19528.60	
12	Lee	Chin	LA	13254	05/15/92	Sales	345.00	17940.00	
13	Naidle	Adam	LA	14321	02/15/94	Sales	243.50	12662.00	
14	Samtanai	Perkash	LA	14354	11/25/95	Sales	215.45	11203.40	
15	Watterson	Cathy	LA	14269	12/15/95	Sales	325.75	16939.00	
16	Graham	Holly	NY	14402	11/01/96	Sales	285.00	14820.00	
17	Rogers	Jane	NY	14024	05/18/95	Sales	310.89	16166.28	
18	Lee	Michael	CHI	14295	03/05/94	Stock	276.00	14352.00	
19	Lee	Randy	CHI	13298	07/25/94	Stock	365.80	19021.60	
20	Palmeri	Marie	CHI	14367	09/01/94	Stock	276.50	14378.00	
21	Seltzer	Al K.	CHI	14931	07/25/96	Stock	255.00	13260.00	
22	Jackson	Martin	LA	14397	10/25/96	Stock	275.00	14300.00	
23	Carson	Laurence	NY	14356	09/30/94	Stock	235.45	12243.40	
24	Hopkins	George	NY	14396	06/10/96	Stock	275.00	14300.00	
25	Valdez	Lina	NY	14385	10/15/96	Stock	265.00	13780.00	
26									
27	**SUMMARY DATA - ADMINISTRATION DEPARTMENT**								
28	Total weekly salaries			2314.26					
29	Average weekly salaries			330.61					
30									
31	**SUMMARY DATA - LOS ANGELES STORE**								
32	Total weekly salaries			2398.15					
33	Average weekly salaries			299.77					
34	Highest weekly salary			375.55					
35	Lowest weekly salary			215.45					
36	Number of employees			8					
37									
38	**SUMMARY DATA - LOS ANGELES ADMINISTRATION DEPARTMENT**								
39	Total weekly salaries			617.90					
40	Average weekly salaries			308.95					
41	Highest weekly salary			342.90					
42	Lowest weekly salary			275.00					
43	Number of employees			2					

Delete summary information

CREATE A PIVOT TABLE

1. Select any cell in list to summarize.
2. Click **Data** menu .... `Alt`+`D`
3. Click **PivotTable**............................ `P`

   —*PivotTable Wizard – Step 1 of 4*—

4. Select source of data:

   - **Microsoft Excel List or Database** .... `M`

   - **External Data Source** .... `E`

   - **Multiple Consolidation Ranges** .... `C`

   - **Another Pivot Table** .... `A`

5. Click `Next >` .... `⏎`

   —*PivotTable Wizard – Step 2 of 4*—

6. Select cells in worksheet containing data source.

   OR

   Type cell reference ....*reference* of data source in **Range** text box.

   NOTE: *Select the **Browse** button if the data source is external. Then select the file containing the data.*

7. Click `Next >` .... `⏎`

   —*PivotTable Wizard – Step 3 of 4*—

8. Create pivot table layout:

   ### To add a field to pivot table:

   - Drag field button onto desired layout area.

   ### To remove a field from pivot table:

   - Drag field button off the layout area.

   ### To move a field to another layout area:

   - Drag field button onto desired layout area.

   ### To change function to apply to field:

   a. Double–click field button in DATA area.

   b. Select **Summarize by** list .... `Alt`+`S`

c. Select desired function .... `↗`
d. Click `OK` .... `⏎`

9. Click `Next >` .... `⏎`

   —*PivotTable Wizard – Step 4 of 4*—

10. Select upper-left destination cell of table in worksheet.

    OR

    Type reference .... *reference* to upper-left destination cell of table in **PivotTable Starting Cell** text box.

    NOTE: *If you leave this blank, Excel creates the pivot table on a new worksheet. Do not place the pivot table where it can overwrite existing data.*

To change proposed pivot table name:

a. Double–click **PivotTable Name:** `_____` .. `Alt`+`N`

b. Type new name .... *name*

11. Select or deselect **PivotTable Options**:

    - **Grand Totals For Columns** .... `Alt`+`C`

    - **Grand Totals For Rows** .... `Alt`+`R`

    - **Save Data With Table Layout** .... `Alt`+`D`

    - **AutoFormat Table** ...... `Alt`+`A`

12. Click `Finish` .... `⏎`

    Pivot table appears.

DISPLAY SPECIFIC PAGE ITEMS IN A PIVOT TABLE

1. Click page field drop-down button.. `▾`
2. Select desired field item ...... `↗`, `⏎`

DISPLAY ALL PAGE ITEMS IN A PIVOT TABLE

1. Click page field drop-down button.. `▾`
2. Select **(All)**.......................... `↗`, `⏎`

UPDATE A PIVOT TABLE

Updates a pivot table to show changes made to source data.

NOTE: *If rows or columns were removed or added to the source data range, you may have to follow the steps to modify a pivot table and change the reference to the source data.*

1. Select any cell in pivot table.

2. Click **Refresh Data** button.......... `!` on Query and Pivot Toolbar.

   OR

   a. Click **Data** menu.......... `Alt`+`D`

   b. Click **Refresh Data**............... `R`

MODIFY A PIVOT TABLE

1. Select any cell in pivot table.

2. Click **PivotTable Wizard** button .. `🔲` on Query and Pivot Toolbar.

   OR

   a. Click **Data** menu.......... `Alt`+`D`

   b. Click **PivotTable** .... `P`

3. If desired, make changes to field layout:

   AND/OR

   - Click `Next >` .... `⏎`

     OR

     Click `< Back` .... `Alt`+`B`

   To change: **PivotTable Wizard**

   Data source .... Step 1

   Reference to source data.......... Step 2

   Fields in layout.......................... Step 3

   Pivot table position, Pivot table name, and Pivot table options...................................... Step 4

   Pivot table options include:
   Grand Totals For Columns,
   Grand Totals For Rows,
   Save Data With Table Layout,
   AutoFormat Table.

4. Click `Finish` .... `Alt`+`F`

MOVE OR REMOVE FIELDS ON A PIVOT TABLE

- In pivot table, drag field button onto desired area in or off pivot table.

NOTE: *Pointer indicates the result of the move as follows:*

- Move field to column ....
- Move field to row ....
- Move field to page ....
- Remove field from pivot table ....

EXERCISE

Consolidate Data

87

NOTES:

Consolidate data

- Excel provides another data handling feature called **Consolidate,** which may be used with a database list or with multiple worksheets. Consolidate is used to condense and summarize the data from one or more source ranges into a consolidation table. The source ranges can be on one worksheet, on several worksheets in the same workbook, or in different workbooks.

- You can use the consolidate feature to summarize data from several database lists. For example, you may have a separate database for each branch which can be summarized with a consolidation table. As long as the data items have the same labels, you can select the source ranges and summarize the data. This is called a **consolidation by category**.

- You can also use the consolidate feature to summarize data from several non-database worksheets that are identical in layout and have data from different departments. For example, a template for an expense analysis is completed by each department which can be summarized on a consolidation table. This is called a **consolidation by position**.

Create a Consolidation Table

- To create a consolidation table, place the cursor in the top left cell of the consolidation table range. Select **Data, Consolidate** and the Consolidate dialog box will display. As shown in the illustration below, you can select the Function to be used and the Reference. The illustration shows the same range on three departmental worksheets being combined. After each source range is selected, the Add button is clicked and the range moves into the All References box. Note that links to the source data may be selected which will update the consolidation table if the source data changes. This feature cannot be used if the data is all in one workbook. The labels selections are used for consolidation by category consolidations.

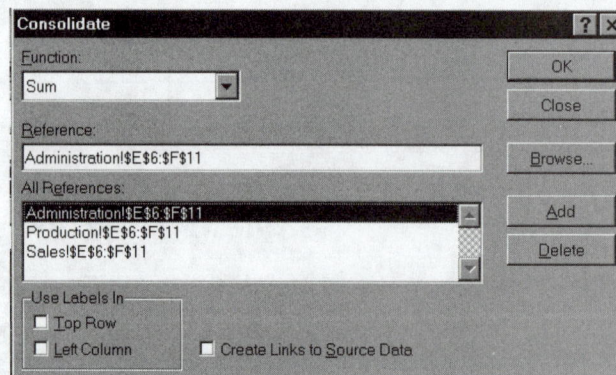

Consolidate [? X]

Function:
Sum ▾

Reference:
Administration!$E$6:$F$11

All References:
Administration!$E$6:$F$11
Production!$E$6:$F$11
Sales!$E$6:$F$11

Use Labels In
☐ Top Row
☐ Left Column   ☐ Create Links to Source Data

[OK] [Close] [Browse...] [Add] [Delete]

CONSOLIDATE DIALOG BOX

In this exercise, Pringle Publishers, Inc., would like to consolidate expense analysis data from the production, sales and administration departments into a consolidated expense report.

EXERCISE DIRECTIONS:

1. Group Sheets 1-4 and create the template as shown at the bottom of this page, or open 💾 **87ANAL**.

2. Ungroup sheets and select Sheet1. Rename sheet to Production.

3. Modify the subtitle to:

   Expense Analysis - Production

4. Enter the data below:

1996 Actual	1997 Estimate
72,956.00	83,500.00
8,950.00	10,150.00
3,865.00	4,400.00
1,751.00	2,000.00
950.00	1,020.00

5. Rename the next two sheets for Sales and Administration.

6. Modify the subtitles to reflect each department.

7. Enter the data below on the Sales sheet and on the Administration sheet.

Sales		Administration	
1996 Actual	1997 Estimate	1996 Actual	1997 Estimate
86,457.00	99,500.00	121,670.00	125,500.00
10,569.00	12,100.00	14,483.00	15,300.00
4,586.00	5,200.00	6,448.00	6,600.00
2,145.00	2,400.00	2,920.00	3,000.00
1,549.00	1,700.00	1,532.00	1,750.00

8. Group the Production, Sales and Administration sheets and total the two columns.

9. On Sheet4, change the subtitle to:

   Consolidated Expense Analysis

10. Rename the sheet to Consolidated Analysis.

11. Consolidate the data from the department sheets onto the consolidation table.

    - Place cursor at E6 on the Consolidated Analysis sheet.
    - Click **Data, Consolidate.**
    - Sum is the default, do not change the function.
    - Click the Reference: box. Select the Production sheet and the range with numeric data (E6.F11).
    - Click Add.
    - Repeat the last two steps for the Sales and Administration sheets.
    - Click OK

12. Print a copy of the workbook.

13. Save and close the workbook; name it **ANAL**.

	A	B	C	D	E	F
1	PRINGLE PUBLISHERS, INC.					
2	Expense Analysis					
3						
4	Expenses				1996 Actual	1997 Estimate
5	Number	Account				
6	510	Salaries				
7	520	Employer Taxes				
8	530	Benefits Plan				
9	580	Office Supplies				
10	590	Telecommunications				
11	Total					
12						

CONSOLIDATE DATA- by Position

Consolidate by position when source data is in the same order and uses identical category labels.

1. If data is in separate workbooks, open and arrange workbooks.

2. Make sure data to consolidate is arranged in the same order.

3. Select destination worksheet.

4. Select range to receive consolidated data.

5. Click **Data** menu .... `Alt`+`D`

6. Click **Consolidate** .... `N`

7. Click **Function** and select summary function .... `F`

8. Click **Reference:** and select (from worksheet) or type source area reference .... `E`

9. Click `Add` .... `Alt`+`A`

Reference is added to All References list.

10. Repeat steps 7 and 8 for each source reference to add.

To create a link to source data:

- Select **Create Links to Source Data** .... `S`

NOTE: You cannot link the data if the destination range is on the same worksheet as the source data.

11. Click `OK` .... `↵`

NEXT EXERCISE

EXERCISE

Summary 88

Marina Ortiz, a friend of yours, has asked you to assist her in organizing a section of her checkbook. You will create a database list which will make it easier for Phyllis to prepare her taxes and keep track of her expenditures.

EXERCISE DIRECTIONS:

1. Create the worksheet at the right, or open 💾 **88CHECK**.

2. Do the following:

    • Set column B to 20, column E to 15, and column F to 11.

    • Use **Fill, Series** on the **Edit** menu to enter the check numbers, then center these values.

    • Center all columns titles and data in columns A, C and F.

3. Sort the database so the FOR entries are in alphabetical order and the date of the checks are in order within each category.

4. Create a database range name.

5. Below the database enter the following title: SUMMARY OF EXPENSES

6. Enter the following pairs of row labels, in column B, with a blank line between each pair:

    Total expenses
    Number of checks written

    Total non-deductible expenses
    Number of non-deductible checks

    Total deductible expenses
    Number of deductible checks

7. Calculate the value referred to by each label and place the result in column D of that row.

8. Using Advanced Filter, create a result list of the deductible expense checks.

    • Place the table three rows below the summary labels.

    • Enter the following heading: DEDUCTIBLE EXPENSES

9. Using Advanced Filter, create a result list that will list the payments made for telephone as well as heat and light:

    • Place this table five rows below the previous table.

    • Enter the following heading: UTILITY EXPENSES

10. Print a copy of the entire worksheet to fit on one page.

11. Re-sort the database data so the checks are in check number order.

12. Save and close the file; name it **CHECK**.

	A	B	C	D	E	F
1			Marina Ortiz			
2			Check Register			
3						
4	NUMBER	PAYEE	DATE	AMOUNT	FOR	DEDUCTIBLE
5	235	Merry Mortgage Co.	10/01/97	553.65	mortgage	N
6	236	FoodShop Grocery	10/05/97	186.65	groceries	N
7		Sally Gregory	10/10/97	25.00	gift	N
8		Dr. Jane Friend	10/15/97	75.00	medical	Y
9		Cancer Care	10/17/97	55.00	donation	Y
10		Glow Utility Co.	10/20/97	103.86	heat and light	N
11		Mr. and Mrs. J. Soto	10/20/97	100.00	gift	N
12		West Telephone Co.	10/29/97	95.43	telephone	N
13		Merry Mortgage Co.	11/01/97	553.65	mortgage	N
14		Dr. William Keene	11/08/97	140.00	medical	Y
15		FoodShop Grocery	11/12/97	192.45	groceries	N
16		Bitex Computer Inst.	11/15/97	850.00	tuition	Y
17		Jason Park Township	11/18/97	475.98	taxes	Y
18		Glow Utility Co.	11/21/97	121.98	heat and light	N
19		Homeless Shelter	11/28/97	100.00	donation	Y
20	▼	Merry Mortgage Co.	12/01/97	553.65	mortgage	N
21		West Telephone Co.	12/05/97	129.87	telephone	N

EXERCISE

Summary

89

> The Noah Auto Sales car dealership needs to organize their transaction data to plan for bonuses, reorders and potential profits. You have been asked to prepare a database list so that Mr. Arc, the manager of the dealership, can easily get this and other information.

EXERCISE DIRECTIONS:

1. Create the database shown on the right, or open 💾 **89NOAH**.

   NOTE: The transactions are coded: S for Sold, L for Leased.

   - Set columns C and E to 14.
   - Left–align column A data.
   - Center column E entries.
   - Format the price data with commas and no decimal places.

2. Sort the data so the salespeople and the items they sold are listed in alphabetical order.

3. Name the database range.

4. Use Advanced Filter to create a result list to list only the cars that were sold.
   - Place the table four rows below the existing data.
   - Enter an appropriate heading for this table.
   - Clear the TRANSACTIONS field from the table.
   - Enter the row label TOTAL below this listing.
   - Calculate the total value of cars sold below the PRICE column.

5. Use Advanced Filter to create a result list to list the cars that were leased.
   - Place the table four rows below the existing data listing.
   - Enter an appropriate heading for this table.
   - Clear the TRANSACTION field from the table.
   - Enter the row label NUMBER OF LEASES below this listing.
   - Calculate the count of cars leased, and place this value to the right of the NUMBER OF LEASES label.

6. Use filters to answer the following questions:
   - ❓ How many cars were sold by Jim?
   - ❓ How many Tigers were leased?
   - ❓ How many Tigers were sold?
   - ❓ How many Road Runners were sold in December?
   - ❓ How many Panthers were sold in December?

7. Use Advanced Filter to create a result list to list all the transactions involving the two models of the TIGER.
   - Place the table four rows below the existing data listing.
   - Enter an appropriate heading for this table.

8. Enter the following summary labels in an available area of the worksheet, and calculate the results using database (list) functions or by using summary totals:

   SALES SUMMARY - RON
   - Total $ Sales
   - Average Sale Price
   - Number of Sales
   - Highest Sale Price
   - Lowest Sale Price

9. Format money values for commas and no decimal places.

10. Re-sort the file so that all items are in chronological order.

11. Print a copy of the worksheet to fit on one page.

12. Save and close the file; name it **NOAH**.

    OPTIONAL: Add enhancements, as desired.

	A	B	C	D	E
1			NOAH'S AUTO SALES		
2			TRANSACTIONS DATABASE		
3					
4	DATE	AGENT	ITEM	PRICE	TRANSACTIONS
5	11/04/97	JAIME	BARACUDA	17,689	S
6	11/04/97	RON	ROAD RUNNER	13,545	S
7	11/04/97	JIM	TIGER	21,760	L
8	11/04/97	PAT	TIGER	22,550	S
9	11/07/97	PAT	PANTHER	15,430	L
10	11/08/97	JIM	BARACUDA	17,565	L
11	11/10/97	RON	PANTHER	15,765	S
12	11/13/97	JAIME	TIGER	22,698	L
13	11/18/97	PAT	ROAD RUNNER	13,675	L
14	11/22/97	RON	TIGER ZX	25,489	S
15	11/24/97	KAREN	BARACUDA	17,986	S
16	11/28/97	JAIME	TIGER	22,435	L
17	12/04/97	JIM	PANTHER	15,999	S
18	12/05/97	KAREN	BARACUDA	17,476	L
19	12/08/97	PAT	ROAD RUNNER	13,999	S
20	12/12/97	JIM	TIGER ZX	26,540	L
21	12/15/97	KAREN	ROAD RUNNER	13,765	S
22	12/18/97	RON	BARACUDA	17,999	L
23	12/22/97	JAIME	PANTHER	15,345	S
24	12/29/97	KAREN	TIGER ZX	25,476	L

NEXT LESSON

LESSON 11

MACRO BASICS

Exercises 90-93

- Create, Name and Run Simple Macros

- Delete Macros

- Change Options for Existing Macro

- Mark Position for Recording Macro

- Visual Basic

- Hide/Unhide a Workbook

- Edit a Macro

- Assign Macro to a Graphic Button

- Select a Macro Button without Running the Macro

EXERCISE 90

■ Create, Name and Run Simple Macros ■ Delete Macros
■ Change Options for Existing Macro ■ Hide/Unhide a Workbook

NOTES:

Create, Name, and Run Simple Macros

■ A **macro** is a series of actions used to accomplish a task and stored for reuse at a later time. It is a way to automate a set of instructions that you need to perform often, such as the entry of commands, formats, formulas and/or labels. An entire list of commands can then be performed with one mouse click or several keystrokes. For example, you can write a macro to create your business heading.

■ Recording a macro involves the following steps:

1. Plan the keystrokes or commands needed to complete the task.

2. Select the cell where the recording will begin.

3. Decide if the macro should use relative references. Select this option if you want the macro to be carried out anywhere on the worksheet in relation to the previously selected cell. Deselect it if the macro should always act on the specific cells in which the macro was recorded.

4. Click **Tools, Record Macro**, name the macro, describe the macro, and set any of the following macro options in the Record New Macro dialog box:

   • Assign the macro to the **Tools** menu and type the menu text.

   • Assign a shortcut key for playing back the macro.

   • Specify where to store the macro.

   • Set the macro language.

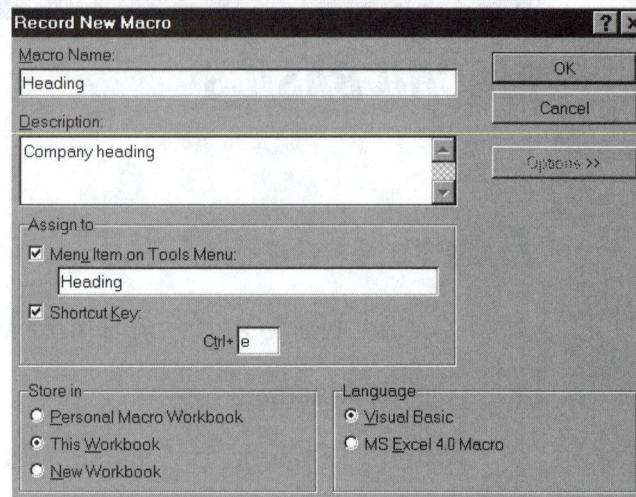

5. When the Ready Recording message is on the status bar, perform the steps to complete the task and/or type data to record.

6. Stop the macro when you are done, by clicking **Tools, Record Macro, Stop Recording.**

■ When you record a macro, it is always stored on module sheets in a workbook. **Module sheets** are special sheets Excel reserves for storing macros. Excel can run any macro contained in any open workbook.

As you will note in the Record New Macro dialog box above, you can store a module sheet and macros in the following workbooks:

• **Personal Macro Workbook** — stores macros in a *hidden* workbook that is always open. Use this option to store macros you will use often and when working with other workbooks. You can use the **Unhide** command on the **Window** menu to view the hidden Personal Macro workbook.

- **This Workbook** — stores macros in the current workbook. Use this option if the macro applies to tasks you will do only on the current workbook.

- **New Workbook** — stores macros on a new or specified workbook. Use this option if you will sometimes apply the macro to tasks in other jobs. You will have to open the workbook containing the macro before running it.

■ When creating a macro, you should describe the macro in the space provided so that you can easily identify its purpose at a later time.

■ When you play back your macro recording or run a macro, Excel carries out the instructions in the macro program. Once a macro has been created and named, you can run (invoke) the macro by doing one of the following procedures:

- Pressing the shortcut key, if you assigned one.

- Selecting **Macros** from the **Tools** menu and selecting the macro from the list.

- Selecting the macro from the **Tools** menu, if you assigned it to the menu.

- Clicking a button to which a macro has been assigned.

Delete Macros

■ If you no longer need a macro, or wish to record it again, you can delete it. To delete a macro, click **Tools, Macro,** then select the macro and click Delete. When you delete a macro, Excel deletes the lines in the module.

■ If you use the Personal notebook to store macros, you will need to unhide it to view or to delete a macro.

> *In this exercise, you will create a vendor list for Gourmet King. Since this list will be updated with new names frequently, certain tasks can be automated using macro commands.*

EXERCISE DIRECTIONS:

1. Create the partial worksheet as shown on the right, or open 💾 **90FOOD**.

2. Adjust column widths as necessary.

3. To enter a macro for the company heading, place the cursor in A1 and use the information provided below:

   - Before beginning, click **Tools, Record Macro, Use Relative References** so that this macro can be used in another location.
   - Click Tools, Record Macro, Record New Macro and set:
   Macro name: Heading
   Description: Company heading
   - Click **Options** and set:
   Assign to Menu Item on Tools menu
   Type menu text: Heading
   Shortcut Key: Ctrl + e (suggested)
   Store in: This Workbook
   - Click OK button.
   - Record the following steps:
     - Type heading "Gourmet King, Inc." (use upper and lower case) in current cell.
     - Format for Bold, 14 point, Century Gothic font.
     - Center across columns.
     - Highlight A2:F2 and format the cells for a heavy line across the bottom of the cells.
   - Stop recording by clicking Tools, Record Macro, Stop Recording.

4. To test and run the macro, switch to Sheet2, place the cursor in cell A1 and press Ctrl+e.

   ✓ *The heading should appear on Sheet2. The width of the heading may vary since there are no columns of data. If there is an error, you can delete the macro using the Tools, Macro dialog box and then record it again. You will learn how to edit a macro in the next exercise.*

5. To run the macro from the **Tools** menu, switch to Sheet3, cell A1, and select Heading from the bottom of the **Tools** menu.

6. To enter a macro for credit limit format, place the cursor on the first number and use the information provided below:

   - **Use Relative References** should be selected.
   - Set:
   Macro name: Limit
   Description: Format credit limit for commas, currency, and no decimals.
   - Set **Options**:
   Shortcut Key: Ctrl + h (suggested)
   Store in: This Workbook
   - Record formatting for currency, commas, and no decimals. (Toolbar buttons can be used.)
   - Stop recording.

7. To test the macro, highlight the remainder of the credit limit numbers, and press Ctrl+h.

8. Add the following data to the list using right mouse and Pick from list to enter the product:

COMPANY	LAST	FIRST	TELEPHONE	PRODUCT	CRED LIMIT
China Tea	Wong	Samuel	212-555-2376	Coffee/Tea	5000
Organics, Inc.	Aloe	Sally	908-555-9812	Produce	6000

9. Use the Limit macro (Ctrl+h) to format the credit limit data.

10. To enter a macro to print the list in compressed format with gridlines, use the information provided below:

   - **Use Relative References** should be selected.
   - Set:
   Macro name: Printsmall
   Description: Prints list with gridlines to fit in daily calendar.
   - Set **Options**:
   Assign to Menu Item on Tools menu
   Type menu text: Printsmall
   Store in: This Workbook
   - Record page setup commands for 75% scaling and gridlines. Record print command.
   - Stop recording.

11. Since the material has already printed, do not test the macro unless you have full access to a printer.
12. To check options set for macros:
    - Select Tools, Macro.
    - Select the Limit macro.
    - Click Options.
    - Click OK.
    - Close the Macro dialog box.

13. To view the macro module sheet:
    - Move to Sheet16 and select Module1.
    - Scroll down the sheet.
    - Select Sheet1.
14. Save and close the workbook file; name it **FOOD**.

	A	B	C	D	E	F
1						
2						
3	VENDORS					
4						
5	COMPANY	LAST	FIRST	TELEPHONE	PRODUCT	CREDIT LIMIT
6	Merlin Products	Florham	Marie	201-555-6598	Specialty	5000
7	TRG Provisions	Bowman	Bill	212-555-6589	Meat/Poultry	9000
8	Coffee Depot	Roast	Sam	212-555-5487	Coffee/Tea	5000
9	Produce Central	Weimer	Carol	617-555-7687	Produce	7000
10	Penzina Candy	Trent	David	908-555-2376	Confections	5000
11	Golly Farms	King	Peter	201-555-1242	Meat/Poultry	10000
12						

RECORD A MACRO

1. If necessary, mark position for recording macro (*see below*).
2. Click **Tools** menu .... `Alt` + `T`
3. Click **Record Macro** .... `R`
4. Click **Record New Macro** .... `R`
5. Type macro name .... *macro name* in **Macro Name** text box.
   NOTE: *A macro name cannot contain spaces.*
6. Click **Description:**
   [   ] .... `Alt` + `D`
7. Type macro description .... *macro description*
8. Click [Options >>] .... `Alt` + `O`

To assign macro to Tools menu:

a. Select ☐ **Menu Item on Tools Menu** .... `Alt` + `U`
b. Click in **Menu Item on Tools Menu:** [   ] .... `Tab`
c. Type menu text .... *menu text*

To assign a shortcut key for playing back macro:

a. Select ☐ **Shortcut Key** .... `Alt` + `K`
b. Click in **Ctrl +** [   ] .... `Alt` + `T`
c. Type letter .... *letter*
   NOTE: *If letter is already in use, Excel will notify you.*

To specify where macro will be stored:

- Select **Store in** option:
  Personal Macro Workbook .... `Alt` + `P`
  This Workbook .... `Alt` + `W`
  New Workbook .... `Alt` + `N`

To set macro language:

- Select ◯ **Visual Basic** .... `Alt` + `V`
  OR
  Select ◯ **MS Excel 4.0 Macro** .... `Alt` + `E`

9. Click [OK] .... `↵`
   *Excel displays a toolbar with a **Stop Macro** button.*

To set recording references to relative or absolute:

a. Click **Tools** menu .... `Alt` + `T`
b. Click **Record Macro** ..... `Alt` + `R`
c. Select or deselect **Use Relative References** ... `Alt` + `U`

10. Execute commands to record.
11. Click **Stop Macro** button .... [■] to end recording.
    *Excel adds a module or macro sheet to the end of the existing sheets in the workbook if you specified **This Workbook**, above.*

RUN A MACRO

*   Press assigned
    shortcut key.......................Ctrl +*letter*
    OR
    a.   Click **Tools** menu ....Alt + T
    b.   Select assigned macro
         name .... ⬆⬇ , ↵
         near bottom of menu.
    OR
    a.   Click **Tools** menu ....Alt + T
    b.   Click **Macro**........................... M
    c.   Select macro name ...... Tab , ↵
         in **Macro Name/Reference** list.
    d.   Click Run ....Alt + R

DELETE A MACRO

If macro is stored in the Personal
Macro Workbook:

*   Unhide the Personal Macro
    Workbook. (see below)

1.   Click **Tools** menu ....Alt + T
2.   Click **Macro**.................................. M

3.   Select macro name.............. Tab , ↵
     in **Macro Name/Reference** list.
4.   Click Delete .... Alt + D

CHANGE OPTIONS FOR EXISTING MACRO

1.   Click **Tools** menu .... Alt + T
2.   Click **Macro**.................................. M
3.   Select macro name.............. Tab , ↵
     in **Macro Name/Reference** list.
4.   Click Options... .... Alt + O
5.   Select **Macro** options:
     Macro options include: *Description,
     Menu Item on Tools Menu,
     Shortcut Key, Function Category,
     Status Bar Text, Help Context ID,
     Help File Name*
6.   Click OK .... ↵

UNHIDE A WORKBOOK

*Use to view the Personal Workbook where
macros are stored.*

1.   Click **Window** menu .... Alt + W
2.   Click **Unhide**................................. U
3.   Select workbook .... ⬆⬇
     to unhide in **Unhide Workbook** list.
4.   Click OK .... ↵

HIDE A WORKBOOK

1.   Select workbook to hide.
2.   Click **Window** menu .... Alt + W
3.   Click **Hide** .... H

NEXT EXERCISE

EXERCISE

■ Mark Position for Recording Macro ■ Visual Basic ■ Edit a Macro
■ Assign Macro to a Graphic Button
■ Select a Macro Button without Running the Macro

91

NOTES:

Mark Position for Recording Macro

■ When you first record a macro, Excel will record the macro in a new module sheet. Any macros created thereafter, in that worksheet, will be entered below the initial macro. If you want Excel to store the macro in a different or specific module sheet, you can follow the procedure to mark the position for recording the macro. You can also record actions within an existing macro.

Visual Basic

■ Excel records your actions in a language called **Visual Basic**. To watch Excel record your actions, you can set up your workbook as follows:

- Open a new window for the workbook.

- Display the module sheet in the duplicate window.

- Arrange the windows so you can see the sheet in which the actions will be recorded next to the module sheet in which Excel will record the actions. Then watch Excel enter each Visual Basic command in the module sheet as you record a macro.

■ Excel provides online help about the Visual Basic macro language. You can find help by selecting the **Help** menu, **Microsoft Office Help Topics, Contents** tab, Getting Started with Visual Basic or Microsoft Excel Visual Basic Reference.

Edit Macros

■ You can edit the macro commands Excel records. For example, when Excel records your command to turn gridlines off, it writes the following line:

ActiveWindow.DisplayGridlines = False

You can edit this line to make the macro turn gridlines on or off depending upon the current state of the active window. To do this you would change the line to read:

ActiveWindow.DisplayGridlines = Not ActiveWindow.DisplayGridlines

The **Not** operator tells Excel to change the DisplayGridlines property to its opposite state, which will act as a toggle when the macro is invoked.

Assign Macro to a Graphic Button

■ In the previous exercise, macros were assigned to shortcut keys or to the menu.

However, you can assign a macro to a graphic button that you place in the worksheet. (Note the illustration of the labeled buttons in the worksheet, on page 320.) This allows you to invoke the macro by clicking the button. To create the button, you will need to use two buttons on the Drawing Toolbar:

Create Button

Lets you create a button to which you can assign an existing macro.

Drawing Selection

Lets you select a macro button without executing the macro.

NOTE: *You can also assign a macro to a custom button on the toolbar. These buttons will always be available if you store the macros in the Personal Macro Workbook. This is a good idea if you are the only person who will use Excel on your computer.*

In this exercise, you will update the FOOD worksheet for Gourmet Giant, Inc. You will create more macros to automate several tasks and assign the new macros to graphic buttons.

EXERCISE DIRECTIONS:

1. Open **FOOD** or open **91FOOD**.

2. Mark position for recording new macro, using **Tools, Record Macro, Mark Position for Recording** on the Module1 sheet in the first available area.

3. Record and name two macros to perform tasks indicated below:

   - Do not select Use Relative References.

   - **Macro name**   **Description**
     SortCompany   Sorts list by company and turns on print preview.

     SortProduct   Sorts list by product and turns on print preview.

   - Do not assign macros to the **Tools** menu or to a shortcut key — you will assign macros to graphic buttons later on.

   - Set option to store macros in the current workbook.

4. Create graphic buttons and assign the appropriate macro to each. Label the graphic buttons as indicated in the illustration.

5. Add the following new vendors to the list:

6. Format the credit limit figures using the Limit macro shortcut keys, Ctrl+h.

7. Place the cursor on the list and test the new macro button for Sort Product

8. Do not print the worksheet.

9. Test the Sort Company button, but do not print the worksheet.

10. To watch a macro being recorded, open a **N**ew Window and arrange the window vertically. In the right window, move to the Module1 sheet and scroll down to the first clear area.

11. Record and name a macro to perform task indicated below:

    - **Macro name**   **Description**
      Gridlines   Turns worksheet gridlines off.

    - Set no options since a button will be created.
      HINT: *Use the Tools, Options menu to remove worksheet gridlines.*

12. Create and label a graphic button for the Gridlines macro.

COMPANY	LAST	FIRST	TELEPHONE	PRODUCT	CREDIT LIMIT
Kate's Cookies	Krumble	Kate	201-555-5923	Confections	1000
Globe Trading	Mariner	Tug	212-555-1200	Specialty	5000

13. Edit the Gridlines macro so that it reads:

    ```
    ActiveWindow.DisplayGridlines = Not
    ActiveWindow.DisplayGridlines
    ```

    NOTE: *The line should appear on one line. Do not include line breaks in the module. There is a space after the word "Not".*

14. Try out the Gridlines macro button. It should turn gridlines on or off each time you click it.

15. Create and label a graphic button for the PrintSmall macro.

16. Use the Print Small button to print the worksheet in compressed format with gridlines.

17. Save and close the file; name it **FOOD**.

	A	B	C	D	E	F	G
1	Gourmet King, Inc.						
2							
3	VENDORS						
4							
5	COMPANY	LAST	FIRST	TELEPHONE	PRODUCT	CREDIT LIMIT	Sort Company
6	China Tea	Wong	Samuel	212-555-2376	Coffee/Tea	$ 5,000	
7	Coffee Depot	Roast	Sam	212-555-5487	Coffee/Tea	$ 5,000	
8	Golly Farms	King	Peter	201-555-1242	Meat/Poultry	$ 10,000	
9	Merlin Products	Florham	Marie	201-555-6598	Specialty	$ 5,000	Sort Product
10	Organics, Inc.	Aloe	Sally	908-555-9812	Produce	$ 6,000	
11	Penzina Candy	Trent	David	908-555-2376	Confections	$ 5,000	
12	Produce Central	Weimer	Carol	617-555-7687	Produce	$ 7,000	
13	TRG Provisions	Bowman	Bill	212-555-6589	Meat/Poultry	$ 9,000	Gridlines
14							
15							
16							Print Small
17					You will create buttons to run macros.		
18							
19							

ASSIGN MACRO TO A GRAPHIC BUTTON

1. Click **Drawing** button.................
   on Standard Toolbar to show
   Drawing Toolbar.

2. Click **Create Button** button.........
   on Drawing Toolbar.
   Pointer becomes a +.

3. Position pointer ....
   where corner of button will be.

4. Drag button outline to desired size.

5. Select desired
   macro...................................... Tab ,
   in **Macro/Name/Reference** list.

6. Click OK ....

7. Click text in button.

8. Edit text as desired.

9. Click anywhere in worksheet.
   *NOTE: If you need to change the
   button text, size or position,
   you need to select the button
   without running the macro
   (see below).*

SELECT A MACRO BUTTON WITHOUT RUNNING THE MACRO

1. Click **Drawing** button.................
   on Standard Toolbar to show
   Drawing Toolbar.

2. Click **Drawing Selection** button .
   to activate it.

---

3. Click any part of button.
   *Excel marks button with a selection
   outline and handles.*

4. Click in button to edit the button text.
   *NOTE: When you have finished editing
   the button, be sure to click
   the **Drawing Selection** button
   again to deactivate it. This will
   let you work with data in cells
   and allow you to run a macro
   assigned to the button.*

EDIT A MACRO

1. Click **Tools** menu .... Alt + T

2. Click **Macro** .... M

3. Select macro name .... Tab ,
   in **Macro Name/Reference** list.

4. Click Edit .... Alt + E
   *Excel places insertion point in macro
   code in module.*

5. Edit macro commands as desired.
   *NOTE: Appendix C contains additional
   information about the Visual
   Basic Macro language.*

6. Select sheet in which macro will be
   executed and try out the macro.
   *NOTE: The next time you run the
   macro, Excel will execute the
   macro code as stored in the
   module. Excel saves the macro
   when you save the workbook.*

MARK POSITION FOR RECORDING MACRO

*Marks starting point in a module where a new
macro will be recorded. Excel will add new
macros below last macro in the module.*

1. Select desired module sheet.
   *NOTE: If module sheet is in the
   Personal Macro Workbook,
   unhide this workbook.*

2. Place insertion point in module where
   macro code will be inserted or new
   macro will begin.

3. Click **Tools** menu .... Alt + T

4. Click **Record Macro**.................... R

5. Click **Mark Position for
   Recording**................................. M

6. Select sheet and cell where recording
   will begin.

7. Record macro.

EXERCISE

Summary

92

You have created worksheets that use worksheet protection. However, it is difficult to know if worksheet protection is on or off, and you would like a faster way to switch between these modes. To automate this task you will create a macro on a new workbook. The macro will use a Visual Basic code to determine the current state of worksheet protection. With this workbook open, you can run the macro to set worksheet protection in any other open workbook.

EXERCISE DIRECTIONS:

1. Open a new workbook.

2. Since the purpose of this workbook is to record and store macros, delete all sheet tabs except Sheet1.

3. Save and name the workbook **MYMACS**.

4. In Sheet1, record a macro to turn worksheet protection on.

   - Set command to Use Relative References.
   - Set these macro options:

     Macro name: Protect_on_off

     Description: Turn protection on or off.

     Store in: This Workbook

     Assign macro to menu.

   - Record command to turn worksheet protection on; do not assign a password.
   - Stop recording the macro and select the module sheet.
   - Edit the macro code so it looks exactly like the macro code shown at the right.

     NOTE: In the macro code illustration, the shaded text shows recorded code. Type the additional code exactly as shown. Excel will color key statements such as Sub and Else automatically. The ← indicates where you must press the Enter key.

   - Notice the underscore character (_) at the end of the first line in the recorded code. This character tells Excel the next line belongs with the line above it. Omit underscore if code can fit on one line.

   NOTE: Appendix C contains information about looking up Visual Basic macro language codes.

MACRO CODE:

```
Sub Protect_on_off() ←
        If ActiveSheet.ProtectContents = True Then ←
                ActiveSheet.Unprotect ←
                MsgBox ("Protection is OFF") ←
        Else ←
                ActiveSheet.Protect DrawingObject:=True, _
                Contents:=True, Scenarios:=True ←
                MsgBox ("Protection is ON) ←
        End If ←
End Sub
```

5. Test the macro on Sheet1. Edit the macro, if necessary.

6. In Sheet1, record macro to type your name and enter the current date and time.

- Set these macro options:

  Macro name: Author

  Description: Type name and insert date and time.

  Store in: This Workbook

  Assign macro to menu.

- Record these commands and entries:

  a. Use GoTo command to activate cell A1.

  b. Enter your full name.

  c. Select cell A2.

  d. Insert current date (Press Ctrl + ;).

  e. Set width of column A to fit the longest entry.

- Stop recording the macro and select the module sheet.

- Edit the macro line that types in the date to:

  `ActiveCell.FormulaR1C1 = Now()`

- Test the macro on Sheet1. Edit the macro, if necessary.

7. Open ⌨ **AGE** or open 💾 **92AGE** and run the Author macro to insert your name and current date and time.

8. Open ⌨ **ZONE** or open 💾 **92ZONE** and test protection macro on its worksheet.

9. Close all workbook files without saving them.

EXERCISE

Summary

93

The BITEC CO. would like to have several macros available in the INCOME workbook on macro buttons. You will create macros and macro buttons. In addition, you will open the MYMACS workbook, created in the previous exercise, and apply macros to this workbook.

EXERCISE DIRECTIONS:

1. Open 🖮 **INCOME** or open 💾 **93INCOME**.

2. Record a macro to format the data for currency with commas and no decimal places.

   - Activate the Use Relative References feature.
   - Macro name: FormatVal
   - Description: Formats money values for currency, with commas and no decimal places.
   - Store in: This Workbook
   - Record commands.
   - Stop recording.

3. Create a macro button and assign the FormatVal macro to the button. Name the button, Format Values.

4. Use the button to format the remaining values.

5. Record a macro to print the data sheet at 120% scaling in landscape mode without gridlines.

   - Macro name: PrintLarge
   - Description: Prints the Data sheet at 120% scaling in landscape mode without gridlines.
   - Store in: This Workbook
   - Record commands.
   - Stop recording.

6. Create a macro button and assign the PrintLarge macro to the button. Name the button, Print Data.

7. If you have easy access to a printer, create an optional third macro to print each chart on a separate sheet. Make a button for this macro.

8. Open 🖮 **MYMACS** or open 💾 **93MYMACS**.

9. Switch to the Income worksheet.

10. Move the Bitec 6 title on the Data sheet from A1 to C1.

11. Run the Author macro to insert your name and current date and time.

12. Test the Gridlines_on_off macro.

13. Save and close the file; name it **INCOME**.

LESSON 12

SUMMARY EXERCISES

Exercises 94-100

- Science/Math
- Finance/Portfolio Analysis
- Accounting/Balance Sheet
- Economics/Decision Making
- Sales Marketing
- Accounting/Depreciation
- Accounting/Financial Reports

EXCEL

EXERCISE
Science/Math (Lookup Table, Formulas, If statements, Worksheets, Series, Hide Data, Enhancements)

94

The Poseiden Import/Export Company is involved in foreign trade of food items. Since many foreign companies use the metric system for measurements and we show both measures on our labels, your supervisor has asked you to create a record of the conversion of metric measurements to U.S. Customary Weights and Measures and vice versa.

In addition, your supervisor would like a price list developed for each lot of merchandise. The markup depends on the number of items in a lot. There is a 35% markup on all items except for those that we have ordered in lots of 1000 units or more, where the markup is only 30%.

EXERCISE DIRECTIONS:

1. Create the worksheet in Illustration A as shown, or open 💾 **94METRIC**.
   - Set column widths, as necessary.
   - Use a series for the Lot numbers.
   - Name the lookup table range, TABLE.
   - Enhance title rows as desired.
2. Find:
   - FACTOR
     HINT: *Use a vertical lookup function to search the TABLE for the desired conversion and the associated factor. The format for a lookup formula is =VLOOKUP(search item, range to search, column position in range, FALSE).*
   - PKG. WT.
     HINT: *ORIGINAL PKG. WT* FACTOR*
   - UNIT
     HINT: *Use a vertical lookup formula to search the TABLE for the desired "CONVERT TO" associated unit.*

3. Copy the heading and the first two columns of this report to Sheet2 and create the second worksheet as shown in Illustration B.
4. Enter the NUMBER of items in the lot and the PRICE per item as per the illustration.
5. Find:
   - TOTAL: The total price for the lot of merchandise.
   - MARKUP: Enter an IF statement that produces a 30% markup on lots of 1000 units or more or a 35% markup on all other lots.
   - RESALE PRICE: TOTAL+MARKUP
6. Find the Totals for this report.
7. Use lines and double lines to enhance the reports.
8. Rename the worksheets, LABELING RECORD and PRICE LIST.
9. Save and close the workbook file; name it **METRIC**.
10. Hide the conversion table on the Labeling Record sheet and print a copy of the workbook.

	A	B	C	D	E	F	G	H
1	**POSEIDEN IMPORT/EXPORT COMPANY**							
2			LABELING RECORD					
3								
4	LOT NO.	PRODUCT	PKG. WT.	UNIT	FACTOR	PKG. WT.	UNIT	
5	23452	Sardines	100	Grams				
6	23453	Fish sauce	715	Grams				
7	23454	Olive oil	3.785	Liters				
8	23455	Flour	2.27	Kilograms				
9	23456	Rice	11.35	Kilograms				
10	23457	Vinegar	950	Milliliters				
11	23458	Coffee	16	Ounces				
12	23459	Tuna	6	Ounces				
13	23460	Fruit Juice	1	Gallons				
14	23461	Maple Syrup	2.5	Pints	▼	▼	▼	
15	23462	Choc. Sauce	1.5	Quarts				
16								
17								
18								
19								
20								
21			**CONVERSION TABLE**					
22			CONVERT	MULT.BY	CONVERT			
23			FROM:	FACTOR	TO:			
24			Gallons	3.785	Liters			
25			Grams	0.035	Ounces			
26			Kilograms	2.2	Pounds			
27			Liters	33.8	Ounces			
28			Milliliters	0.0338	Ounces			
29			Ounces	28.3495	Grams			
30			Pints	0.473	Liters			
31			Pounds	0.454	Kilograms			
32			Quarts	0.946	Liters			
33								

ILLUSTRATION A

	A	B	C	D	E	F	G
1	**POSEIDEN IMPORT/EXPORT COMPANY**						
2			PRICE LIST				
3							RESALE
4	LOT NO.	PRODUCT	NUMBER	PRICE	TOTAL	MARKUP	PRICE
5	23452	Sardines	1440	0.35			
6	23453	Fish sauce	2400	1.10			
7	23454	Olive oil	288	5.40			
8	23455	Flour	500	0.95			
9	23456	Rice	200	3.65			
10	23457	Vinegar	720	1.95			
11	23458	Coffee	1800	0.95			
12	23459	Tuna	1440	0.38			
13	23460	Fruit Juice	288	0.96			
14	23461	Maple Syrup	500	2.20	▼	▼	▼
15	23462	Choc. Sauce	288	1.85			
16							
17	TOTALS						

ILLUSTRATION B

EXERCISE 95

Finance/Portfolio Analysis (Formulas, Charting, Enhancements)

NOTES:

- A **portfolio** is a varied group of investments in stocks and/or bonds.

- **Commission** is a fee charged for buying stock. It is added to your cost.

- **Market value** is the current price of a traded security. If you compare market value to the cost of your security, you can determine your "paper" profit or loss. This is known as a paper profit or loss since you must sell the stock to actually earn the profits.

> As an active investor in the stock market, you would like to evaluate your portfolio each month. In this exercise, you will create a portfolio analysis for October and chart your paper profits and losses.

EXERCISE DIRECTIONS:

1. Create the worksheet shown on the right, using wrapped column headings, or open 💾 **95FOLIO**.

2. Use your name as the owner of the portfolio.

3. Set column widths as necessary.

4. Find:
   - TOTAL COST
   - CURRENT MARKET VALUE
   - $ PROFIT OR LOSS
   - % PROFIT OR LOSS (based on TOTAL COST)
   - Totals of TOTAL COST, CURRENT VALUE, $ PROFIT OR LOSS columns
   - % OF PORTFOLIO (based on total CURRENT MARKET VALUE)
   - Total of % OF PORTFOLIO column

5. Enhance the worksheet using Autoformat and make any additional format and alignment changes.

6. Create an embedded pie chart illustrating the % OF PORTFOLIO column. Add appropriate titles and labels. Explode the PILGRIM FUND pie section.

7. Place the chart below the worksheet and add the following text note to the left of the graph:

   The Pilgrim Fund investment is showing over 60% profit.

8. Create an embedded column chart using stock symbols and comparing the Unit Cost and Unit Price columns. Add appropriate legends, titles and data labels.

9. Save the workbook file; name it **FOLIO**.

10. Print a copy in landscape mode.

11. Close the workbook file.

   ❓ Which stock is most profitable? Least profitable?

   ❓ Which stock represents the largest percentage of the portfolio? Smallest percentage?

   ❓ What is your recommendation for future sales/purchases of your currently held stocks?

	B	C	D	E	F	G	H	I	J	K	L
1				*(YOUR NAME)*							
2			MONTHLY PORTFOLIO ANALYSIS - OCTOBER								
3											
4	STOCK NAME	SYMBOL	QUANTITY	UNIT COST	COMMIS-SION	TOTAL COST	CURRENT UNIT PRICE	CURRENT VALUE	$ PROFIT OR LOSS	% PROFIT OR LOSS	% OF PORTFOLIO
5											
6	PILGRIM FUND	PIL	500	15.92	0.00		25.76				
7	GENES TECH	GET	200	34.50	98.40		36.25				
8	RAINBOW FUND	RAI	300	23.54	0.00		29.42				
9	KAISER AL.	KAL	100	15.25	35.00		14.75				
10	WINGS AIRLINES	WIA	150	64.75	127.50		55.50				
11	TEX INC.	TEX	250	43.00	135.76		56.00				
12	GTTE	GT	125	32.00	48.25		31.00				
13	IBBM	IB	50	95.00	52.55		89.00				
14	SUN CITY PFD.	SCI	200	25.50	56.00		25.25				
15	HUGHES SEMI	HSM	100	13.50	35.00		18.50				
16											
17	TOTALS										
18											
19											

EXERCISE

Accounting/Balance Sheet (Copy Template Sheet, 3-D References, Consolidate Data)

96

NOTES:

- A **balance sheet** is an accounting form that shows what a company owns (ASSETS), what the company owes (LIABILITIES) and how

much the owners are worth (EQUITY) if the company paid its debts and went out of business.

Web Electronics is a large company that has several separate divisions. Each division requires its own balance sheet each month. As an assistant in the Accounting Department, you have been asked to prepare a single balance sheet that summarizes all of the divisions, a consolidated balance sheet, and a balance sheet that compares the divisions, a comparative balance sheet.

EXERCISE DIRECTIONS:

1. Create the worksheet template for a balance sheet shown in Illustration A on the right.

   - Set column widths as necessary.
   - Create lines exactly as shown.
   - Enhance the title lines as desired.
   - Enter a formula to find TOTAL ASSETS, TOTAL LIABILITIES, TOTAL LIAB and EQUITY.

   NOTE: Zeros will appear until data is entered.

2. Rename Sheet1; name it **BAL**.

3. Delete Sheet2 through Sheet16.

4. Copy the BAL sheet four times.

5. Rename sheets as follows:

BAL	**SUMMARY**
BAL (2)	**MODEM**
BAL (3)	**SOFTWARE**
BAL (4)	**REPAIR**
BAL (5)	**COMPARISON**

6. Select the MODEMS sheet and add data for the MODEM DIVISION using the data shown in Illustration B on the right.

   - Change second line of the title to read: MODEM DIVISION.

7. Select the SOFTWARE sheet and add data for the SOFTWARE DIVISION using the data shown in Illustration B on the right.

   - Change second line of the title to read: SOFTWARE DIVISION.

8. Select the REPAIR sheet and add data for the REPAIR DIVISION using the data shown in Illustration B on the right.

   - Change second line of the title to read: REPAIR DIVISION.

9. On the COMPARISON sheet:

   - Move the Liabilities and Capital sections below the assets so that the all the labels are in column A.
   - Change second line of the title to read: COMPARATIVE BALANCE SHEET.
   - Create four column headings, using word wrap, beginning in Column D, under the date, that read: MODEM DIVISION, SOFTWARE DIVISION, REPAIR DIVISION, TOTAL

10. Copy the Balance Sheet data from each division sheet into the appropriate column on the Comparison sheet. (Since data is arranged in two columns on the division sheets, each copy will be a two-step process.)

11. Find the horizontal Total for each item.

12. Find the Total Assets, Total Liabilities, Total Liabilities and Equity for all columns.

13. Create a column chart comparing the Assets for the three divisions. Add appropriate labels, headings and legends.

14. Select the Summary sheet.

15. Use consolidate feature or 3-D references to consolidate all the Asset ranges into the summary sheet.

16. Use consolidate feature or 3-D references to consolidate all the Liability and Capital ranges into the summary sheet.

17. Format all money values for two decimal places.

18. Print a copy of the workbook.

19. Save and close the workbook file; name it **WEB**.

	A	B	C	D	E	F	G
1			**WEB ELECTRONICS**				
2			CONSOLIDATED STATEMENTS				
3			BALANCE SHEET				
4			JUNE 30, 19--				
5							
6		**ASSETS**			**LIABILITIES**		
7							
8	CASH				ACCOUNTS PAYABLE		
9	ACCOUNTS RECEIVABLE				NOTES PAYABLE		
10	INVENTORY				TOTAL LIABILITIES		
11	FURNITURE						
12	EQUIPMENT				**CAPITAL**		
13	BUILDINGS						
14	LAND				NED WEBER, CAPITAL		
15							
16	**TOTAL ASSETS**				**TOTAL LIAB AND CAPITAL**		
17							

ILLUSTRATION A

	A	B	C	D	E	F	G	H	I	J	K
1				MODEM DIVISION			SOFTWARE DIVISION			REPAIR DIVISION	
2	ASSETS										
3	CASH			9000			5600			12000	
4	ACCOUNTS RECEIVABLE			15680			22450			39600	
5	INVENTORY			12500			9600			5990	
6	FURNITURE			4300			5500			14000	
7	EQUIPMENT			16900			11400			61000	
8	BUILDING			84500						72000	
9	LAND			65000						50000	
10											
11	LIABILITIES										
12	ACCOUNTS PAYABLE			12900			10400			15678	
13	NOTES PAYABLE			115000			8000			134780	
14											
15	NED WEBER, CAPITAL			79980			36150			104132	
16											

ILLUSTRATION B

EXERCISE

Economics/Decision Making (Formulas, Copying, Editing, Page Breaks Named Ranges, Linking Data, Charting, Enhancements)

97

The President of the Elitepog Manufacturing Company has retained your services as a managerial consultant. The company produces an upscale version of a popular toy. They have asked you to develop some sales, price and profit projections so they can make critical decisions for establishing unit price and advertising budgets. As a consultant, you know it is sometimes possible to increase sales and profits if your advertising budget is increased.

You have two advertising plans to test to determine if it is wise to recommend increasing Elitepog Manufacturing's advertising budget. To complete the supply and demand analysis, some important information is established:

- *It is estimated that the daily demand for widgets is 1000 units. For every increase of $1 in the selling price, Widget Manufacturing will lose 40 units of sales volume. The following formula accurately describes the daily demand for the product: 1000 - (SELLING PRICE x 40).*

- *Variable costs, which are costs that fluctuate with sales, are $1 per unit.*

- *Fixed costs, which remain constant, are $1,200 per day.*

EXERCISE DIRECTIONS:

1. Create the worksheet as shown, or open 💾 **97POG**.

2. Find:
    - PROJ. VOLUME
      HINT: 1000 -(SP x 40).
    - PROJ. REVENUE
      HINT: Selling Price X Volume.
    - VARIABLE COSTS
      HINT: Volume X $1.
    - FIXED COSTS
      HINT: $1200 per day.
    - TOTAL EXPENSES
      HINT: Variable Costs + Fixed Costs +
              Advertising Expense.
    - BASIC PROJECTED PROFIT
      HINT: Revenue - Total Expenses.

   To test advertising plan A:

   NOTE: This plan will increase unit sales by 10%.

    - Copy the entire table and titles to A25.
    - Edit the third line of the title to read:
      ADVERTISING PROMOTION A-INCREASE
      SALES BY 10%.
    - Change the ADV. EXPENSE column values to
      $200 for each selling price.

- Edit PROJ. VOLUME formula to reflect a 10%
  increase in sales.
  HINT: Use (1000 - (SP x 40)) x 1.10

   To test advertising plan B:

   NOTE: This plan will increase unit sales by 15%.

    - Copy the range A25:H45 to A48.
    - Edit the third line of the title to read:
      ADVERTISING PROMOTION B-INCREASE
      SALES BY 15%.
    - Edit the ADV. EXPENSE column values to $500
      for each selling price.
    - Edit PROJ. VOLUME formula to reflect a 15%
      increase in sales.

3. Enter page breaks between worksheets and a footer
   that includes the page number, date and filename.

4. Print a copy of the three-page report.

5. To compare the results of the three advertising
   budgets, you will need to combine the profit
   data on a new sheet tab. To identify the data, create
   the following named ranges:

    - A8:A20   SELL_PRICE
    - H8:H20   BASIC_PROFIT
    - H32:H44   PROFIT_PLANA
    - H55:H67   PROFIT_PLANB

6. Rename the sheet containing the data; name it
   Report Data.

7. On Sheet2, create the summary worksheet titles as shown below:

ELITEPOG MANUFACTURING COMPANY				
SUMMARY OF PRICE/PROFIT PROJECTION				
Selling Prices	BASIC PROFIT	PROFIT PLAN A	PROFIT PLAN B	

8. Use Copy and Paste Special to create pasted links to named ranges and enter each range below appropriate column title in Sheet2.

9. Rename Sheet2; name it **Summary**.

10. Create a 3-D column chart showing the profits under each plan for each price from $10 to $17. Use appropriate titles and legends.

11. Enhance the workbook sheets:

   - Highlight the results shown at the $13 price level by outlining the data.

   - Enhance the titles and column headings.

   - Add a graphic, if available.

   - Use FormatPainter to copy formats to Report Data sheet.

   - Add, to the left of the chart, the following note in a text box:

     We recommend a unit price of $13 and the adoption of advertising Plan A.

12. Save the workbook file; name it **POG**.

13. Print one copy of the workbook.

14. Close the workbook file.

15. From the chart data, answer the following:

   ❓ What happens to profits under each advertising plan when the projected price exceeds $13?

   ❓ If the price was reduced to $12 due to market considerations, would you still recommend Plan A?

	A	B	C	D	E	F	G	H	I
1			ELITEPOG MANUFACTURING COMPANY						
2			POG PRICE/PROFIT PROJECTIONS						
3			BASIC ADVERTISING BUDGET						
4									
5	PROJECTED			TOTAL	TOTAL			BASIC	
6	SELLING	PROJ.	PROJ.	VARIABLE	FIXED	ADV.	TOTAL	PROJECTED	
7	PRICE	VOLUME	REVENUE	COSTS	COST	EXPENSE	EXPENSES	PROFIT	
8	5					0			
9	10					0			
10	11					0			
11	12					0			
12	13					0			
13	14					0			
14	15					0			
15	16					0			
16	17					0			
17	18					0			
18	19					0			
19	20	▼	▼	▼	▼	0	▼	▼	
20	24					0			
21									

EXERCISE

Sales Marketing (Lists, Subtotals, Database Functions, Filters)

98

You are the owner of a local sneaker store, Runner's World, with a small department selling sportswear apparel. Since this is a new line to the shop, the garments have not yet been inventoried. You are to create a list to record all purchases in this department as of March 31, 1997. You will then create reports to summarize the list information.

In addition, you will need to determine the items that should be reduced in price to promote quick sale. According to store policy, prices must be marked down 20% on items in stock over 40 days, and garments must be reordered when inventory falls below 50%.

EXERCISE DIRECTIONS:

1. Create the list shown on the right, or open
   🖫 **98RUN**.
   - Set column widths appropriately.
   - Format the COST column for two decimal places.
   - Enter the labels SELL PR., NO. SOLD, % SOLD, GROSS PROFIT in columns G through J.

2. Find SELL PR. for each item.

   HINT: Markup is 40% of cost. Selling price is COST x 40% + COST or COST x 1.4

3. Format appropriately.

4. Find remaining items:
   - NO. SOLD

     HINT: NO. PURC. - ON HAND
   - % SOLD

     HINT: NO. SOLD/NO. PURCHASED
   - GROSS PROFIT

     HINT: (SELLING PRICE - COST) x NO. SOLD

5. Format appropriately.

6. Name the list ITEMS. Include column titles.

7. Sort the list so all vendors (Sort By field) are in alphabetical order and items (Then By field) are in alphabetical order within vendor names.

8. Use Advanced Filter to extract from the list items to be reordered (items that sold more than 50% of inventory).
   - Insert four rows above the list and set up a criteria range there to indicate % SOLD>.50 condition.
   - Copy the records to the range beginning at A40.

- Label the extracted list appropriately.
- Print a copy of this report.

9. Use Advanced Filter to extract from the original list items that have been in stock for more than 40 days as of March 31, 1997. We would like to reduce the selling price of these items by twenty percent.
   - Set up criteria range as follows:
     DATE REC.
     ="<"&DATE(97,3,31)-40

     NOTES: In the criteria, the & (ampersand) combines the less than sign (<) with the result of the date expression (DATE(97,3,31)-40. The serial value resulting from the date expression appears.

     *If you see **#VALUE!** and not **<35480**, check that the **Transition Formula Evaluation** setting is deselected. To do this, click **Options** on the **Tools** menu. Select the Transition tab, then click the option to deselect it.*

- Copy the records to the range beginning at A58.
- Label the extracted list appropriately.
- Delete the last three fields in the extracted list.
- Add a new field to the extracted list in column H; name it NEW SELL PR.
- Find new selling price (SELL PR. x .8).
- Format appropriately.
- Print a copy of the new list.

10. To analyze purchases and sales of merchandise from OLYMPICS, one of our vendors, enter the summary labels below in an available area of the worksheet:

- RUNNER'S WORLD
- SPORTSWEAR SUMMARY DATA
- ANALYSIS OF OLYMPICS PURCHASES AND SALES
- Total Items Purchased
- Total Items Sold
- Total Gross Profit
- Average % Sold
- Average Gross Profit per item

11. Set up criterion for VENDOR and use appropriate database functions to calculate the indicated values for the original list. Use OLYMPIC as the criterion.

12. Format appropriately.

13. Print a copy of the summary data.

14. Save and close the workbook file; name it **RUN**.

OPTIONAL: Add enhancements to the lists and summary data.

	A	B	C	D	E	F	G	H	I	J	K
1			RUNNER'S WORLD								
2			SPORTSWEAR DIVISION								
3											
4	ITEM	VENDOR	NO. PURC	ON HAND	DATE REC.	COST	SELL PR.	NO. SOLD	% SOLD	GROSS PROFIT	
5	JOG SUIT-WOMEN/L	DCNY	10	3	02/15/97	30.00					
6	JOG SUIT-WOMEN/M	DCNY	15	7	02/15/97	30.00					
7	JOG SUIT-WOMEN/S	DCNY	15	12	02/15/97	30.00					
8	JOG SUIT-WOMEN/XL	ADIOS	4	2	02/15/97	30.00					
9	BODY LEOTARD/L	JUMPSKIN	10	1	01/19/97	20.00					
10	BODY LEOTARD/M	JUMPSKIN	25	12	01/19/97	20.00					
11	BODY LEOTARD/S	JUMPSKIN	10	2	01/19/97	20.00					
12	JOG SUIT-MEN/L	SPIKEE	20	4	01/10/97	25.00					
13	JOG SUIT-MEN/M	SPIKEE	15	12	01/10/97	25.00					
14	JOG SUIT-MEN/XL	SPIKEE	10	8	01/10/97	26.00					
15	NYLON SHORTS/L	SPIKEE	10	6	02/09/97	8.00					
16	NYLON SHORTS/M	SPIKEE	15	11	02/09/97	8.00					
17	NYLON SHORTS/S	SPIKEE	10	9	02/09/97	8.00					
18	NYLON SHORTS/XL	SPIKEE	8	8	02/09/97	8.00					
19	SWEATPANTS/L	OLYMPIC	20	17	03/14/97	7.00					
20	SWEATPANTS/M	OLYMPIC	25	19	03/14/97	7.00					
21	SWEATPANTS/S	OLYMPIC	12	7	03/14/97	7.00					
22	SWEATPANTS/XL	OLYMPIC	12	10	03/14/97	7.00					
23	SWEATSHIRT/L	OLYMPIC	60	20	01/29/97	10.00					
24	SWEATSHIRT/M	OLYMPIC	50	20	01/29/97	10.00					
25	SWEATSHIRT/S	OLYMPIC	30	20	01/29/97	10.00					
26	SWEATSHIRT/XL	OLYMPIC	25	15	01/29/97	10.00					
27	T-SHIRT/L	CHAMP	40	10	02/28/97	6.00					
28	T-SHIRT/M	CHAMP	30	2	02/28/97	6.00					
29	T-SHIRT/S	CHAMP	15	5	02/28/97	6.00	▼	▼	▼	▼	
30	T-SHIRT/XL	CHAMP	15	4	02/28/97	6.00					

EXERCISE

Accounting/Depreciation (Formulas, IF Statements)

99

NOTES:

- An **asset** is something of value that is owned.

- **Depreciation** is a decrease in value of an asset because of use and passage of time.

- **Salvage value** is the estimated amount that can be recovered at the end of the life of an asset.

- **Book value** is the current value of an asset. It is calculated by subtracting from the asset cost the total depreciation from all years owned.

- **Straight-line depreciation** is a method of calculating annual depreciation that results in charging an equal amount of annual depreciation expense for every year.

For example, an asset costs $1,000, has a salvage value of $200 and has an estimated life of eight years. Using the straight-line method, the annual depreciation would be $100 per year (1000-200)/8=100.

- Depreciation is calculated for this problem based on the **Half Month method**. This states that if the equipment is purchased between the first and fifteenth of a month, depreciation is calculated for the entire month. If equipment is purchased between the sixteenth and end of the month, depreciation is not calculated until the next month.

In this exercise, Mark and Jane Thomasville, both attorneys, need to prepare a depreciation schedule for their office equipment. This information is needed to prepare financial statements and tax returns.

EXERCISE DIRECTIONS:

1. Create the worksheet as shown on the right, or open 💾 **99DEPR**.

2. Do the following:

   - Set column widths as necessary.
     - ✓ *Note that each part of the date (month, day, year) is in its own column.*
   - Underline the row six column titles.
   - Use fonts, styles and color to enhance the heading area.
   - Format the money columns for two decimal places.

3. Find for all assets:

   - ANNUAL DEPR.

     Depreciation is calculated using straight-line method.

     HINT: *(COST - SALVAGE VALUE)/ LIFE OF ASSET IN YEARS*

   - FIRST YR. NO. OF MONTHS

     Depreciation is calculated for the time that the equipment is owned using the half month method (see notes above).

     HINT: =IF(DAYS>15,12-MONTH, 12-(MONTH-1))

   - FIRST YR. PARTIAL DEPR.

     The depreciation for the first year of ownership based on the number of ownership months and the established annual depreciation.

     HINT: *(ANNUAL DEPR./12) x FIRST YR. NO. OF MONTHS*

   - DEPR. 1995, DEPR. 1996 and DEPR. 1997

     The appropriate depreciation value, for each asset, is determined by when that asset was purchased. If the asset was purchased in the current year, the depreciation value is the same as the FIRST YR. PARTIAL DEPR. If the asset was purchased in a prior year, the depreciation value is the ANNUAL DEPR.

     An IF statement can be used, copied and edited for each of the different depreciation years.

HINT: =IF(YR=DEPR. year,
FIRST YR. PARTIAL DEPR.,
ANNUAL DEPR.)

NOTE: You should enter DEPR. year as a
constant (i.e, 95, 96 or 97).

- BOOK VALUE

  *The cost of the asset less the total depreciation
  from all ownership years represents the current
  book value.*

4. Find:

- COST TOTALS for 1995, 1996, 1997
  and ASSETS.

- TOTALS for DEPR.1995, DEPR.1996,
  DEPR.1997 in the appropriate columns.

- BOOK VALUE at the end of 1997.

5. Format all money columns for two decimal places
   and delete extraneous zeros that may have
   appeared after formulas were entered.

6. Print a copy so it fits on one page.

7. Save and close the workbook file; name it **DEPR**.

   ❓ What is the total value of all the assets at the time
   of purchase?

   ❓ What is the total depreciation or loss in value for
   the years 1995? 1996? 1997?

   ❓ What is the book value of all assets?

	A	B	C	D	E	F	G	H	I	J	K	L	M	N
1						MARK AND JANE THOMASVILLE, ATTORNEYS AT LAW								
2						DEPRECIATION SCHEDULE								
3														
4		D				ESTIMATED	LIFE OF		FIRST YR.	FIRST YR.				
5	M	A	Y	ASSET		SALVAGE	ASSET IN	ANNUAL	NO. OF	PARTIAL	DEPR.	DEPR.	DEPR.	BOOK
6	O	Y	R	DESCRIPTION	COST	VALUE	YEARS	DEPR.	MONTHS	DEPR.	1995	1996	1997	VALUE
7														
8	4	3	95	DESK AND CHAIR	1020.00	200.00	8							
9	5	16	95	FILE CABINET #25	375.00	75.00	8							
10	6	14	95	FILE CABINET #48	750.00	150.00	8							
11	10	15	95	TYPEWRITER	600.00	100.00	8							
12	12	10	95	CALCULATOR	150.00	45.00	5							
13				TOTAL 1995										
14														
15	5	2	96	DESK AND CHAIR	650.00	125.00	8							
16	6	20	96	COMPUTER	2700.00	700.00	5							
17	7	10	96	LASER PRINTER	1300.00	300.00	5							
18	9	19	96	FILE CABINET #34	540.00	100.00	8							
19	11	5	96	CONSOLE	1200.00	225.00	8							
20				TOTAL 1996										
21														
22	1	28	97	COMPUTER TABLE	485.00	95.00	5							
23	5	5	97	FILE CABINET #42	550.00	100.00	8							
24				TOTAL 1997										
25														
26				TOTAL ASSETS										

EXERCISE

Accounting/Financial Reports (3-D reference, Worksheets, Enhancements)

100

Blossom's Blooms is a floral contractor who summarizes his records each month using a Trial Balance. All the account balances are entered on the Trial Balance and then used in the financial reports. Mr. Blossom would like you to set up a Trial Balance sheet that would automatically send the values to the appropriate locations on the Financial reports as the Trial Balance is created.

EXERCISE DIRECTIONS:

1. Open 💾 **100TB** or

   Create the Trial Balance in Illustration A on Sheet1.

   Create the Income Statement in Illustration B on Sheet2 (do not include the numbers).

   Create the Balance Sheet in Illustration C on Sheet3 (do not include the numbers).

2. Group all three sheets:

   Enhance the three heading lines to 14 point Bold.

3. On the Trial Balance:

   Enter a formula to find the balanced totals.

   Format borders as illustrated.

   Format numbers for commas with no decimal places.

   Name the sheet: Trial Balance - May.

4. In the Income Statement:

   Bold each section heading. (Income, Expenses, Net Income).

   Enter a 3-D reference to enter the Fees Income from the Trial Balance to the location indicated.

   Copy the formula down for Rental Income.

   Enter a sum formula to find Total Income in Column F.

   Enter a 3-D reference to enter the Salary Expense from the Trial Balance to the location indicated.

   Copy the formula down for all expenses.

   Enter a formula to find Total Expenses in Column F.

   Enter a formula to find Net Income in Column F.

   Format borders as indicated.

   Format numbers for commas with no decimal places.

   Rename the sheet: Income Statement - May.

5. On the Balance Sheet:

   Bold each section heading (Assets, Liabilities, Capital).

   Enter a 3-D reference to enter Cash from the Trial Balance to the location indicated.

   Copy the formula down for Accounts Receivable and Supplies.

   Continue entering 3-D references for remaining Assets and Liabilities.

   Find the book value of the building by subtracting the Accumulated Depreciation from the Building value and enter the answer in Column F.

   Enter a formula to find Total Assets.

   Enter a formula to find Total Liabilities.

   Enter a 3-D reference for Bud Blossom, Capital and Bud Blossom, Withdrawals to enter the values from the Trial Balance.

   On the Net Income/Net Loss line enter a 3-D reference to enter the number from the bottom line of the Income Statement.

   Enter a formula to find Total Capital using the Capital, Investments, Withdrawals and Net Income data.

   Enter a formula to find Total Liabilities and Capital.

   Format the borders as indicated.

   Format numbers for commas with no decimal places.

   Rename the sheet: Balance Sheet - May.

6. Copy the three sheets so that they follow these sheets.

7. Rename the sheets:

   Trial Balance - June
   Income Statement - June
   Balance Sheet - June

ILLUSTRATION A

	A	B	C	D	E	F
1			Blossom's Blooms			
2			Trial Balance			
3			May 31, 199-			
4						
5	Account				Debit	Credit
6	Number	Account			Balances	Balances
7	101	Cash			18,000	
8	110	Accounts Receivable			8,000	
9	120	Supplies			1,500	
10	150	Building			57,000	
11	155	Accumulated Depreciation				12,000
12	201	Accounts Payable				6,300
13	202	Mortgage Payable				15,000
14	301	Bud Blossom, Capital				34,000
15	305	Bud Blossom, Withdrawals			10,000	
16	401	Fees Income				42,400
17	402	Rental Income				2,000
18	501	Salary Expense			12,000	
19	502	Utilities Expense			2,500	
20	503	Interest Expense			1,200	
21	504	Advertising Expense			1,000	
22	505	Miscellaneous Expense			500	
23						

ILLUSTRATION B

	A	B	C	D	E	F
1			Blossom's Blooms			
2			Income Statement			
3			For the month ended May 31, 1995			
4						
5	Income:					
6		Fees Income			42400	
7		Rental Income			2000	
8		Total Income				
9						
10	Expenses:					
11		Salary Expense			12000	
12		Utilities Expense			2500	
13		Interest Expense			1200	
14		Advertising Expense			1000	
15		Miscellaneous Expense			500	
16		Total Expenses				
17	Net Income					

ILLUSTRATION C

	A	B	C	D	E	F
1			Blossom's Blooms			
2			Balance Sheet			
3			May 31, 199-			
4						
5		Assets				
6	Cash					18000
7	Accounts Receivable					8000
8	Supplies					1500
9	Building				57000	
10	Accumulated Depreciation of Building				12000	
11	Total Assets					
12		Liabilities				
13	Accounts Payable					6300
14	Mortgage Payable					15000
15	Total Liabilities					
16		Capital				
17	Bud Blossom, Capital				34000	
18	Add: Investments					
19	Less: Bud Blossom, Withdrawals				10000	
20	Add: Net Income/Net Loss				0	
21	Total Capital					
22	Total Liabilities and Capital					

8. Enter the June Balances on the Trial Balance sheet as follows:

101 Cash	12000	
110 Accounts Receivable	21000	
120 Supplies	3280	
150 Building	57000	
155 Accumulated Depreciation		13000
201 Accounts Payable		4480
202 Mortgage Payable		14500
301 Bud Blossom, Capital		51200
305 Bud Blossom, Withdrawals	18000	
401 Fees Income		55000
402 Rental Income		4000
501 Salary Expense	22000	
502 Utilities Expense	5000	
503 Interest Expense	2000	
504 Advertising Expense	1200	
505 Miscellaneous Expense	700	

9. Change Dates to June 30 on all June reports.

10. Check June statements for accuracy.

11. Print a copy of May and June Statements with footers that include filename and sheet name.

12. Save and close the file; name it **TB**.

APPENDIX

Appendices A—F

APPENDIX A

GLOSSARY

3-D reference A reference to cells in other sheets in a workbook.

Absolute reference A type of cell reference that will not change when copied or moved. An absolute reference contains a dollar sign ($) before the row and/or column reference, e.g., $A$2.

Active cell The cell that is ready to receive data or a command.

Add-ins Special programs that can be used with Excel to extend its capabilities.

Advanced filter An Excel feature that displays or extracts records from a list based on a specified criteria such as employees that live in New York.

AutoFilter An Excel feature that makes it easy to show specific records in a list.

AutoCalculate An Excel feature that provides the sum, average, count, max or min functions for a range of numbers on the status line. The answer can not be copied to another location.

AutoComplete An Excel feature that will complete an entry, after typing a few letters, based on entries you have already made in that column.

AutoCorrect An Excel feature that will correct common typing errors. Words or codes may be added to the AutoCorrect dictionary so that your specific entries can be corrected.

AutoFit An Excel feature that sets the column width to the widest entry in the column.

AutoFormat An Excel feature that provides sample worksheet formats with font, style, color and layout settings.

AutoSum An Excel feature that makes it easy to total values in a worksheet.

Buttons   Symbols on a toolbar which represent tasks or actions and are used in conjunction with a mouse to access the tasks or actions.

Cell   A single location on a worksheet.

Cell borders   Line styles that border the edges of cells in a worksheet.

Cell reference   A column letter and row number, e.g., A1 or F12.

Cell Tips   A new feature that will allow you to add explanatory notes to any cell. A cell with a CellTip has a red dot in the upper right-hand corner.

Charting   Preparing a visual interpretation of data in the form of column, line, stacked column, or pie chart.

ChartWizard   An Excel feature that provides a series of steps with prompts that guide you through the process of creating a chart.

Column(s)   The vertical portions of the worksheet, e.g., A, B, C, etc. There are 256 columns in a worksheet.

Column heading(s)   The area at the top of a worksheet that indicates the column letters. Column headings also act as controls for sizing or hiding columns.

Column width   Refers to the size of a cell. A cell may be made wider or more narrow than its default size of nine characters.

Copying   Reproducing data from one location to another.

Data Map   Geographical data can be plotted and customized on maps that are provided with Excel. The Data Map Control feature allows you to customize your presentation.

Data marker   A symbol in a chart that represents a value.

Data series   A set of related data markers in a chart.

Data table   A data table used to evaluate different solutions to a problem based on specific input values or variables.

Database functions	A set of built-in formulas that perform calculations or special operations on records in a list.
Default	Settings which are preset by Excel but may be modified by the user. For example, column width settings.
Dialog box	A box which appears on the screen after a menu item is selected and contains settings to be changed.
Drag and Drop	An action that lets you perform tasks, such as copying a cell, by moving an object or data with the mouse to another object or location.
Editing	Changing the contents of a cell.
External reference	A reference to cells in another workbook.
Extract data	The process of copying a subset of a data range to another worksheet or workbook.
Field names	Column labels that appear in the first row of a list and identify the content of each column.
File	A saved workbook.
File protection	An Excel feature that lets you protect a workbook file when others attempt to open it.
Filename	The name given to a saved workbook.
Fill series	An Excel feature that allows for fast entry of sequential numbers in a column or row.
Font	A set of characters that share a design and name. Fonts come in varying sizes and styles.
Format	Using special commands to display worksheet data in the style, numeric format or alignment that makes the best presentation.

Formula

A mathematical expression that makes new values by combining numerical values with operators (plus, minus, etc.) Formulas may contain cell references, operators and functions.

Freeze panes

An Excel feature that keeps row or column titles in view while you scroll to other parts of a worksheet.

Function

A built-in formula that performs calculations or special operations.

Function Wizard

An Excel feature that provides you with a series of steps with prompts that guide you through the process of creating a function.

Global

A command affecting the entire worksheet.

Goal Seek

An Excel feature that changes a value in a problem so a formula using the value results in a specified answer.

Graphic objects

Items, such as lines, circles and boxes, that you can add to a worksheet or chart.

Graphing

Preparing a visual interpretation of data in the form of column, line, stacked column chart or pie chart.

Gridlines

In a worksheet, gridlines define the boundaries of cells. In a chart, gridlines mark increments on a value axis.

Label

A cell entry that begins with a letter or label prefix. Labels cannot be used in ordinary calculations.

Label prefix

The apostrophe (') character that precedes a cell entry to format a number as text.

Link

A feature enabling the user to connect two or more files so the linked file automatically updates when changes are made to the source file.

List (Database)

A table containing similar sets of data. Excel treats each row in a list as a record and each column as a field. Labels in the first row indicate the field names.

Lock cells An Excel feature that lets you restrict use of specific cells in a worksheet when worksheet protection is on.

Logical function A function that answers a true/false question and calculates data according to the answer.

Logical operator Symbols, such as > <, used in formulas or criteria ranges to evaluate a condition.

Lookup function A type of function that you can use to retrieve data from a list.

Macro A series of recorded actions that automates an Excel task.

Module The name of the macro sheet that is created in your current workbook to contain macro commands. Module sheets are numbered.

Named range A defined area of a worksheet that has been given a name.

Non-adjacent range A selection of cells that do not exist next to each other in a worksheet.

Numerical data Data that can be calculated.

Open The process of accessing a saved file.

Page break A division in a worksheet that marks the end of one printed page and the beginning of another.

Pivot table An interactive tool used to analyze information in a list.

Protect A feature that restricts access to worksheet data or a workbook file.

Range A rectangular group of adjacent cells in a worksheet that may be identified with a cell reference such as AB:D5.

Record A row in list that makes up a related set of data, such as an employee's name, address and phone number.

Relative reference   A type of cell reference that will change when copied or moved.

Transpose   The layout of data will be changed from row to column orientation or vice versa.

Typestyle   A selected font attribute, such as bold, italic or underlined, for example.

Value   A numerical or formula entry on the worksheet used in calculations.

Visual Basic   The language that is used to record macro commands.

Windows   The graphic environment that allows you to use Excel and other Windows-based programs simultaneously.

Workbook   An Excel document which may contain worksheets, charts and module sheets.

Worksheet   A columnar spreadsheet, containing 256 columns and 16,384 rows, used to calculate or analyze data. By default there are sixteen worksheets in a workbook.

Wrap text   A method of formatting text so that it fits on more than one line in a cell or other text area.

Replace   An Excel feature that lets you replace existing information quickly with another entry.

Row(s)   The horizontal portions of the worksheet, e.g., 1, 2, 3, etc. There are 8,192 rows in a worksheet.

Row headings   The area to the left of a worksheet that indicates row numbers. Row headings also act as controls for sizing or hiding rows.

Save   Stores a copy of the workbook on disk.

Scroll   A vertical or horizontal screen movement which displays portions of the spreadsheet that exist beyond the limits of the screen.

ScrollTips   When you click and drag a worksheet to another part of the worksheet, the ScrollTips will show the row or column as you scroll to the new location.

Series   A set of values that are grouped together.

Sheet tabs   Controls that let you select sheets in a workbook.

Sheets   Units of a workbook, such as worksheets, charts and modules.

Sort   The process of arranging records in a list in a particular order according to the contents of one or more columns.

Spelling   An Excel feature that checks the words in a worksheet and suggests replacement words when misspelled words are found.

Styles   Combinations of formats that have names.

Template   A skeleton worksheet containing labels and possibly formulas which may be reused with different data. Excel provides templates or model worksheets or you may create an original template.

Template Wizard   The Template Wizard helps you to link cells in the Template to fields in an Excel list, or database.

Toolbar   A set of buttons that carry out commands when clicked.

APPENDIX B

FUNCTIONS

A **function** is a built-in formula that performs a special calculation automatically. Like formulas, functions require an *equal sign* (=) as the first character in the cell entry. Excel identifies functions by the *function name* followed by a *left and right parentheses* which may include a *set of arguments*. No spaces separate a function name from the first parentheses.

The **arguments** are the names for the variables (references to values or the values themselves) the function needs to return an answer. *Commas* are used to separate the arguments (shown in bold below) in a function.

EXAMPLE: =AVERAGE(**B2,B3,70**) + SUM(**A1:A20**)

In this example, the first character is an equal sign (=) and the results of two functions (AVERAGE and SUM) are totaled. The arguments in the AVERAGE function are B2, B3 and 70. The argument in the SUM function is the range A1:A20.

Functions may be typed in directly or entered using the Function Wizard. The **Function Wizard** will step you through the entry of the function and its arguments.

To use Function Wizard to create a function:
1.   Select cell to contain formula.
     OR
     a.   Double-click cell containing formula.
     b.   Click formula where function will be inserted.
2.   Click **Function Wizard** button f_* on Standard Toolbar or formula bar.
     OR
     a. Select **Insert** menu.
     b. Select **Function**.
     — Function Wizard Step 1 of 2 —
3.   Select a category in **Function Category** list.
4.   Select a function in **Function Name** list.
5.   Select [Next >].
     — Function Wizard Step 2 of 2 —
6.   Select desired argument box.
7.   Type data.
     Depending on the function, enter the following kinds of data:
     ● **numbers (constants)** — *type numbers (integers, fractions, mixed numbers, negative numbers) as you would in a cell.*
     ● **references** — *type or insert cell references.*
     ● **named references or formulas** — *type or insert named references or formulas.*
     ● **functions** — *type a function or click* **Function Wizard** *button f_* (to left of argument box) to insert a function into an argument (nest functions).*
     The Function Wizard describes the current argument, indicates if the argument is required, and shows you the result of the values you have supplied.
8.   Repeat steps 6–7, as needed.

9. Select [Finish].

10. Type or insert remaining parts of formula.

    OR

    Press **Enter**.

Select function category. →

Function Wizard – Step 1 of 2   ? ☒

Choose a function and press Next to fill in its arguments.

Function Category:
- Most Recently Used
- All
- Financial
- Date & Time
- Math & Trig
- Statistical
- Lookup & Reference
- Database
- Text
- **Logical**
- Information

Function Name:
- AND
- FALSE
- **IF**
- NOT
- OR
- TRUE

Select function. ←

IF(logical_test,value_if_true,value_if_false)

Specifies a logical test to perform.

[Help] [Cancel] [< Back] [Next >] [Finish]

Function Wizard – Step 2 of 2   ? ☒

IF   Value: 0

Specifies a logical test to perform.

Value_if_false (optional)

is the value that is returned if logical_test is FALSE.

value the function will return ←

instructions for active argument →

logical_test	fx	B3=D3	TRUE
value_if_true	fx	B3+D3	0
value_if_false	fx	"They are not equal."	"They are not equ

[Help] [Cancel] [< Back] [Next >] [Finish]

arguments ←

FUNCTION WIZARD EXAMPLE

The Function Wizard organizes functions into descriptive categories:

CATEGORY	USED TO
Most Recently Used	List functions used recently.
All	List all functions in alphabetical order.
Financial	Analyze investments, cash flow, depreciation, etc.
Date & Time	Calculate values relating to date or time.
Math & Trig	Perform algebraic and trigonometric calculations.
Statistical	Perform statistical analysis on table of values.
Lookup & Reference	Locate the contents of a cell.
Database	Perform calculations related to database tables.
Text	Manipulate text entries.
Logical	Determine if a condition is true or false.
Information	Determine information about cells, the operating system, status of the Solver utility, etc.

*NOTE: A more detailed description of a selected function may be obtained by clicking the **Help** button from the **Function Wizard** dialog box.*

APPENDIX C

VISUAL BASIC

A **macro** is a set of instructions (a program) that you create and save to automate repetitive tasks. Macros may be invoked (played back, or run) to expedite the entry of commands, formulas, labels or a series of format settings.

When you record a macro, Excel writes the actions in **Visual Basic Language** or **code** in a module sheet. The module sheet is added to your workbook. The macro code is placed within a **Sub** and **End Sub** statement which names the macro and marks the beginning and end of the macro commands.

MACRO EXAMPLE:

```
' Bolditalics Macro
' Macro to format text for bold and italic.
'
' Keyboard Shortcut: Ctrl+h
'
Sub Bolditalics()
        Selection.Font.Bold = True
        Selection.Font.Italic = True
End Sub
```

EXPLANATION OF MACRO EXAMPLE:

Lines beginning with apostrophes (')	indicate comment entries that will not be executed.
`Sub Bolditalics()`	marks and names the beginning of the macro subroutine. Bolditalic is the macro name.
`Selection.Font.Bold=True`	sets text in selected cell to Bold.
`Selection.Font.Italic=True`	sets text in selected cell to Italics.
`End Sub`	marks end of subroutine.

As discussed in Lesson 11, macros may be created by recording them. If you follow directions in Exercise 91, to open a duplicate window, you will be able to view the entry of the macro while it is being recorded. This is a good way to learn how the macros are created.

Another way to create a macro is to enter or type it. Some macros cannot be recorded and must be entered using Visual Basic code. When you type macro codes, Excel formats key words like **Sub** and **End Sub,** automatically. If you need to divide a line that belongs together, you can type an underscore (_) character at the end of the line.

To determine what the appropriate Visual Basic code words are, you can refer to Help Topics information about the language as follows:

1. Click **Help** menu.

2. Click **Microsoft Excel Help Topics**.

3. Select Contents sheet.

4. Select Getting Started with Visual Basic or Microsoft Excel Visual Basic Reference.

5. Select desired topic.

6. Select specific subtopic, such as property name or statement name, for detailed information.

   NOTE: Every topic on the contents menu contains submenus that can be explored to find the specific function, object, property or statement desired.

FINDING HELP ON VISUAL BASIC

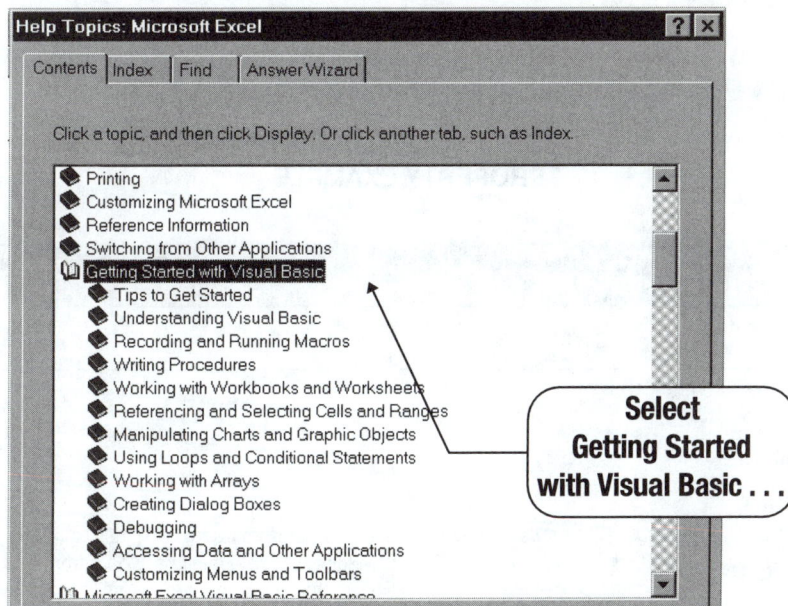

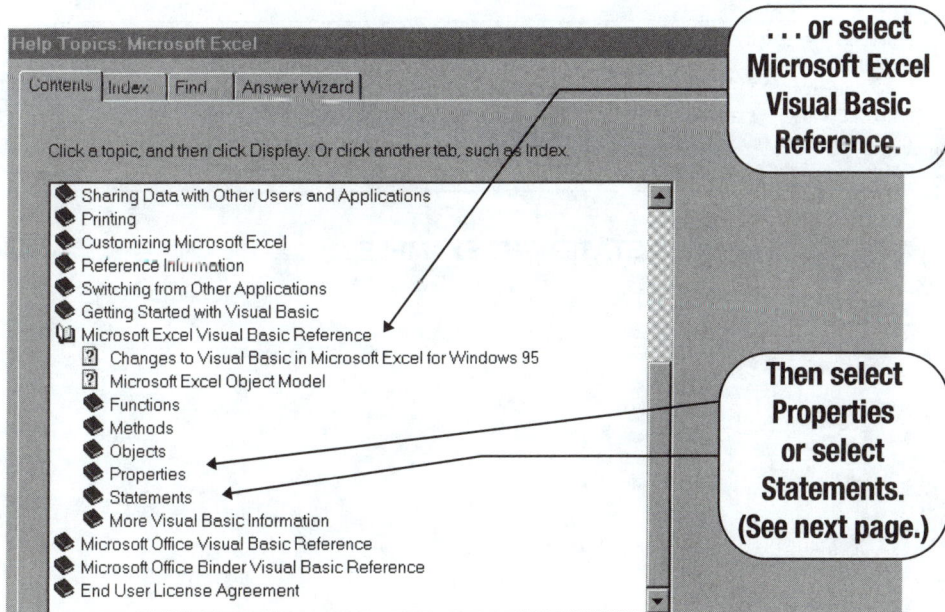

Help Topics: Microsoft Excel

Contents | Index | Find | Answer Wizard

Click a topic, and then click Display. Or click another tab, such as Index.

- Printing
- Customizing Microsoft Excel
- Reference Information
- Switching from Other Applications
- Getting Started with Visual Basic
  - Tips to Get Started
  - Understanding Visual Basic
  - Recording and Running Macros
  - Writing Procedures
  - Working with Workbooks and Worksheets
  - Referencing and Selecting Cells and Ranges
  - Manipulating Charts and Graphic Objects
  - Using Loops and Conditional Statements
  - Working with Arrays
  - Creating Dialog Boxes
  - Debugging
  - Accessing Data and Other Applications
  - Customizing Menus and Toolbars
- Microsoft Excel Visual Basic Reference

> **Select Getting Started with Visual Basic . . .**

Help Topics: Microsoft Excel

Contents | Index | Find | Answer Wizard

Click a topic, and then click Display. Or click another tab, such as Index.

- Sharing Data with Other Users and Applications
- Printing
- Customizing Microsoft Excel
- Reference Information
- Switching from Other Applications
- Getting Started with Visual Basic
- Microsoft Excel Visual Basic Reference
  - Changes to Visual Basic in Microsoft Excel for Windows 95
  - Microsoft Excel Object Model
  - Functions
  - Methods
  - Objects
  - Properties
  - Statements
  - More Visual Basic Information
- Microsoft Office Visual Basic Reference
- Microsoft Office Binder Visual Basic Reference
- End User License Agreement

> **. . . or select Microsoft Excel Visual Basic Refercnce.**

> **Then select Properties or select Statements. (See next page.)**

Microsoft Excel Visual Basic

Help Topics | Back | Options

ActiveCell Property

See Also | Example | Applies To

Accessor. Returns a **Range** object that represents the active cell in the active window (the window on top) or in the specified window. If the window is not displaying a worksheet, this property fails. Read-only.

Remarks

If you do not specify an object qualifier, this property returns the active cell in the active window.

Be careful to distinguish between the active cell and the selection. The active cell is a single cell inside the current selection. The selection may contain more than one cell, but only one is the active cell.

The following expressions all return the active cell, and are all equivalent.

```
ActiveCell
Application.ActiveCell
ActiveWindow.ActiveCell
Application.ActiveWindow.ActiveCell
```

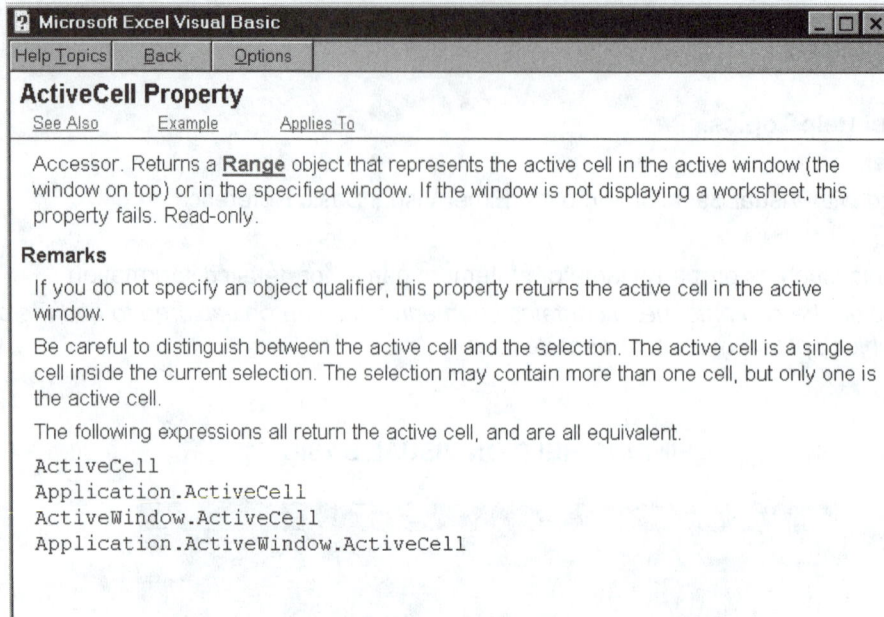

PROPERTY EXAMPLE

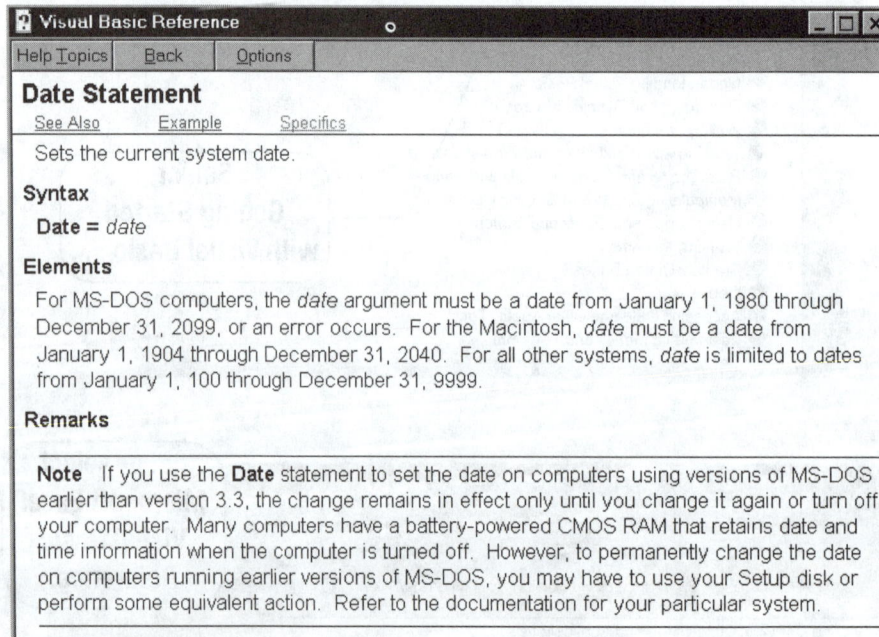

Visual Basic Reference

Help Topics | Back | Options

Date Statement

See Also | Example | Specifics

Sets the current system date.

Syntax

Date = *date*

Elements

For MS-DOS computers, the *date* argument must be a date from January 1, 1980 through December 31, 2099, or an error occurs. For the Macintosh, *date* must be a date from January 1, 1904 through December 31, 2040. For all other systems, *date* is limited to dates from January 1, 100 through December 31, 9999.

Remarks

Note If you use the **Date** statement to set the date on computers using versions of MS-DOS earlier than version 3.3, the change remains in effect only until you change it again or turn off your computer. Many computers have a battery-powered CMOS RAM that retains date and time information when the computer is turned off. However, to permanently change the date on computers running earlier versions of MS-DOS, you may have to use your Setup disk or perform some equivalent action. Refer to the documentation for your particular system.

STATEMENT EXAMPLE

APPENDIX D

TOOLBARS

A **toolbar** is a set of buttons that allows mouse users to select frequently-used commands without accessing the menu system.

By default, Excel automatically displays the Standard and Formatting toolbars just below the menu bar.

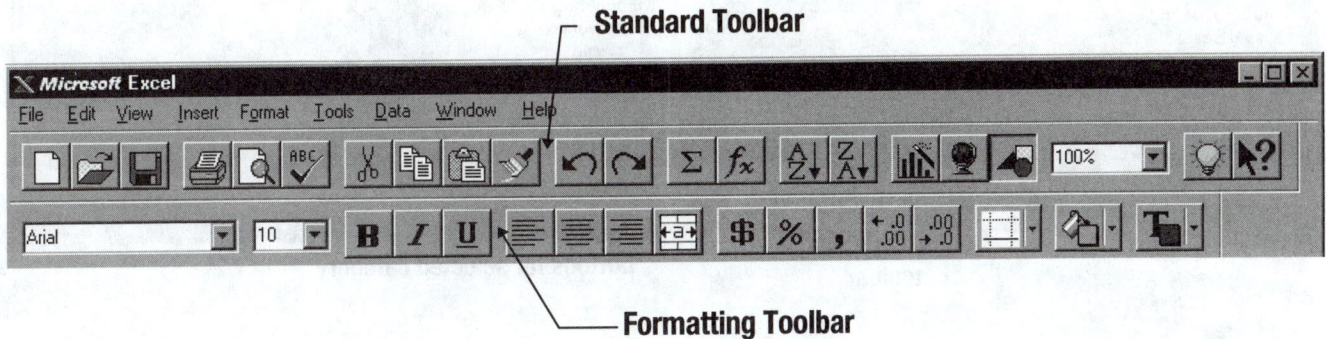

Standard Toolbar

Formatting Toolbar

Excel comes with thirteen toolbars. Each toolbar contains buttons that can help you do specific kinds of tasks quickly.

The Excel toolbars:

Auditing

Chart

Drawing

Formatting

Forms

Full Screen

Microsoft

Query And Pivot

Standard

Stop Recording

TipWizard

Visual Basic

WorkGroup

APPENDIX D

The Toolbars command on the View menu lets you create custom toolbars and modify existing toolbars. Note the illustration below.

Select toolbar to display

customize instructions

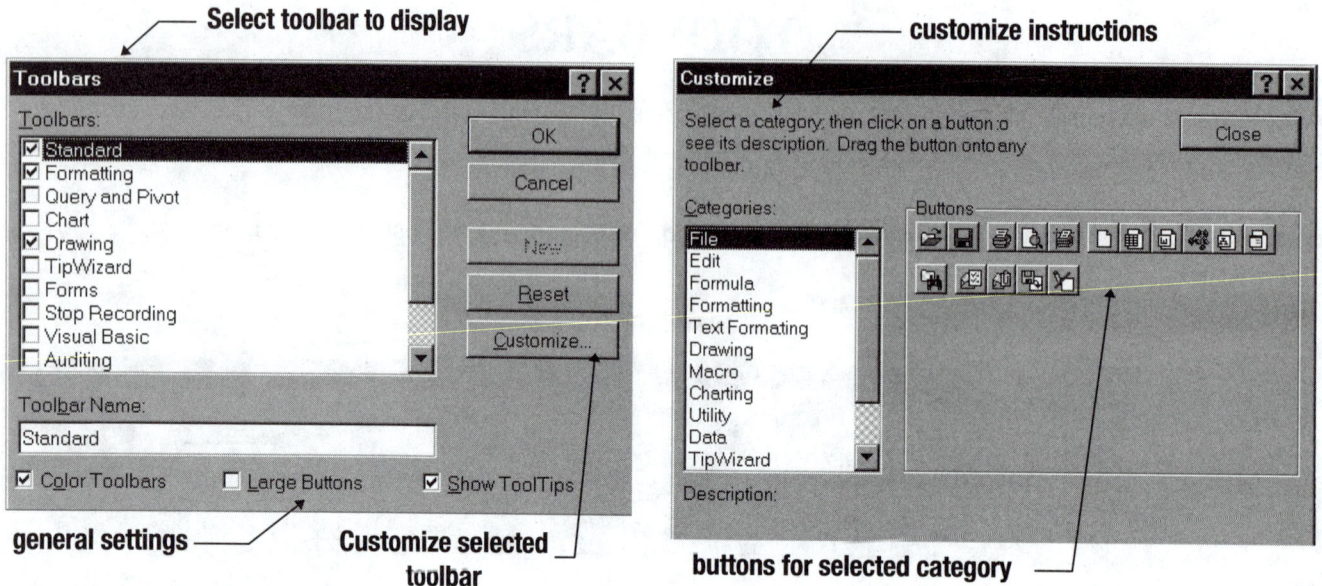

general settings

Customize selected toolbar

buttons for selected category

Excel provides the following procedures to enhance and customize your toolbar activities:

- Show the purpose of a toolbar button.
- Show or hide a toolbar.
- Move a toolbar.
- Switch between a floating or docking toolbar.
- Size a floating toolbar.
- Set general toolbar options, such as the color and size of the toolbars.
- Create a customized toolbar.
- Delete a customized toolbar.
- Restore a built-in toolbar.
- Change width of a toolbar drop-down list.
- Move a toolbar button.
- Copy a toolbar button.
- Add or remove toolbar buttons.
- Copy image of a toolbar button to another button.
- Change image of a toolbar button.
- Restore image of a toolbar button.

To show purpose of a toolbar button:

Rest pointer on desired toolbar button.

The button name appears below the button and a description appears on the Status Bar.

To use a toolbar button:

Click the button.

To access the toolbar shortcut menu:

1. Right–click a blank area on any toolbar.

2. Click desired menu option:

   - Standard, Formatting, Chart, Drawing, Forms, Visual Basic, Auditing, WorkGroup, Microsoft

   - Toolbars

   - Customize

To show or hide a toolbar:

1. Click **View** menu.

2. Click **Toolbar**.

3. Select or deselect desired toolbar(s) in **Toolbars** list.

   ***Toolbars* list items include:** *Standard, Formatting, Query and Pivot, Chart, Drawing, TipWizard, Forms, Stop Recording, Visual Basic, Auditing, WorkGroup, Microsoft, Full Screen*

4. Click OK .

To move a toolbar:

You can dock a toolbar (between the menu bar and the formula bar or on the edges of the Excel window), or have it float as a separate window. Toolbars containing a drop-down list (i.e., the Formatting Toolbar) cannot be docked on the left or right edge of the Excel window.

1. Point to a blank area on toolbar.

   OR

   Point to title bar of floating toolbar.

2. Drag toolbar outline onto desired workspace position or desired docking position.

   NOTE: Excel shifts existing toolbars when you move a toolbar into a docking position.

To switch between a floating or docking toolbar:

Double–click a blank area on toolbar.

To size a floating toolbar:

1. Point to border or corner of floating toolbar.

   Pointer becomes one of the following: ⬰ ⬍ ⬌ ⬲ .

2. Drag toolbar outline to desired size.

To set general toolbar options:

1. Click **View** menu.
2. Click **Toolbars**.
3. Select or deselect toolbar options:
   - Color Toolbars
   - Large Buttons
   - Show ToolTips
4. Click `OK`.

To create a customized toolbar:

1. Click **View** menu.
2. Click **Toolbars**.
3. Type a unique toolbar name in **Toolbar Name:** `_____`.
4. Click `New`.

   Excel displays an empty toolbar and opens the Customize dialog box.

   To add a button to the new toolbar:

   a. Click a category in **Categories** list.

      To see a button's description:

      1. Click desired button in **Buttons** box.
      2. Read description at bottom of dialog box.

   b. Drag desired button onto new toolbar.
   c. Repeat steps a–b, as needed.
5. Click `Close`.

To delete a customized toolbar:

1. Click **View** menu.
2. Click **Toolbars**.
3. Select toolbar to delete in **Toolbars** list.
4. Click `Delete`.
5. Click `OK` to confirm deletion.
6. Click `OK`.

To restore a built-in toolbar:

1. Click **View** menu.

2. Click **Toolbars**.

3. Select built-in toolbar to restore in **Toolbars** list.

4. Click [Reset].

    *NOTE: If you do not see the **Reset** button, you have selected a customized toolbar, not a built-in toolbar. Customized toolbars cannot be reset.*

5. Click [OK].

To change width of a toolbar's drop-down list:

1. Right–click a blank area on toolbar.

2. Click **Customize**.

3. Click border of [▾] on toolbar in Excel window to change.

    Excel surrounds drop-down list box with a thick border.

4. Point to left or right border of drop-down list box to size.

    Pointer becomes a ↔ when positioned correctly.

5. Drag box outline left or right.

6. Click [Close].

To move a toolbar button:

Groups a button with other buttons, adds space between buttons, moves a button to a new position on a toolbar, and moves a button to another toolbar. If you are moving a button to another toolbar, both toolbars must be in view.

1. Right–click a blank area on toolbar.

2. Click **Customize**.

3. Drag button outline to desired location on current or other toolbar.

4. Click [Close].

To copy a toolbar button:

NOTE: If you are copying a button to another toolbar, both toolbars must be in view.

1. Right–click a blank area on toolbar.

2. Click **Customize**.

3. Press **Ctrl** and drag button outline to desired location on current or other toolbar.

4. Click [Close].

To add or remove toolbar buttons:

1. Right–click a blank area on toolbar.
2. Click **Customize**.

   To add a button:

   a. Click category in **Categories** list.

      To see a button's description:

      1. Click desired button in **Buttons** box.
      2. Read description at bottom of dialog box.

   b. Drag desired button to desired position on toolbar.

   c. Repeat steps a–b, as needed.

   To remove a button:

   Drag button off toolbar.

3. Click [Close].

To copy image of a toolbar button to another button:

NOTE: Both the source and destination buttons must be in view.

1. Right–click a blank area on toolbar.
2. Click **Customize**.
3. Click source button on toolbar.
4. Click **Edit** menu.
5. Click **Copy Button Image**.
6. Click destination button on toolbar.
7. Click **Edit** menu.
8. Click **Paste Button Image**.
9. Click [Close].

To change image of a toolbar button:

NOTE: You can copy an image (bitmap or picture) from another application onto the clipboard, and then paste the image to the button. Follow steps 1–3 below, then click Paste Button Image from the shortcut menu.

1. Right–click a blank area on toolbar.
2. Click **Customize**.
3. Right–click button on toolbar to change.
4. Click **Edit Button Image**.

   To erase entire image:

   Click [Clear].

   To change or add colors:

   a. Click a color in **Colors** box.
   b. Click or drag through each pixel to color in **Picture** box.
   c. Repeat steps a–b, as desired.

   To move image:

   Click arrow button in direction to move image.

5. Click [OK].

To restore image of a toolbar button:

1. Right–click a blank area on toolbar.
2. Click **Customize**.
3. Right–click button on toolbar to restore.
4. Click **Reset Button Image**.
5. Click [Close].

APPENDIX E

ERROR MESSAGES

Below is a list of error values that may appear in a cell when Excel cannot calculate the formula value.

#DIV/0!   Indicates that the formula is trying to divide by zero.

          In formula: • *Divisor is a zero.* • *Divisor is referencing a blank cell or a cell that contains a zero value.*

#N/A   Indicates that no value is available.

          In formula: • *An invalid argument may have been used with a LOOKUP function.* • *A reference in an array formula does not match range in which results are displayed.* • *A required argument has been omitted from a function.*

#NAME?   Indicates that Excel does not recognize the name used in a formula.

          In formula: • *A named reference has been deleted or has not been defined.* • *A function or named reference has been misspelled.* • *Text has been entered without required quotation marks.* • *A colon has been omitted in a range reference.*

#NULL!   Indicates that the intersection of two range references does not exist.

          In formula: • *Two range references (separated with a space operator) have been used to represent a non-existent intersection of the two ranges.*

#NUM!   Indicates a number error.

          In formula: • *An incorrect value has been used in a function.* • *Arguments result in a number too small or large to represent.*

#REF!   Indicates reference to an invalid cell.

          In formula: • *Arguments refer to cells that have been deleted or overwritten with non-numeric data. The argument is replaced with #REF!.*

#VALUE!   Indicates the invalid use of an operator or argument.

          In formula: • *An invalid value, or a referenced value, has been used with a formula or function, i.e., SUM("John").*

Circular   A message that indicates formula is referencing itself.

          In formula: • *A cell reference refers to the cell containing the formula result.*

          NOTE: *If a circular reference is intended, you can select Options from the Tools menu, then select Iteration from the Calculation tab. Iteration is an instruction to repeat a calculation until a specific result value is met.*

APPENDIX F

WORKSHEET PLANNING GRID

	A	B	C	D	E	F	G	H
1								
2								
3								
4								
5								
6								
7								
8								
9								
10								
11								
12								
13								
14								
15								
16								
17								
18								
19								
20								
21								
22								
23								
24								
25								
26								
27								
28								
29								
30								
31								
32								
33								
34								
35								
36								
37								
38								
39								
40								
41								
42								
43								
44								
45								
46								
47								
48								
49								
50								
51								
52								
53								
54								
55								
56								
57								
58								
59								
60								

INDEX

INDEX

INDEX

INDEX

367

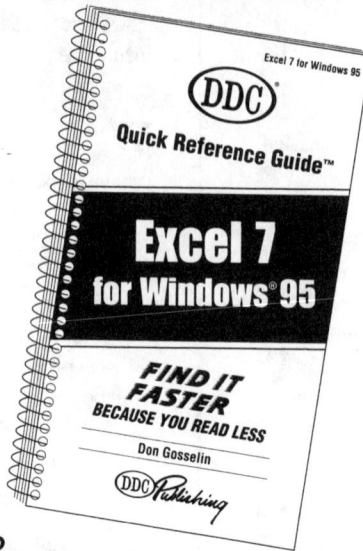

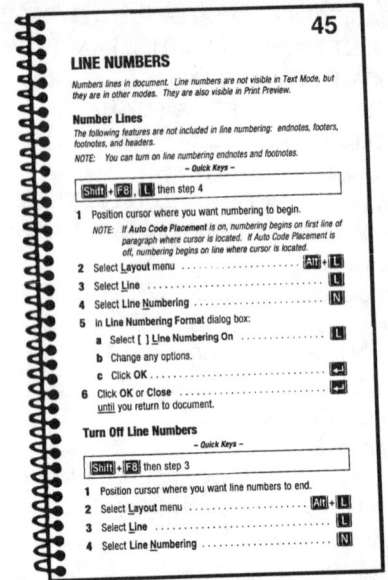

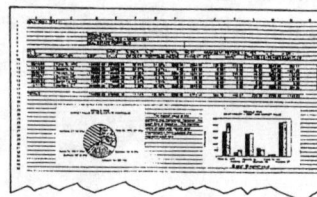

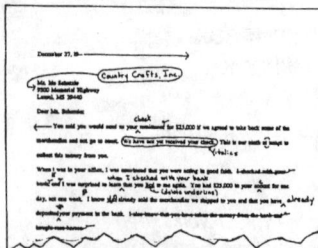

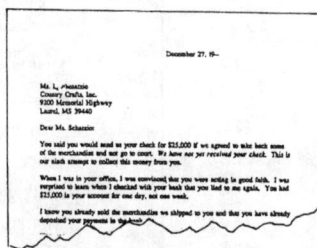

MATERIALS

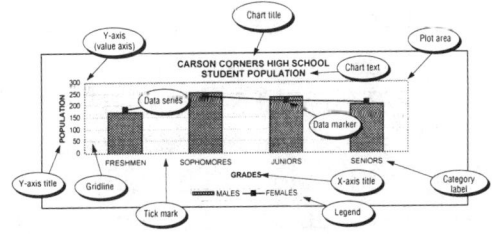

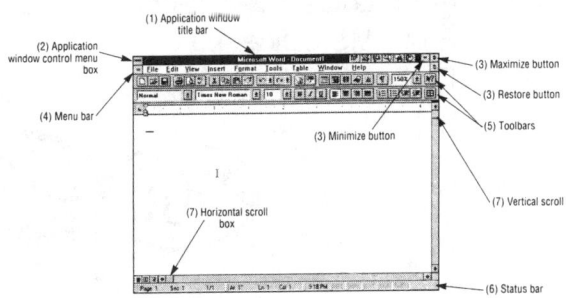

Transparencies For Training

Talk to your students with the screen illustration in front of you, and they will see what you are explaining. Every word has double impact when you point to the screen element you are discussing. Nothing beats the visual it all boils down to this: Do you want to teach quickly, or do you want to teach slowly? What's your teaching time worth?

If this screen was sitting on your projector, large as life, and you had your pointer, how would you go about explaining spreadsheets?

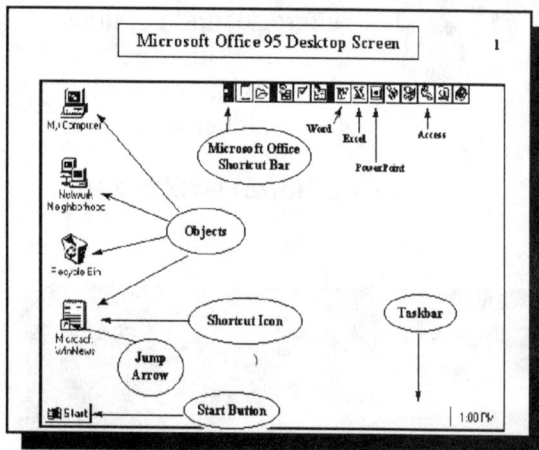

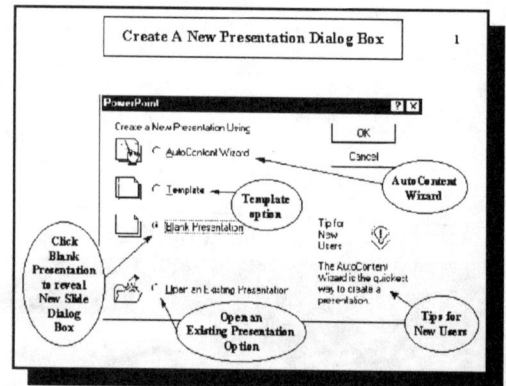

Price $50 ea. Each set contains 20 transparencies, index sheet, & album.

F-44	Access 7	F-45	PowerPoint 7 for Windows 95
F-36	DOS 5-6.22	F-35	Windows 3.1 & 3.1
F-37	Excel 5	F-41	Windows 95
F-43	Excel 7 for Windows 95	F-38	Word 6
F-33	Lotus 1-2-3 DOS	F-47	Word 7 for Windows 95
F-46	Lotus 1-2-3 Windows Rel. 5	F-39	WordPerfect 5.1 DOS
F-34	Lotus 1-2-3 Windows	F-31	WordPerfect 6.0 DOS
F-40	MS Office 4.3	F-32	WordPerfect 6.0 Win
F-48	MS Office Windows 95	F-42	WordPerfect 6.1 Win
		F-49	Works 4 Windows 95

DDC *Publishing*

275 Madison Avenue, New York, NY 10016
Ph.: 800-528-3897, Fax: 800-528-3862

More Fast-teach Learning Books

Did we make one for you?

Title	Cat. No.
Corel WordPerfect 7 for Win 95	Z12
DOS 5–6.2 (Book & Disk)	D9
DOS + Windows	Z7
Excel 5 for Windows	E9
Excel 7 for Windows 95	XL7
INTERNET	Z15
Lotus 1-2-3 Rel. 2.2–4.0 for DOS	L9
Lotus 1-2-3 Rel. 4 & 5 for Windows	B9
Microsoft Office	M9
Microsoft Office for Windows 95	Z6
Windows 3.1 – A Quick Study	WQS-1
Windows 95	Z3
Word 2 for Windows	K9
Word 6 for Windows	1-WDW6
Word 7 for Windows 95	Z10
WordPerfect 5.0 & 5.1 for DOS	W9
WordPerfect 6 for DOS	P9
WordPerfect 6 for Windows	Z9
WordPerfect 6.1 for Windows	H9
Works 3 for Windows	1-WKW3
Works 4 for Windows 95	Z8

DESKTOP PUBLISHING LEARNING BOOKS	
Word 6 for Windows	Z2
WordPerfect 5.1 for DOS	WDB
WordPerfect 6 for Windows	F9
WordPerfect 6.1 for Windows	Z5

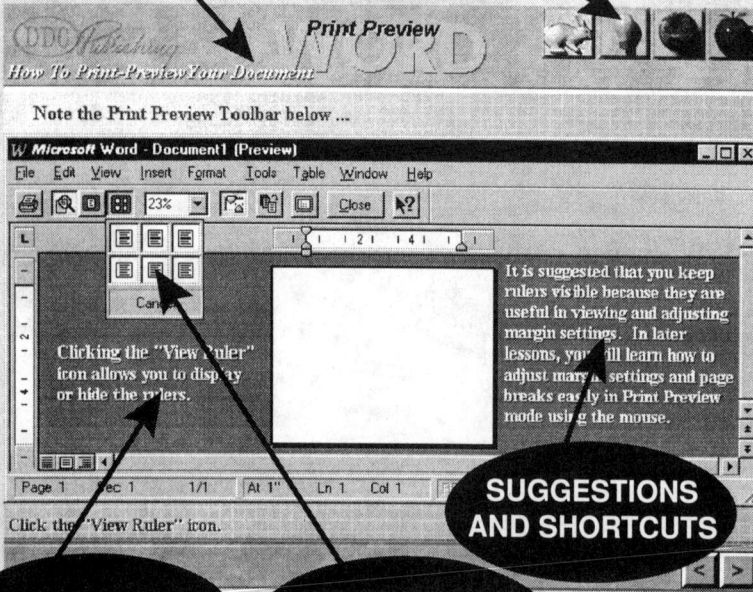

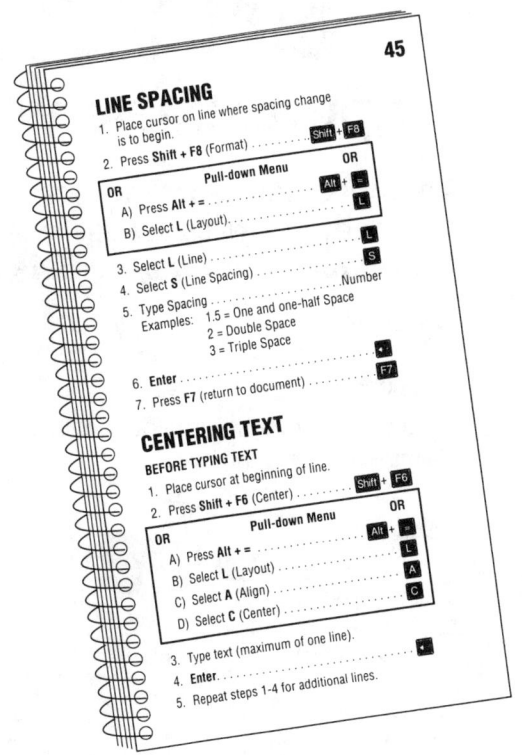

Short Course Learning Books
Approximately 25 hours of instruction per book

We sliced our learning books into short courses, *introductory* & *intermediate.*

- We extracted pages from our Fast-teach Learning books and created shortened versions.
- Each book comes with a data disk to eliminate typing the exercise.

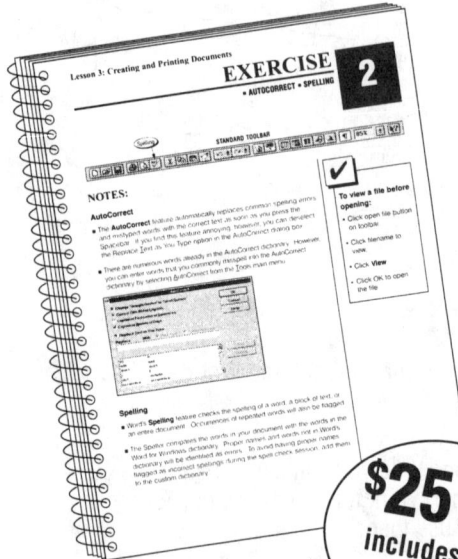

$25 EACH includes book and data disk

FREE CATALOG
AND
UPDATED LISTING

We don't just have books that find your answers faster; we also have books that teach you how to use your computer without the fairy tales and the gobbledygook.

We also have books to improve your typing, spelling and punctuation.

Return this card for a free catalog and mailing list update.

DDC Publishing
275 Madison Avenue,
New York, NY 10016

☐ Please send me your catalog and put me on your mailing list.

Name _____

Firm (if any) _____

Address _____

City, State, Zip _____

Phone (800) 528-3897   Fax (800) 528-3862

SEE OUR COMPLETE CATALOG ON THE INTERNET @: http://www.ddcpub.com

FREE CATALOG
AND
UPDATED LISTING

We don't just have books that find your answers faster; we also have books that teach you how to use your computer without the fairy tales and the gobbledygook.

We also have books to improve your typing, spelling and punctuation.

Return this card for a free catalog and mailing list update.

DDC Publishing
275 Madison Avenue,
New York, NY 10016

☐ Please send me your catalog and put me on your mailing list.

Name _____

Firm (if any) _____

Address _____

City, State, Zip _____

Phone (800) 528-3897   Fax (800) 528-3862

SEE OUR COMPLETE CATALOG ON THE INTERNET @: http://www.ddcpub.com